Classics and the Us‹

Classical Receptions

Series Editor: Maria Wyke, University College London

The ancient world did not end with the sack of Rome in the fifth century AD. Its literature, politics, and culture have been adopted, contested, used and abused, from the middle ages to the present day, by both individuals and states. The Classical Receptions Series presents new contributions by leading scholars to the investigation of how the ancient world continues to shape our own.

Published

Classics and the Uses of Reception
Edited by Charles Martindale and Richard F. Thomas

In Preparation

Sex: From Ancient Greece to the 21st Century
Alastair Blanshard

Ancient Rome and Modern America
Margaret Malamud

Antiquity and Modernity
Neville Morley

The Ancient World in Popular Culture
Maria Wyke, Margaret Malamud, and Lloyd Llewellyn-Jones

Classics and the Uses of Reception

Edited by

Charles Martindale
and
Richard F. Thomas

Blackwell
Publishing

© 2006 by Blackwell Publishing Ltd

BLACKWELL PUBLISHING
350 Main Street, Malden, MA 02148-5020, USA
9600 Garsington Road, Oxford OX4 2DQ, UK
550 Swanston Street, Carlton, Victoria 3053, Australia

The right of Charles Martindale and Richard F. Thomas to be identified as the
Authors of the Editorial Material in this Work has been asserted in accordance
with the UK Copyright, Designs, and Patents Act 1988.

First published 2006 by Blackwell Publishing Ltd

1   2006

Library of Congress Cataloging-in-Publication Data

Classics and the uses of reception / edited by Charles A. Martindale and
Richard F. Thomas.
p. cm. — (Classical receptions)
Includes bibliographical references and index.
ISBN-13: 978-1-4051-3146-9 (alk. paper)
ISBN-10: 1-4051-3146-2 (alk. paper)
ISBN-13: 978-1-4051-3145-2 (pbk. : alk. paper)
ISBN-10: 1-4051-3145-4 (pbk. : alk. paper)
1. Classical literature—History and criticism—Theory, etc.
2. Reader–response criticism.   3. Arts, Classical.   I. Martindale, Charles.
II. Thomas, Richard F., 1950–   III. Series.
PA3013.C597 2006
880.09—dc22
2005030975

A catalogue record for this title is available from the British Library.

Set in 10/13pt Galliard
by Graphicraft Limited, Hong Kong
Printed and bound in Singapore
by C.O.S. Printers Pte Ltd

The publisher's policy is to use permanent paper from mills that operate a sustainable
forestry policy, and which has been manufactured from pulp processed using acid-free
and elementary chlorine-free practices. Furthermore, the publisher ensures that the text
paper and cover board used have met acceptable environmental accreditation standards.

For further information on
Blackwell Publishing, visit our website:
www.blackwellpublishing.com

Contents

Figures

Notes on Contributors

William W. Batstone is an Associate Professor of Greek and Latin at Ohio State University. He has published on Latin poetry and prose from the Roman republic to Horace and Virgil. He is currently working on the performance of self and identity in Roman comedy, finishing a book on Caesar (forthcoming, Oxford University Press), and starting a translation of Sallust (Oxford University Press). His primary interest is in how literature can be said to have value and meaning.

Katie Fleming is a temporary Lecturer in Classical Studies at Queen Mary College, University of London. Her teaching and research interests are in both Greek and Latin literature and culture, and the classical tradition (particularly in the twentieth century).

Simon Goldhill is Professor of Greek at the University of Cambridge. His most recent books include *Who Needs Greek? Contests in the Cultural History of Hellenism* (Cambridge University Press, 2002), *Love, Sex and Tragedy: How the Ancient World Shapes Modern Life* (John Murray/Chicago University Press, 2004), and *The Temple of Jerusalem* (Profile Press/Harvard University Press, 2004).

Lorna Hardwick is in the Department of Classical Studies at the Open University, UK, where she is Professor of Classical Studies and Director of the Reception of Classical Texts Research Project. Recent publications include *Translating Words, Translating Cultures* (Duckworth, 2000), *Reception Studies* (Oxford University Press, 2003), an on-line database of modern productions of Greek drama with critical evaluations of modern primary sources used in documenting performance (<http://www2.open.ac.uk/ClassicalStudies/GreekPlays>), and articles on Greek drama and poetry in postcolonial contexts. She is currently preparing a monograph on the relationship between receptions of classical texts and broader cultural shifts.

Kenneth Haynes teaches in the Department of Comparative Literature at Brown University. He recently published *English Literature and Ancient Languages* (Oxford University Press, 2003) and is now coediting with Peter France *The Oxford History of Literary Translation in English*, volume 4: *1790–1900*. He is also editing and translating a selection of Johann Georg Hamann's essays for the Cambridge Texts in the History of Philosophy.

John Henderson, Professor of Classics, University of Cambridge and fellow of King's College, is the author of *The Triumph of Art at Thorvaldsens Museum: Løve in København* (Museum Tusculanum Press, 2005) and of books on Phaedrus, Seneca, Statius, Pliny, Juvenal and his nineteenth-century editor, John Mayor, and Roman gardening. Essays on Roman literature and history are collected in *Fighting for Rome* (Cambridge University Press, 1998) and *Writing Down Rome* (Clarendon Press, 1999). In the pipeline are *Plautus, Asinaria: The One about the Asses* (University of Wisconsin Press), *Isidore's Creation: Truth from Words* (Cambridge University Press), and *Oxford Reds: Classic Commentaries on Latin Classics* (Duckworth).

Ralph Hexter was, for the preceding decade, Professor of Classics and Comparative Literature at the University of California, Berkeley. He is now Professor of Classics and Comparative Literature and President of Hampshire College in Amherst, Massachusetts. His publications include *Ovid and Medieval Schooling* (1996), *Innovations of Antiquity*, coedited with Daniel Selden (1992), and articles on topics from Virgil to Verdi. He is currently working on various intersections of classical reception, sexuality, and theatre in the fifteenth through the twentieth centuries.

Craig Kallendorf is Professor of English and Classics at Texas A&M University. His research interests include the classical tradition, the history of the book, and the history of rhetoric. His most recent publications include *Virgil and the Myth of Venice: Books and Readers in the Italian Renaissance* (Clarendon Press, 1999) and *Humanist Educational Treatises* (Harvard University Press, 2002).

Helen Kaufmann taught Latin Literature and Language in the Classics Department at the University of Fribourg, Switzerland until recently. She is now a Senior Lecturer at Ohio State University. She wrote a commentary on Dracontius' *Romul.* 10 (*Medea*) (forthcoming). Her research interests include Bacchylides, (late) Latin poetry and the reception of ancient motifs in the contemporary world.

Duncan F. Kennedy is Professor of Latin Literature and the Theory of Criticism at the University of Bristol. His research interests lie in Latin literature, modern responses to the Roman world, critical and discourse theory, Virgil, Ovid, and Lucretius. His publications include *The Arts of Love: Five Studies in the Discourse of Roman Love Elegy* (Cambridge University Press, 1993) and *Rethinking Reality: Lucretius and the Textualization of Nature* (University of Michigan Press, 2002).

Miriam Leonard is a Lecturer in Classics at the University of Bristol. Her research interests are in the reception of classics in modern European thought. Her publications include articles and essays on reception theory and the role of the ancient world in Cixous, Derrida, Irigaray, and Lacan. She is author of *Athens in Paris: Ancient Greece and the Political in Post-war French Thought* (Oxford University Press, 2005) and coeditor with Vanda Zajko of *Laughing with Medusa: Classical Myth and Feminist Thought* (Oxford University Press, 2005).

Alexandra Lianeri is the Moses and Mary Finley Fellow at Darwin College, Cambridge University. She has published articles in the fields of classical reception, translation studies, and the history of historiography. She is currently working on a monograph exploring the role of Athenian democracy in the history of political thought and coediting a book on translation and the concept of "the classic."

Genevieve Liveley is a Lecturer in Classics at the University of Bristol. Her teaching and research interests are in Latin literature and culture, gender and sexuality, and the classical tradition. Her publications include articles and essays on Ovid's *Metamorphoses*, feminism in the classics, and contemporary critical theory. She is the author of *Ovid: Love Songs* (Duckworth, 2005) and is currently working on a book on postfeminism and the classical tradition.

Charles Martindale, Professor of Latin at the University of Bristol, has written extensively on the reception of classical poetry. In addition to the theoretical *Redeeming the Text: Latin Poetry and the Hermeneutics of Reception* (Cambridge University Press, 1993), he has edited or coedited collections on the receptions of Virgil, Horace, and Ovid, as well as *Shakespeare and the Classics* (Cambridge University Press, 2004). His most recent book is *Latin Poetry and the Judgement of Taste: An Essay in Aesthetics* (Oxford University Press, 2005).

Siobhán McElduff took her doctorate from the University of Southern California and teaches at Harvard-Westlake School in Los Angeles. Her research interests include the reception of classics amongst non-elite groups and translation in the Roman empire. She has published articles on Senecan tragedy (with John Fitch) and on Terence and translation (forthcoming).

Pantelis Michelakis is Lecturer in Classics at the University of Bristol. He is the author of *Achilles in Greek Tragedy* (Cambridge University Press, 2002) and the *Duckworth Companion to Euripides'* Iphigenia at Aulis (Duckworth, 2006). He has coedited *Homer, Tragedy and Beyond: Essays in Honour of P. E. Easterling* (SPHS, 2001) and *Agamemnon in Performance, 456 BC–AD 2004* (Oxford University Press, 2005). He is currently working on the reception of Greek tragedy in modern theatre and cinema.

James I. Porter is Professor of Greek, Latin, and Comparative Literature at the University of Michigan. He is the author of *Nietzsche and the Philology of the Future* (Stanford University Press, 2000) and *The Invention of Dionysus: An Essay on the Birth of Tragedy* (Stanford University Press, 2000), and editor, most recently, of *Classical Pasts: The Classical Traditions of Greece and Rome* (Princeton University Press, 2005). His current projects include *The Material Sublime in Greek & Roman Aesthetics* and *Homer: The Very Idea*, a study in the production of the memory of Homer from antiquity to the present.

Elizabeth Prettejohn is Professor of History of Art at the University of Bristol. She has a special interest in the reception of ancient art in the modern period. Her publications include *Sir Lawrence Alma-Tadema* (1996), *Frederic Leighton: Antiquity, Renaissance, Modernity* (1999, with Tim Barringer), and *Beauty and Art 1750–2000* (2005). Future projects include a book on *The Modernity of Ancient Sculpture*.

Timothy Saunders completed his PhD at the University of Bristol in 2001. His research interests include ecological literary theory, reception theory, Latin literature, and modern poetry. He has published essays on pastoral poetry, contemporary art, and the Russian poet Joseph Brodsky, and is currently researching the reception of antiquity in twentieth-century Russian poetry.

Mathilde Skoie is Senior Lecturer in Latin at the University of Bergen. She is interested in Roman poetry, mainly elegy and pastoral, and its reception. She has published a monograph on the scholarly reception of the elegiac poet Sulpicia, *Reading Sulpicia: Commentaries 1475–1990* (Oxford University Press, 2002) and is coediting a volume on pastoral, *Reinscribing Pastoral in the Humanities: Essays on the Uses of a Critical Concept* (forthcoming, Bristol Phoenix Press, 2006).

Richard F. Thomas is Professor of Greek and Latin at Harvard University. His interests are generally focused on Hellenistic Greek and Roman literature, on intertextuality, and on the reception of classical literature in all periods. Recent books include *Reading Virgil and His Texts: Studies in Intertextuality* (University of

Michigan Press, 1999) and *Virgil and the Augustan Reception* (Cambridge University Press, 2001). He is currently working on a commentary to Horace, *Odes* 4 and a coedited volume on the performance artistry of Bob Dylan.

Tim Whitmarsh is Reader in Greek Literature at the University of Exeter. A specialist in literary and cultural theory and the Greek texts of the Roman empire, he is the author of *Greek Literature and the Roman Empire* (Oxford University Press, 2001), *Ancient Greek Literature* (Polity Press, 2004), and *The Second Sophistic* (Oxford University Press, 2005). He is currently working on a book titled *Reading the Self in the Ancient Greek Novel* (forthcoming, Cambridge University Press).

Vanda Zajko is Senior Lecturer in Classics at the University of Bristol. She has wide-ranging interests in the reception of classical literature and her recent publications include "Homer and Ulysses" in the *Cambridge Companion to Homer* (2004) and " 'Petruchio is Kated': Ovid and The Taming of the Shrew" in *Shakespeare and the Classics*, ed. Martindale and Taylor (Cambridge University Press, 2004). Her coedited volume *Laughing with Medusa: Classical Myth and Feminist Thought* will be published by Oxford University Press in 2005.

Introduction

Thinking Through Reception

Charles Martindale

pro captu lectoris habent sua fata libelli

Terentianus Maurus, v.1286[1]

In *Redeeming the Text* (1993) I issued what was in effect a manifesto for the adoption of reception theory within the discipline of classics, a position at that time controversial.[2] Since then there has been a significant expansion of activities (including undergraduate and postgraduate courses) carried out under the banner of "reception," particularly in the UK, and to a lesser extent in the USA where, for example, there are always reception panels at the annual conference of the American Philological Association (in continental Europe generally work so designated is more likely to be pursued outside departments of classics). One sign of the change of attitude was the decision by Cambridge University Press in the mid 1990s that Cambridge Companions to ancient authors should contain a substantial reception element.[3] Another was the addition of "reception," in 2001, to the categories of work specified within classics in the Research Assessment Exercise (RAE), which periodically grades the research of all university departments in the UK. Reception within classics encompasses all work concerned with postclassical material, much of which in other humanities departments might well be described under different rubrics: for example, history of scholarship, history

---

1 Quoted Schmidt (1985) 67.
2 Martindale (1993). That book is particularly indebted to 20th-century German hermeneutics, to Derrida, and to Eliot; I would now work with a genealogy for reception that goes back, through writers like Pater, to Kant's great Critiques. For those who not only believe in originary meanings but also think they are easy of attainment, I would point out that my reading of *Redeeming the Text* differs in almost every case from the various other receptions of it in this book.
3 So far Easterling (1997); Martindale (1997a); Hardie (2002); Fowler (2004); Freudenburg (2005) – others are to follow.

of the book, film and media studies, performance history, translation studies, reader-response and personal voice criticism, postcolonial studies, medieval and Neo-Latin, and much else besides (the essays in this volume are designed to gesture towards the range of these pursuits, but it would have been impossible to cover them all, without sacrificing the focus on methodology).

Reception has thus helped to challenge the traditional idea of what "classics" is (something most classicists, including myself, simply took for granted 30, or even 20 years ago), prompting reflection on how the discipline has been constituted, variously and often amid dispute, over past centuries. It is not merely a matter of looking at what happened to classics after what we now like to call "late antiquity," but of contesting the idea that classics is something fixed, whose boundaries can be shown, and whose essential nature we can understand on its own terms. Many classicists (though by no means necessarily the majority) are in consequence reasonably happy, if only to keep the discipline alive in some form, to work with an enlarged sense of what classics might be, no longer confined to the study of classical antiquity "in itself" – so that classics can include writing about *Paradise Lost*, or the mythological *poesie* of Titian, or the film *Gladiator*, or the iconography of fascism.[4] However, most Anglophone classicists (whatever they may claim) remain largely committed to fairly positivistic forms of historical inquiry, the attempt through the accumulation of supposedly factual data to establish the-past-as-it-really-was, of the kind I criticized in *Redeeming the Text*. To my thinking this commitment is mistaken. This is partly because such positivism is conceptually flawed for reasons some of which I hope will emerge in the course of this introduction. But it is partly also for pragmatic reasons because, given the overwhelmingly "presentist" character of the contemporary scene, a classics which overinvests in such historicist approaches may not attract tomorrow's students, or achieve any wider cultural significance. Historical positivists also miss the opportunities for much fascinating work, including work that is historical in a wider sense. When I went to university in 1968, the "New Criticism" at least provided alternative protocols of reading to the then dominant combination of historicism and philology, but the New Criticism is now excoriated by all, leaving various forms of historicism, within classics at least, largely unassailed.

Although reception studies flourish, indeed in the UK constitute perhaps the fastest-growing area of the subject, there has been little discussion about the value of such work, and the weaknesses, or strengths, of particular methodologies used within it. Following an exploratory panel we organized at the meeting of the American Philological Association in 2003, Richard Thomas and I designed, through this book, to start a wider debate about the uses of reception within classics. To focus the discussion, we circulated among the contributors William Batstone's "provocation," the paper he delivered at the APA (placed first in the current collection), and met in Bristol to discuss the issues it raises and the different

4 So Beard and Henderson (1995).

models used by other contributors. After these two public events contributors exchanged and commented on each other's contributions in what was very much a collaborative research project. But there is no party line, no attempt to find a general "solution" to the problems involved. Instead, the reader will find a wide variety of approaches, perspectives, and demonstrations over the whole field currently constituted within the word "reception" (for reasons of space, and because it involves a partly different set of problems, we decided to exclude reception within antiquity, itself an important and fast-growing area of study[5]).

One symbolically important date for the student of reception is April 1967,[6] when Hans Robert Jauss delivered his inaugural lecture at the University of Constance, "What is and for what purpose does one study Literary History?", somewhat hubristically echoing the title of Schiller's inaugural at Jena in 1789, but substituting "literary" for Schiller's "universal." Jauss argued for a paradigm shift in literary interpretation which he called *Rezeptionsästhetik* (sometimes translated as "the poetics of reception").[7] It was to be one that would avoid the mistakes of Russian Formalism on the one hand (which paid insufficient attention to the sociology and historicity of literature) and of Marxism, with its grim historical determinism, on the other, while also building on their insights. The new model would acknowledge the historicity of texts, but also allow for the aesthetic response of readers in the present (any present of reading). It thus involved a significant turn to the reader (something which was to characterize a whole range of literary approaches over the remaining years of the century, for example the reader-response criticism associated with the American theorist, Stanley Fish[8]). A "text" – and here I am using the word in the extended poststructuralist sense, that could mean a painting, or a marriage ceremony, or a person, or a historical event – is never just "itself," appeals to that reified entity being mere rhetorical flag-waving; rather it is something that a reader reads, differently. Most versions of reception theory stress the mediated, situated, contingent (which of course does not mean the same as arbitrary) character of readings, and that includes our own readings quite as much as those of past centuries. There is no Archimedean point

---

5 See Hardwick (2003a) ch. 2; for a compelling example of such work see Graziosi (2002).

6 Jauss's lecture had an enormous influence in Germany, much less elsewhere. This helps to explain why Anglo-American classics has been so slow to respond to the challenge of reception theory, whereas other aspects of contemporary theory, poststructuralism in particular, had (in however limited a sense) their effect from the early 1980s.

7 See Robert Holub, "Reception Theory: School of Constance," in Selden (1995) 319–46, p. 320. The lecture was subsequently retitled "Literary History as a Provocation to Literary Scholarship," and under that title included in Jauss (1982a), ch 1. Holub (1984), in Methuen's New Accents series, remains the best introduction to reception in general. For an account (somewhat unsympathetic) of some of the difficulties in Jauss's (constantly shifting) position see Nauta (1994).

8 See for a general survey Selden (1995) chapters 9–13. Fish's seminal *Is There a Text in This Class?* was published in 1980, but its genesis goes further back.

from which we can arrive at a final, correct meaning for any text. In Jauss's own words, the meaning of a text involves "a convergence of the structure of the work and the structure of the interpretation which is ever to be achieved anew," and that meaning is "a yielded truth – and not a given one – that is realized in discussion and consensus with others."[9] Jauss's approach owes a great deal to the hermeneutics espoused by his teacher Hans-Georg Gadamer (himself a pupil of Heidegger). Modifying Gadamer's idea of the fusion of horizons of text and reader, Jauss speaks of "the horizon of expectation" of the text, "an intersubjective system or structure of expectations"[10] (membership of a genre would be an obvious example), which enters, and may substantially modify, the different "horizon of expectation" of the reader.

A clear consequence of all this for classicists is, in the words of Julia Gaisser, author of an exemplary study of the reception of Catullus in the Renaissance,[11] "the understanding that classical texts are not only moving but changing targets." We are not the direct inheritors of antiquity. As Gaisser colourfully puts it, such texts "are not teflon-coated baseballs hurtling through time and gazed up at uncomprehendingly by the natives of various times and places, until they reach *our* enlightened grasp; rather, they are pliable and sticky artifacts gripped, molded, and stamped with new meanings by every generation of readers, and they come to us irreversibly altered by their experience."[12] On this model the sharp distinction between antiquity itself and its reception over the centuries is dissolved. A particular historical moment does not limit the significance of a poem; indeed the same Roman reader might construe, say, an ode of Horace very differently at different historical junctures – texts mean differently in different situations. One objection to historicism thus becomes that it is not historical enough.[13] The complex chain of receptions has the effect that a work can operate across history obliquely in unexpected ways. The aesthetic critic Walter Pater gives an illuminating instance of operations of the kind in his essay on Michelangelo:

> The old masters indeed are simpler; their characteristics are written larger, and are easier to read, than the analogues of them in all the mixed, confused productions of the modern mind. But when once we have succeeded in defining for ourselves

9   Segers (1979–80) 84, 86.
10 Holub in Selden (1995) 323.
11 Gaisser (1993).
12 Gaisser (2002) 387 (I would myself demur at Gaisser's totalizing "irreversibly" – the possible future of interpretation is never known).
13 So Bradshaw (1987) 96: "Even if we were so perverse as to want to read *Hamlet* as though Goethe and Mackenzie, Turgenev and Freud had never existed we still could not do so, any more than we can see what our grandparents saw in photographs of our parents as children – the intervening writers have shaped the sensibilities we bring to *Hamlet*. Trying . . . to cut out the intervening commentary by seeing the play in strictly 'Elizabethan terms' is *un*historical as well as aesthetically impossible."

those characteristics, and the law of their combination, we have acquired a standard or measure which helps us to put in its right place many a vagrant genius, many an unclassified talent, many precious though imperfect products of art. It is so with the components of the true character of Michelangelo. The strange interfusion of sweetness and strength is not to be found in those who claimed to be his followers; but it is found in many of those who worked before him, and in many others down to our own time, in William Blake, for instance, and Victor Hugo, who, though not of his school, and unaware, are his true sons, and help us to understand him, as he in turn interprets and justifies them.[14]

Such insights (could we call them "truths"?[15]) necessarily elude the positivist, but they can emerge, given a critic of Pater's subtlety, from the practices of reception.

Given the stress, within reception, on the situatedness and mediated character of all readings, there is no necessary quarrel between reception and "history" (that most elusive of jargon terms) – though, for the reasons we have just seen, Jauss was hostile to what he called "dogmatic historicism and positivism."[16] Indeed one value of reception is to bring to consciousness the factors that may have contributed to our responses to the texts of the past, factors of which we may well be "ignorant" but are not therefore "innocent";[17] hence the importance of possessing reception histories for individual texts. A poem is, from one point of view, a social event in history, as is any public response to it. But we also need to avoid privileging history over the other element in Jauss's model, the present moment in which the text is experienced, received, partly aesthetically (though that moment too is always potentially subject to historicization). If we respect both elements, our interpretations can become "critical," self-aware, recognizing our self-implication, but they will not thereby (necessarily) stand forever. History, as Duncan Kennedy well puts it, "is as much about *eventuation* as it is about original context"; and he continues "that is what 'Reception Studies' seeks to capture, and what the model of historicism prevalent in classical studies, with its recuperation of the notion of 'reception' for an original audience, seeks to eschew."[18]

My own view is that reception, on a Jaussian model, provides one intellectually coherent way of avoiding both crude presentism ("the reading that too peremptorily assimilates a text to contemporary concerns"[19]) and crude historicism. Antiquity and modernity, present and past, are always implicated in each other, always in dialogue – to understand either one, you need to think in terms of the

---

14   Pater (1980) 76.
15   They are not, of course, "facts."
16   Segers (1979–80) 84.
17   I take my terminology from McGann (1985) 87 (McGann offers a spirited defense of what we might call "historicist" reception studies).
18   Kennedy (2001) 88.
19   Armstrong (2003) 29.

other. James Porter, arguing that classics "so far from being an outmoded pursuit" is "essential and vital," observes that "modernity *requires* the study of antiquity for its self-definition: only so can it misrecognize itself in its own image of the past, that of a so-called classical antiquity."[20] But that is only to give half of the picture, for the reverse is also true (moreover, to use the word "misrecognize" rather than "recognize" is to move too swiftly to a particular hermeneutic stance – we might prefer "(mis)recognize"). This is no new insight. In "We Philologists" (1875) Nietzsche writes, "This is the antinomy of philology: *antiquity* has in fact always been understood *from the perspective of the present* – and should the *present* now be understood *from the perspective of antiquity?*"[21] Charles Baudelaire, in what became a founding text for Modernism and theories of modernity, "The Painter of Modern Life" (1863), sees antiquity and modernity as always interpenetrating, superimposed.[22] He starts by arguing that "beauty is always and inevitably of a double composition," an eternal element, and "a relative, circumstantial element, which will be, if you like, whether severally or all at once, the age, its fashions, its morals, its emotions." The second element is the element of modernity, "the ephemeral, the fugitive, the contingent."[23] Baudelaire would almost certainly have recalled a passage about Pheidias' building programme in Athens from Plutarch's *Life of Pericles*:

> So then the works arose, no less towering in their grandeur than inimitable in the grace of their outlines, since the workmen eagerly strove to surpass themselves in the beauty of their handicraft. And yet the most wonderful thing about them was the speed with which they rose . . . For this reason are the works of Pericles all the more to be wondered at; they were created in a short time for all time. Each one of them, in its beauty, was even then and at once antique; but in the freshness of its vigour it is, even to the present day, recent and newly wrought. Such is the bloom of perpetual newness, as it were, upon these works of his, which makes them ever to look untouched by time, as though the unfaltering breath of an ageless spirit had been infused into them.[24]

Thus from the moment of their creation the Parthenon sculptures were both old and new. But even in the work of the illustrator Constantin Guys, Baudelaire's "painter of modern life" himself, whose rapidly executed sketches brilliantly

---

20 Porter (2003) 64.
21 Cited Porter (2000) 15.
22 Benjamin (1983) 87.
23 Baudelaire (1964) 3, 13. See also Benjamin (1983), ch. 3, "Modernism," esp. 81 ("Modernity designates an epoch, but it also denotes the energies which are at work in this epoch to bring it close to antiquity"), 84 (though Benjamin underestimates the complexity of Baudelaire's thought on these matters).
24 *Pericles*, ch. 13 (translation by Bernadotte Perrin, from the Loeb Plutarch, vol. 3); I am grateful to Jim Porter for drawing my attention to this passage.

caught (or should that be catch?) the fleeting contingencies and ephemera of the modern world, the eternal element necessarily enters in, because Guys drew, not directly from life, but from memory (and even if he had drawn from life, it would still have involved a mental image, an element of idealization, of the mediated), and, equally importantly, because the immediacy of the moment of modernity has been frozen in a finished work of art, destined to become itself antiquity to our modernity. As Baudelaire puts it, "for any 'modernity' to be worthy of one day taking its place as 'antiquity,' it is necessary for the mysterious beauty which human life accidentally puts into it to be distilled from it."[25]

The desire to experience, say, Homer in himself untouched by any taint of modernity is part of the pathology of many classicists, but it is a deluded desire (even were such a thing possible, it could not satisfy, for it would no longer be "we" who were reading Homer). Pater, himself a classicist but one well versed in literature and philosophy generally, makes the point with characteristic suavity in his review of the poems of William Morris (*Westminster Review*, 1868):

> The composite experience of all the ages is part of each one of us; to deduct from that experience, to obliterate any part of it, to come face to face with the people of a past age, as if the middle age, the Renaissance, the eighteenth century had not been, is as impossible as to become a little child, or enter again into the womb and be born. But though it is not possible to repress a single phase of that humanity, which, because we live and move and have our being in the life of humanity, makes us what we are; it is possible to isolate such a phase, to throw it into relief, to be divided against ourselves in zeal for it, as we may hark back to some choice space of our own individual life. We cannot conceive the age; we can conceive the element it has contributed to our culture; we can treat the subjects of the age bringing that into relief. Such an attitude towards Greece, aspiring to but never actually reaching its way of conceiving life, is what is possible for art.[26]

The religious language that saturates the passage suggests that Pater felt in full the lure of the idea of an originary experience (according to Christ, if we are to enter the kingdom of heaven, we must become as little children), but he also knew the limits, and the advantages, of the possible. Accordingly he commends Morris, in his retelling of the old Greek stories, for eschewing a pastiche, and therefore fake, classicism in a merely antiquarian spirit, as well as, conversely, something that is "a disguised reflex of modern sentiment." We cannot read Morris's Greeks either as stock classical characters or as "just like us" in some vision of eternal

---

25 Baudelaire (1964) 13–14. For the whole argument see Prettejohn (2005) 102–9.

26 Pater (1868) 307. The essay, in shortened form and retitled "Aesthetic Poetry," was included in the first (1889) edition of *Appreciations* (Pater (1913)). Throughout this section I am indebted to a lecture by Elizabeth Prettejohn, "Homer and Beauty in Victorian Art."

human nature; instead the "early-ness" of Greek myth is interpreted through the earliest stirrings of the Renaissance in late medieval art and literature. By thus setting the medieval against the Hellenic Morris creates "a world in which the centaur and the ram with the fleece of gold are conceivable," even if "anything in the way of an actual revival must always be impossible."[27] The medievalism makes it evident that Morris's project is neither "a mere reproduction"[28] nor one of unthinking modernization, erasing the difference between past and present. What we have in Morris is a kind of "double-distancing"[29] (like the multiple-distancing in the passage from Pater's essay on Morris quoted above), and the friction between the various historical layers evoked allows the construal of our relationship to the past to be made in a sophisticated way.

For a classicism to be successful, in Pater's terms, it needs to be significant in both its classical aspect and in its modern one, not to subsume either one into the other. Indeed modernity can be modern only insofar as it postdates or supersedes the past, the embedded traces of which are, indeed, the very proof of modernity. Thus Pater shows us we cannot have antiquity without modernity; such a view would give us a classics that does not belong merely to the past, but to the present and the future.[30] In general Pater's thought is always dialectical in just this way. He is drawn to historicism, attracted by the absence within it of absolute values, the underlying relativism; but he also believes in the "House Beautiful," as something that exists in the present and is (at least potentially) alive for us, not in the form of some coercive Western tradition but as a sodality of artists who communicate across the ages.[31] So Pater's friend, the poet Swinburne, could communicate with his "brothers"[32] from other centuries:

27 Pater (1868) 300, 305, 307.
28 Pater (1868) 300.
29 I borrow this term from Michael Ann Holly, who used it in a response at the conference " 'Old Fancy or Modern Idea'?: Re-inventing the Renaissance in the 19th Century," organized by the University of Plymouth Art History Research Group and held in the Victoria and Albert Museum, 10–11 September 2004.
30 Cf. Prettejohn (2002) 121, on the paintings of Alma-Tadema: "the naïveté is ours, if we believe that a representation of the past can magically conjure the represented era without any participation of the representing one, and even more so if we thought that our own conceptions of the Roman past were somehow more 'objective' than those of the Victorians."
31 Pater (1913) 241: "that *House Beautiful*, which the creative minds of all generations – the artists and those who have treated life in the spirit of art – are always building together, for the refreshment of the human spirit" (from the Postscript). Pater anticipates, though in a much less authoritarian form, the arguments of T. S. Eliot's famous essay "Tradition and the Individual Talent" (1919), another key text for students of reception (Eliot (1951)).
32 His "sisters" too, among whom he numbered Sappho and Christina Rossetti.

My brother, my Valerius, dearest head
Of all whose crowning bay-leaves crown their mother
Rome, in the notes first heard of thine I read
      My brother.
No dust that death or time can strew may smother
Love and the sense of kinship inly bred
From loves and hates at one with one another.
To thee was Caesar's self nor dear nor dread,
Song and the sea were sweeter each than other:
How should I living fear to call thee dead,
      My brother?[33]

Things that have had value from different times and places in the past are available in the here and now, with the result we are not doomed either to a narrow and relentless presentism or to any form of historical teleology.

I have said that, since 1993, few have attempted, within classics, to theorize reception, or explore how such studies should best be pursued; indeed reception has been largely turned back into a form of positivist history, often of a rather amateurish kind. (The principle needs to be this: research on, say, the Victorians must be credible to Victorianists as well as classicists.) An exception to this reluctance to theorize is Simon Goldhill, who argues, in *Who Needs Greek?*, for a move away from a primarily literary approach to investigate broader cultural formations, "an extended range of cultural activities."[34] This seems to be part of a wider trend to collapse reception into cultural studies; witness the title of a recent collection from outside classics, *Reception Study: From Literary Theory to Cultural Studies*.[35] Goldhill's chapter on Plutarch shows both the strength and the blind-spots of his approach. From the Renaissance to the early nineteenth century Plutarch was one of the most admired ancient authors. The *Lives* was one of three works given to Frankenstein's monster to teach him about humanity and its ways (the other two were *Paradise Lost* and Goethe's *The Sorrows of Young Werther*). However Plutarch then suffered a catastrophic decline in reputation from which he has not yet recovered (though his appropriation by other writers, for example Shakespeare for his Roman plays, ensured his continued if subterranean presence). Nietzsche dismissed him as a "trivial latecomer," while the German ancient

---

33   "To Catullus," included in Gaisser (2001). This excellent volume is part of the useful Penguin Poets in Translation series, sadly now discontinued; other volumes treat Homer, Horace, Juvenal, Martial, Ovid, Seneca, and Virgil.

34   Goldhill (2002) 12.

35   Machor and Goldstein (2001); so too Hardwick (2003a) 5: "Reception studies, therefore, are concerned not only with individual texts and their relationship with one another but also with the broader cultural processes which shape and make up those relationships."

historian B. G. Niebuhr called the *Lives* "a collection of silly anecdotes."[36] Plutarch, it thus might seem, is exactly the kind of author who invites resuscitation through reception studies. Goldhill is primarily interested in what Plutarch shows us about being Greek in the Roman world, about cultural self-definition.[37] He does not seem to envisage the possibility that Plutarch could be truly alive again for us, other than as part of a purely historical inquiry. At one point he comments, "A modern reader *must* be bored by Plutarch"[38] – like so many of our current historicists Goldhill is, in his heart, a Hegelian, sharing Hegel's belief in the relentless and progressive forward march of *Geist*. Goldhill concludes his discussion thus:

> The title of this chapter posed the question "Why Save Plutarch?" not so that I can answer simply "because he is a good and interesting writer whose huge influence in pre-nineteenth-century Europe and America requires attention rather than ignoring, especially if writers of the stature of Rousseau, Shakespeare, Emerson are to be fully appreciated." Rather, it is because this question opens up the issue of cultural value itself, and of our inevitable complicity with its construction.[39]

The trouble with this formulation is that, for such a purpose, countless other writers would do just as well. To my thinking Goldhill's account ignores too much of what constitutes Plutarch's special "virtue" (Pater's word, in *The Renaissance*, for the unique aesthetic character of an artwork). As a result of that virtue, the distinctive quality of the *Lives* that held the imaginations of readers in the past, Plutarch at least once changed the world, as the scholar and literary critic Arthur Quiller-Couch, in a defense of the value of Greek, observed:

> I warn my countrymen . . . that gracious as the old Greek spirit is, and, apt to be despised because it comes jingling no money in its pocket, using no art but intellectual persuasion, they had wiselier, if only for their skins' sake, keep it a friend than exile or cage it. For, embodying the free spirit of man, it is bound to break out sooner or later, to re-invade . . . You may think this a fancy: but I warn you, it is no fancy. Twice the imprisoned spirit has broken loose upon Europe. The first time it slew over half of Europe an enthroned religion; the second time it slew an idea of monarchy. Its first access made, through the Renascence, a Reformation: its second made the French Revolution. And it made the French Revolution very largely (as any one who cares may assure himself by reading the memoirs of that time) by a simple translation of a Greek book – Plutarch's *Lives*. Now Plutarch is not, as we estimate ancient authors, one of the first rank. A late Greek, you may call him, an ancient

36   I take all this fascinating information from Goldhill (2002) 246–7, 284.
37   Goldhill (2002) 261 and *passim*.
38   Goldhill (2002) 292.
39   Goldhill (2002) 293.

musical at close of day:

> an easy garrulous tale-teller. That but weights the warning. If Plutarch, being such a man, could sway as he did the men who made the French Revolution, what will happen to our Church and State in the day when a Plato comes along to probe and test the foundations of both with his Socratic irony? Were this the last word I ever spoke, in my time here, I would bid any lover of compulsory "Natural Science" – our new tyranny – to beware that day.[40]

Quiller-Couch shares the dominant estimate of Plutarch of his time. But for some reader who dares break through the *Zeitgeist*, somewhere, who knows? Plutarch might yet change the world again. I fear too that, if we abandon a serious commitment to the value of the texts we choose for our attention and those of our students, we may end by trivializing reception within the discipline; already a classics student is far more likely to spend time analysing *Gladiator* than the *Commedia* of Dante. I find this trend worrying. This is not to decry the study of a wide range of cultural artefacts (there are many more good things in the world than the canon knows), and certainly not to criticize the study of film or even of popular culture. It is simply to say that we form ourselves by the company that we keep, and that in general material of high quality is better company for our intellects and hearts than the banal or the quotidian (often we use the latter, archly and somewhat cheaply, merely to celebrate our own cultural superiority). We need to believe in the value of what we do, and whatever we do we need to do it in full seriousness, not in any spirit of cynicism or condescension.

It is worth asking if the concept of "reception" today serves any useful purpose, now that the word's power to provoke has largely subsided. Simon Goldhill thinks it "too blunt, too *passive* a term for the dynamics of resistance and appropriation, recognition and self-aggrandisement" that he sees in the cultural processes he explores.[41] Perhaps so, but it is worth remembering that reception was chosen, in place of words like "tradition" or "heritage," precisely to stress the *active* role played by receivers. Reception can still serve the interests of a wider range of those receivers than classics has traditionally acknowledged, by recovering or rescuing diverse receptions. In that sense there could be said to be an egalitarian politics of reception. Lorna Hardwick talks of the power of such a classics to decolonize the mind[42] (though we should beware of complacency in that regard); certainly part of the potential virtue of reception is a commitment to pluralism. Yet we have to make choices amid the sheer diversity of the procedures and assumptions that reception embraces, or on occasion occludes. For some, reception is defined in terms of its postclassical subject matter, for others (including myself)

---

40 Quiller-Couch (1943) 192–3.
41 Goldhill (2002) 297; so too Hall (2004) 61.
42 Hardwick (2003a) 110.

it is a way of doing classics that is at odds with the positivism of much that is now labelled "reception." I have argued throughout this introduction that reception involves the acknowledgement that the past and present are always implicated in each other. Others rather hope, through reception, to strip away accretions, and see antiquity for itself with greater clarity:

> Although sharing with more familiar and traditional approaches to Classical schol-
> arship a commitment to advancing collective understanding of Greek and Roman
> antiquity, this new approach is also quite distinct: it is set apart by its conviction
> that the ancient texts can only ever be truly understood in the social and cultural
> contexts which originally produced them if the layers of meaning which have
> become attached to them over the intervening centuries are systematically excavated
> and brought to consciousness . . . By considering how individual texts, authors,
> intellectual currents and historical periods have been "received" in diverse later con-
> texts, this approach enhances the clarity with which texts can be seen when returned
> to their original producers, now separated, to an extent, from the anachronistic
> meanings imposed upon them.[43]

I have already given reasons against such an approach, and there are others. How could one ever know if one had truly stripped away all the layers of "anachron-ism" in this process of intellectual ascesis? And, even could one do so, what would be left might turn out to be rather evidently impoverished. If we strip away all "accretions," we don't get the "original truth" but something much more insub-stantial (we need a method for "adding" something as well as acknowledging losses). We shall not, for example, find a "real" Sappho if by that we mean one for which there is convincing corroborating evidence from her own time (we have anyway only about 3 percent of what she wrote). We may sneer at Wilamowitz's view that Sappho ran a girls' school; but is a widespread current view that she created "a cohesive social group for women" any less transparently ideological?[44] Our self-implication is more than usually self-evident in such cases, and why should we seek to pretend otherwise? Whatever the case in Archaic Lesbos, the certainty is that Sappho is now a lesbian (as Emily Wilson wittily puts it, "it is only a slight exaggeration to say that Baudelaire, through Sappho, invented modern lesbian-ism, and Swinburne brought it to England"). Should we give up all this richness – in exchange for little or nothing?[45]

---

43   Rowe et al. (2003) 3; so too Hardwick (2003a) 3: "This kind of study has proved
      valuable in that it has enabled people to distinguish more readily between the ancient
      texts, ideas and values and those of the society that appropriated them."
44   See Wilson (2004) 27–8 (the subsequent quotation is from p. 27).
45   For Sappho's reception see, *inter alia*, DeJean (1989); Dubois (1995); Greene
      (1996); Prins (1999); Reynolds (2001); Reynolds (2003), though much still remains
      to be uncovered.

What's in a name? In the years to come people may, or they may not, find "reception" a useful label for certain scholarly activities. But the issues raised by Jauss's *Rezeptionsästhetik* will not readily go away. Two things above all I would have classics embrace: a relaxed, not to say imperialist, attitude towards what we may study as part of the subject, and a subtle and supple conception of the relationship between past and present, modern and ancient. Then classics could again have a leading role among the humanities, a classics neither merely antiquarian nor crudely presentist, a classics of the present certainly, but also, truly, of the future.

1

Provocation

The Point of Reception Theory

William W. Batstone

All meaning is constituted or actualized at the point of reception.[1] This, the founding claim of reception study, seems hardly contestable. After all, what meaning is there that is not already a received meaning? As a result, reception study can include perspectives as diverse as those of the editors of this volume: the one finds in reception theory both the enrichment of meaning by the reception of the past and the liberation of meaning for the individual reader in the present;[2] the other finds in the practical history of Virgil's reception a distortion of Virgil's original vision and brings historicist and methodological tools to bear on that reception in order to correct our understanding.[3] Both approaches, however, seem to me to share a strong commitment to the subjectivity of the reader. Whether we are correcting the omissions and suppressions of readers like Goebbels and Dryden or imagining the redemption of the text in a reader who accepts her historicity, commits herself to the text, and finds the "Love that moves the sun and the other stars,"[4] we seem to have assumed something about reading and reception that can bear further discussion, and what we have assumed is the point of reception. And in doing this the project has, I believe, often betrayed the point of reception theory. In other words, the project has become yet another effort to place ourselves above rather than in the complexity of reading and writing.

My interest in reception theory, then, is in the point of reception and how we might think about it within the same postmodern discourses that have directed our attention away from the *mens auctoris* and the "text itself" toward the historicity and biases that constitute our being in the world and our access to understanding. I can only offer a brief outline of some of the considerations that

---

1   Martindale (1993) 3.
2   Martindale (1993).
3   Thomas (2001).
4   Martindale (1993) 106.

are part of my thinking about this, a thinking that is still in process. Like all texts this is a pastiche of other texts in words that are not my own.[5]

I begin with the linguisticality of the world which takes us back to Heidegger and Gadamer. "Language is the fundamental mode of our being-in-the-world and the all-embracing form of the constitution of the world." ". . . [W]ords and language are not wrappings in which things are packed for the commerce of those who write and speak. It is in words and language that things first come into being and are."[6] This means that in terms of our consciousness, language precedes the world. It is the medium into which we are born and it carries with it values and meanings that reach as far back into the past as they do into the future. This is possible because from within language meaning is not arbitrary; metaphor is connected to metaphor, metonymy to metonymy and the briefcase has long ceased to carry the lawyer's briefs while the word still does. This does not, of course, mean that the "briefcase" essentially carries "underpants" or "legal briefs," only that you cannot get the "briefs" out of the "briefcase." Any symbolic system carries with it its history, its future and play. "We can only speak and think in and through a particular language that we did not create, so that we are always thinking and speaking in a medium that is structured for us (historically) without its being mapped to the world in such a way that reveals the world without a point of view or with a *universal* point of view."[7]

But, while language from within language is not arbitrary, it is not fixed either; it is filled with play, like the play of a door on its hinge, and this play facilitates the self-renewing give and take of the game of meaning.[8] It is in this play that the child comes to language and to consciousness. She plays with the play of language. Like adolescents who play with social roles and future identities; like the clever slave who plays with the plot. And this play is an act of world construction and of self-construction, one that proceeds in part from mimesis and in part from figuration: it is always a play with difference, but it is also the play that allows difference to become part of identity: the child plays with the heft, the value and force of "ma ma" or of "I love you," she plays with the counter-move those moves precipitate.

---

5   In fact, this essay was written for oral presentation and was not so much the product of research and investigation as the result of reflection on the work of Heidegger, Gadamer, Bakhtin, Barthes, Derrida, Kristeva, and others whom I have read over the years. No attempt has been made to fill out the huge secondary bibliography, and individual quotes are sometimes more the result of whom I happened to be reading at the time of writing than they are indicative of the most influential or important thinkers on the particular topic.

6   Heidegger (2000) 15.

7   Hahn (2002) 51.

8   See, further, Gadamer (1998) 101–34; (1976) 66.

The process of coming to language and coming to consciousness combines what Kristeva referred to as the semiotic pulse of drive and desire[9] with the logical and syntactic organization of linguistic signification. It includes the operations of the imaginary, the identification strategies (introjection and projection) that are necessary for the subject to come forth and to make use of other processes like condensation and displacement.[10] Consciousness, then, is not only linguistic and symbolic, but to a large degree precipitated by the unconscious (which, as we know from Freud and Lacan is not only structured like a language but structured by language). Consciousness, then, is structured by the drives and desires we suppress for the sake of the images and mirages we identify with. Among these drives and passions we should never underestimate the passion for ignorance, a passion that seems to support and underwrite the other great passions of love and hatred. But, "When does the child become master of language?," Gadamer asks. The answer is clearly, "Never." The gathering of meaning is "the ongoing game in which the being-with-others of men occurs"[11] – and not only that but it is the game in which the being-with-self occurs.

But this process of coming to language is not merely a kind of permeation of consciousness with language as if it were a dye: in your teal and magenta world you become teal and magenta. We are always shaping and being shaped by the questions we are asking; we are always, as Heidegger likes to say, "underway." But, if our consciousness takes place in a language that precedes us in a world into which we are thrown, how can our own difference, our own meaning take place? Language and mimesis bring with them two powerful tools. First, there it is an entailment of mimesis and iterability that the imitation is not in the same place as the exemplar. This has two implications. Words always mean differently: if I want you to understand my words, I want you to understand them from your position. I want you to understand differently. But, by the same token, my words, words which are never mine to begin with, are also always only mine: that is, what I say here and now, in this place and time, can never be said again, not by me or by you, not even if we repeat these words. The event will always be different. For Bakhtin, this is the ground of responsibility and it creates the nature of the event of self.[12] As a result, in repetition and in play, language acquisition, which includes hearing our own words in the mouth of another, which includes our inner dialogue, is always an act of mimesis and appropriation, always both similar and different. In the event, we receive and give back to the common world, and what is most personal is paradoxically and simultaneously most public and common. Second, the acquisition of language is not just the acquisition of words or narratives, of images and prejudices and interpretive protocols. It is the

---

9   See Kristeva (1984) 19–106; (1996) 19–27.
10 See Kristeva (1995) 103–106.
11 Gadamer (1976) 56.
12 See Bakhtin (1993).

acquisition of figures, of ways to use and abuse language, of lies and irony and metaphor and metonymy. This means that, wherever consciousness goes, language has already been. This means that part of the heft of learning to say "I love you" is learning to write those words in the wind and the water. In fact, these three words, the most intimate and desired of words, can help summarize our being in language: they are words that have been in and out of the mouths of count-less lovers and countless liars, and we want them in our mouths and in our ears; they are shifty words made with shifters, and always understood from the other person's point of view, that complex point of reception where semiosis and symbol, projection and repression intersect. (We have already suppressed much of what we do not know.) And so, if language is consciousness and language never stops, then "heterogeneity within signification points to heterogeneity within the speaking subject; if language is a dynamic process then the subject is a dynamic process."[13]

Reading then is the complex act of hearing the words of another, which is the complex act of making them fit within the linguistic structure and context (that is, history and genetics) of our own consciousness – it brings new contexts and analogies that are understood by virtue of old contexts and figures. It may uncover ideas that were already ours but of which we were ignorant; it may bring the familiar into unforeseen combinations. It may require the invention of new metaphors or new blindnesses just as it can stir old passions and refigure for-gotten stories.

The point of reception conceived in this way, is not some thing-like point "within" the consciousness of the objective Thing-like reader; it is not some organic entity (like "brain") that precedes the text; it cannot be isolated or stopped any more than identity is isolated within me or language can be stopped and placed under "my" control. The point of reception is the ephemeral interface of the text; it occurs where the text and the reader meet and is simultaneously constitutive of both. ("The house was quiet and the world was calm . . . The words were spoken as if there was no book" (Wallace Stevens[14]).) At the point of reception the text comes alive as the consciousness of the reader. In this way, "to understand what the work of art says to us is . . . a self-encounter."[15] We lose ourselves in the hori-zon of the other (that is, in the words that are the traces of that otherness). We play the other as we did as a child. But in representing the other, we play our-selves. In the theatre of plurality we find the fiction of identity. That is because we cannot understand what we do not understand, and so, when we come to understanding (of any thing, of the other) we come to self-understanding. But the "Other makes the subject other to itself."[16] And so we find the uncanny at

13   Kristeva (2002) xviii.
14   Stevens (1972) 279.
15   Gadamer (1976) 101.
16   Kristeva (2002) xviii.

the heart of the familiar. "Meaning is constituted through an embodied relation with another person . . . it is constituted in relation to an other and it is beyond any individual subjectivity."[17]

This process has important implications. Just as the pattern of language is already found within the body, so the social relation inhabits the psyche: the logic of alterity, then, is already found in consciousness. Reading, then, like geopolitics,[18] requires that we learn to live with the return of the repressed other within our own psyches, to experience ourselves as subjects in process, subjects on trial, to experience the repressed other within. This is how we learn to live with others who are not merely other, and this is how we articulate an ethical relationship between conscious and unconscious, self and other, citizen and foreigner, identity and difference; this is how we live with ourselves – not as the reader and his book that are one in the quiet of night, but as the reader and his book that are both same and different, that meet at the point of reception.

If the point of reception is this merger of the poet's words and my own, the point where the neoteric tri-kolon crescendo reverberates in our imagination of Cicero's own reading,[19] "quot sunt, quotque fuere, Marce Tulli / quotque post aliis erunt in annis" ("as many as are and as many as have been, Marcus Tullius, and as many as will be in years to come"), we can see, I think, how our reading always changes the text and how the text always changes us. And so, it is not a contradiction to say, on the one hand, that all understanding is self-understanding, made possible only by the foreknowledge and prejudices of our being in the world, and, on the other, that a text can change one's life. "For self-understanding only realizes itself in the understanding of a subject matter"[20] – that is, it has the structure of alterity – and that "The self that we are does not possess itself"[21] – that is, we are what happens. "One must take up into himself what is said to him in such fashion that it speaks and finds an answer in the words of his own language."[22] – that is in words inhabited by the reader's prejudices, desires, blindnesses, and imaginary. "When it does begin to speak, however, it does not simply speak its word, always the same, in lifeless rigidity, but gives ever new answers to the person who questions it and poses ever new questions to him who answers it."[23] The text like the reader is always changing, always the same.

Now, if it is right to think of understanding and self in this way, then we are, as Bakhtin already said, an event, a project thrown into the world and caught between the imperfect of our past and the future perfect of our present (our desire).

---

17 Kristeva (2002) xviii.
18 Kristeva (1991) 169–92.
19 See Batstone (2002) 116–17.
20 Gadamer (1976) 55.
21 Gadamer (1976) 55.
22 Gadamer (1976) 57.
23 Gadamer (1976) 57.

This is the point of reception: where words, not my words, not your words, intersected with the past (memory, tradition, even individual history, and, of course, the unconscious) and the future (desire, chance, and ideology) are repeated in the future perfect of the present. The iterability of the text insures that it always eludes (plays out and out-plays) the maker; but it always eludes the receiver as well. When I have changed – and I will – it will be there and a new "I" will make it flicker with presence and absence or with the fulness of being, a sublime or an abjected object.

So, what are the consequences or implications of this view? First of all, if it is true to say that while the material text remains the same, the received text always changes, then the text is never redeemed – or, perhaps better, it is always being converted. If reading like the self is always open, if it is always an act of self-understanding (which cannot *not* be a mirage) and of world construction (which cannot *not* be political), we may always ask, "Why stop here?" It would seem that every reading is, as Nietzsche said in 1880, a will to power.[24] When done publicly, not only does it add to the possible voices of meaning (to the figures and language in the theatre of plurality), but it establishes a curriculum and projects a future. Goebbels was right, and that is why Thomas believes in the suppression of Goebbels' reading. And this is also true of the practical suggestions made by *Redeeming the Text*.

The claim, "What else indeed could (say) 'Virgil' be other than what readers have made of him over the centuries?"[25] is itself subject to both its own historicity and its political ambition. In other words, it is an effort to change the point of reception. This is true, first of all, at the *curricular* level, where we can note that many of the readers that concern Thomas's book are strikingly absent from *Redeeming the Text*. How might Goebbels or Mussolini or even Stauffenberg figure within the claim that Virgil can only be what readers have made of him? These readers require an oppositional reading, a reading that suppresses their ambitions. And, secondly, since history, like reception, is always open, it is up to us to determine not just what the importance of Dryden's reading is, but what Dryden means. The past is still before us and we must always write the history of reception.

Another aspect of the politics of reception appears in the pleasure of the text that Martindale imagines: namely, *the reader* who finds in dialogue with the text the Love that moves the sun and other stars. As fetching and powerful as this image is, we might hesitate before its autoerotic implications. We might recognize that other readers construct their texts to fill other desires: the *fetishistic* reader who reads the divided text, the text of stiletto heels and tongues and the curve of phrase; the *obsessive* reader who gives himself to the secondary codes and the metalanguages of his text; the *paranoic* reader who constructs and consumes the complicated and devious secrets of the text; and the *hysteric* who throws himself

24 Nietzsche (1980) 487, borrowed by Barthes (1975) 62.
25 Martindale (1993) 10.

across the body of the text and is ravished.[26] And to this list we could add
the intellectual pleasures of mimesis, the diversionary pleasures of escapism, the
kathartic pleasures of Aristotelian tragedy, and the hectoring pleasures of a
puritan sermon.

Finally (and I am not pretending to be complete), reception theory positions
us to question every will to power that stops the meaning of the text or the history
of reception. I mean by this more than philological interrogation (although there
are many questions to be raised). I have in mind something a little more elusive,
but related. If all understanding is self-understanding and if the self is always a
project caught between an imperfect past and the future perfect desire of the present, then within the language of consciousness and understanding something is
always suppressed and always revised. It is, after all, how we construct a psyche,
how we imagine an identity, how we live with ourselves as we make promises and
create worlds. And, it is how we read and understand. This means that the very
trope according to which the Augustan reading is optimistic pamphleteering in
contrast to an ambivalent reading is itself not only an asymmetrical construction
of alternatives, but itself a suppression. Why could there not be an ambivalent-
Augustan reading? Or a redemptive-Augustan reading? If Goebbels' Virgil amid
the plans for the Holocaust is anathema, what about the Confederate Virgil –
Turnus defending the institution of slavery from the imperialistic *Libertas* of the
Roman North? And why should our ambivalence not make us ambivalent about
ambivalence? Sometimes it is the time for action and ambivalence is an indulgent
and destructive luxury. But, no matter where you turn something is suppressed,
and, whatever it is, it is you. And that is not really all that bad. For, as Lacan
liked to point out, the suppressions of the unconscious not only mean that we
are worse than we believe, but also that we are better than we know.

So reception theory, it seems to me, opens up the political discussion. It raises
important questions about text, reading, meaning, and understanding, questions
that I think need to be considered in terms of the point of reception: what
Heidegger called *Dasein*. But reception theory cannot itself provide normative
answers regarding reception because the past is always imperfect, always awaiting
tomorrow to become what it will have been. The point of reception theory, then,
is to return reception and the point of reception to its important work of self-
understanding and world construction, to the important work of changing the
point of reception.

26 See Barthes (1975) 62–3.

Part I
Reception in Theory

2

Literary History as a Provocation to Reception Studies[1]

Ralph Hexter

The majority of essays in the present collection take up questions of reception with a decided emphasis on central theoretical questions. What, for example, does a focus on reception contribute to our ability to read, understand, and interpret works of the past, in the case of this volume, primarily so-called "classical" literary texts from ancient Greece and Rome? One might say, then, that in our approach to reception, we are coming to grips with the larger question of hermeneutic possibility or, rather, possibilities, since a number of the essays pluralize reception along various significant parameters, among them gender and class. Whether this is actually just another mode of philology pure and simple remains to be seen; surely it is not, if by "philology" is understood an anti-historicist positivism, but in its longer history, "philology" has usually been much broader than that. She was, after all, thought by Martianus Capella to be a bride fit for no less a hermeneut than Mercury ("De Nuptiis Mercurii et Philologiae").

My aim here is to focus attention on a possibly subordinate issue, one that, come to think of it, seems to have received surprisingly little attention: reception history in the sense of reception historiography, and in particular, reception studies organized around the reception tradition of a single author's works. When reception studies as such were inaugurated, which one might date to Hans-Robert Jauss's essay to which I allude in my title,[2] the idea of reorganizing the writing of literary history by shifting focus from author to reader, from "influence" to reception, was a central one. Indeed, it was programmatic. Jauss's own approach had its roots in phenomenology (for example, his key phrase "horizon of expectation" (*Erwartungshorizont*)) and an even longer history of hermeneutics, both

---

1 The title is intended as an homage to Hans Robert Jauss's original provocatory address now some 35 years in the past.

2 "Literaturgeschichte als Provokation der Literaturwissenschaft" (in Jauss (1994) 144–205). A somewhat less than ideal English translation appears in *Toward an Aesthetic of Reception* (Jauss (1982a)).

philosophical and biblical; in fact, almost immediately writing emerged that either developed the literary-historical parameters of Jauss's provocative essay[3] or emphasized the hermeneutic axis. Jauss himself was as interested in "reception" for its axiological potential: in other words, as a source for aesthetic judgments.[4] However, the historical and even the aesthetic dimensions of "reception theory" and even "reception history" faded in the face of the growing emphasis on the reader qua reader, obviously the cornerstone of any reception-based approach but now the focus of analysis and systematization all its own. The impulse in this direction derived also from Germany, specifically from Wolfgang Iser, like Jauss at work in Konstanz,[5] who popularized the term "reading process" (*Lesevorgang*), but its elaboration occurred primarily in English studies (Iser's own field) and first in the United States (where Iser soon started teaching and publishing).[6] Focus on the reader *à la* Iser in the field of English found ready resonance. It had a glorious precursor in I. A. Richards,[7] and almost simultaneous with Iser's first publications a home-grown American tradition of reader-focused analysis sprang to life.

While focus on the reading process is not necessarily ahistorical, for readers are perforce historical actors, some noted work in the English tradition has de-emphasized the historical.[8] More Jaussian and thus, in my sense, more historical is the early writing of Stanley Fish, focused in that phase of his career on the seventeenth century.[9] Subsequent studies in the English tradition have focused

3   Born the same year as Jauss's essay was the journal *New Literary History*. Ralph Cohen (1974) anthologizes a number of significant pieces printed in the early years of *NLH*. In German, note Gunter Grimm (1977). An early attempt at an overview is the first edition of Rainer Warning (1994), published in 1975. Both Warning's and Grimm's volumes have extensive bibliography of the work up to their respective dates of publication. An indispensable English-language orientation in the first 15 years of reception theory is that of the Germanist Robert C. Holub (1984).

4   In the original "Literaturgeschichte" (Jauss (1994)), note the famous essay on *Madame Bovary*. Also in 1968, Jauss, a medieval Romance philologist in the great tradition of Auerbach and Spitzer, edited *Die nicht mehr schönen Künste: Grenzphänomene des Ästhetischen* (Jauss (1968)). His own attempt at systematizing a reception-based aesthetic emerged as *Ästhetische Erfahrung und literarische Hermeneutik* (Jauss (1982b)); its first part, issued in 1977, was translated into English as *Aesthetic Experience and Literary Hermeneutics* (Jauss (1982c)).

5   Iser (1971); in English, Iser (1978b). His own further work and reception is primarily based in the United States.

6   His next book, Iser (1978a), followed almost at once. A collection that well displays the impact of this line of criticism is Suleiman and Crosman (1980).

7   Richards (1929).

8   For example, the more psychologically focused readerly analysis (and thus in a sense more in the Richards tradition) represented by Holland (1975).

9   I think first and foremost of Fish (1971 and 1972), virtually contemporary with Iser's publications. Among his later, more theoretical elaborations of reader-based analysis is Fish (1980).

attention on reading in earlier societies with different textual and publication processes, not to mention different modes of literacy, as well as in different communities (to pick up a term of Fish's) of readers, most importantly, in my view, women.[10]

This by no means exhausts the streams of reader-based analyses in the 1970s and early 1980s. Umberto Eco came to the analysis of the reader's role from semiotics,[11] hardly a surprise, since no system of sign theory can do without a recipient, explicit in Jauss and his fellow German theorists. In contrast, the French tradition seems somewhat bipolar. On the one hand, before 1968 (and Jauss) is Robert Escarpit's *Sociologie de la littérature*, which could be read, at least in retrospect, as an early contribution to reception history.[12] After 1968, one could certainly point to many of Roland Barthes's most influential works as performances of literary analysis from a readerly perspective. Though different in style of representation, *S/Z*, codes and all, has its surprisingly Jaussian dimensions.[13]

As this volume and earlier works of so many of its contributors amply establish, if classics as a field was somewhat slow to embrace wholeheartedly new literary critical modes that focused on the reader, it has long since made up for lost time. The manifold investigations of intertextuality, which has to a large extent remapped the entire field of Roman literary studies, are oriented around the textual experiences and repertoire of readers (and authors as readers), though some of the "early adopters" of reception, or at least of readerly analysis, within classics exhibit interest in a broader range of areas, from hermeneutics and narratology to gender, sexual, and nationalist politics.[14]

I think it valuable, even from the very "middest" of current rich work that digs deeply in certain fields within the large land of "reception," to reflect back on

10 A good starting point, but only that, is Schweickart and Patrocinio (1986). A full exploration in this area would range from Fetterley's "resistant reader" (1978) through the conceptualization of "reading like a man" (Dinshaw (1989), esp. 28–64). A recent investigation of reading, literacy, and gender in the early modern period is Ferguson (2003).

11 Eco (1979).

12 Escarpit (1964). Even if one sees this as more a contribution to the "history of taste," in general no complimentary term, in fact, Jauss's own individual analyses not only contribute to but are in part based in *Geschmacksgeschichte*. An uncannily contemporary example of *Geschmacks-* and *Rezeptionsgeschichte* to which I will return is Dörrie (1968).

13 Barthes (1970); in English, Barthes (1974). See also Foucault (1977); Barthes (1973); in English, Barthes (1975). A relatively early survey that sought to emphasize the poststructuralist overtones of the school of reader-response analysis was Tompkins (1980).

14 Bartsch (1984); Block (1984); Winkler (1985); Slater (1990); Hexter (1990); Selden (1992), as well as Hexter (1992) in the same volume. Two important collections from this period are Pedrick and Rabinowitz (1982) and Woodman and Powell (1992).

earlier explorations and other avenues taken, or at least started, within this capacious and oh-so-malleable territory. One of the literary historical industries that long predates modern reception studies is that of tracing the tradition of a single author. Studies of this sort are legion, for example, the hoary examples of Domenico Comparetti's work on Virgil, Spargo's more narrow study of Virgil the magician, or Rand's *Ovid and His Influence*.[15] Such studies were, as Rand's title makes explicit, pursued as histories of "influence," so that, with the reorientation of perspective called for by Jauss and others (and in the wake of the general embarrassment about literary history itself), studies of such literary traditions became perforce reception-based inquiries. And rightly so. That I do not mean to dispute.

Since it has been for some time an area of my interest and activity, let me remain with Ovid, and use the opportunity afforded me here to air some of the most fundamental methodological questions that trouble – or should trouble – all of us who write chapters in the *Nachleben* of a classical author, or any author for that matter. The problem need not (necessarily) inhere in any single chapter. In other words, Jauss would permit us (and in his work often exemplifies) the reconstruction of a single moment of reception on or along a particular historical "horizon of expectation." So, to pick a fairly well-known example, one might certainly write a focused study of the *Ovide moralisé*, by far the most influential of medieval translations of Ovid's *Metamorphoses* into any vernacular, whereby one understands translation as it was practiced in the Middle Ages, at least for literary works, as offering considerable freedom for reduction, expansion, and adaptation. The immediately preceding clause already begins the work of setting the *Ovide moralisé* in its original horizon of expectations, explaining to modern readers what fourteenth-century readers would even without thinking understand about the work even before they actually encountered it. Jeremy Dimmick dedicates two pages of his survey "Ovid in the Middle Ages: Authority and Poetry" to it, well describing it as "an Ovidian and post-Ovidian museum, under Christian curatorship."[16]

> It incorporates earlier French adaptations, including the *Philomena* sometimes attributed to Chrétien de Troyes (6.2183–3840). Its expanded account of the Trojan War brings in material from the *Heroides*, and more unlikely sources: when Paris has made his judgement in favour of Venus (11.1473–2400), she provides him with commandments of love which précis the *Ars amatoria*, and the whole scene seems to be modelled on Amant's homage to the god of love in Guillaume de Lorris' *Roman de la Rose*.[17]

---

15   Comparetti (1896); in English, Comparetti (1908 and 1997); Spargo (1934); Rand (1963). From the same period is Munari (1960).
16   Dimmick (2002), with discussion of the *Ovide moralisé* concentrated in pp. 278–80; cited here is p. 279.
17   Dimmick (2002) 279.

As Dimmick indicates, in coming to understand the *Ovide moralisé* we need to expand our interpretive horizons[18] across the whole Ovidian canon, including not only other "Ovidiana" but their own individual reception traditions, along with the sequence of commentaries above all on the *Metamorphoses*.[19] His references to Chrétien and the *Roman de la Rose* point to yet other horizons that also must be taken into account, here – as often in the case of classical authors in the medieval period and later – the horizons of vernacular literary tradition(s).

Dimmick highlights here, in line with his program, points where the vernacular tradition is already heavily invested in Ovid – Chrétien as (likely) adapter of Ovidian tales, Guillaume de Lorris, author of the first portion of *Roman de la Rose*, with its fountain of Narcissus. This is precisely the point at which I want to ask the question that troubles me: where do we draw the line? Granted, all historical work involves setting boundaries, but I want to put in question the seeming inevitability that when we set out to write a history of Ovidian reception, even of one era,[20] we as a matter of course privilege the Ovidian linkages that both precede and follow any work that appears in our sequence. The *Ovide moralisé* also incorporates non-Ovidian material, from Statius' *Thebaid* in book 9, for example. Should we not, at least in some ideal version of such an account, find a way to calibrate the reception of Ovid with that of Statius (not to mention Virgil)?[21] Even seemingly Ovidian episodes have wider fields. Another

18 These horizons are not the same, of course, as the horizons of expectations of the *Ovide moralisé's* first audience, but as interpreter one seeks to elaborate interpretive horizons that permit us to reconstruct and understand the historical horizon(s). There may be a function of mirroring in this; in the ultimate act of aesthetic appreciation and judgment, the horizons are, in Jauss's project, to "melt" (*verschmelzen*), but as historical interpreters we hold short of liquefaction.

19 Beyond Pierre Bersuire (Petrus Berchorius), whose *Ovidius moralizatus* – the fifteenth book of his expansive *Reductorium morale*, the entirety written with preachers in mind – has intense and complex interconnections with the *Ovide moralisé*, one could expand one's purview to what was by this time a good century and a half of explanatory commentary and allegorizations (natural-scientific, euhemerist, moral, and overtly Christian) by such named sources as Arnulf of Orléans, John of Garland, and Giovanni del Virgilio. Bersuire, early versions of whose commentary may have contributed material to the *Ovide moralisé*, himself incorporated material from the *Ovide moralisé* into the last of the stages (1342). See further, Hexter (1989), esp. 53–6.

20 A recent example would be the valuable survey by Ziolkowski (2005).

21 The impact of Statius' *Thebaid* and even the fragmentary *Achilleid*, epics only recently returning to the center of critical attention, in the Middle Ages can hardly be overstated. Even before the period of which I have been speaking, the reception of Statius "interfered" in significant ways with the reception of Virgil and Ovid. If I had focused this essay more on the Virgilian tradition, I would be making the point that while Macrobius and Fulgentius, for example, have their places in any history of the reception of the *Aeneid*, neither of them is as significant for understanding the *Roman*

twelfth-century episode like the *Philomena* incorporated into the *Ovide moralisé* is the *Pyramus and Thisbe* (*Ovide moralisé* 4.219–1169). A full account would want to bring in the entire complex of *Pyramus and Thisbe* exercises popular in schools.[22] What we have seems very much like a large room where the voices of these texts echo and reecho. The risk of cacophony cannot put us off from realizing that the music we make ourselves hear is a simplification. Can we achieve at least polyphony?

And should we not also be setting the *Ovide moralisé* in the context of all the vernacular options available to its first audience, whether for edification or entertainment? (As if the boundaries there were easily drawn!) Then of course we must take into account the wider history of the years during which the *Ovide moralisé* was put together (1316–28) and consider what its special significance may have been for Jeanne, wife of Philip V, who seems to have been its intended recipient. Not only what we might imagine her to have made of it, but what its makers might have wanted her to make of it, hoping to anticipate her desires (rightly or wrongly). In an earlier note I referred to the work's "first audience," and by definition there was one. But it is important to realize that the modern edition on which we all rely[23] tends to obscure the significant variation among manuscripts, each of which permits us a perspective and purchase on its reception even as it complicates any account of that reception. There were multiple *Ovides moralisés*.[24]

We may grant, and of course we must grant, that every historian faces the challenge of drawing some boundaries about his or her study. Perhaps everything is connected, but some connections are more significant than others, and we look to historians to make precisely that claim, explicitly and implicitly, in their works, starting with their choice of focus, their organization of the material, and their

---

d'Eneas* as is knowledge of the history of the reception of Statius' *Thebaid* and, above all, of the *Roman de Thèbes*. And were we to proceed thence to Heinrich van Veldeke's *Eneit*, we would need to draw in a swarm of other romances, in Middle High German and in Old French as relevant. And so on, *ad infinitum*.

22 Edited by De Boer (1921); cf. Glendinning (1986).
23 De Boer (1966 [1915–18]).
24 Cf. Jung (1994); he lists some 23 manuscripts (pp. 170–1), suggesting that a thorough study of the tendencies of each manuscript remains a desideratum. As in the case of commentaries, where each manuscript even of an attributed commentary can exhibit differences, sometimes small, sometimes large, each manuscript is a witness – in the truest sense of the word – to a different instance of reception and in turns allows us to reconstruct a potentially distinct horizon of expectation, so each of the *Ovide moralisé* manuscripts could let us read a different refraction of Ovid, and all the other figures and texts behind the *Ovide moralisé*, as many as our analytic procedures and minds can allow us to perceive. I leave to the side the fifteenth-century history of prose reworkings of the *Ovide moralisé*.

narrative. What I am raising as a concern here is that by revisiting – with no seeming end in sight – the reception traditions of classical literature rather unimaginatively author by author, and repetitively for an author like Ovid,[25] we are deepening channels and fortifying ways of thinking we ought rather to be conceiving as temporary assemblages that should give way to yet other imaginary constructions.

Of such studies, whether an individual author's monograph surveying or collective endeavors organized around the reception tradition of a single classical text or author, I believe we must pose the question: precisely what historical connections obtain between subsequent readings of a given work (or subsequent readers of an author's works)? As I began to suggest in the case of the *Ovide moralisé*, above, are not all texts historically fully and only to be explained in the moment and against the horizon of their arising? That moment may be replete with earlier readings, but it will be the business of the reception historian (if I can use that term) to instance the degree to which those earlier readings are alive in the historical moment in question.

The questions I am raising about reception history here are in some ways not new. They are essentially the questions that already in the third quarter of the twentieth century were being raised about the historicity of "literary history" *tout court*.[26] My concern extends beyond the worry that reception histories of the sort I have been describing may in the end be no more than a sequence of individual moments that we are, if for no reason other than habit, privileging, to the fear that, in organizing such by tracing readings of a single author's work or works, we are organizing such chronicles in a maximally irrational way. Again, are separate instances of Ovidian reception part of the same history, and if so, how? Some are clearly hard to link historically in any meaningful way. What has, for instance, Maximus Planudes' Greek metaphrasis of Ovid's *Metamorphoses* to do with Caxton's English version? And in other cases where there are clear linkages, there are inevitably complex doublings of reception histories, crossings and amplifications, that one would also need to take into account. How does one, for instance, sort out and distinguish, for, say, French readers from the later fourteenth century onwards, the impact of the *Ovide moralisé* (itself an instance of the reception of the *Metamorphoses* along with *Metamorphoses*-commentaries and

25 In addition to Hardie (2002), there is also Boyd (2002), to which I, too, contributed an essay.

26 Not that this ended the enterprise. See Martindale (1996) for a trenchant critique of a more recent grand outing of Latin literary history with, along the way, many observations I find very much in the spirit of my essay. Perkins (1992) is an indispensable discussion of the enterprise of literary history, though he quite intentionally treats "literary histories of reception and impact" only briefly in his introduction (23–7); relevant to my focus in this essay is his observation that "[r]eception history is acutely vulnerable to the difficulties of structuring and grouping" (27).

other parerga, not to mention other vernacular octosyllabic works) from direct
encounters with the Latin *Metamorphoses* (holding constant, for the moment, issues
of manuscript presentation, not to mention marginal commentaries that might
accompany the poem itself) in subsequent readings and renderings of Ovid's poem,
in French and many other European vernaculars?[27]

One can worry and worry and not write, and one could of course write and
not worry. Neither course seems at all advisable. One must worry and write, write
despite the worries. What we can do is construct future projects in reception history such that they are in no way blind to these difficulties but rather, by facing
the challenges, in a variety of ways seek to overcome them. No solution will be
total; each will be a partial evasion. Perhaps the most important point will be, in
fact, the very variety of the strategies, so that the picture that might begin to emerge
will be suggestive of a three-dimensional one by virtue of its multi-ocular focus.
Nor will it be a steady or even a very bright one; it will be flickering, and the
flickering will remind us of the impossibility of complete success.

One obvious approach is to focus on one work by Ovid. As noted, of course,
one can never separate the reception of the *Amores*, say, or the *Ars amatoria* from
the reception of "Ovid," including his biography, real and imagined. One gets
some sense of the "thickness" a thoroughgoing history of one of Ovid's major
works would attain from the monumental survey by Heinrich Dörrie of the *Heroides*-
mania which raged across Europe in the fifteenth through eighteenth centuries.[28]
Even if, in that magisterial chronicle, there can be no full accounting of the way the
taste for the "heroick epistle" fits into a full program of reading and writing (much
less viewing visual images, listening to music) in which fans of the *Heroides* and
its multitudinous offspring engaged, it remains in my mind one of the most successful full, if inevitably partial, accounts of a major chapter of Ovidian reception.

Again: one might imagine a sequence of projects each of which takes one instance
of Ovidian reception – as I began ever so slightly to do with the *Ovide moralisé*
above, or once tried to do with an earlier and much more marginal bit of Ovidiana[29]
– and tries to construct the horizon(s) of expectations along which it emerged,
and not merely the Ovidian ones. One could also imagine an Ovidian reception
project that focused on a series of years – for example, 817, 1000, 1130, 1278,
1380 – and tried to write a thick description of the literary context for the reception of Ovidian works in each of those years. Probably one would be wise to pick
a geographic focus as well for each of these studies, because it goes practically

27   For example, the *Metamorphoses of Ovid* translated in 1480 by William Caxton (but
     never published by him), which constitutes the first complete English version of any
     Ovidian work, turns out not to be an Englishing of Ovid's Latin at all but, rather, a
     rendering of the *Ovide moralisé*, and of a particular fifteenth-century version of the
     Ovide moralisé at that (now London, BL MS Royal 17.E.iv).
28   Dörrie (1968).
29   Hexter (1988).

without saying that the reception of Ovid does not proceed smoothly across Europe. Especially in the earlier centuries, some works are available in only one place; even later, different commentary traditions prevail in different areas,[30] and there are different emphases of tastes among Ovidian works, not to mention the very different vernacular horizons. Theoretically, one could imagine an army of scholars writing such dossiers for every year for every place. Then might our history be complete, though I have a strong sense that we would find ourselves in a Borgesian gyre of one sort or another. Could anyone in any generation ever read the sum total of histories that would thereby be created?

I have myself along the way toyed with other strategies. Rather prosaically, I fear, in "Ovid in the Middle Ages: Exile, Mythographer, Lover,"[31] I tried, conforming to the style and sense of the edited collection, to model my account of medieval Ovidian reception on Ovid's highly varied corpus itself, which has never permitted his reception to be viewed as a homogeneous entity. I somewhat arbitrarily constructed a triple focus, with a section devoted in turn to each of the three aspects evoked in the piece's subtitle. The very fact that each section highlighted a different set of works from the Ovidian canon, and that each had a different temporal center of gravity, so to speak, itself constituted a definite statement about the contours of Ovidian reception. Perhaps the best that can be said about this strategy is its very arbitrariness; at least in that way it pointed to the flickering nature of the image, almost advertising it rather than attempting to conceal it. Somewhat more boldly, in an essay entitled "Ovid's Body,"[32] I used the corporal theme of the volume to which I was contributing as an opportunity to play with some analogues of reception, from the imitative stylization of "drag" fashion houses of Harlem (at least as known to a wider audience from the 1990 film *Paris Is Burning*) to the prosthetic addition of medieval pseudo-Ovidiana, especially the serio-comic and often scabrous *De Vetula*. If the latter seems, in retrospect, not much more than a bad joke itself, the former strikes me to have potential precisely because of its frankly ludic nature. The analogy to which I pointed brought out an element of stylization that I think explains much of the creative reception of Ovid in high medieval Latin poetry, and in the legendary houses, and those who perform in them, we have perhaps a sense of the ludic spaces in which it might after all be true to say that geographically scattered and historically distant admirers of Ovid come together, to play. There might be other possible analogies for transhistorical and thus imaginary reading communities in which members in later days are aware of their predecessors, "faith communities," for example, but the ludic has much more appeal.

So let the games begin.

---

30 Hexter (1986).
31 Hexter (2002).
32 Hexter (1999).

3

Discipline and Receive; or, Making an Example out of Marsyas

Timothy Saunders

For some reason, the past doesn't radiate such immense monotony as the future does. Because of its plenitude, the future is propaganda. So is grass.

Joseph Brodsky[1]

I   Reception Fables

Towards the beginning of *Redeeming the Text*, Charles Martindale offers a close reading of Shelley's "Ozymandias" in order to illustrate some of the key concerns of his book. "We could interpret this poem" he suggests "as a fable about reception."[2] This practice of illustrating a critical theory through a reading of a literary text is by no means confined to reception studies. It could, however, prove especially problematic in this context. For not only do such examples have the capacity to say either too much or too little about the theories they are supposed to illustrate; they also promise to bring straight back into play those very presuppositions about the nature of texts, reading and history which reception theory in particular might wish to resist.[3]

The "fable about reception" which Martindale narrates during his reading of "Ozymandias" appears to avoid this conundrum through the emphasis it places on dialogue. Meaning is to be construed as a product of dialogue and this dialogue is to be characterized as genuinely open-ended and susceptible to change. "My reading of the poem," Martindale concludes, "in the light of reception theory, becomes itself a tiny part of the dialogical processes of its reception and thus of

---

1   Brodsky (1986) 7.
2   Martindale (1993) 3.
3   For more on the problems posed to reception theory by the practice of exemplarity, see also the essays by Miriam Leonard and Duncan Kennedy in this volume.

any argument about its meaning. *Meaning,* could we say, *is always realized at the point of reception.*"[4] Above all, the introduction of Shelley's "Ozymandias" at the outset of *Redeeming the Text* is intended to "begin the conversation" which, it is hoped, will contribute to the hermeneutic practices of the future.[5] More than a decade on, the terms upon which this conversation has been carried out so far have not always lived up to its preliminary promise. It is the contention of this essay that it is precisely the use of ancient texts as "examples" or "illustrations" in the construction of any such reception fables which has conversely constrained the potential of this conversation. It is rather by construing the artefacts of antiquity as in some way "anecdotal" to this dialogue, I suggest, that reception-based hermeneutics can once again lay claim to that radical vision of the future of which it has previously, and on occasion, allowed itself to dream.

II Receiving Marsyas

The reception fable to be narrated here emerges from a reading of the figure of Marsyas. This figure receives its most familiar retelling in book 6 of Ovid's *Metamorphoses*:

> Sic ubi nescio quis Lycia de gente virorum
> rettulit exitium, satyri reminiscitur alter
> quem Tritoniaca Latous harundine victum
> adfecit poena. "quid me mihi detrahis?" inquit;   385
> "A! piget, a! non est" clamabat "tibia tanti!"
> clamanti cutis est summos direpta per artus,
> nec quicquam nisi vulnus erat: cruor undique manat;
> detectique patent nervi, trepidaeque sine ulla
> pelle micant venae; salientia viscera possis   390
> et perlucentes numerare in pectore fibras.
> illum ruricolae, silvarum numina, fauni
> et satyri fratres et tunc quoque carus Olympus
> et nymphae flerunt, et quisquis montibus illis
> lanigerosque greges armentaque bucera pavit.   395
> fertilis immaduit madefactaque terra caducas
> concepit lacrimas ac venis perbibit imis;
> quas ubi fecit aquam, vacuas emisit in auras.
> inde petens rapidum ripis declivibus aequor
> Marsya nomen habet, Phrygiae liquidissimus amnis.   400

4 Martindale (1993) 3.
5 Martindale (1993) 2.

So when someone had told of the destruction of the Lycian peasants, another remi-
nisced about the satyr who, playing on Minerva's pipe, was defeated and punished
by Apollo. "Why do you tear me from myself?" he said. "Ow! I repent, ow!" he
kept on shouting "a pipe is not worth as much as this!" But as he cried out, the
skin was ripped away from the top of his limbs, he was all wound: blood flows on
every side, his nerves lie exposed and his veins tremble and glisten without any skin
to cover them; you could count the dancing organs and sinews glittering clearly in
his breast. Him the country-dwelling fauns, spirits of the woods, lamented and his
brother satyrs and Olympus, dear to him even then; the nymphs also wept for him,
as did anyone who grazed wool-bearing flocks or horned herds on those mountains.
The fertile earth was soaked and, soaking, gathered their fallen tears and drank them
into her deepest veins. Changing these to water, she sent them forth into the open
air. From there a river, which runs down swiftly to the sea through its sloping banks,
has the name "Marsyas," the clearest river in Phrygia.[6]

(Ovid, *Metamorphoses* 6.382–400)

As a story about reception, Ovid's account of Marsyas contains a considerable exemplary value. In the here and now of his present retelling, Marsyas retains little, if
anything, of his original identity. He emerges instead as a figure whose nature
and existence have been largely created for him by his various receptions: by the
unknown narrator who reminisces about his fate (383); by Apollo, who flays him
into a ghastly caricature of the lyre, the very instrument he competed against with
his pipe and whose victory precipitated his present predicament (384–91);[7] and
by the crowd of mourners whose tears soak into the earth and are subsequently
emitted back into the air to form the river which bears the name "Marsyas"
(392–400).

Martindale remarks of this passage that "no critical account I have seen even
begins to offer any explanation of its curious impact, at the point of reception."[8]
He suggests that the "massive progeny" engendered by this story, and in particular Titian's *Flaying of Marsyas*, can offer us such an account instead. This suggestion will be followed up further in the sections to come. But the perspectives
offered by the tradition it has engendered do not constitute the only way of reading this tale at the point of reception. Rather, Ovid's story can itself suggest a
reception-based reading of the hermeneutics at work in its own exegesis. What
insights into the supposed inadequacies of alternative critiques might then be made
available to us if we treat the story at *this* point of its reception?

Ovid's account of the flaying of Marsyas often strikes critics as unnecessarily
grotesque and flippant. It intersperses bucolic and baroque, humour and horror,

---

6 All translations are my own, unless otherwise indicated.
7 For the analogy between Marsyas' flayed body and Apollo's lyre, see Feldherr and James
   (2004) 82–3 and 96–7.
8 Martindale (1993) 63.

with seemingly tasteless abandon. It therefore falls to those who wish to uphold Ovid's rendition here to resolve these apparent inconsistencies and aberrations. The opening paragraph of Andrew Feldherr and Paula James's recent article, significantly entitled "Making the Most of Marsyas," represents a case in point:

> Ovid's account of Marsyas at *Metamorphoses* 6.382–400 invites completion. The tale itself is but partially told and demands to be supplemented by other texts and other tales within the *Metamorphoses*. This task, in turn . . . involves the reader in juggling contradictory judgments on the tale's protagonists and the nature and purpose of the narrative itself.[9]

Feldherr and James are perhaps unusually explicit in their assumption that reading Ovid's tale of Marsyas necessarily involves completing it. Their approach is, however, representative of a broader critical practice. According to this practice, the ancient world comes to be viewed as a kind of jigsaw puzzle. A few pieces may currently be missing; the puzzle may not until now have been put together in quite the right way; but in either case the possibility still remains that one day that text or that world will again be restored to its original plenitude. In the case of Marsyas, the play on "remembering" and "re-membering" has become such a critical commonplace that it has all but established a direct correlation between these two activities. A reception-based reading, by contrast, might prefer to preserve the joke, but pull the punch-line.

As an example of this, one might cite the temptation to discern a direct lineage between a satyr who competed against Apollo with his pipe and a river in Phrygia. Andrew Feldherr, for one, argues that the clarity of the river identifies an "underground tradition" which circumvents Apollo's intervention and returns the name Marsyas back to its source in the satyr.[10] This ignores, however, the series of disjunctions which Marsyas' metamorphosis entails. Above all, the river which bears the name "Marsyas" does not issue directly from the blood of the satyr, but rather from the tears of the onlookers. It comes into being as an indirect consequence of the process of his remembering. Try to follow the river Marsyas all the way back to its source, this image implies, and you are at least as likely to find your way back to the beginnings of your own modes of recollection and recovery as you are to any original, or even predominantly Ovidian, satyr. The story of Marsyas, in other words, whether it is Ovid's Marsyas, Titian's, Feldherr's, mine, or anyone else's, is here inescapably indivisible from the story of its reception. And that, one might add, may well be its point.

---

9 Feldherr and James (2004) 75.
10 Feldherr and James (2004) 81–2. Feldherr's observation that Ovid's river remembers the satyr through the Latin form ("Marsya") of the Greek name, however, encourages the reception-based reading outlined here.

III Marsyas Receiving

The progression of events which leads up to the transformation of Marsyas from satyr to river involves a number of, often oblique, metamorphoses. First Marsyas is remembered; then flayed; then lamented; whereupon the tears of those lamenters are soaked up by the earth; until finally the earth transforms these tears into the river which now bears his name. The version of reception theory illustrated in the previous section suggests that, while it may once have been possible to track Marsyas' transformation forwards from satyr to river, it is now no longer possible to make the same journey in the opposite direction. Each of his various receptions has rendered the prospect of ever encountering an authentic or original Marsyas again utterly obsolete. Viewed from the point of reception, to remember Marsyas is to reconstruct rather than restore him.

This reading of the text suggests that the practice of reception places under immediate erasure any idea we might still entertain of restoring an object to the status it enjoyed prior its reception. It is worth noting, however, that this text also has something to say about the fate awaiting those who actually do the "receiving." For the pipe with which Marsyas competes against Apollo is one he has "received" from Athena (hence its epithet *Tritoniaca*). According to the version of the story which Ovid himself offers in the third book of the *Ars amatoria*, Athena, having first invented the pipe, catches sight of her distorted features as she is playing it, throws the pipe away and exclaims "non es mihi tibia tanti!" ("You are not worth so much to me as this, pipe!" 3.505). When Marsyas echoes these words in the *Metamorphoses*, his citation sounds parodic and this makes him seem all the more like a mimetic caricature. As Andrew Feldherr concludes: "the satyr really has lost the capacity for self-representation, and we might be tempted to reinterpret his initial words in the following way: 'Why do you strip the "me" from me?' "[11]

Interpreted in this way, a reception-based hermeneutics threatens to deprive both the received and the receiver of their respective identities. Indeed, if reception is to be construed primarily as a form of reader-response theory, then any focus on Marsyas' audience would appear to bear this out. Instead of looking directly at Marsyas and his suffering, we find ourselves responding instead to its response (whether that response resides with other critical accounts or with the group of onlookers represented in Ovid's *Metamorphoses* and elsewhere). At the same time, this focus on other people's reactions can conversely serve to distance us from making a genuine commitment to our own readings and responses. *Quid me mihi detrahis?*

---

11 Feldherr and James (2004) 79.

IV Dialogue

For the most part, reception-based approaches tend to resist committing themselves either to wholly objective or to wholly subjective interpretations of the past. Their strategies for doing so may differ in each instance, but at some point they are likely to end up characterizing the process of interpretation as one of exchange and, more specifically, as a dialogue.[12] In this way, apparent alterities are brought together in the hope of achieving a radical dialectic: between past and present; text and reader; the timeless and the time-bound; sameness and difference; continuity and rupture; subject and object; aesthetics and philology; and so on. The consequence of privileging dialogue in this way is almost invariably to reconfigure the object of knowledge which emerges as a kind of hybrid. This would appear to break up the concept of an originary, stable text which is one of reception theory's primary targets, but it could also be this very principle of hybridity which allows for the return of some of the same essentialisms which the theory itself set out to dismiss. In the case of Ovid's story of Marsyas, for example, it is remarkable how readily its role as a discrete and clearly discernible source text for all other accounts of the satyr is both presupposed by many reception-based approaches and then immediately reinscribed by them through their dialogic interpretative practices.

In accordance with its dialogic principles, reception theory suggests that we should no longer conceive of a text as a kind of Platonic Ideal of which our interpretations are more or less imperfect reflections, but rather as something far more changeable and mobile.[13] As it happens, such a static conception of literature and interpretation is by no means entirely accurate as a description of Plato's own writings. These are themselves largely composed as dialogues and would consequently appear to be all the more receptive to reception theory. In the *Symposium*, for instance, the drunken Alcibiades compares Socrates with Marsyas (215a–222b) and, in one application of the analogy, simultaneously justifies the status of Plato's own works as receptions of Socrates' words:

> But you produce the same effect [as Marsyas] with your words only, and do not require the flute: that is the difference between you and him. When we hear any other speaker, even a very good one, he produces absolutely no effect upon us, or not much, whereas the mere fragments of you and your words, even at second hand, and however imperfectly repeated, amaze and possess the souls of every man, woman and child who comes within hearing of them. (215c–d)[14]

---

12 See, for instance, Jauss (1982a) 69–70; Martindale (1993) 101–6; Hardwick (2003a) 4.

13 Jauss (1982a) 28; Martindale (1993) 17.

14 Translated by Jowett (1994).

Not every aspect of this passage evidently fits favorably as an illustration of reception theory. Plato's writings are, on this description, still only fragments, imperfectly repeated, of a perfect and full, hypostasized original. (The entailment of this is that the processes of dialogue and the projection of Platonic Ideals are, perhaps, harder to keep apart in practice than in theory.) At the same time, Alcibiades' rhetoric also implies a certain selectivity in the application of his figures. Not all words or fragments benefit as much from their reception as others. It just so happens that Socrates' words and deeds, recharacterized in this satyric form and preserved within the framework of a Platonic dialogue, represent examples of ones that do.

In any case, it is precisely the occasional lack of fit between Marsyas and his purported analogue in Socrates which forms such an intoxicating feature of Alcibiades' speech as a whole ("that is the difference between you and him," he admits here). Socrates himself, however, rejects the analogy outright. Alcibiades' dialectic is just a ruse, he suggests, since the figure of Marsyas applies much more obviously to the narrator of the story and his own hidden agenda than it does to its ostensible target in Socrates:

> "You are sober, Alcibiades," said Socrates "or you would never have gone so far about to hide the purpose of your satyr's praises, for all this long story is only an ingenious circumlocution, of which the point comes in by the way of the end: you want to get up a quarrel between me and Agathon . . . But the plot of this Satyric or Silenic drama has been detected, and you must not allow him, Agathon, to set us at variance." (222c–d)

One might be tempted to read this exchange between Socrates and Alcibiades here as an amusing send-up of reception theory's dialogic pretensions. For how genuinely dialogic are the dialogues in which this theory purports to engage? In a manner akin to Socrates' retort to Alcibiades, it could be charged that the use of Ovid's story as an exemplary "fable about reception" is itself invalidated through its very deployment in that capacity. It is this, one might suggest, which has prevented, or at least preceded, the proper exegesis of the tale. Like Ovid's satyr, the meaning of this passage as a whole has entered the arena already defeated (*victum*). Making an example out of Marsyas is equivalent to punishing him all over again. He has been flayed and disfigured to such an extent that he once more reflects the instruments of his torture. Except that this time it is not Apollo's lyre which has done the damage, but reception theory's supposed commitment to hybridity and exchange. Could this be what it really means to state that any "reading of the poem, in the light of reception theory, becomes itself a tiny part of the dialogical processes of its reception and thus of any argument about its meaning"?

V Received Wisdom

The problems and possibilities offered by a dialogic approach to the past are likewise illustrated vividly by Dante's invocation of the figure of Marsyas at the opening of the *Paradiso*:

> O buono Apollo, all'ultimo lavoro
> fammi del tuo valor sì fatto vaso,
> come dimandi a dar l'amato alloro.   15
> Infino a qui l'un giogo di Parnaso
> assai mi fu; ma or con amendue
> m'è uopo intrar nell'aringo rimaso.
> Entra nel petto mio, e spira tue
> sì come quando Marsïa traesti   20
> della vagina delle membra sue.

O good Apollo, for the last labour make me such a vessel of your power as you demand for the gift of your loved laurel. So far the one peak of Parnassus has sufficed me, but now I have need of both, as I enter on the arena which remains. Come into my breast and breathe there as you did when you drew Marsyas from the scabbard of his limbs.

(Dante, *Paradiso* 1.13–21)

In this prayer, Dante expresses his desire to be extracted from his own historical and material context in order to be enabled to sing of the paradise beyond. It is perhaps somewhat perverse, then, that he should choose to articulate this desire in terms which bring that historical context immediately back into play. Indeed, if anything, the ongoing dialogue with antiquity which has already constituted such a prominent feature of the first two books of the *Divina Commedia* is now to be intensified. In order to enter and sing of paradise, Dante will need both peaks of Parnassus rather than just the one.

The invocation of the figure of Marsyas at this juncture consequently constitutes a daring, if somewhat surprising, move. At the same time, it offers us a probing model for thinking through some of reception theory's own ambitious goals and its preferred methodology for bringing them about. For it remains uncertain whether a reception-based hermeneutics can ever break truly free from the constraints of those critical practices with which it has committed itself to engage. In Dante's dialogue with antiquity, the figure of Marsyas which emerges is assumed to transcend the initiating conditions of its dialogue and to become instead a fully redeemed reenactment of the crucifixion and resurrection of Christ. The true figure of Marsyas, that is, is the one which remains when all else has been stripped away. It is not the Marsyas who is fashioned out of the customary scholarly desire to piece him back together again.

It remains to be seen whether reception theory can bring about a comparable transfiguration of its texts and figures. At the very least, the similarities it bears towards the procedures of the *Commedia* are both promising and yet cause for some concern. For in the Christianized world-view at work throughout Dante's *Commedia*, meaning is there also generated within both a spatial and a temporal framework, as individuals offer their own, historically contingent and ideologically engaged, readings of God's Book. To this extent, in Dante too meaning is realized anew at the point of reception and in Dante too it accordingly displays a certain topicality. But it is a meaning which can nonetheless still be deemed "good" or "bad," "right" or "wrong" in the light of divine revelation. Reception theory may well be able to avoid the consequences of such an evidently constrained, and often oppressive, dialectic if it is prepared to abandon the kind of theological and holistic hermeneutic structures which bring such dialectics into play. In so doing, however, it simultaneously runs the risk of rendering the content of its own "received wisdom" all but obsolete. Instead of offering a mode of interpretation which can engage with questions of value as well as philological fact, as Hans Robert Jauss advocated,[15] the knowledge acquired through reception theory could then in practice come to consist of little other than a descriptive record of those several receptions which have, in a purely value-free zone, continued to take place.

VI Figures of Reception

The previous sections have proceeded upon the supposition that the story of Marsyas has the capacity to narrate an exemplary fable about the hermeneutics of reception. The figure of Marsyas seems especially well suited for this role, since – like the practice of exemplarity itself[16] – his is both an ancient figure and one which has been invoked by artists and writers of all periods, including the contemporary one. At the same time, the story of Marsyas also appears to address some of the aspirations and procedures which are most obviously associated with reception practice at the present moment. Ovid's Marsyas, for instance, serves as an illustrative example of a text which responds well to a consideration of the role of its audience, while Dante's articulates the desire for a reading and writing practice which can break free of its current historical constraints and which can consequently transfigure the objects of its study rather than merely repeat them.

Yet the figure of Marsyas also "stretches to breaking point" the tensions inherent in reception theory as it has been practiced so far.[17] For all its apparent commitment to a genuine dialogic exchange (no matter how antagonistic or amicable that

15 Jauss (1982a) 5.
16 On the ancient practice of exemplarity see Hardwick (2003a) 23–6; but see also 90f. for the distinction between *exemplum* and *paradeigma*.
17 Martindale (1993) 63 makes much the same observation.

proposed dialogue is supposed to be), reception has a tendency to turn that dialogue into a conversation almost exclusively about itself. From this, indeed, may stem the sense of circularity which can readily be attributed to some of its readings, in which the foundational belief that "all meaning is realized at the point of reception" serves both as their introduction and conclusion.

Part of the problem can be attributed precisely to the way in which texts such as Ovid's story of Marsyas are sometimes "made examples of" by reception practice. It is as if this practice lays claim to a belief displayed both in Alcibiades' exposition of Socrates' satyric qualities and throughout Dante's critical and poetic writings: that a beautiful truth often lies hidden beneath a deceptive surface.[18] Whereas in Dante the truth hidden deep in ancient texts could be revealed in the light of Christian revelation, now it is the point of reception which promises to award us the necessary perspective.

If such an account of reception is indeed to be deemed in any way representative, then this theory too would have proved itself to be both teleological and totalitarian in its instincts. It too would have displayed a desire for plenitude in its enactment. It could, indeed, be argued that, in its most voracious form, reception theory has the capacity to devour everything set before it, including other readings and other theories. According to this version, all acts and all interpretations would henceforth have to be characterized as acts of reception. It is in this form, in which all meaning is located both at and as its point, that reception threatens to swallow even itself.

Paul Hamilton most probably has some such version as this in mind when he argues that "the preservation of reception-theory as an abstract model rather than the description of specific interventions in literary or cultural traditions encapsulates what these interventions are opposing."[19] Hamilton himself appears to be quite confident that the critical deployment of individual examples remains adequate to the task of sustaining the impetus of such interventions and, in so doing, of resisting some of reception theory's more totalitarian tendencies. It is his description of an "anecdote," however, which suggests a far more radical device: "By anecdote," he writes, "is meant something precisely unrepresentative, non-mimetic, juxtaposed to rather than figurative of the thing to which it is illustratively adjacent."[20] Could this prove to be reception theory's redeeming device?

VII   Reception Futures

It is one of the central claims of reception studies that they have had, and should continue to have, the effect of liberating classical texts and images for a diversity

---

18   See, for instance, Plato *Symposium* 221d–e and Dante *Convivio* 2.1.2–3.
19   Hamilton (2003) 186.
20   Hamilton (2003) 145.

of future refigurations.[21] By refusing to accept the writings of the past as in any way "dead literature," moreover, these studies may also claim to have restored these writings to much the same roles in the world as those they originally enjoyed at the time of their first appearing.[22] Reception, one might say, gives antiquity back its future.

At the same time, one of the futures looked towards by reception theorists extends far beyond anything achieved in practice to date. Instead of remaining content with replacing the question "What did the text say?" with the further question "What does the text say to me, and what do I say to it?"[23] reception theory, in common with several other instances of hermeneutic inquiry, occasionally dreams of a moment of redemption, or even apocalypse. When that future comes, all previous techniques and methodologies will finally fall back into their long-awaited obsolescence and interpretation will take place under a new heaven and over a new earth. At the present moment, however, and also in common with certain other models of hermeneutics, reception theory remains trapped in, rather than transcendent of, those methodological procedures it strives to resist but into which it continues to recur. Its adherence to a belief in dialogue and hybridity by no means resolves the dichotomies, alterities, and numerous aporias which have consistently bedevilled attempts to render up the past in the present; rather, it intensifies them. It is, indeed, through its continued metacritical dialogue with those essentializing and positivistic positions it overtly opposes, and as a consequence of the hybrid methodologies which then emerge from this dialogue, that reception theory is itself prevented from constituting that moment of redemption (or apocalypse) towards which it must instead, and for the time being, continue to work.

Indeed, reception theory would appear to entail the conclusion that it is precisely our ignorance of the future which seriously constrains and contextualizes our knowledge of the past.[24] It is because the future contains the capacity for change and even redemption that the past can likewise continue to be different, and possibly better, in that future. The moral content thus awarded to reception through its forward-looking glance is exactly what provides it with its critical urgency and point in the present moment. At least in its anecdotal form, in which its figures would be allowed to intervene in highly individualized contexts and not as representatives of a more generalized abstract position, its ongoing capacity to critique the orthodoxies and standardized readings of contemporary critical practices, including those of reception itself, should continue to be harnessed and deployed.

What this might mean in practice should differ from case to case. In each instance, however, reception theory's principal conclusion that "meaning is always realized

---

21   Hardwick (2003a) 109.
22   See the preface to Hardwick (2003a).
23   Jauss (1982a) 146.
24   Jauss (1982a) 60.

at the point of reception" will genuinely have to constitute the beginning rather than the end of any of the interpretative stories it proceeds to tell. The selection of figures, texts, and art works which appear to illustrate most readily the central tenets of this theory should in turn be deployed to reconfigure those tenets and their illustration in art. Figures of reception are not to be called upon solely to act as mere seconds to one side of the dialogue in which reception theory purports to engage; rather, they should serve to question, and eventually break away from, the very terms of the debate itself. In this, the studies of these figures' receptions would themselves have a significant, and potentially destabilizing, role to play.

The results of such reception-based critiques could well prove to be utterly unexpected and may even end up disrupting several of reception theory's own most hallowed principles; but for a critique whose goal is a future which cannot, by necessity, yet be described, anything less would exemplify once again its potentially indefinite, self-recurring defeat.

4

Text, Theory, and Reception

Kenneth Haynes

Since the Renaissance (and fitfully before), classical texts have figured not only within literature and the other arts but also in the formation of social groups, the discussion of politics and religion, and the emergence of scholarship. These diverse aspects of reception should not be conflated. From the sixteenth and seventeenth centuries to the early twentieth, the classics were instrumental in the education of European elites and provided one of the main sources of their social distinction. By the nineteenth century, classics in several European countries helped to identify and form not only elites but also an important segment of the middle class (the professional, as opposed to the commercial, class); in Victorian Britain the class structure was marked, to a large extent, by knowledge of Greek and Latin among the elites, Latin among gentlemen, and English among the rest.[1] Supported historically also by other institutions, especially the schools and universities, the Anglican Church, to some extent the legal and medical professions, and eventually the civil service, knowledge or at least some acquaintance with the classics could be assumed of a significant fraction of the literate public. This knowledge was defended in a variety of ways – as liberal, disinterested, character-building, and so forth, though these ideologies were repeatedly contested.[2]

Classics have frequently served as a point of reference in political and social thought, though here too many interests were at stake for classical texts to function in any simple way. The eighteenth century could not agree whether Horace was an exemplar of moral independence or a toady to his patron because its own attitudes toward patronage were mixed;[3] the nineteenth century was not sure what to think about ancient sophists because it was not sure what to think about liberals.[4]

---

1   See Stray (1998) 74 and *passim*.
2   See e.g. Waquet (2001).
3   See Stack (1985) 6–7.
4   See Turner (1981) 264–83.

Because high culture has usually been sponsored by elites, the classics have played a central role in European literature through the many forms of translation, imitation, and inspiration. But the reception of classics was not limited to the high literacy of elites. By the nineteenth century, when classical literacy was broader than before, more popular literary vehicles – the novel, bestselling poems like Macaulay's *Lays of Ancient Rome* – were on easy terms with classical learning. And it was not just literature that was engaged with the classics; the arts in general, and especially painting, continually made reference to antiquity, and by the nineteenth century a good deal of popular painting was also doing so.

Finally, the reception of classics is bound to the history of scholarship, which includes the institutions that have supported it (humanist offices, the Anglican Church, academies, the civil service, schools, and universities), the formation of the problems which scholarship has understood itself to be solving, the processes of rationalization which emerge when confronting a continuously growing body of commentary, and the history of the notions of truth and expertise within which scholarship operated.

In thinking about the relation between the reception of a classical text and the institutions, ideology, artistic activity, and scholarship that make this reception possible, two errors should be avoided: either denying any autonomy to the different domains of reception (as, for example, when scholarship or the art work is described as entirely ideological, solely an example of the will to power) or refusing to see the different domains as related to and constrained by others.

Another danger is that of confounding questions which should remain distinct, or which arguably should remain distinct. For example, the question of what a classical text meant – either to members of its original audience or to readers in subsequent periods in history – is not in principle unrecoverable, though we may happen to lack evidence to treat it persuasively. The question of what a text means now, however, is another matter. Whether a work has the capacity to help us to form an understanding of the world that orients us toward moral action (even when it does so negatively by showing us how not to behave) is not a question which can be answered by historical scholarship. Finally, there is the question of the aesthetic beauty of a work, its formal qualities and its intrinsic value, which cannot be determined either by historical scholarship or by the present meaning of a work. Or at least that is how a Kantian will speak of the matter, insisting that questions of knowledge, morality, and aesthetic beauty are distinct.

I intend to take "meaning" as my focus in this chapter. What does it mean to interpret a classical work, how is the meaning of a text received or produced? Two major twentieth-century debates may shed light on this question: the debate between Hans-Georg Gadamer and Jürgen Habermas on the universality of hermeneutics on the one hand and the so-called "rationality debate" between Peter Winch and a number of anthropologists on the other. I hope to relate the first debate to the major literary dispute over the interpretation of the *Aeneid* and the second debate to the interpretation of Achilles in the *Iliad*. It is not my intention to contribute

directly to the debates themselves, but rather to describe the nature of the disagreement, and in particular to scrutinize instances when theory (including
historicism) has been adduced to constrain interpretation.

That the worlds of ancient writers and modern readers are marked by different institutions, social relations, concepts, beliefs both passive and active, and
experiences is Gadamer's starting point. He seeks to describe this difference not
as an obstacle to understanding but as productive of understanding. The attitude
of historicism that sees these differences solely as obstacles to be removed by scholarship is misconceived, according to Gadamer, because differences may be so deeply
implicit to our identity that we do not have the option to dismiss them and besides
we are often not aware of them. Adopting from Heidegger the description of *Dasein*
as fundamentally thrown or projected, Gadamer insists that the "concrete bonds
of custom and tradition" correspond to our own potential futures, including future
understanding. We do not have an unconstrained ability to choose our own futures,
and since that which constrains (but also makes possible) our future projection
has preceded us,[5] the role of tradition will be central to Gadamer's analysis.

From our tradition we have inherited our prejudices, a word which Gadamer
seeks to rehabilitate:

> In fact history does not belong to us; we belong to it. Long before we understand
> ourselves through the process of self-examination, we understand ourselves in a self-
> evident way in the family, society, and state in which we live . . . That is why the
> prejudices of the individual, far more than his judgments, constitute the historical
> reality of his being.[6]

It is inevitable then that in trying to understand a text someone will project a
provisional understanding onto the text[7] on the basis of those prejudices, though
it is important to stress that fore-projections, like prejudices, are capable of being
revised. Prejudice should be seen as a provisional judgment, a judgment that has
been "rendered before all the elements that determine a situation have been finally
examined."[8] It is not possible to "separate in advance the productive prejudices
that enable understanding from the prejudices that hinder it and lead to misunderstandings" because our prejudices are not at our free disposal.[9]

It was the Enlightenment that discredited prejudice and reduced it to indicate
a false or unfounded judgment. It does this through its own unexamined prejudice: "the fundamental prejudice of the Enlightenment is the prejudice against
prejudice itself."[10] It imputes to reason rather than tradition the source of all

5   Gadamer (1993) 270.
6   Gadamer (1993) 276–7.
7   Gadamer (1993) 267.
8   Gadamer (1993) 270.
9   Gadamer (1993) 295.
10   Gadamer (1993) 270.

authority,[11] failing to recognize that "reason exists for us only in concrete, historical terms."[12] Under its influence, tradition came to be regarded as prejudiced in the pejorative sense and its authority as illegitimate. Along with prejudice, Gadamer seeks to rehabilitate authority and tradition. "That which has been sanctioned by tradition and custom has an authority that is nameless, and our finite historical being is marked by the fact that the authority of what has been handed down to us – and not just what is clearly grounded – always has power over our attitudes and behavior."[13] The authority of tradition comes from its role in constituting who we are, from the fact that it is already present in all attempts at understanding.

Interpretation is undertaken by people who necessarily belong to a tradition. It must therefore "start from the position that a person seeking to understand something has a bond to the subject matter" and that the person has or acquires "a connection with the tradition from which the text speaks."[14] Gadamer, that is, places a knowledge of the historical reception of a text at the center of the process of understanding that text. Not, however, in order to bridge the historical distance between author and reader, which is impossible. The "real meaning of a text" does not depend solely on the historical contingencies of the author and his original audience but is "co-determined also by the historical situation of the interpreter and hence by the totality of the objective course of history."[15]

The text then is not to be read as an expression of life but to be taken seriously as having a claim to truth. Its temporal distance from us is not something to be bridged by transposing ourselves into an alien age and to think alien thoughts; that was the naive assumption of the historicists. Rather, temporal distance is a "positive and productive condition enabling understanding";[16] it lets the "true meaning of the object emerge fully," an infinite process since "the discovery of the true meaning of a text or a work of art is never finished."[17] Truth, here, is not the objective truth of the sciences but the new understanding that arises from the productive encounter between text and interpreter. This occurs when interpreters do more than project a historical horizon (and so find themselves alienated in a past consciousness) but rather insist also on their own present horizon of understanding.[18] The goal of understanding is the fusion of the horizon of the present (formed by the past) and the horizon of the past (which has to be recovered in that present formed by that past).

11   Gadamer (1993) 272.
12   Gadamer (1993) 276.
13   Gadamer (1993) 280.
14   Gadamer (1993) 295.
15   Gadamer (1993) 296.
16   Gadamer (1993) 297.
17   Gadamer (1993) 298.
18   Gadamer (1993) 306–7.

In his review of *Truth and Method*, Habermas sees many advantages in the hermeneutical description of understanding. It relies on ordinary language (as opposed to general linguistic theories) but is not limited to particular language games (as opposed to Wittgenstein); that is, it functions by making use of the "tendency to self-transcendence embedded in linguistic practice."[19] Our ordinary language is ambiguous and incomplete, and intersubjective communication is therefore always breaking down. "Hermeneutic understanding is applied to the points of rupture; it compensates for the brokenness of intersubjectivity."[20] In our ordinary experience, when communication breaks down, interpretive processes are set in motion to reestablish understanding.[21] Gadamer's image of horizon captures a basic fact about language: it is not closed but can in principle include what is at first foreign and incomprehensible.[22] Habermas is most impressed by the relevance of hermeneutics to action:

> Hermeneutic understanding is structurally oriented toward eliciting from tradition a possible action-orienting self-understanding of social groups. It makes possible a form of consensus on which communicative action depends. It eliminates the dangers of a communication breakdown in two directions: vertically, in one's own tradition, and horizontally, in the mediation between traditions of different cultures and groups.[23]

Habermas also begins to sketch a critique of Gadamer. First, against the rehabilitation of prejudice, he notes that a prejudice which sees itself as a provisional judgment subject to future modification no longer functions as prejudice.[24] What is historically pre-given to us is altered when it is taken up in reflection. Knowledge is rooted in particular tradition, but this does not mean that the claims of tradition cannot be rejected. The authority of tradition is qualitatively different before and after reflection.[25] Second, Habermas indicates that there are limits to the hermeneutical method. Language is not only a medium of communication; it is also a medium of domination and social power.[26] Intended and symbolically transmitted meaning is not the whole of intersubjectivity, and social action must be understood in an objective framework that is not merely interpretive.[27]

19   Habermas (1977) 336.
20   Habermas (1977) 341.
21   Habermas (1977) 338.
22   Habermas (1977) 342.
23   Habermas (1977) 353.
24   Habermas (1977) 358.
25   Habermas (1977) 358.
26   Habermas (1977) 360.
27   Habermas (1977) 361.

Gadamer, in his response, insists that hermeneutics is indeed universal. There is no objective framework that can be represented outside of language. And since societal reality, with all its concrete forces, must be represented in consciousness by means of language,[28] discussions and analyses of it must be hermeneutical. This insistence prompted Habermas to a fuller development of what he takes to be the limits of hermeneutical understanding. Prejudices are not just randomly distributed; sometimes communication is *systematically* distorted, particularly in order to disguise and protect the workings of power. Habermas believes that hermeneutics reaches the limit of its efficacy at this point.[29] It is not enough to interpret the "what" of distorted expressions; they can only be understood in terms of the "why" – the initial conditions for the systematic distortion itself.[30]

Their disagreement might be more broadly characterized in other ways, for example as to whether or not there is a dichotomy between facts and values. For the Kantian Habermas, there is such a divide, and hermeneutics applies only to the domain of values and meanings; the objective framework in which communication occurs may be discovered, not just interpreted. For the Heideggerian Gadamer, there is no such divide because the world as it is revealed to us already has a structure in which we find that facts and values co-inhere; hermeneutics, therefore, is universal. Their disagreement is also related to the question of whether rationality is universal. If it is not, if, as Gadamer claims, reason "is not its own master but remains constantly dependent on the given circumstances in which it operates,"[31] then we must always be committed to hermeneutical understanding because we cannot presuppose what notion of reason is operating in or behind a given statement.

Critical disputes about Virgil's *Aeneid* in the second half of the twentieth century have centered, sometimes loudly, on the meaning of the poem, that is, with its correct interpretation. Insofar as the poem's meaning is at issue, the Gadamer–Habermas debate is relevant. From a Gadamerian perspective, the present concerns of interpreters, far from being extraneous or intrusive, are intrinsically constitutive (that is, co-constitutive) of Virgil's meaning, which is always being formed anew. The reception of Virgil is not a sequence of misreadings continually corrected by the progress of scholarship but rather a demonstration that a great art work is *toujours en acte*, its truth never finished. Habermas, though he would eschew the term "truth" here and speak instead of valid norms for social action, would also find the present meaning of a text has an open-ended character. However, he would insist on an additional area of investigation outside of hermeneutics. Whether in the course of their reception classical texts have provided valid norms for behavior and self-understanding is a question that must be

28 Gadamer (1976) 35.
29 Habermas (1980) 189.
30 Habermas (1980) 194.
31 Gadamer (1993) 276.

answered in awareness of the pressures of ideology, patronage, and social formation.

However, in neither case are the formal qualities of the *Aeneid* relevant, and so we may find something deeply dissatisfying about this way of describing the critical reception of the *Aeneid*. The problem is on both sides. Gadamer and Habermas are concerned with meaning; in his analysis, Gadamer refers to the "true meaning," the "real meaning," and "the message" of utterances, while Habermas's focus on the message is yet more sustained. Often discussions of the *Aeneid* have also concentrated on the meaning of the poem. R. A. Brooks, in an essay which might be seen as the first contribution to the "Harvard school" of interpretation,[32] refers to the "knots of meaning which unify the poem," though the plural is significant. Recently, a classicist referred to these debates as "the most important modern disputes over Virgil's ethical and political viewpoint,"[33] where "viewpoint" not only emphasizes the meaning of the poem but anchors that meaning in Virgil's intention.

Yet works of art have formal characteristics that distinguish them from other kinds of utterances; they cannot be reduced to their meanings without losing this distinction. Replacing texts with their interpretations is not a happy way to treat literature, even if those interpretations are regarded as necessarily provisional. Perhaps Kant offers a helpful alternative. For Kant, art is not concerned with concepts but with the relations among concepts, and therefore it is not a mode of knowledge; art does not appeal to interest, and so it is not a kind of morality.[34]

Turn again to the *Aeneid*. Conflicting concepts, that is meanings, are present: Rome is an eternally necessary idea of civilization, civilization places large and perhaps impossible demands on the civilized, the civilized must fight monsters but run the risk of becoming monstrous in doing so. Rather than attempting to secure a meaning, readers ought to be concerned with the relation of meanings. That is, the literary value of a work comes from its ability to adjudicate among meanings and not merely to represent them. These judgments are effected by formal means, by word choice, narrative, meter, and all the ways which good literary criticism has always shown to be the case. The relation among meanings is not normally indeterminate or exactly poised, though it sometimes is; Marvell's Horatian ode is often read in this way.

There are advantages to describing literary criticism in this way. For one thing, it restores the role of authorial agency without using it to underwrite meaning. It is the author who builds in words a structure of forces, and consequently a serious reader must accept as factors the diverse impulses of the work; still, how they are evaluated or weighed will vary, depending on the experiences of readers and on their historical situation.

32   Reprinted as Brooks (1966) 143–63.
33   Fantham (1997) 200 n. 35.
34   Kant (1987) 48–51, 53–4.

For another, this emphasis brings to the foreground the question of aesthetic value. Equating literature with representation does not give a criterion for distinguishing bad literature from good, propaganda from art. Focusing on the relation among concepts rather than the representation of concepts forces criticism to be concerned with questions of aesthetic value. One thing we find in the greatest works of literature, like the *Iliad* and the *Aeneid*, is a high degree of self-critique, an ability to anticipate objections, an indication why something is so and not otherwise, where that "otherwise" may be explicitly present in the work or implicitly given by its context. This is the case also in lesser works; for example, literary encomia may be no more than flattery, but they may also, by depicting the world as it should be, have a hortatory or even subversive effect. In literature such a distinction (it has been called the difference between ideology and utopia[35]) cannot be found in meaning alone.

Finally, disputes about judgments are different in kind from disputes about representation. If the disagreement is over Virgil's viewpoint, he is either pro- or anti-empire, and the interpretive gulf is wide. If the dispute is concerned with the correct weighing of balancing forces, critics may find they share more in common. A dispute between an optimistic and a pessimistic reading has nowhere to go. But if the focus is on judgment, then an optimistic reading must concentrate on dissociating itself not from pessimism but from a poorly judged optimism, in the form for example of crass triumphalism or self-serving opportunism. Likewise a pessimistic reading should dissociate itself from a poorly judged pessimism, as in for example a sentimental inflation of the status of victims or an irresponsible escapism from the necessity of power.

The large body of admirable literary criticism about the *Aeneid* has always done this; I object here only to a self-description that is sometimes found in criticism, rather than to its practice. For some critics, rejecting meaning as the area of critical concern has seemed to imply that literature must therefore be meaningless. But this must be understood differently, not as a deprivation, since literary works do have meanings, but as relocating the attention to how those meanings are related formally. Kant does not see literature as a producer of agreeable feelings or as belonging to a private aesthetic realm. To insist on the primacy of judgment does not relegate art to aestheticism.

There is a confusion in Gadamer. How the meanings of texts evolve over time is an important aspect of reception studies, but Gadamer (like Heidegger) believes that the crucial meanings and values by which social actors orient themselves come specifically from works of art and in particular from those great works of art seen as inaugurating a tradition. To some extent this is true: historically, literary works have been pressed into the service of meaning-formation (though religious and moral-philosophical works have contributed more directly), and so the history of the meaning of art works is a proper subject of reception. This

---

35 In Ricoeur's sense; see Ricoeur (1986) and also Haynes (2001).

history, however, should not be considered an adequate response to the work. Gadamer's attempt, via Heidegger, to retrieve the question of aesthetic truth truncates the specific faculty of art (nonetheless, hermeneutics is unavoidable in responses to literature because meanings must be identified before the relations of meanings can be established).

I anticipate the objection that I am describing only one kind of literature, hardly aesthetics in general. Perhaps by insisting on reflective judgment I depreciate all but self-conscious writing. Gadamer, for example, could respond that the faculty of critical judgment valued here is no more than prejudice for sentimental over naive writing, in Schiller's sense. In more modern terms, it might be objected that while immanent self-critique might be found in the literary products of a highly literate culture it may well be absent from the oral compositions of a non-literate culture. For a test case, consider another famous crux of literary interpretation, Achilles' response to the emissaries in book 9 of the *Iliad*. Achilles tells Phoenix that he has no need to be honored by the Achaeans because he has been honored by the dispensation of Zeus, *phroneô de tetimêsthai Dios aisêi* (*Iliad* 9.608). In some readings of the poem, Achilles here steps outside the cultural code of heroic honor, a code which he explicitly rejects in his prior response to Agamemnon (see, for example, Whitman[36]). Others, still influenced perhaps by Bruno Snell's description of Homeric characters, reject that reading as anachronistically imputing to Achilles modern forms of subjectivity and interiority. Modern commentators are divided. Some (for example Willcock[37] and Griffin[38]) take the prepositional phrase to mean "by my worldly status," while another (Hainsworth[39]), finding the rhetoric "more impressive than clear," cautiously concludes that "the implication may be that Akhilleus now has no use for the earthbound conceptions of Agamemnon." The debate is a wide one, involving questions not only of the history of subjectivity but also of the interpretation of Homeric religion. The specific crux here, however, is critical to a reading of the poem as a whole. Should the line be read as the expression or representation of a heroic code, or does it also interrogate the limits of that code by imagining how to live worthily after rejecting the consolations it would offer?

As with the question of how to read Virgil, I am not attempting to resolve the debate. Nonetheless, it may be useful to examine the theoretical position from which it is alleged that Homeric man could not skeptically interrogate fundamental aspects of his culture. Is the ability to reject or revise fundamental convictions a highly specialized phenomenon, or is it more general? How should we understand Achilles' words?

36   Whitman (1965) 183.
37   Willcock (1978) 1.283.
38   Griffin (1995) 141.
39   Hainsworth (1993) 140.

The rationality debate among philosophers and anthropologists was set in motion in 1964 with an essay by the Wittgensteinian philosopher Peter Winch[40] attacking a famous work by the social anthropologist E. E. Evans-Pritchard (1937). This debate, by some accounts still ongoing, has involved a number of contributors, including the philosophers Habermas and Alasdair MacIntyre as well as several anthropologists.[41] There have been two main and related foci of the debate: how to understand a very foreign culture and whether rationality is universal.

Evans-Pritchard tried to make sense of a Zande ritual that was at first unintelligible to him. When a misfortune happens to a particular person, the Azande assume witchcraft is involved. They can give specific naturalistic reasons for the event, but they have an additional area to investigate, the question of why the misfortune happened at a particular time and to a particular person. This was due to witchcraft, and the perpetrator can be identified by poisoning a chicken. A complex system of institutional procedures ensures that the oracle functions vitally within the society, having an emollient effect on tensions between peers and reinforcing the status of the prince. Witchcraft beliefs likewise function socially, and there is no incentive to examine internal contradictions in the Zande system of beliefs.

Winch objects on Wittgensteinian grounds that Evans-Pritchard has misunderstood the Azande because he does not understand them as they understand themselves; he is not playing the same "language-game" as they play. Evans-Pritchard's attention to contradiction and his claim that witchcraft has no "objective reality" distance him from the forms of Zande life; instead, he has imported Western notions of logic and scientific causality where they do not belong. For Winch those are highly context- and language-dependent. We can only know what is real by how it shows itself in the language,[42] but Evans-Pritchard depends on a scientific notion of the real where contradiction, for example, is troubling; he commits, that is, a category-mistake.[43] There is nonetheless a problem for Winch. How is understanding across language-games possible at all? His answer is that to understand the mystical thought of the Azande it will be necessary to translate it not into Western scientific discourse but more appropriately into Western philosophical and religious attitudes.[44]

Winch's critique is itself vulnerable to attack. In a recent assessment, Horton is severe. There is no evidence that the Azande are contemplative mystics; their interest in witchcraft is like our interest in science – oriented toward "explanation, prediction, and control."[45] Religion is not generally aimed at ends very different from those of science and technology, though this is the case in Western history

40   Reprinted as Winch (1970) 78–111.
41   See further two basic anthologies, Wilson (1970) and Hollis and Lukes (1982).
42   Winch (1970) 82.
43   Winch (1970) 93.
44   Winch (1970) 107–9.
45   Horton (1993) 145.

after Newton.[46] The cooperative endeavor of explanation, prediction, and control that secures and protects the resources which make human existence possible requires something like the common Western conception of rationality, including our everyday notions of causality, truth, falsity, agreement with reality, space, time, persons, non-persons, material objects, and so on.[47] There is no alternative rationality in primitive societies to the one we know, and although most societies have some sectors of life in which something like mysticism may operate, those sectors are carefully constrained by the ordinary striving to meet biological needs.[48] Belief in the Trinity does not ordinarily pose a problem to mathematics.

Winch's argument that contradiction does not matter from within the Zande language-game is also vulnerable, and this brings us back to the question of how to interpret Achilles' words. Faced with a contradiction or other adverse experience, are the Azande willing to revise core beliefs? Mostly not, and certainly much less so than scientists. However, even scientists, when they have confidence in a theory, tend to greet evidence that goes against its predictions with *ad hoc* excuses, such as the carelessness of operators, impure materials, etc.[49] That is, radical reorientations in core beliefs tend to be rare. This is not in itself a difference between modern and primitive, but a fact about core beliefs. The model of rule-following in a language-game which Winch employs is not workable because the deviation from rules observable in all human society is missing from his account, and we cannot *a priori* assume that such deviations are themselves rule-bound.[50] "Readiness to learn and openness to criticism" are not "idiosyncratic features of our own culture."[51] Anthropologists have emphasized the improvisatory character of human culture,[52] the ability of even very closed societies to revise themselves under conditions of necessity.

There is no anthropological or philosophical reason to deny that skepticism is a permanent human possibility. We have, that is, no theoretical or historical reason that would require Achilles to endorse a heroic code of behavior. We are left with nothing better than literary criticism to understand Achilles' words.

46   Horton (1993) 155, 158.
47   Horton (1993) 141.
48   Horton (1993) 154.
49   Horton (1993) 150.
50   MacIntyre (1970) 122.
51   Habermas (1984) 1.62.
52   For example, Held (1951).

5

Surfing the Third Wave?

Postfeminism and the Hermeneutics of Reception

Genevieve Liveley

A brief history of feminism might look something like this. Until the late eighteenth century, the social, cultural, and political shores of the pre-feminist world were quiet, only occasionally struck by storms – such as the late medieval *querelle des femmes* – stirred up by early feminist thinkers and writers. In 1792, with the publication of Mary Shelley Wollstonecraft's *Vindication of the Rights of Women*, pre-feminist shores were washed by the first wave of modern feminism and first wave feminists, driven by the winds of revolution in France, wrote of and worked for the right to claim legal identity and independence for women, campaigning for suffrage and abolition causes. In the second half of the twentieth century, the second wave of feminism pounded European and American shores, as second wave feminists of the 1960s and 1970s further claimed the legal right to equality for women, writing of and campaigning for women's liberation from patriarchal oppression. Pinpointing the death of first wave feminism to the moment at which women won the vote, second wave feminists dismissed the "old feminism" as individualist and reformist, and as incompatible with the collectivist and revolutionary spirit of the "new feminism." In the mid 1980s, a third wave began to break as a new generation of feminists started to question the emphasis upon sisterhood and oppression in the second wave, dismissing as "victim feminism" the politics and theory of the previous generation. Privileging difference, individuality and self-reflexivity in their theory and praxis, third wave feminists began to highlight the heterogeneity of feminist thinking and the diversity of "feminisms" now emerging in the wake of the second wave.[1]

Thanks to Duncan Kennedy, Charles Martindale, and Vanda Zajko for showing me other ways to read between the waves.

1 Of course, other stories of feminism might look very different. In particular, third wave or postfeminism has been identified as emerging from critiques of "academic feminism" and "white feminism" by women of color and self-styled "third-world feminists." On the contentious issue of feminism's three "waves," see Coppock, Haydon, and Richter

Although charged by its critics with reversing the advances made by the feminist movement and of steering us back to a pre-feminist world, third wave feminism or postfeminism as theory and praxis can be seen explicitly to acknowledge its indebtedness to the history of feminism. The label "third wave" is preferred by many feminists precisely because of the relationship with previous movements and moments in the history of feminism that it suggests. As Sarah Gamble argues in her essay "Postfeminism":

> It may be . . . that third wave feminism is capable, as post-feminism is not, of describing a position from which past feminisms can be both celebrated and critiqued, and new strategies evolved. The state of economic, political and technological flux which characterizes modernity presents opportunities and dangers for women which the feminists of the first and second wave could not have imagined.[2]

Yet, the term "postfeminism" with its controversial prefix need not necessarily describe a denunciation of former feminist models. It can connote the rejection of an earlier feminist phase, or a relapse back to a past phase, but it can also signal the reconfiguration of feminism to reflect changing contexts and conditions.[3]

In her 1985 study of postfeminism and modernity, *Gynesis*, Alice Jardine asked how the concept and practice of feminism might profit from this new model of postfeminism. Looking forward to the future of third wave feminist theory and praxis she questioned whether feminism might be redefined and redirected and whether literary criticism's relations with male and female engendered texts might be reconfigured so as to reconceptualize a new kind of feminist hermeneutics – one "able to give up its quest for truth; capable of self-reflection on its own complicity with inherited systems of representation."[4] For Jardine, a modern feminist or postfeminist hermeneutics – like Gadamer's "proper hermeneutics"[5] – must be willing and able to reflect upon its situatedness, the historicality of its position. Only when it is capable of demonstrating the workings of history within its (and our) own understanding can such an interpretative strategy be deemed effective – thus, only when feminist theory and praxis is capable of reflecting upon its own "horizon" (the shifting line between past, present, and future) can feminism as hermeneutic be effective.

    (1995); Friedman (1991); Gamble (2001b); Heywood and Drake (1997); Hodgson-
    Wright (2001); Modleski (1991); Sanders (2001); Siegel (1997); Thornham (2001);
    and Whelehan (1995). On feminism in classics, see Rabinowitz and Richlin (1993);
    Skinner (1986); and the special edition of *Helios* (1990).
2   Gamble (2001a) 54.
3   Cf. Gamble (2001a) 44–5.
4   Jardine (1985) 63.
5   Gadamer (1975).

It now seems timely to ask: has the third wave concept and practice of feminism or postfeminism, with its promise of new feminist engagements with male-engendered texts, enabled this hermeneutics? Does third wave or postfeminism (however complicit in its own chronologically informed epistemology and self-reflexive periodization) provide an opportune moment from which to scrutinize the theory and praxis of feminism in classics – a point of reception at which we may be capable of self-reflection upon our own complicity with the systems of representation and reception that we inherit, inhabit, and bequeath?

Re-crossing the Great Void

Jardine's own writing offers a potential prototype for the new model of post-feminist theory and praxis that she looks towards in *Gynesis*: a scholarly text that is also an allegorical narrative, a history of feminist thinking, a map of feminist hermeneutics, and a work of reception – reflecting upon the relation of postfeminist literary critical engagements with male-authored texts to pre-feminist engagements with male-authored texts. Indeed, Jardine shows herself to be particularly sensitive to the continuities and correlations no less than to the divisions and differences between early feminist thinking (as demonstrated in early modern writings such as Christine de Pisan's *La cité des dames*), twentieth-century or second wave feminist theory and praxis (as evinced in the writings of Cixous, Irigaray, and Kristeva), and the postfeminist or third wave feminist hermeneutics that characterize and inform her own work.

Jardine considers "the necessary first step to reading and rereading" contemporary women theorists and fiction writers to be the rigorous reading and rereading of the men who have influenced these women's texts.[6] Thus, she explicitly elects to reread Lacan, Derrida, and Deleuze rather than Cixous, Irigaray, or Kristeva, in the hope of escaping "the clouds of rhetoric surrounding the interpretations of what these women were 'really' writing, doing, or prescribing."[7] Furthermore, in Jardine's quest to locate the canonical fathers of contemporary French feminism and to examine their legacy for the future of feminism and feminist criticism, she reveals the complicity of much contemporary feminist theory and praxis – including her own engagement with psychoanalytic, philosophical, and fictional texts by male writers – with inherited systems and structures of representation and interpretation. Noticing some of the principal blind-spots in contemporary feminism on both sides of the Atlantic, she observes that French feminists and theorists are frequently accused by American feminists "of reverting to 'essentialist' definitions of woman, of being hopelessly enamoured of 'male theoretical

6   Jardine (1985) 264.
7   Jardine (1985) 260–1.

structures' (especially philosophical ones), natural definitions of woman, and so on."[8] But she notices that correspondingly, to many French women, American academic feminists can seem "blind to the ways in which capitalist, patriarchal ideology governs their thinking; that they are more worried about tenure for their work *on* women than they are about working *with* women to change symbolic structures."[9] Each group, it seems, can see the blind-spots of the other but finds it hard to see its own.

For Jardine, however, a modern feminist hermeneutics must be "capable of self-reflection," particularly upon its complicity with the inherited hermeneutic structures and systems that it seeks to challenge. Yet, as her own study shows, *distance* – whether temporal or spatial – is required to facilitate such reflection. The point of self-reflection in this model depends, like the point of reception, upon a process of displacement. Indeed, Jardine endeavours to pinpoint her own displaced position on the feminist map with some precision. She not only locates her rereadings and writings as those of a "displaced" American feminist reflecting upon French texts and theory in France, but also situates those texts and her rereadings in the temporal space of their production – a period "of intellectual crisis" during which "major cultural critics were calmly announcing the 'historicization' (death) of feminism as a movement."[10] Thus, it is from this moment and from this horizon that Jardine sets out to explore the postfeminist landscape of modernity.

Situating the present horizon of her own feminist position as a line marking the "death" of second wave feminism as concept and practice and the birth of postfeminism, Jardine makes an interesting move. As she endeavours to look towards the future direction of a new postfeminist hermeneutics, she looks back to the first feminist hermeneutics and its reception in medieval and Renaissance Europe, allegorizing modern postfeminism as a new or ongoing mode of the early modern "feminism" of the *querelle des femmes*. She proposes that the contemporary crisis of modernity and its concomitant challenges for feminism and postfeminism represents "nothing less really than a new kind of *querelle des femmes*: a strangely new and urgent emphasis on 'woman,' a willing blindness to the *endoxes* of its history and contemporary contexts; the uses of woman as part of a strategy of radical reading and writing."[11]

Historicizing the concept and practice of feminism, Jardine looks back to a key moment of epistemological and hermeneutic crisis in Western culture – the transitional period between the Middle Ages and the Renaissance – to trace a connection between "the first concerted adventure of feminism"[12] and the new postclassical secular European state. Jardine's point of coincidence and correlation,

---

8   Jardine (1985) 15–16.
9   Jardine (1985) 15–16.
10 Jardine (1985) 17.
11 Jardine (1985) 102.
12 Albistur and Armogathe (1977) 67.

however, turns out to mark a pivotal moment in the history of reception studies no less than in feminist or women's history.

The *querelle des femmes* initiated by Christine de Pisan in *La cité des dames* which prompted heated debates between early feminists, humanists, and clerics about the status of women, was conceived specifically as a response – a work of reception – to the antifeminist rhetoric of *Le Roman de la rose*, itself a canonical work of classical reception. Begun in the early thirteenth century by Guillaume de Lorris and later completed by Jean de Meun, the allegorical *Le Roman de la rose* was conceived unequivocally by de Lorris as a new *Ars amatoria* (*Roman* 1.37–9). Indeed, de Lorris names himself explicitly as the "modern" heir of Catullus, Gallus, Tibullus, and Ovid, in a literary lineage drawing directly upon *Amores* 3.9 and *Tristia* 4.10.53–4. Rejecting this classical inheritance and its antifeminist representation of women, in *La cité des dames* Christine de Pisan conceived an alternative literary tradition and what would later be identified as the first feminist hermeneutic – a hermeneutic of reception and allegorization.

Shifting her horizon from the past to the future, Jardine offers her own allegory of the theory and praxis of third wave or postfeminism with a short story from Walter Abish's *In the Future Perfect*.[13] In this story, the hero is compelled to set out on a journey across the Great Void of the North African desert to find his lost father and to claim an inheritance, leaving behind Track, the woman whose body is tattooed with a map that charts his path across the Great Void to an oasis called Blitlu. To guide him in his journey the hero has only an "old book" about deserts – written by an army general and titled, like Abish's story, *Crossing the Great Void* – into which Track has inserted a slip of paper giving directions – "up until now correct" – to Blitlu. Jardine focuses particularly upon the scene in which the hero and Track part:

> It was the last time he saw her.
> Are you thinking of going back to Blitlu, he asked?
> Can I drop you here . . . I don't want to run into your Uncle, she said.
> My uncle . . . How do you know my uncle?
> He's everybody's uncle, she said, condescendingly.[14]

For Jardine, the crucial questions raised by this parting are whether Track will accompany the hero on his journey and if not, where and with whom she will chose to go instead. Appropriating the story as a self-conscious allegory of her own postfeminist mapping of the meetings and divergences of modern feminism and postfeminist hermeneutics, Jardine asks: "Among all the pathways, roads, tracks, and spaces in Abish's short story, all crisscrossing their ways through false images, illusions, and misconnections, which direction might or should the feminist critic

---

13   Compare with Batstone's "the future perfect in the present."
14   Abish (1977) 107.

take?"[15] Her subsequent charting of the late twentieth-century course of feminist thinking in France and America explores some of the different directions that feminist criticism has already taken and might yet take, considering particularly the interdisciplinary companions that feminists have and might yet elect to travel with at different stages of their journey.

Yet this story may also be seen to raise questions about the fundamental validity of any quest to recover a lost father or an inheritance, the dependence of any hero upon the authority of an "old book," the difficulties of attempting to read a map inscribed on a woman's body – the particular difficulties faced by a woman attempting to read a map tattooed on her own back – and the hermeneutic challenge presented to reader and traveller alike by a set of directions which have been "up until now correct" but may no longer be so. Indeed, these are the concerns that emerge in Jardine's own quest for a new form of postfeminist hermeneutics, one focused upon something other than representations of and by women, prepared to concede its traditional quest for truth and reality, ready to give up its search for a lost or stolen inheritance – a postfeminist hermeneutics of reception.

Rescuing Creusa

In the same year as the publication of Jardine's *Gynesis*, feminist theorist Rachel Blau DuPlessis appropriated a similar story of a hero's quest, in this case to serve as an allegory for the marginalized position of second wave feminism in mainstream academic scholarship. In a rereading of Virgil's *Aeneid* 2.707–44, DuPlessis focuses in particular upon the part of the story in which the hero and his wife are separated:

> The torch is passed on. His son clutches his hand, his crippled father clings to his back, three male generations leave the burning city. The wife, lost. Got lost in burning. No one knows what happened to her, when they became the Romans. She became the Etruscans?[16]

DuPlessis rereads and rewrites Virgil's foundation story from a second wave feminist perspective as a literary-critical allegory, rescuing Creusa from Virgil and from the flames of Ilium, in order to recuperate this shadowy female figure not as one of the first female victims of Rome's embryonic power but as the founder of a new city, a new race, and a new language. In DuPlessis' rereading and retelling of Virgil's story, Creusa is "lost" by Aeneas and thus lost to the future history of Rome, but through being lost she becomes the founding mother of the Etruscan people – a subordinate and alien race whose non-Roman Latin language DuPlessis

---

15   Jardine (1985) 51.
16   DuPlessis (1985) 271.

figures as an allegory of feminist literary-critical discourse, a "meta-discourse" both familiar and alien, subordinate and subversive to mainstream literary criticism.

DuPlessis' appropriation of Creusa was subsequently itself reappropriated by feminists working in the discipline of classics, most explicitly by Marilyn Skinner and her fellow contributors to the 1986 special issue of *Helios*, "Rescuing Creusa: New Methodological Approaches to Women in Antiquity" – a collection of essays on feminism and classics that set out "to rescue Creusa and transport her safely to a new homeland."[17] Skinner's reappropriation of the story of Creusa offered a self-reflexive allegory of the marginalized and subordinate yet independent position of feminism in mainstream classical scholarship, and was to establish a rhetoric of reappropriation, reconstruction, revision, and rescue as the prevailing discourse of second wave feminist studies in classics – a rhetoric of reception. It also raised expectations and questions about the future direction of feminist studies in classics: From what and whom has Creusa been rescued? What are the motives and future plans of her rescuers? And, having been rescued, is Creusa to follow Aeneas on his journey – and if not, where and with whom will she decide to go instead? Moreover, at Skinner's exhortation to feminists in classics that "It is time to sail for Caere," for "already we have abandoned the citadel, counted our numbers, taken stock of our resources and equipped our boats,"[18] other questions might be raised: What does it mean to abandon the citadel? What are the resources available to feminist scholarship in classics and which companions are to be counted among its crew?

Skinner's discussion of contemporary endeavors in classics to "rescue" Creusa offers some revealing answers to these questions. Her historicizing representation of the shape of second wave feminism in classics suggests that its rescue mission had been launched at a timely moment, just as the citadel was indeed about to fall. Reflecting Jardine's attention to historical "coincidences" – moments of epistemological and hermeneutic crisis in Western culture at which feminist voices appear to gain authority and legitimacy – Skinner suggests that, at roughly the same time as the introduction of feminism as a new field of research into classical studies, the discipline itself experienced such a period of crisis. Her introduction dates the formal recognition of "Women in Antiquity" as a legitimate and independent field of research in classics to the spring of 1973 – when the first special issue of a classical journal devoted to this area was published by *Arethusa*.[19] At around this time, Skinner argues, classical studies experienced a "far-reaching intellectual shift" towards a phase that she terms "postclassicism" – a period of epistemological and ideological crisis in which the discipline began to acknowledge "the idea of all cultural artefacts and systems as broadly accessible 'texts' open to multiple and even conflicting readings, and to a flexible and pluralistic

17   Skinner (1986) 6.
18   Skinner (1986) 6.
19   *Arethusa*, 6 (1) (Spring 1973).

notion of our disciplinary activity in which feminism, like other interpretative strategies, [became] one strong voice in a richly polyphonous semiotic discourse."[20]

As she traces her allegory of the late twentieth-century map of feminist scholarship in classics, exploring some of the different directions that feminist research in the field had already taken and might yet take, Skinner considers in particular the interdisciplinary companions that feminists have chosen to take with them on their journey. Among the number accompanying feminism in its classical quest, she lists "anthropology, English, and modern language studies, history and sociology,"[21] while among the resources equipping the boats set for Caere, she also includes "structural and symbolic anthropology, the history of *mentalité*, poststructuralist literary theory, Freudian and Lacanian psychoanalysis, neo-Marxism, and feminist theory."[22] There is one striking omission from this number, however, an absent presence among the crew. Unacknowledged by Skinner, reception theory – encompassing reader-response criticism, reading as allegory, theories of dialogue, histories of reading, canon formation, and hermeneutics – was already steering the fleet to Caere.

Re-appropriating the Text

In the same year as the publication of Jardine's *Gynesis* and DuPlessis' "For the Etruscans," the APA panel of the Women's Classical Caucus controversially scheduled for its annual meeting the topic of "Re-appropriating the Text: The Case of Ovid." Following papers by Leslie Cahoon on the *Amores*, Florence Verducci on the *Ars amatoria*, and Frederick Ahl on the *Metamorphoses*, Phyllis Culham presented an explosive response – challenging the panel and its audience to consider: "How is one to relate to a literary-historical documentation of the past, which not only was male-generated, but has been honed carefully in the transmission through the ages to take on an ever more androcentric shape?"[23] The focus of Culham's response and the vigorous debate that it sparked, subsequently revised and published in 1990 in a special edition of *Helios*, centered upon the validity of feminist receptions and reappropriations of male-authored canonical classical texts. This new *querelle des femmes* articulated many of the same concerns regarding the concept and practice of feminism in classical scholarship as those raised in Jardine's *Gynesis* and in "Rescuing Creusa," and similarly looked to reception theory for direction.[24]

---

20 Skinner (1986) 4.
21 Skinner (1986) 4.
22 Skinner (1986) 4.
23 This summary of the debate is formulated by Keuls (1990) 221.
24 Five of the eight essays collected in the 1990 *Helios* special edition refer to the 1986
    "Rescuing Creusa" anthology. Culham and McManus also cite Alice Jardine's *Gynesis*.

Participants in both the "original" APA event and its *Helios* "translation" debated whether the central concern of modern feminist scholarship should – or ever could – be "the recovery of women's lived reality," and whether the trend in contemporary feminist scholarship in classics to recuperate male-authored, canonical texts represented a collusive act of "collaboration with authoritarianism."[25] Challenging the validity of any quest to discover the truth about women's lived reality with the counter-claim that lived reality is always mediated and its representation always already textual, participants in the debate demonstrated a direct engagement with a range of issues pertinent to reception studies – particularly reader-response criticism, histories of reading, and canon formation.

Phyllis Culham's polemical position paper maintained that any approach to the study of women in antiquity that denigrated or excluded women's experience of lived reality "could not logically be termed feminist, however effective it might be as literary or historical criticism."[26] Questioning, therefore, the decision by a feminist organization such as the Women's Classical Caucus to schedule the topic of "Reappropriating the Text: The Case of Ovid" for discussion at its annual meeting, Culham asserted that:[27]

> The sort of critical distancing that denigrates women's lived reality is finally disadvantageous, because it assigns feminists the role of *re*acting, *re*reading, *re*sponding. It is difficult, in fact, to see how feminist efforts to reappropriate this male-authored text ultimately differ from the rereadings which produced Ovidius Christianus, Ovide Moralisé, and Ovid the Neoplatonist.

Among the published essays that *re*acted, *re*read, and *re*sponded to Culham's text, Mary-Kay Gamel was the only interlocutor in the debate to respond directly to Culham's claim that feminist reappropriations of Ovid do not ultimately differ from the medieval and early modern receptions that allegorized, parodied, and moralized his writings. She argued:

> That the *motivation* for my rereading of Ovidian texts is similar to that which produced *Ovide moralisé* I acknowledge. Whether the *results* of my rereading are more or less appropriate to the texts themselves, or to feminist analysis, others will judge. The variety of readings ancient texts have received proves not that all readings are equally valid or that these texts are "timeless" but that readings, like texts, are located within history.[28]

---

25 Culham (1990) 161. Culham's criticism of feminist literary critics entering a "mutually congratulatory relationship with the text they are judging" (162) borrows its formulation from Jardine (1985) 147, but fails to recognize that Jardine's *Gynesis* is concerned precisely with reappropriating male-authored texts.

26 Culham (1990) 161.

27 Culham (1990) 162.

28 Gamel (1990) 172; emphases in original.

The central tenet of reception theory, and of reception as hermeneutic, tells us that "*meaning is always realized at the point of reception*," and that "we read *from the present interest*."[29] Phyllis Culham's quest to rescue Creusa, to recover the truth about "women's lived reality" in ancient Greece and Rome misses the point then – that such "truth" is constituted always and only at the point of its reception. The "reality" of women's lives is "realized" – made real – retrospectively from the point of reception.[30] And this is the case whether that "point" is located with cultural historians reading material artefacts from antiquity or literary critics reading classical literary texts produced by canonical male authors. From this perspective, which allows us to see one of the critical blind-spots in feminist quests to rescue Creusa, we see that feminist efforts to recover the reality of women's lived experience, or to reappropriate the texts of canonical male authors do *not* ultimately differ from the sort of rereadings that produced Ovidius Christianus, Ovide Moralisé, or Ovid the Neoplatonist. Nor, perhaps, do they differ from those rereadings and reappropriations of classical texts that produced *Le Roman de la rose*, *La cité des dames*, *Tales from Ovid*, or even Ovid's own *Heroides*.

Yet the force of Culham's condemnation is seemingly leveled at feminists for responding to classical texts, not merely in the context of literary criticism, but in the tradition of literary reception. Her hostility towards feminist rereadings of canonical authors such as Ovid seems to have been directed, moreover, by a conviction that these reappropriations are products of a special interest group or groups, the products of and for their time. Culham demonstrates no sympathy with any notion of the "potentiality" of textual interpretation (such as that proposed by Jauss) – the idea that feminist interpretations of a classical author such as Ovid might be "always already" authorized by the text and only wait to be released.[31] The assumption underlying Culham's argument seems to be that feminist rereadings of classical texts are fundamentally *mis*readings, that feminist appropriations of canonical texts are *mis*appropriations.

Feminist readers and readings have been particularly vulnerable to charges of misreading and misappropriation in their endeavors to engage critically with classical texts. Yet, as Charles Martindale points out,

> The common complaint that feminist readings emphasize some details at the expense of others misses the mark, since this is something all interpretations do – *and must do*. And in general feminists do not occlude their *interestedness*.[32]

It is a risk, however, that in making explicit this "interestedness" – the position of *present interest* from which feminist rereadings and reappropriations are produced

29 Cf. Martindale (1993).
30 I owe this formulation to Duncan Kennedy.
31 Jauss (1982a). Alison Sharrock identifies the trend of "releasing" readings as a new strand of feminist criticism in classics (2002) 101 n. 25.
32 Martindale (1993) 13.

– such interpretations are thus unable to appeal to (and so lose the appeal *of*) any sense of timelessness or universality in their approach to classical texts. Hence the continuing risk that feminist interpretations of any text render themselves vulnerable to the type of criticism leveled by Culham: that they are offered only a temporary authorization by and within the broader literary community, and that they await their own moment of reception when another set of readers will judge whether to grant or withhold continued authority. It is worth noting that among the resources Skinner saw equipping the boats set for Caere, "the history of *mentalité*" appears not to have survived the journey, and is no longer regarded as a useful critical companion for classicists. Is this, perhaps, the fate that Culham fears may lie ahead for feminist theory and praxis? This concern reflects Stanley Fish's assertion that a literary institution "at any one time will authorize only a finite number of interpretative strategies"[33] but is also compatible with Gadamer's view that "It is part of the historical finiteness of our being that we are aware that after us others will understand in a different way."[34] It is hard to see, then, how feminist literary criticism ultimately differs from any other mode of reading or reception in this respect. Certainly, feminist criticism meets the Fishian benchmark for the respectability of any literary-critical enterprise, "that it be, or at least be able to present itself as, *distinctive*"[35] – but the same might also be said of the medieval tradition of allegoresis that produced *Ovide moralisé*. Moreover, the etymology of *respectability* reminds us that an interpretative strategy such as feminist literary criticism depends not (only) upon the esteem of its peers for authorization, but upon the regard of those who come after and "look again" at its products and processes.

Perhaps here, as Amy Richlin suggests, classics as a discipline has something distinctive of its own to contribute to a postfeminist hermeneutics – and to postfeminism and the hermeneutics of reception: "a long view."

> We are used to noting trends over the two thousand year period which is our own domain, along with the fifteen hundred years that came after. In this perspective, capitalism is a flash in the pan. On such a large scale, local-historical differences do not seem so significant, or so different.[36]

Whether feminism, from this perspective, appears only as a "flash in the pan" depends upon the length of view we take. Alice Jardine's model of postfeminist hermeneutics adopts a relatively "long view," seeing the late twentieth-century *querelle des femmes* between second and third wave feminists, between feminist theorists and activists, and between Anglo-American and French feminists, as "reflecting" the

---

33   Fish (1980) 342.
34   Gadamer (1975) 336.
35   Fish (2001) 38; emphasis in original.
36   Richlin (1993) 284.

fourteenth-century *querelle des femmes* – clearly illustrating the point that on a large enough temporal scale, "local-historical differences" such as those mapped by feminists of the first, second, and third waves do not appear so very different. Jauss allows for an even longer view, in which feminist readings "released" from classical texts are always already authorized by their classical authors. In this view, Ovid launches perhaps the earliest feminist mission to "rescue Creusa" in *Heroides* 7, when his pregnant Dido reminds us of the fate of "pretty Iulus' mother," carelessly left behind to burn when Aeneas leaves Troy (*Heroides* 7.84).

If a modern feminist or postfeminist hermeneutics must be willing and able to reflect upon the historicality of its position, and if feminism as hermeneutic can become effective only when it proves itself capable of reflecting upon its own horizon (the shifting tide line between first, second, and third waves), then such a long view becomes essential. For it is this long view that provides the necessary distance and displacement to facilitate such self-reflection. And if the contentious prefix "post" can point to feminism's past, present, and future trajectory, then it can also direct us to a point of reception at which we can recognize and re-negotiate the systems of representation, reading, and reception that we inherit, inhabit, and bequeath.

6

Allusion as Reception

Virgil, Milton, and the Modern Reader

Craig Kallendorf

It is common knowledge that fragments of the *Aeneid* are embedded in *Paradise Lost*, but surprisingly, over 300 years of critical activity has yet to clarify either the full extent of the relationship or what it might mean for our understanding of the two poems. Milton's first commentator, Patrick Hume, began the practice of identifying the Latin root of an unusual word in *Paradise Lost* and then citing passages from the *Aeneid* in which that word is used, generally without further comment. As Richard Thomas has reminded us, however, such references must then be interpreted.[1] Unfortunately those critics who have proposed interpretive patterns in Milton's allusions to Virgil remain divided on the most fundamental of issues. Davis Harding, for example, claimed that Satan rewrites Turnus, serving like his model as epic antagonist;[2] C. M. Bowra and Francis Blessington, however, linked Satan to Aeneas, but with different interpretations, with Bowra claiming that Satan indeed takes on Aeneas' grandeur but as part of Milton's larger critique of the value system of ancient epic,[3] while Blessington saw Satan as a parody of Aeneas, a posturer who fails to attain the nobility of his model.[4] In the face of such disagreement Charles Martindale has suggested that Milton's relationship to Virgil is exaggerated, or at very least needs to be defined much more precisely.[5]

Some disagreement, of course, is part of the normal business of literary criticism, but problems of this magnitude suggest an aporia in theory, some fundamental operating premise that has not been thought through carefully enough. It happens that the past several decades have seen a good deal of theoretical discussion of allusion. Earlier debates about the importance of authorial intention took a decisive turn in the 1960s, when Julia Kristeva introduced the

---

1 Thomas (1986) 174.
2 Harding (1962) 44–51.
3 Bowra (1948) 229–30.
4 Blessington (1979) 1–8.
5 Martindale (2002) 107.

term "intertextuality" to highlight the relationship between two texts without reference to authorial subjectivity. Structuralist critics helped fill out the implications of this approach,[6] but among classicists, authorial subjectivity returned through the back door in the work of Gian Biagio Conte, who recognized a reconstructed author writing for an implied reader whose literary experience allowed for the recognition of intertextual references. More recent work is beginning to acknowledge Martindale's assertion that "meaning is always constructed at the point of reception"[7] and to privilege the role of the reader in defining the meaning of allusions.[8] I shall begin here, but propose a somewhat different model that focuses on the relationship between the modern critic and the alluding author as two different but interconnected readers. The validity of this model, I believe, is confirmed by its ability to guide us to a new appreciation of the role of the *Aeneid* in *Paradise Lost*.

A number of poststructuralist responses to intertextuality have focused attention on a reader who in some way or other does more than passively recognize a reference embedded in a text. As early as 1966, Earl Wasserman suggested that allusion "ought to be defined broadly enough to include a creative act by the reader"; that is, as Pucci puts it, the reader "constitutes the allusion" and "makes meaning." The reader of an allusion "configures on his own terms the interpretive outcomes of this connection . . . [T]he language of the allusion makes possible but does not determine the creation, function, or conceivable interpretations of the allusion."[9]

The consequences of this approach depend on something that has been noticed but not adequately explored, the fact that there are two readers operating in allusion: the critic who notices an allusion and the author who wrote it. The alluding author begins the process by reading an earlier text, then working out an interpretation of that text. As he or she begins writing, the new text unfolds in dialogue with the old one, in such a way that the potential meaning of one or more words resonates against their original usage in another text, where they meant something that is seen as relevant again. The critic, the second reader, works backwards and recreates this process as he or she is able to understand it, reading the second text and coming to a preliminary idea about what it means, then noticing a relationship to an earlier text that the author could have known, then going back and forth between the two to reconstruct the author's reading of the first text on the basis of the allusions and what they appear to reveal. Schematically the process might be represented like this:

text[1] (T^1) — [reading of author (R-A)] — text[2] (T^2) — reading of critic (R-C)

---

6   Allen (2000).
7   Hinds (1998) 47–51.
8   Fowler (2000) 111, 130; Edmunds (2001) xi–xx, 39–62, 133–69; Pucci (1998) 3–48.
9   Pucci (1998) 22, 43, 36.

I have placed R-A in brackets to indicate that it is normally a reconstruction of a reading that is not available in the same way as R-C is. The critic will have his or her own reading of T^1 that may be independent of T^2, and certainly was so before the allusion was noticed, but the recreation of R-A also generates a reading of T^1 through the filter of T^2.

To help explain this model and its significance, I suggest four axioms:

(1) The active agent in recognizing and interpreting allusion produces R-C and, by extension, R-A, and has to work within the hermeneutic possibilities for T^1 and T^2 as he or she understands them. In other words, R-C is always the result of a critic who is situated, in time and place, as a member of an interpretive community that fosters some hermeneutic options for given texts and discourages, even blocks off, others. The common interpretations of T^1 will foreground some lines and scenes in the mind of the reader-critic, who will be more likely to recognize and attribute meaning to them in T^2 than the lines and scenes from T^1 that are neglected by comparison within his or her interpretive community.[10]

(2) R-A is not the product of Iser's implied reader, the appropriate and sympathetic receiver of the cues embedded in T^1 by its author,[11] but is instead a construct that emerges from the recognition of fragments of T^1 in T^2 and the effort of the reader-critic to interpret their significance in T^2 in relation to their original significance in T^1. Often, especially with older works, this construct is all there is. The recreated reader-author, however, can merge with the author as actual reader if relevant external evidence like criticism of T^1 or a copy of T^1 annotated by the reader-author can be found.[12] In cases like this, the reader-author's actual reading of T^1 provides a check on the constructed R-A, supplementing and, if necessary, correcting the work of the critic.

(3) Some allusions will remain local, a fragment of one text embedded in another that serves primarily to enrich verbal texture, but the most richly rewarding allusive contact will be systematic, one of a number of references that contribute substantially to meaning.[13] Classicists have tended to focus on local allusions,[14] but Joseph Farrell uses the relationship between Homer and Virgil to suggest that more attention should be paid to systematic allusions in cases when "a totalizing relationship" has been created.[15] References that enter an allusive system have the added advantage of the system as a guide to their interpretation – that is, the understanding of any given allusion from T^1 in T^2 can be checked at least in part against the understanding of other allusions from T^1 in R-A for plausibility and coherence.

10 Pucci (1998) 44.
11 Iser (1978b) 37–8.
12 Kallendorf and Kallendorf (2000).
13 Hebel (1991).
14 Hinds (1998) 101.
15 Edmunds (2001) 154.

(4) In allusion meaning flows both chronologically backwards as well as chronologically forwards.[16] In other words, R-C is created when the critic reads backwards, first reading T², then T¹ through it. However R-A is recreated in a reciprocal process by which T¹ and the critic's provisional understanding of it are pulled forward into T² and the critic's provisional understanding of it, with both matrices of meaning being adjusted and readjusted as the critic moves between the two texts to recreate R-A. Quoting Pope, Rudat refers to this as a "'mutual commerce' between alluding and allusive contexts, an intense interaction that seems to go both ways."[17]

In order to test the value of this model, let us now turn to Virgil and Milton.

As Francis Blessington has noted, *Paradise Lost* begins *in medias res* just like the *Aeneid*, when a figure of manifest grandeur is driven by divine wrath across a body of water, then forced to explore a new land in search of a new home.[18] Indeed Satan's first words to Beëlzebub, "If thou beest hee; But O how fall'n! how chang'd / From him . . ." (*PL* 1.84–5), echo Aeneas' words when he first saw Hector's ghost, "ei mihi, qualis erat, quantum mutatus ab illo / Hectore qui redit . . ." ("Oh this / was Hector, and how different he was / from Hector back from battle"; *Aen.* 2.274–5), making us wonder right away if Satan is a new Aeneas. Initially the answer seems to be "yes," for Satan concludes this speech with another conspicuous gesture toward Aeneas:

> So spake th' Apostate Angel, though in pain,
> Vaunting aloud, but rackt with deep despair . . .
> (*PL* 1.125–6)

> Talia uoce refert curisque ingentibus aeger
> Spem uultu simulat, premit altum corde dolorem.
>   (These are his words; though sick with heavy cares,
> he counterfeits hope in his face; his pain
> is held within, hidden.)
> (*Aen.* 1.208–9)

16   Kallendorf (1994); Fowler (2000) 130.
17   Rudat (1981) 46.
18   Blessington (1979) 6–7. There are two main modern sources for parallels between *Paradise Lost* and the *Aeneid*: the index to Patterson's Columbia edition of the *Works of Milton*, under the lemma "Vergil" in the second index volume ((1931–40) 2026–9), and the appendix to Verbart's *Fellowship in Paradise Lost* ((1995) 253–302). Both are extremely helpful, but neither is complete, so I have returned to the commentators of the long eighteenth century, whose sensitivity to classical allusion is often greater than that of modern readers (Oras (1967) 5–21). I have relied primarily on the editions of Hume (1695), Bentley (1732), the Richardsons (1734), Newton (1750), and Todd (1809), but will not normally reference each parallel to avoid overburdening the notes. Translations of the *Aeneid* are by Mandelbaum (1971).

Then God withdraws the hail and thunderbolts from the fiery lake of Hell (*PL* 1.169–77), just as Neptune calmed the seas and ceased to afflict Aeneas in the famous "Quos ego . . ." scene at the beginning of the *Aeneid* (1.124ff.). Another series of allusions links Satan to Aeneas in Carthage. As Satan prepares to speak to the other fallen devils, "attention held them mute" (*PL* 1.618), just as when Aeneas began to tell his story to Dido, "conticuere omnes intentique ora tenebant" ("A sudden silence fell on all of them; / their eyes were turned, intent on him"; *Aen.* 2.1). Similarly the description of Pandaemonium, which Satan observes in *PL* 1.728ff., recalls the description of Dido's palace, which Aeneas observed in *Aen.* 1.710ff., even down to the same number of lamps (*Aen.* 1.726–7); what is more, the devils swarming to the newly constructed Pandaemonium (*PL* 1.768–76) are depicted in terms of the famous bee simile that described the Carthaginian builders (*Aen.* 1.430ff.).

Book 2 of *Paradise Lost* rewrites Virgil's *descensus ad inferos*, suggesting that Satan in Hell parallels Aeneas in the underworld. In counseling war, Moloch claims that there will be no problem leaving Hell because "Th' ascent is easy then" (*PL* 2.81), echoing the Sibyl's advice to Aeneas, "facilis descensus Auerno" ("easy – / the way that leads into Avernus"; *Aen.* 6.126). *PL* 2.528ff. is clearly based on *Aen.* 6.653ff., suggesting that the devils in Hell parallel the blessed in Virgil's Elysian fields. When Satan announces his plan to leave Hell in search of Adam, he again describes the challenges of the journey in reference to Aeneas' descent to Hell, noting that "long is the way / And hard, that out of Hell leads up to light" (*PL* 2.432–3; cf. *Aen.* 6.128–9, "sed reuocare gradum superasque euadere ad auras, / hoc opus, hic labor est," "But to recall your steps, to rise again / into the upper air: that is the labor; / that is the task"), with the ninefold restraint of Hell's fiery adamantine gates (*PL* 2.436) recalling the details of Virgil's underworld (*Aen.* 6.439, 552) and the "four infernal Rivers" (*PL* 5.575ff.) giving a pronounced Virgilian flavor to Milton's Hell. Satan is also linked to Aeneas through references to other books of the *Aeneid*, brandishing his dart in *PL* 2.786, for example, like Aeneas on his way to kill Turnus in *Aen.* 12.919.

By this point, Satan appears to be a new Aeneas, described in terms and situations that link him systematically to Virgil's hero. The allusions diminish in book 3, where decorum perhaps makes it more difficult to link God's discussions with Jesus to classical literature; as Newton explained, ". . . Milton's divine Persons are divine Persons indeed, and talk in the language of God, that is in the language of Scripture."[19] In book 4, however, the allusive pattern resumes. Satan finds Adam and Eve in "A Silvan Scene" (*PL* 4.140) that closely resembles the "siluis scaena coruscis" ("the backdrop . . . a black / grove thick with bristling shadows"; *Aen.* 1.164) of the Libyan shore on which Aeneas landed.

Signs that something may be wrong with this interpretation, however, begin to appear. When Satan enters Paradise, he is compared to a wolf entering a sheepfold

---

19 Newton (1750) 1.211.

(*PL* 4.183–92), a comparison that echoes *Aen.* 9.59–66, but which links Satan not to Aeneas, but to Turnus.[20] Milton's first description of Adam (*PL* 4.288–94), in turn, recalls Virgil's description of Aeneas (*Aen.* 1.588–93), although Adam's hyacinthine locks are perhaps closer to Odysseus'.[21] Our sense of confusion grows when Adam's first words to Eve, "Whom fli'st thou?" (*PL* 4.482), clearly echo Aeneas' last words to Dido in Virgil's underworld (*Aen.* 6.466, "quem fugis?" "whom do you flee?"), suggesting again that perhaps Adam, not Satan, is the new Aeneas.[22] A reader who has noticed these clues will therefore not be totally unprepared when Milton settles the matter definitively in the final 25 lines of book 4. We see Satan, "and on his Crest / Sat horror Plum'd" (*PL* 4.988–9), which recalls the Chimaera on the helmet of Turnus in *Aen.* 7.785–6. Then God hung "his golden Scales" (*PL* 4.996–7) in heaven, just as Jupiter had done before the final battle in the *Aeneid*, so that Satan, who must lose in his confrontation with the angels who have come to Adam's defense, is associated with Turnus, who had to lose to Aeneas so that Italy could be established. The confrontation ends by associating Satan with Turnus in a way that anyone who has ever read the *Aeneid* will recall instantly: Satan

> fled,
> Murmuring, and with him fled the shades of night.
> (*PL* 4.1014–15)

> uitaque cum gemitu fugit indignata sub umbras.
> (and with a moan
> his life, resentful, fled to shades below.)
> (*Aen.* 12.952)

Until almost the very end of book 4, the clues suggest that Satan is the new Aeneas, the hero of Milton's rewritten *Aeneid*. But the clues are there to deceive: Satan is not the new Aeneas, but the new Turnus, just as he was in a group of minor (and now unread) epics written by Crashaw, Fletcher, and Beaumont, Milton's literary milieu from his Cambridge days.[23]

As long ago as Dryden, readers of *Paradise Lost* have been tempted to see Satan as the hero of the poem, even though they know that, theologically speaking, this cannot be. Part of Satan's appeal, I submit, is the strength of his association with Aeneas, the hero of the greatest epic of the ancient world and the one whose virtues are most compatible with Christian values. In Stanley Fish's now famous phrase, however, such a reader has been "surprised by sin,"[24] having allowed

20   Blessington (1979) 86–7.
21   Harding (1962) 69–72.
22   Verbart (1995) 2.
23   Burrow (1993) 251–2.
24   Fish (1967) 1–56.

himself or herself momentarily to be taken in by appearances and to forget what must be true, that the evils of Satan cannot really be associated with the virtues of Aeneas. Reading *Paradise Lost*, like living in the world, is a dynamic process in which perceptions must be corrected against the eternal verities. And for Milton the stakes were high: "The rewards for reading that text were not earthly jouissance but eternal joy; the punishment for inept reading was eternal perdition."[25] Richardson understood at least part of this when he tried to explain that Milton sent his Cherubim from the ivory gate, the portal of false dreams by which Aeneas left the underworld at the end of the first half of the *Aeneid*, because what he had just written "was to be consider'd only as a Pure Fiction, and Poetical Invention, . . . [and] did not Answer the End."[26] Indeed the entire Virgilian underpinnings as they had been presented so far "did not Answer the End." We must therefore look elsewhere for the rewritten Aeneas in *Paradise Lost*.

Milton, like Virgil, tells parts of his story out of chronological order, so that the account of the battle in Heaven which led to Satan's expulsion does not come until book 6. Here there is no question about it: Satan is associated with Turnus, not Aeneas. At the decisive *aristeia* between Michael and Satan, the "Uplifted imminent" (*PL* 6.317) of both warriors' swords comes from *Aen.* 12.728–9, "corpore toto / alte sublatum consurgit Turnus in ensem" ("Turnus . . . / rises up to his full height; with sword / uplifted"). In the next lines Satan's sword is broken by Michael's, which was taken from the armory of God (*PL* 6.320ff.), just as Turnus' sword was broken by Aeneas', which he had also received from a deity (*Aen.* 12.731ff.). A little later a collective reference to Satan's army, "so thick a Cloud / He comes" (*PL* 6.539–40), recalls the references to Turnus' troops as "nimbus peditum" ("like a cloud . . . of the infantry"; *Aen.* 7.793) and "nubem belli" ("the cloud of war"; *Aen.* 10.809).

Who, then, is the new Aeneas? In this context one might like to say "Jesus," whose army conquers Satan's and who, as Addison pointed out, could make sense as the hero of *Paradise Lost*.[27] In Milton's allusive system, however, this identification does not work. Satan's opponent in the *aristeia* in book 6 is Michael, not Jesus, and when Jesus on occasion is linked with a textual reference to the *Aeneid*, the association is generally not with Aeneas. In book 3, for example, Jesus offers himself in place of Adam to fulfill the terms of divine justice, using a repeated "mee . . . mee" that recalls the "me . . . me" of Nisus and Euryalus' mother (*PL* 3.236–8; *Aen.* 9.427, 493–4).

There is another option, however. At the beginning of book 5, Raphael descends from God to warn Adam to keep his sexual passion from deflecting him from his proper duty to those who will come after him. When Milton writes "Like

25 Wood (1991) 204.
26 Richardson (1734) 178–9.
27 Addison (1720) 547.

Maia's son [Mercury] he stood" (*PL* 5.285), he makes the link to the *Aeneid* explicit (cf. *Aen*. 4.238ff.), and Adam later addresses Raphael as "Divine Interpreter" (*PL* 7.72), which recalls the description of Mercury as "interpres diuum" in *Aen*. 4.378. If Raphael, not Satan, is the new Mercury, then Adam might be the new Aeneas for whom we are searching, with Eve being a new Dido.

And indeed, they are. As Verbart notes,[28] Adam and Eve consummate their union in language that recalls the union of Dido and Aeneas, such that "the Earth / Gave sign of gratulation" (*PL* 8.513–14; cf. *Aen*. 4.165–8). And for Adam, as for Aeneas, the relation between sex and duty is crucial. At *Aen*. 4.265–76 Mercury reminded Aeneas that he had put the lesser before the greater in indulging his passion at the expense of his duty. He therefore had to break off his union with Dido and leave Carthage so that he could found Italy, as the gods had commanded. Raphael likewise warns Adam that "attributing overmuch to things / Less excellent" (*PL* 8.565–6) is a mistake and that Eve is "worthy well / Thy cherishing, thy honoring, and thy love, / Not thy subjection" (*PL* 9.568–70). Again, lest the point be missed, Raphael repeats it on his way out: "take heed lest Passion sway / Thy Judgment to do aught, which else free Will / Would not admit" (*PL* 8.635–7). In other words, Adam must be careful not to make Aeneas' mistake and elevate his passion for Eve above his willing obedience to God.[29]

Milton's story continues to unfold in Virgilian terms. At *PL* 5.48ff., Eve's distress at not finding Adam when she wakes up recalls Dido's dreams of being abandoned (*Aen*. 4.465ff.). And when the Fall takes place, it does so in decidedly Virgilian terms. When Eve eats, the earth responds much as it had at Dido's marriage:

> Earth felt the wound, and Nature from her seat
> Sighing through all her Works gave signs of woe,
> That all was lost.
> > (*PL* 9.782–4)

> prima et Tellus et pronuba Iuno
> dant signum; fulsere ignes et conscius aether
> conubiis summoque ulularunt uertice Nymphae.
> > (Primal Earth
> and Juno, queen of marriages, together
> now give the signal; lightning fires flash,
> the upper air is witness to their mating,
> and from the highest hilltops shout the nymphs.)
> > (*Aen*. 4.166–8)

When Adam hears that Eve has eaten, his blood runs cold and his joints relax (*PL* 9.888–91), linking him to Aeneas in several places, in the storm that opened

---

28 Verbart (1995) 127–30.
29 Blessington (1979) 25–33.

the *Aeneid* (1.92), in front of Polydorus, the bleeding bush (*Aen.* 3.29–30), after a dream in which the gods told him his destiny lay not in Crete, but in Italy (*Aen.* 3.175), and (most importantly) in response to Mercury's warning (*Aen.* 4.279–80).[30] Eve is "now to Death devote" (*PL* 9.901), linking her yet again to Dido, who was "pesti deuota futurae" ("doomed to face catastrophe"; *Aen.* 1.712).[31] Adam in turn resolves to die with her, "not deceiv'd, / But fondly overcome with Female charm" (*PL* 9.998–9), which is compatible with the sentiment of *Aen.* 4.412, "improbe Amor, quid non mortalia pectora cogis!" ("Voracious Love, to what do you not drive / the hearts of men?"). He eats, and "Earth trembl'd from her entrails, as again / In pangs" (*PL* 9.1000–1), reechoing the passage in which the earth responded to the "sin" of Dido and Aeneas (*Aen.* 4.166–8). Now Death offers "a passage broad, / Smooth, easy, inoffensive down to Hell" (*PL* 10.304–5), another echo of "facilis descensus Auerno" ("easy – / the way that leads into Avernus"; *Aen.* 6.126).

Once again Satan attempts to clothe himself in the image of Aeneas, returning to his legion of devils in Hell within a cloud (*PL* 10.441ff.), from which he bursts out as Aeneas had in his entry to Carthage (*Aen.* 1.439ff.); now, however, he can no longer deceive and is immediately turned into a snake (*PL* 10.504ff.).[32] Adam remains the new Aeneas, "arming to overcome / By suffering" (*PL* 11.374–5) as Nautes had urged Aeneas to do in *Aen.* 5.710. Michael appears in order to remove the mists from Adam's eyes (*PL* 11.411ff.) as Venus did for Aeneas at the fall of Troy (*Aen.* 2.603–5). He gives Adam a vision of all that his descendants would accomplish, much as Anchises gave Aeneas a vision to encourage him: in fact, "Things by thir names I call, though yet unnam'd" (*PL* 12.140) echoes *Aen.* 6.776, "haec tum nomina erunt, nunc sunt sine nomine terrae" ("These will be names that now are nameless lands"; *Aen.* 6.776). The vision ends with Jesus, who will "bound his Reign / With earth's wide bounds, his glory with the Heav'ns" (*PL* 12.370–1), placing him in the same position as Augustus in Virgil's prophecy (*Aen.* 6.791ff.).

So encouraged, Adam and Eve trudge away from Paradise out into the world. And one last time, they do so in Virgilian terms, for over the receding gates stood the fiery arms and faces of the divine beings (*PL* 12.641–4; cf. 12.589–94), recalling the gods and goddesses that the departing Aeneas saw above the walls of Carthage (*Aen.* 5.1–7).[33] Unlike Aeneas, Adam has a companion, but both have fallen, and a lifetime of toil awaits them both.

30   Verbart (1995) 291–2. Verbart (1995) 292 notes that in the final lines of the poem (*Aen.* 12.951–2) Turnus' "limbs also slacken, which is part of Virgil's strategy to link him with Aeneas at this point in the story through shared imagery and verbal allusion."
31   Verbart (1995) 122–3.
32   Fallon (1984).
33   Verbart (1995) 72.

Milton has created a poem which must be read in the same way as sinners move through a fallen world: dynamically, and attentively, for appearances often deceive the unwary. The story of *Paradise Lost* is also the story of the *Aeneid*, and one of the attentive reader's jobs is to figure out how pagan poetry can support Christian truth. A good reading will escape the temptation to see Satan as the new Aeneas and settle on Adam, who, like Aeneas, allowed passion to invert his priorities temporarily but is sent on his way again to try to live in accordance with divine will.

It is now time to clarify R-A, Milton's reading of the *Aeneid*. For a reader of Virgil in 2006, there are two major lenses through which the *Aeneid* can be interpreted. The first stresses the obstacles that Aeneas overcame on his journey and the success he had in articulating the values that would come to be associated with imperial Rome. By the end of the poem he has overcome the forces of anger and rage, both within himself and as represented by the people who oppose him, so that Aeneas serves as the ideal hero of ancient Rome and the *Aeneid* celebrates the achievements of Augustus and his age. This approach is often referred to as "optimistic." Another approach, however, stresses that Aeneas himself was often inconsistent in attaining the values he was searching for, especially in the last scene of the poem, which is reinterpreted as a key failure in which Aeneas surrendered to the very voices of barbarism and fury within himself that he had struggled throughout the poem to suppress. This approach, which is sometimes called "pessimistic," sometimes the "Harvard school" reading, blurs the boundaries within the poem and listens sympathetically to Aeneas' opponents as well as to Aeneas.[34] It is worth noting that the distinction between the two approaches is not absolute – the "optimists" certainly recognize that success comes at a price in the *Aeneid*, while the "pessimists" in turn do not argue that the cost is so high that Rome should never have been founded – but for the sake of clarity and brevity, it is important to recognize a basic difference in what the two groups of readers choose to emphasize.

So how, then, did Milton read the *Aeneid*? Unfortunately Milton's copy of Virgil has not been located,[35] and unfortunately again, Milton's comments on the *Aeneid* in his other published works are casual and reveal very little about how he read the poem.[36] Almost from the beginning, however, the prevailing (although unexamined) assumption has been that Milton was an "optimistic" reader. In writing about *Paradise Lost* for the *Spectator*, Addison was adamant that "Aeneas is indeed a perfect Character."[37] Writing over two centuries later, Davis Harding said essentially the same thing,[38] and twenty years ago James Sims concurred: "As illustrated by the works of Camões and Milton, Renaissance writers saw Virgil

---

34   Kallendorf (1999a) 391–2.
35   Patterson (1938) 18.557–84; Verbart (1995) 99 n. 1; Martindale (2002) 108–9.
36   Riley (1929); Martindale (2002) 107–8.
37   Addison (1720) 538.
38   Harding (1962) 35.

as a greatly gifted propagandist for the Rome of his emperor and patron Augustus."[39]

This approach, however, does not explain much of what we have noticed so far. Fewer than 75 years after the initial publication of *Paradise Lost*, Bentley saw the problem quite clearly, as his comments on *PL* 9.13–9 show:

> . . . Sad task, yet argument
> Not less but more Heroic than the wrath
> Of stern *Achilles* on his Foe pursu'd
> Thrice Fugitive about *Troy* Wall; or rage
> Of *Turnus* for *Lavinia* disespous'd,
> Or *Neptune's* ire or *Juno's*, that so long
> Perplex'd the *Greek* and *Cytherea's* Son . . .

The inclusion of Turnus in this list is remarkable, given that the same Renaissance reading of the *Aeneid* that equated Aeneas with virtue also equated his opponent with vice; as Bentley put it, "Silly, as if the *Aeneid* was wrote for *Turnus's* Sake and Fame, and not for *Aeneas's* whose Name it bears."[40] Bentley had a simple solution for the problem caused by lines that complicated the straightforward "optimistic" reading of the *Aeneid* that he attributed to Milton: he excised them, using the circular argument that lines suggesting sympathy for Turnus could not have been written by Milton because they provide evidence for a reading of the *Aeneid* that was not Milton's. Modern readers who do not wish to go to this extreme are forced to argue that since Adam gave into temptation and Aeneas "had resisted temptation or at least had extricated himself from it before his irresponsibility had consequences fatal to his mission,"[41] "it is the contrast with the Virgilian epic that we are left with at the end" of *Paradise Lost*.[42] As Verbart puts it, Adam and Eve share a fate which is ultimately happy, resting in a happy matrimony that makes it difficult to condemn Adam's love for Eve; Aeneas, on the other hand, is left in miserable loneliness.[43]

As I attempted to recreate R-A (Milton's reading of the *Aeneid*), however, by moving from T^2 (*Paradise Lost*) to T^1 (the *Aeneid*) and back again, this is not what the allusions seemed to be stressing: Adam's love for Eve led to his fall, which parallels Aeneas' inappropriate affair with Dido. Both poems, in other words, stress the failure of their hero and the consequences of that failure. The critics in the paragraphs above, however, were forced into their position by a key piece of external evidence: at the time they were writing, it was generally assumed that the "pessimistic" reading of the *Aeneid* did not come into existence until after

39 Sims (1982) 335.
40 Bentley (1732) 266–7.
41 Porter (1993) 115.
42 Blessington (1979) 42.
43 Verbart (1995) 238–46.

World War II and that the only reading of the *Aeneid* that was available to Milton was the "optimistic" one, no matter how badly it seemed to fit the allusive system connecting the two poems. Richard Thomas, however, has shown that readers in antiquity were already struggling to make Virgil into the straightforward optimist that many of them thought he should be,[44] and this inability to fit all pre-modern readings of the *Aeneid* into the Procrustean bed of "optimistic" interpretation became more pronounced as the years passed. Joseph Sitterson, Jr. suggested over a decade ago that Ariosto's *Orlando furioso* is actually based in a "pessimistic" reading of the *Aeneid*,[45] and I have shown that this same reading can be found in a group of scholars and poets of the early Italian Renaissance as well as in *La Araucana*, a sixteenth-century Spanish epic that was also written in imitation of the *Aeneid*.[46]

The "pessimistic" reading of the *Aeneid*, in other words, was available to Milton and is, I believe, the one that structures his allusive system. Admittedly I find this position easy to adopt because I am writing at a time when this interpretation is widely accepted among Anglophone scholars, but, as the first axiom of my theoretical model suggests, I can only interpret from within my temporal and geographical situation. External evidence does not contradict my recreation of R-A, which was constructed through close textual analysis (my second axiom). Some of Milton's allusions provide little more than verbal texture, but in the end the totalizing relationship from which R-A was constituted produces a coherent allusive system embracing *Paradise Lost* and the "pessimistic" *Aeneid* (my third axiom). And as my fourth axiom suggests, meaning flows both ways. Rather than a contrast between the two poems, a dynamic allusive system in which a sinful Adam parallels a "sinful" Aeneas enriches our reading of both poems, allowing us to see both an Aeneas whose repeated efforts to do what is right take on the resonances of the Christian effort to follow God and an Adam who provides the pattern for all people to follow as he loses sight of his proper priorities, makes a mistake, accepts the consequences of that mistake, and heads off to try again.[47] The reading of *Paradise Lost* that is strengthened by its allusive ties to the *Aeneid* is therefore both more and less revolutionary than the one that has Milton simply rejecting the classical tradition,[48] in that it argues that *Paradise Lost* simultaneously rewrites the *Aeneid* by accepting its central argument, but also rewrites it by producing an "argument / Not less but more Heroic" (*PL* 9.13–4).

---

44 Thomas (2001).
45 Sitterson (1992).
46 Kallendorf (1999a); Kallendorf (2003).
47 The analysis of which way meaning flows here is enriched by the fact that, as Fish points out, *Paradise Lost* was composed after the *Aeneid*, but since Adam was the first man, the events that Virgil portrayed had to have happened after the events in Milton's poem, so that in this sense *Paradise Lost* is "earlier" ((1967) 37).
48 Steadman (1967) v.

As the essays in this volume suggest, reception studies have finally received a secure home within the field of classics. The analysis of Virgilian allusions in *Paradise Lost*, however, warns us that scholars must proceed with some caution in this area. Unless we think carefully about what we are doing, the temptation is to assume that a given classical text was read in the past very much as it is today – in other words, to conflate the reading of the critic (R-C) with the reading of the author (R-A). The growing body of scholarship in the classical tradition, however, warns us against doing this. To take but two examples, few people today would read the *Iliad* as a guide for fashioning gentlemanly conduct, as Edmund Spenser did, or a Senecan tragedy as a warning to the upper classes that they should behave virtuously, as William Shakespeare did. Yet these were valid readings in the past, and any study of the allusive relationships between Homer and Spenser or Seneca and Shakespeare should unfold from within the general framework of the second author's reading of the first. The model set forth in this essay provides a way for this to be done, so that the classicist's traditional preoccupation with allusion might lead to even more satisfying results in the future.

7

Hector and Andromache

Identification and Appropriation

Vanda Zajko

The distinctive contribution made by psychoanalysis to debates about the point of reception is its insistence on the psychic investment in literary tropes. For the psychoanalytic critic, the separation of the form of a literary text from the motivations, desires, and interpretations of its readers makes no sense, since it is the relation between language and the libidinal structures of the self that accounts for the effect of narrative. The complexity of the interaction between text and subject, the focus of reception theory, is articulated by psychoanalysis in terms which emphasize the mutuality of their influence and so, as a mode of criticism, it potentially mediates between what might be characterized as extreme formalist and reader-response perspectives. It is, of course, not the only critical discourse to occupy such a position. But it is unique in its development of a vocabulary specifically designed to conceptualize and describe these interactive processes, a vocabulary which is sometimes employed by literary critics without much precision or rigor.

Identification is an example of just such a term; relied on in a wide variety of contexts to help account for the mysterious way in which readers may sometimes experience themselves as being transformed by their intimacy with a literary text, it has entered into common parlance and is seldom interrogated or explained. In the words of Marshall W. Alcorn:

> Identification . . . is a complex and unwieldy concept. The term applies equally well to situations where we imagine ourselves as different from what we are, as we try to imagine ourselves as like another, and situations where we imagine others as different from what they are, because we want them to be like ourselves. In the former case, we try to change ourselves in order to be more like others. In the latter case, we try to change – or perceive others differently – in order to treat them like ourselves. Identification is crucial for all rhetorical functions, but the term *identification*

I would like to thank the editors of this volume and Miriam Leonard for their helpful comments on this piece.

oversimplifies the complexity of the psychological processes involved in responding to the discourse of others.[1]

This chapter aims to revitalize the concept of identification by probing its particular usage in psychoanalytic contexts. More specifically, it will ask how the relationship which develops between a reader and a character might contribute to an explanation for the persistent way in which certain texts, and not others, continue to give pleasure to very different readers across the ages. Of the many branches of psychoanalysis, it will focus for the most part on object-relations theory, which concentrates on the individual's very first bodily and psychic encounters and emphasizes the way in which infantile mental life is conducted as a continual relationship between the self and the world. Taking these early examples of interaction as a model for the dynamics of the reading process allows us to develop the argument that, when readers assimilate and are transformed by particular aspects of literary figures, they are tracing the pattern of early object relationships. Debates about the formation and transmission of canons more often than not prioritize cultural and institutional structures, but there is a place too for consideration of processes internal to the subject. If some literary texts can be shown to have had a more consistently potent effect on readers than others, a psychoanalytic understanding of character might help to explain why.

Psychoanalytic literary criticism has sometimes been attacked for its tendency to reduce or degrade literature by applying to it a body of preconceived insights and ideas. From another perspective, doubt has been cast on its efficacy as a project by the claim that psychoanalysis itself is nothing but literature. The debate over what Peter Brooks refers to as "the status of the 'and' linking psychoanalysis and literary text"[2] continues to be a live one. It can be argued, however, that, from its beginnings, psychoanalytic literary criticism has been a complex enterprise characterized by a joint interest in both form and content, and by an emphasis on the dynamics of reception. For example, in his first text to deal explicitly with literature, "Psychopathic Characters on the Stage," written between 1905 and 1906 (although it was published posthumously), Freud is insistent that the effect of literature cannot be explained in terms of content alone: rather it is produced by the interaction of the psyche of the reader or spectator with the psyche of the author and the characters in the text. In "Creative Writers and Day-Dreaming," written between 1907 and 1908, he makes it clear that form is important because the very *ars poetica* of the writer lies in his ability to present his material in such a way as to overcome the readers' feelings of repulsion, which is "undoubtedly connected with the barriers that rise between each single ego and the others."[3] A psychoanalytic aesthetic, then, has always combined a content which allows for

1   Alcorn (1994) 2.
2   Brooks (1994) 34.
3   Freud (1907–8) 140.

engagement with shared fantasies and fears with a skillful manipulation of form. From this expanded perspective, psychoanalytic texts function in ways that are at times analogous to literary texts, in that they are analysable in terms of the same psycho-dynamic processes, and at others, as a special category of intertexts that offer a particularly engaged viewpoint:

> Psychoanalysis is not an arbitrarily chosen intertext for literary analysis, but rather a particularly insistent and demanding intertext, in that mapping across the boundaries from one territory to the other both confirms and complicates our understanding of how mind reformulates the real, how it constructs the necessary fictions by which we dream, desire, interpret, indeed by which we constitute ourselves as human subjects. The detour through psychoanalysis forces the critic to respond to the erotics of form – that is, to an engagement with the psychic investments of rhetoric, the dramas of desire played out in tropes. Psychoanalysis matters to us as literary critics because it stands as a constant reminder that the attention to form, properly conceived, is not a sterile formalism, but rather one more attempt to draw the symbolic and fictional map of our place in existence.[4]

The choice to engage in psychoanalytic criticism is one which entails a commitment to a sense of the importance of the convergence of literature and life, to the enhancement of "an understanding of human subjects as situated at the intersection of several fictions created by and for them."[5] This commitment involves recognition both of the particularity of the fictions which make up the individual, and their significance to and interpretability within wider communities. The potential of psychoanalysis to traverse this broad territory makes another valuable contribution to reception theory. Stanley Fish, in the introduction to *Is There a Text in This Class?*, refers to a stage in his own intellectual development when he feared that "subjectivity was an ever present danger and that any critical procedure must include a mechanism for holding it in check."[6] He describes the process of ridding himself of this fear as a reformulation of the category of reader where "the reader is identified not as a free agent, making literature in any old way, but as a member of a community whose assumptions about literature determine the kind of attention he pays and thus the kind of literature 'he' 'makes.' "

This kind of reformulation emphasizes that the *activities* of the community define its identity. The arbitrariness of wayward subjective judgment is contrasted with the judgments made by the community, which promotes interpretations that serve its own interests and effectively polices its own disciplinary limits. In a more recent essay Fish offers a description which elaborates upon the depersonalization of his idealized group of readers:

4   Brooks (1994) 43–4.
5   Brooks (1994) 26.
6   Fish (1980) 9.

When I use words like "institution" or "community" I refer not to a collection of independent individuals who, in a moment of deliberation, *choose* to employ certain interpretive strategies, but rather to a set of practices that are defining of an enterprise and fill the consciousness of the enterprise's members. Those members include the authors and speakers as well as their interpreters.[7]

Again, this description emphasizes practices and strategies rather than individuals, and the role of interpersonal dynamics is downplayed. Nor is any attempt made to account for the mechanisms which might coerce or enable people to become, or to feel themselves, part of such "a community." The depersonalization extends to authors too, since readers are "at once constrained and enabled by the same history that burdens and energizes those whom they read."[8] It is as though the transaction at the heart of the reading process can be envisaged only if the personalities of those involved are removed from the picture, if there is no danger of the subjectivity which has been "held in check" breaking free and running amok amidst all sorts of unconstrained interpretations.

The rhetoric of depersonalization is relatively familiar in most areas of literary criticism, and the fear of subjectivity that Fish's account betrays is representative of a general sense that, for interpretations to be authoritative, they must not be overly tainted by what might be described as personal experience. And yet the impossibility of a purely "personal" reading is widely acknowledged too, given the common emphasis on the textuality of the self which is also readily conceded. The relation between the individual and the collective, which is central to a Fishian model of reception, is fundamental to every account of literature which seeks to establish the transformative power of texts, and it could be argued that any theory of how particular works gain influence must to some extent be conducted at the level of the personality, if that relation is to be explored satisfactorily. Once again we can argue that, although psychoanalysis is not the only discourse which is preoccupied with the discursive production of the self, it is unique in its vigorous explication of the means by which the individual comes to consciousness, and in its theorization of what remains inaccessible. If the processes involved in the acculturation of individuals are not entirely within their control (and here of course the operations of language are more often than not cited as determinant), there is more reason than ever to try belatedly, from within culture, to give some account of them.

The last couple of paragraphs have in effect sought to gloss the proposition made by Will Batstone in his position paper sent to contributors that "the point of reception is the ephemeral interface of the text; it occurs where the text and the reader meet and is simultaneously constitutive of both." Batstone declares that his specific interest is in how we might think of reception theory "within the same

---

7 Machor and Goldstein (2001) 36.
8 Machor and Goldstein (2001) 37.

postmodern discourses that have directed our attention away from the *mens auctoris* and the 'text itself,' " and it could be argued that one of the significant differences between his approach and my own is that he utilizes a psychoanalytic vocabulary that privileges Lacanian insight in response to the pressures of combining a notion of subjectivity with a postmodern discourse that is self-conscious about its own textuality and historicity. In terms of the reception of Freud, Lacan is undoubtedly a preeminent figure, but, as other essays in this volume demonstrate, dominant traditions of reception can sometimes function to obscure alternative traditions which have proved themselves persuasive within lesser-known periods and communities. Part of the project of this essay is to rehabilitate a strand of the reception of Freud which has latterly been little discussed within academic circles (although, interestingly, it has remained prevalent within the interpretative community constituted by practicing psychoanalysts), and so to render usable its concepts for a reception-based literary theory.

Let us start by considering a psychoanalytic concept of character. As outlined above, Freud began by stressing the interactive aspect of the reading process and highlighting its status as a complex psychological event. Whether dealing with the work of the most popular authors, in which there is usually one hero who is the unequivocal centre of interest, or of the writers most highly esteemed by the critics, whose stories involve a more varied cast, Freud makes explicit the connection that is forged between the ego of the reader and the imaginative figures he encounters.[9] He does not here use the term "identification," but it is clear that some such concept is key for him in the account he gives of why certain kinds of literature are more potent than others. The sense of identification as a psychological process "whereby the subject assimilates an aspect, property or attribute of the other and is transformed, wholly or partially, after the model the other provides"[10] is amplified and refined, not in works dealing with literary texts, but in those which hypothesize the mental state of the newborn infant and its journey towards maturation.[11] It is from this rich and suggestive material that the various psychoanalytic models of child development have evolved, together with a vocabulary that describes the processes whereby the human subject is constituted through its imitation, or rejection of, "objects" or "part-objects." Literary criticism employs terms such as "empathy" to encapsulate the force of the connection a reader may perceive between herself and a literary character, and "appropriation" to describe an interpretation of a text which is deemed to be more about the "reader" than "the text itself." Psychoanalytic lexis utilizes "introjection,"

9   Freud (1907–8) 137–8 and *passim*.
10 Laplanche and Pontalis (1973) 205.
11 It is not possible in this context to provide a thorough overview of the development of this concept in Freud, but two very important works are "On Narcissism: An Introduction" and "Group Psychology and the Analysis of the Ego." In the latter Freud attempts a typology of various kinds of identification.

"projection," and "projective identification" to conceptualize the ways that the boundaries between self and object are sometimes fleetingly confused to allow this kind of connection to be realized, and so the categories of "reader" and "the text itself" are submitted to concentrated scrutiny.

If we think about the relationship between literary text and reader in terms of object relations, we accept the adoption of concepts formulated to describe infantile mental processes for the elucidation of adult ones, and allow them their freedom from the context of a theory of development. They can then be regarded as largely unconscious mechanisms, involving shifts and fluctuations in the mental representations of the adult which may lead to alterations in a person's sense of self. We are, of course, dealing with metaphors, in this case the metaphors of boundary, incorporation, and exclusion, which can be valuable in helping us to articulate something of the reading process which we cannot directly observe. These particular metaphors are implicit too in the etymology of the more familiar literary-critical terms that were mentioned above. Even when the focus of interpretation is ostensibly not on character, a reading of a literary text invariably involves some consideration of its affective power, of how far a text may "draw in" a reader, or the extent to which a reader may "lose herself in" the text. If we think, in this context, of the description of identification offered above, we may want to argue, in the words of Marshall W. Alcorn, that "strong identification is what makes literature literary."[12]

If identification is a broad term encompassing several varieties of movement between the self and the object, projection and introjection are more sharply focused, and their resonance can best be grasped in relation to each other, as they are intimately connected within the psychic economy. Projection involves the attribution to the representation of the object of qualities derived from aspects of the self that are perceived as threatening or uncomfortable. Initially, it plays an important part in developing the infant's capacity to differentiate between internal and external worlds, but in later life it serves primarily a defensive function, allowing for the unwanted aspects of one's own self-representation to be assigned to the mental representation of another person. Introjection entails the reciprocal attribution to the self-representation of qualities that are perceived as desirable and are derived from aspects of the other person. Neither process implies a conscious manipulation of apparent reality, but rather such distortion as does occur is an interpretative distortion of the significance of that reality. What we are dealing with are mechanisms which operate internally to promote an individual's sense of self-esteem and encourage a sense of relatedness within a wide social context.

Projective identification is a term first introduced by Melanie Klein in her 1946 paper "Notes on Some Schizoid Mechanisms," and it has subsequently evolved to occupy a central position within many psychoanalytic fields. It can be viewed as a more complex form of projection, whereby the person into whom the unwanted

12   Alcorn (1994) 116.

feelings are being projected begins to experience the feelings involved. As such, and at best, it initiates the possibility for empathetic communication between two people and becomes a mode of communication which enables a person to be free, temporarily, of unmanageable feelings until such a time as they are returned to her, having been successfully "contained" by someone else.[13] Thomas Ogden has defined projective identification as "the way in which one person makes use of another person to experience and contain an aspect of himself,"[14] and it is this sense of the discovery of oneself in the representation of another that suggests the analogy with what happens when we read. Such an analogy depends on the recognition of the vitality of literary characters, on an acknowledgment of their capacity to sense and think and breathe. It also depends on concurrence with the view that, to cite Batstone citing Gadamer, "to understand what the work of art says to us is . . . a self-encounter," in the course of which our self may change.

It is important to keep in mind the idea that the "operations of the imaginary" described in the preceding paragraphs are not wholly conscious or within our control. Hélène Cixous, in an important essay, rejects any concept of character that collaborates with the interpretation of literary scenes undertaken "under the aegis of masterdom."[15] She argues that if it is regarded as a commercial transaction, the outcome of which is known in advance, the process of identification between a reader and a character becomes complacent and inert, and it helps to sustain an outmoded conception of literary creation:

> By definition, a "character," preconceived or created by an author, is to be *figured out*, understood, read: he is presented, offered up to interpretation, with the prospect of a traditional reading that seeks its satisfaction at the level of a potential identification with such and such a "personage," the reader entering into commerce with the book on condition that he be assured of getting paid back, that is, recompensed by another who is sufficiently similar to or different from him – such that the reader is upheld, by comparison or in combination with a personage, in the representation that he wishes to have of himself . . . The ideology underlying this fetishization of "character" is that of an "I" who is a *whole* subject (that of the "character" as well as that of the author), conscious, knowable; and the enunciatory "I" *expresses himself* in the text, just as the world is *represented* complementarily in the text in a form equivalent to pictorial representation, as a simulacrum.[16]

In contrast to this moribund operation, Cixous proposes that we work with character in a way that retains the idea of the "subject" as an effect of the unconscious. The centrality of some notion of character to the interpretability of

13   This idea of containment was a significant development of Klein's position and is particularly associated with Wilfred Bion. See Bion (1959) and (1962).
14   Ogden (1982) 6.
15   Cixous (1974) 384.
16   Cixous (1974) 385.

literature is reinforced throughout her essay, as she argues that a probing of its significance leads inevitably to consideration of the nature of fiction itself:

> To be more precise, it is with the removal of the question of "character" that the question of the *nature of fiction* comes to the fore, as well as the examination of subjectivity – through fiction, in fiction, and *as fiction*: where the term "fiction" should not be taken simply (in the sense of *borne in mind*) as part of a pair of opposites, which would make it the contrary of "reality." Here, rather, it would appear that subjectivity as reality is continuously worked over by fiction, because of several factors: the surplus reality produced by the indomitable desire in the text; that which, beginning with the subject, tears itself away, through desire, from what already exists (*le déjà-là*), from the *donnée*, to project itself out into what does not yet exist (*le non-encore-là*), into the unheard-of; and the *imaginary*, secreted by a subjectivity that has always been disturbed, changeable, literally populated with a mass of "Egos."

For Cixous, writing her essay in the 1970s, it was vital to remove the term "character" from the dominant literary-critical vocabulary in order to break free from some of its associations. To replace it with "subjectivity" was to allow the multiple textual selves of psychoanalysis and poststructuralism to shake up the orthodoxy of a "pure representationalism" and to opt for "the incessant agitation of literary practice rather than its theses and its stability."[17] The contemporary situation is somewhat different, and now an alternative strategy might best achieve the disquieting effect that Cixous strove for. These days, it is the decentered subject which has become the orthodoxy, and, as an orthodoxy, it can sometimes result in the kind of inert and self-satisfied criticism which merely responds to literature according to cultural demand. Cixous's most important suggestion is not that we should avoid certain words in perpetuity, but that we should practice a literary criticism which takes very seriously the capriciousness of the unconscious.

The sense of the unconscious as always operative, and yet never predictable, has to be central to any psychoanalytic concept of character. The accounts of the mental processes given above should not, therefore, be regarded as offering the solution to the problem of the representation of personality. In his response at the APA panel, Duncan Kennedy characterized reception as "an act that retrospectively captures elusive meaning." If we think about this formulation, we might argue that psychoanalytic theory is always already a theory of reception. In a manner similar to the way that the reception critic "retrospectively reifies text and subject, makes of them 'things,' endowing them with a nature, a telos and immanent meaning, existing in concealment, but 'discovered' in a revelatory moment in the act of reception to have been there all along," the psychoanalytic critic belatedly attempts to preserve and elucidate the mysterious dynamics of the internal world. And psychoanalysis, like reception theory, has the capacity to

17 Cixous (1974) 384, 383.

challenge the comfortable position of epistemological certainty that Kennedy referred to, since the idea of the unconscious vigorously ensures that "the real is not characterized by plenitude . . . but is felt most vividly by us in relation to *what we do not yet know*."

In conclusion let us think through these ideas in relation to a particular literary text, namely the incident of the leave-taking between Hector and Andromache in Homer *Iliad* 6.369–502, one of the most popular and influential literary scenes from antiquity over the centuries, within very different cultures. The couple meet, not in a domestic setting, but at the Scaean gates, and Andromache is accompanied by a servant holding the baby Astyanax. Hector is described as smiling in silent pleasure at the sight of his son but Andromache is crying. It is she who speaks first in an attempt to dissuade her husband from returning to the fighting, and then Hector replies in a slightly shorter speech, affirming his commitment to continuing to defend Troy. When he has finished speaking he picks up his son, who shrinks back into his nurse's arms frightened by the plumes on his father's helmet, and prays to Zeus concerning the child's future. The episode ends with Hector telling Andromache to return to her domestic work while he returns to the war, and she does so, reluctantly, mourning the loss of her husband even though he is still alive.

Many critics have discussed the shifting tenor of the couple's interaction as their contrasting attitudes emerge. Geoffrey Kirk, for example, comments that "the recurrent and deliberate conjunction of two styles normally kept distinct, even if not completely so, is certainly significant: the severe and heroic on the one hand, the intimate and compassionate on the other." He points out that "an analogous counterpoint operates between the rhetorical scale and style of the speeches and the naturalistic detail of certain elements within them; as also between the use of the traditional formular language of epic description and its adaptation from time to time to give startling moments of human insight."[18] For the purposes of this discussion, the shifts in rhetorical stance and style must be scrutinized as indicators of fluctuating psychic investment, both in terms of the dynamics evolving between the two protagonists, and of the identificatory positions made available to the reader.

Andromache begins by complaining to Hector that he does not have sufficient pity for their son, or for her, since he is not taking seriously enough the impact of his inevitable death on their future. She endeavors to arouse compassion in him, first by emphasizing the completeness of her reliance on him in the absence of a natal family, and then by reminding him at some length of what happens to a warrior's family when the warrior is overcome by his enemy. Her choice of illustration here is highly emotive, since she chooses to recount the death of her father and brothers at the hands of Hector's own chief rival, Achilles. She then delivers some famous lines which again underscore her dependency on him and

18   Kirk (1990) 219.

which contain a striking assertion that for her he fulfills the roles of all significant and intimate relationships:

> Hektor, thus you are father to me, and my honoured mother,
> You are my brother, and you it is who are my young husband.
> Please take pity upon me then, stay here on the rampart,
> That you may not leave your child an orphan, your wife a widow . . .[19]

Her speech ends, not on this emotional high-point, but with a suggestion of how he might best defend the city by regrouping the army in front of a weak section of its walls. Far from being an unmediated outpouring of spousal devotion, these lines are skillfully constructed and coolly delivered. Their composure has provoked disquiet amongst commentators who struggle to reconcile the Andromache who dares to advise her husband on matters of generalship with her earlier, more pitiful, self-representation. Aristarchus, for example, athetized the lines and Pope drew attention to their beautiful artifice, suggesting that Andromache does not here talk "like a soldier" but "like a woman, who naturally enough makes use of any incident that offers, to persuade her lover to what she desires."[20] The critics' drive to discount or diminish Andromache's words at this point can be argued to enact their own discomfort at the identificatory positions they are invited to inhabit. Psychoanalytic criticism here begins to break down the distinction between two different understandings of the processes of reception, between Hector and Andromache's reception of each other, and the scholarly receptions of the scene.

In his response, Hector declares that whilst he is mindful of Andromache's concerns, his own most pressing anxiety is the shame he will feel if he does not fight: even the fact that he knows Troy will fall does not affect his sense of obligation. In an echo of the words of Andromache quoted above, he imagines the slaying of his own father, mother, and brothers, and claims that the thought of their deaths does not distress him so much as the thought of his wife being taken off to Greece as someone else's slave. He pictures, in the future, a stranger who, on observing her in tears, will comment to himself as follows:

> "This is the wife of Hektor, who was ever the bravest fighter
> of the Trojans, breakers of horses, in the days when they fought about Ilion."[21]

He thus envisions that his own glory will bring glory to his wife in the future, even as he suggests that her lack of him in such circumstances will be another source of grief. As Nancy Felson and Laura Slatkin have recently commented: "In his sympathetic imagining of Andromache's grievous future, Hector gives

---

19 *Iliad* 6. 429–32, trans. Lattimore (1951).
20 See Pope's commentary on l. 550 of the passage.
21 *Iliad* 6. 460–1, trans. Lattimore (1951).

priority to marital devotion over even filial or warrior bonds. Yet that sympathy is conditioned by loss and grief, and the oddly contorted temporality of its expression – alternately prospective and retrospective – seems to elide any hope of its enjoyment in the present."[22] How, then, are we to evaluate this pair of speeches in terms of its success as an empathetic exchange?

Andromache is quite explicit, both at the beginning and end of her address, about the fact that Hector's lack of pity is something she is striving to remedy. The emphasis on her isolation, both in the present and as anticipated in the future, effectively establishes Hector as the only figure in her internal world whom she can make use of to experience herself. In the same way that Hector's speech moves forwards and backwards in time, she looks forwards to a bleak existence without him, but also refers to the past in her lengthy digression about her family's death. Her narration of this story is complex, and can be said to ape in miniature the dynamics of the larger scene: she tries to sway her audience of one by offering him the potential to identify with Achilles in the role of victorious warrior, since an understanding of the way such a warrior behaves will allow him to experience more fully the depth of horror at her fate; but there is also the potential for him to identify with her father and brothers, since it is Troy, his city, which will be captured, and his family, amongst them Andromache, who will be slaughtered or enslaved.

Hector, as "reader" of the tale, could have reacted by introjecting the feelings of fear and misery projected by his wife and begun to experience them potently himself. He would then have been able to demonstrate an understanding of her position and engage with her empathetically so that they could, however fleetingly, enjoy their relationship "in the present." In fact, this does not happen. Although he declares himself to be preoccupied with what will become of her, there is something peculiarly self-centered about the scene of the stranger he imagines, and there is very little sense that he has been even partially transformed by anything he has heard. As Pat Easterling notes, "we are not surprised to find that Hector, for all his pity and love, in fact rejects Andromache's advice and goes to fight on the plain as he intended."[23] The impression of his impermeability is sustained when, in the course of his prayer to Zeus, he requests that Astyanax will one day be recognized as a better fighter than his father and will "bring home the blooded spoils, and delight the heart of his mother."[24] In the context of what Andromache has said such a description of her probable delight must surely be a projection.

The sentence from Easterling quoted above is typical of the scholarship on the scene in that, even as it makes the point that Andromache has not been persuasive, it does seem to accept that Hector feels pity and love. In terms of its

22   Felson and Slatkin (2004) 100.
23   Easterling (1984) 2.
24   *Iliad* 6.481, trans. Lattimore (1951).

reception, the episode has become an exemplar of marital devotion and an interpretation which emphasizes the couple's lack of interaction may seem incredible
or wilfully perverse. It is interesting, then, that Sophocles, a close reader of Homer,
reworks the passage to produce a debate in the *Ajax* which is frequently cited
as an instance of non-communication between two people and that its difference
from Homer is what is usually invoked.[25] Just as Andromache's narrative about
her family opens up different identificatory positions for Hector, Homer's narrative too provides the opportunity for conflictual identifications, and it is in this
capacity that some of its greatness lies.

25 Sophocles, *Ajax* 430–524.

8

Passing on the Panpipes

Genre and Reception

Mathilde Skoie

In chapter 10 of Jacopo Sannazaro's pastoral romance *Arcadia* a priest takes a group of herdsmen on a guided tour of Pan's sacred grove. The most prominent item in this grove is Pan's pipe. According to the priest's intertextually loaded narrative, this pipe, created after the pursuit of Syrinx, belonged to Theocritus and Virgil in turn. It is now hanging from a branch as a challenge to potential pastoral poets. In the epilogue, however, it is the narrator himself who bids farewell to his pastoral pipe, hoping that another shepherd will take it up, as he himself is going on to write loftier verse and play on an even bigger pipe. In this way Sannazaro explicitly positions himself as a literary successor of Virgil and Theocritus within a specific generic framework. Furthermore, he signals that what the next pastoral poet should do is to pick up this pipe. Thus Sannazaro describes the writing of pastoral as a matter of piping on the pastoral instruments of your forerunners. New pastoral poetry is presented as the result of a meeting between the ancient and the modern poet. The new poet literally gives life to the old form by breathing into the old instrument. This description of the writing of pastoral might be figured as a model of the process of reception. In this chapter I shall take a closer look at the mechanisms involved in this pastoral relay, and at some of the implications of these mechanisms for our notion of what constitutes genre.

Pastoral Poetry: Eclectic Eclogues

Sannazaro's narrative is perhaps the most explicit *mise en scène* of the pastoral process at work. However, already Virgil's references to Theocritus in the *Eclogues* clearly place the poet in a literary succession. Likewise, the transfer of the pipe at *Eclogue* 5.85 from the older to the younger shepherd might indeed be read as part of the same relay.[1] Furthermore, stress on this kind of placement is a feature

---

1   To make the parallel even clearer, many read the voice of Menalcas in *Ecl.* 5.85 as that of Virgil; cf. Hubbard (1998) 68–9. Another pipe-transfer takes place in *Ecl.* 6.69.

followed also in pastoral criticism.[2] Pastoral poetics has often focused on the pastoral tradition due to the problem that pastoral is an ancient genre only in retrospect. As late as Quintilian, Virgil and Theocritus are placed alongside writers of epic and didactic poetry (*Institutio Oratoria* 10.1.55–7).[3] Furthermore, although pastoral in the vague sense seems a familiar and recognizable subject, it has proved hard to pin down a specific definition of the genre – in particular since it has expanded into so many other genres, such as pastoral drama and pastoral romance. It has therefore often been easier to turn to the history of reception than to any essentializing definition.[4]

According to established tradition, pastoral originated with Theocritus when posterity gave name and preference to those portions of his poetry where herds-men figured prominently – whether done deliberately by an editor, through poetic imitation of specific parts, or a combination of the two.[5] What we are dealing with then is a process of concentration and selection. This is precisely what we see at work in Virgil's foregrounding of the parts of Theocritus which deal with herdsmen in his *Eclogues*.[6] Several scholars have therefore argued for a definition of pastoral as some kind of selective reception.[7] However, this definition might not be quite adequate: Virgil does not simply reduce Theocritus, he also adds other elements to his pastoral concoction, for example, he adds a Callimachean tenor in his rejection of epic (*Ecl.* 6), he includes allusions to (or bits of) the con-temporary elegiac poet Gallus (*Ecl.* 10), he adds references to Lucretius (*Ecl.* 6), and he introduces a contemporary political scene (*Ecls.* 1 and 9). Hence Virgil's selection involves not only the exclusion of the "un-pastoral" parts of Theocritus, but also the inclusion of other forms of poetry and other kinds of subject mat-ter. Likewise, the reception of Virgil's *Eclogues* shows how poets have both selected from the Virgilian model and from completely different traditions. The most obvious example is perhaps the merging of a Virgilian subject with Christian

2 Most recently Hubbard (1998).
3 Although Ovid, *Met.* 1.674ff. might indicate a perception of pastoral as some kind of "closed and self-sufficient discourse," see Martindale (1997c) 108 and Conte (1994) 116.
4 Patterson (1987) simply gives up a definition and rather focuses on the reception of Virgil, while in one of the most recent attempts at a definition, Alpers (1997), who comes up with a definition revolving around the representative shepherd, spends most of his book looking at the historical variations of this representative anecdote and their relations to each other.
5 See Gow (1950) lix–lxii, Hunter (1999) 26–8, and Clausen (1994) xx.
6 Virgil does also refer to the "non-pastoral" poems, e.g. Id. 11 in *Ecl.* 2, and Id. 2 in *Ecl.* 8. In both these cases the Theocritean material is distinctively "pastoralized," i.e. they are placed within a distinctively pastoral framework. Their pastoral quality is signaled already in the first lines of the poems; cf. *pastor* in *Ecl.* 2.1, and the pastoral muse in *Ecl.* 8.1.
7 Fuhrmann (unpublished MS quoted in Iser 1993a), 16 and Martindale (1997c) 108.

elements in later religious eclogues.[8] Thus nowhere is this selection limited to selecting from a specific sphere.

To emphasize that the selection is drawn from a variety of spheres we therefore need to adjust slightly the definition of pastoral as a process of selective reception. It seems germane here to play on the fact that Virgil's pastoral poetry usually goes under the name "eclogues," traditionally interpreted as selections. However, to indicate that the selection may be drawn from several spheres, I would like to appeal to a more specific meaning of the term "eclogue," that is, as implied in the term "eclectic" which by definition precisely emphasizes that the selection is drawn from a variety of sources. This meaning of the term highlights more clearly the inclusive power of pastoral poetry and the creative importance of the new contexts. Thus, rather than a process of selective reception, I would argue that we are dealing with a process of eclectic reception.

Towards a Generic Understanding of Pastoral

The definition of pastoral poetry as a genre belongs primarily to neoclassical criticism.[9] Yet, an important step on the way is Julius Caesar Scaliger's *Poetices libri septem* (1561). He was one of the first in the modern period to make a theory of genre a major organizing principle of his poetics. Even though genre is a main premise, he starts with a literary history of each genre in chronological order (book 1). In this section he only offers a brief description of the genre focusing on the *pastor otiosus* (6B).[10] According to Scaliger this *otium* produces two kinds of song: the monologic love-song and the amoebean song-competition. Then he moves on to the generic terminology. He explains the term "idyll" from the mimetic nature of the genre and "eclogue" as an indication of selection made by later cognoscenti. Scaliger himself is selective in the way he only treats works in Latin. His work was generally thought of as a manual for neo-Latin poets.[11] Vernacular pastoral romance and pastoral drama are therefore outside his scope (hence Sannazaro's Latin piscatorial eclogues are mentioned, but not his *Arcadia*). Yet, he also emphasizes an eclectic element to pastoral when it comes to subject matter: "Pastoralia . . . cuiuscumque generis negotium semper retrahant ad agrorum naturam" (Pastoral works continually reduce material of every kind to a rural

---

8   A very popular thing in the Middle Ages; see Cooper (1977).

9   Most prominently perhaps: René Rapin, *Dissertatio de Carmine Pastorali* (1659), Bernard le Bouyer de Fontenelle, *Discours sur la nature de l'églogue* (1688), Alexander Pope, *A Discourse on Pastoral Poetry* (1717). For an overview see Halperin (1983) 33, and Loughrey (1984). Of course we have scattered comments on the genre in commentaries and other poetics; see e.g. Cooper (1977) and Hulubei (1938) 1–20, but I am here thinking of more systematic generic studies.

10 All references to the text are to the facsimile edn. by Buck (1964).

11 See Buck (1964) xii.

character, 150A).[12] The subject matter is manifold (*materia multiplex*, 7A, and *varia*, 150A) and also drawn from non-pastoral realms such as the town.[13]

The most influential neoclassical poetical treatise, Nicolas Boileau-Despreaux's *Art Poétique* (1674), also takes this generic approach, and like Scaliger Boileau begins the generic section with pastoral. This treatise, which is a standard item on any bibliography dealing with early modern poetics, is however rarely listed by those who deal with the history of *pastoral* poetics.[14] Yet, its influence regarding the bad reputation of baroque pastoral poetry and the fact that for a long time it was the sole general poetics on the curriculum should not be underestimated.[15] As this poetics does not limit its scope to neo-Latin poetry, it also had to deal with a baroque or postclassical pastoral "wilderness" which could be witnessed not only in poetry, but also in parts of works or whole works in other genres (novels and drama).

The sixteenth and the first third of the seventeenth century witnessed an enormous flourishing of pastoral literature.[16] Scholars who have worked on pastoral in this particular period label the fascination in terms of a "formidable craze" and "being on the borderline to madness."[17] The pastoral fashion penetrated the French *bourgeoisie* to such an extent that Charles Sorel can write a parody of the genre (*Le Berger Extravagant*, 1623), and Molière let one of his characters raise the question "Pourquoi toujours des bergers?" (Why always shepherds?).[18] The seventeenth century responded to this question by offering the first treatises solely on the subject. Most notably France in the mid seventeenth century offered several

---

12   Martindale (1997c) 108 reads this passage as an indication of "selection and concentration," putting the emphasis on *retrahant*. I would also emphasize the varied sources pastoral takes in (*cuiuscumque generis negotium*), further emphasized in 150A (see n. 13 below).

13   "Iccirco praeter nemora et agros, siquid ex urbe oblatum canant," 150A.

14   It is noteworthy that none of those who otherwise offer quite full historical overviews of pastoral poetics mention him, e.g. Loughrey (1984), Halperin (1983), and Rosenmeyer (1969).

15   Macé (2002) 10: "Il est vrai que la production poétique de l'âge baroque a longtemps souffert d'un certain discrédit, dû en grande partie aux traditions scolaires françaises, souvent tributaires des jugements peu amènes de Boileau." Cf. the relative scarcity of scholarship on French baroque pastoral poetry in the bibliography of Macé (2002).

16   The most famous works: Sannazaro, *Arcadia* (1504); Montemayor, *Diana* (1559); Spenser, *Shepheardes Calendar* (1579); Sidney, *Arcadia* (1590); Guarino, *Il Pastor Fido* (1590); Honoré d'Urfé, *Bergeries* (1593); Shakespeare, *As You Like It* (1599/1600); Milton, *Lycidas* (1637); Poussin, *Et in Arcadia Ego* (1637–9) (painting). For the French poetic scene, see the frequency of pastoral poetry in collections of baroque poetry, e.g. Blanchard (1969).

17   Van Elslande (1999), dustjacket and 1.

18   Monsieur Jourdain in *Le bourgeois Gentilhomme* (1670), act I, scene ii.

significant contributions to the development of pastoral criticism.[19] Pastoral also played an important part in the quarrel between the ancients and moderns.[20] Yet, by the mid seventeenth century the heyday of pastoral in France was clearly over. Pastoral poetry simply did not come as spontaneously as before. One response to this was to quit writing pastoral poetry (a route followed by many). Another was to turn pastoral into a philosophical genre as Bernard le Bovier de Fontenelle did in his *Eglogues* and argued for in his essays.[21] Yet another was to turn towards "real rustic life" as Rousseau later did. An obvious solution regardless of position is of course eclectic reception in the sense laid out above. And although the selections could vary, Virgil was a standard ingredient. As one scholar remarks in the case of the French neoclassical situation, "à travers ses picoteries on en revient toujours à Virgile."[22] The question, however, is which Virgil the different poets and scholars turn to.[23]

Returning to Virgil: The Ideal Shepherdess

The description of the pastoral poem takes up the first 37 lines of Boileau's treatment of the smaller genres in chanson 2. This song is viewed by critics as the least interesting of the songs in the *Art Poétique*.[24] The general perception of Boileau's standard of excellence is that he thinks the really good writer is the one who writes in accordance with ancient rules. Yet this view needs to be somewhat nuanced. In fact Boileau himself warns against excess in this respect himself (4.78–80). Furthermore, the rules set up are far from straightforwardly ancient ones.[25] I shall in the following argue that his pastoral rules are based on a reading of the

19 Most notable are the critical works by Guillaume Colletet (1657), Gilles Boileau (1657), René Rapin (1659), and Fontenelle (1688).

20 Niderst (1991) even designates a separate category of the *querelle* which he names *la querelle de la pastorale*. In particular, the debate between René Rapin (on the side of the ancients) and Fontenelle (on the side of the moderns) took place in relation to pastoral.

21 *Poésies Pastorales* (1688), *Discours sur la nature de l'églogue* (1688), *Digression sur les Anciens et les Modernes* (1688).

22 Niderst (1991) 107.

23 As noticed by Cooper in the case of medieval pastoral: "there is no single medieval eclogue tradition . . . The one line of contact common to them all was the *Bucolics*, but even they were interpreted in different ways and provided no single pattern of authority" (Cooper (1977) 8).

24 See e.g. Pocock (1980) 96.

25 This is perhaps not so surprising given the lack of ancient theory about the genre. This was, however, perceived as a particular problem in relation to neoclassical doctrine. As Rapin put it in his dissertation on pastoral (1659): "This must needs be a hard Task, since I have no guide, neither Aristotle nor Horace, to direct me" (Rapin (1947) 16).

ancient pastoral texts which clearly positions itself in relation to, and is inspired by, contemporary poetics and poets.

Since the *Art Poétique* is a verse treatise in the style of Horace's *Ars Poetica* the critic follows his model and puts his own readings into play by describing a pastoral poem through writing one (vv. 1–10):

> Telle qu'une bergère, au plus beau jour de fête,
> De superbes rubis ne charge point sa tête,
> Et, sans mêler à l'or l'éclat des diamants,
> Cueille en un champ voisin ses plus beaux ornements
> Telle, aimable en son air, mais humble dans son style,   5
> Doit éclater sans pompe une élégante Idylle.
> Son tour, simple et naïf, n'a rien de fastueux
> Et n'aime point l'orgueil d'un vers présomptueux.
> Il faut que sa douceur flatte, chatouille, éveille,
> Et jamais de grands mots n'épouvante l'oreille.   10

> (As a fair Nymph, when Rising from her bed,
> With sparkling Diamonds dresses not her head;
> But, without Gold, or Pearl, or costly Scents,
> Gathers from neighb'ring Fields her Ornaments:
> Such, lovely in its dress, but plain withal,
> Ought to appear a Perfect *Pastoral*:
> Its humble method nothing has of fierce,
> But hates the ratling of a lofty Verse:
> There, Native beauty pleases, and excites,
> And never with harsh Sounds the Ear affrights.)[26]

The chanson opens with a simile likening pastoral to the ideal shepherdess; lovely but plain (vv. 1–10). [27] Through a description of her appearance (adorned with

---

26 All English translations are by Sir William Soame, revised by John Dryden, first published in 1683 (text used: University of Virginia Electronic Text Center). Notice that the translation is not a particularly close one, e.g. *bergère* (v. 1) is translated with "nymph" rather than "shepherdess," *Grâces* (v. 27) translated with "Gods" rather than "Graces," etc.

27 The attentive reader would perhaps object to this being a description of pastoral, as the technical terms in the passage are *idylle* (v. 6) and *églogue* (v. 35). However, this only reflects the terminological fluidity at the time. According to contemporary dictionaries and commentaries, there was a complete anarchy regarding pastoral terminology, and there was no substantial difference between the competing terms *pastoural, poesie pastorale/champêtre, idylle/idyllie,* and *églogue.* Thus the Soame/Dryden translation (v. 6) of *idylle* as "pastoral" is perfectly appropriate (indeed modern editions of Boileau's text often give this passage the heading "Poésie pastorale"). For commentaries on this, see e.g. Delaporte (1970) 5–6, Gidel (1872) 2.309, and cf. *pastoural* and *idyllie* in e.g. Huguet, *Dictionnaire de la langue Française du seizième siècle* (Paris 1973).

flowers rather than jewels) and gait (*simple et naïf*) Boileau fleshes out the characteristics of pastoral. Already here we see the merging of a classical usage and a contemporary horizon. The likening of a genre to a woman reminds the classically trained reader of Ovid's fleshing out of elegy and tragedy in *Amores* 3.1 and 9.[28] At the same time Boileau draws upon contemporary texts: commentators list several contemporary influences, most prominently Charles Cotin's poetics from 1666, which has a description of a pastoral gone wrong, using the image of an overdressed countrywoman,[29] while the pastoral poet Jean Régnauld de Segrais (one of the few pastoral poets Boileau approved of) used a similar construction in a description of a shepherdess in a pastoral poem.[30]

The balance between the lofty and the lowly is further illustrated by examples of excess in either direction (vv. 11–19):

> Mais souvent dans ce style un rimeur aux abois
> Jette là, de dépit, la flûte et le hautbois;
> Et, follement pompeux, dans sa verve indiscrète,
> Au milieu d'une églogue entonne la trompette.
> De peur de l'écouter, Pan fuit dans les roseaux;   15
> Et les Nymphes, d'effroi, se cachent sous les eaux.
> Au contraire cet autre, abject en son langage,
> Fait parler ses bergers comme on parle au village.
> Ses vers plats et grossiers, dépouillés d'agrément,
> Toujours baisent la terre et rampent tristement: 20
> On dirait que RONSARD, sur ses pipeaux rustiques,
> Vient encor fredonner ses idylles gothiques,
> Et changer, sans respect de l'oreille et du son,
> Lycidas en Pierrot, et Philis en Toinon.

> (But in this stile a Poet often spent,
> In rage throws by his Rural Instrument,
> And vainly, when disorder'd thoughts abound,
> Amid'st the Eclogue makes the Trumpet Sound:
> *Pan* flyes, Alarm'd, into the neighb'ring Woods,
> And frighted Nymphs dive down into the Floods.
> Oppos'd to this another, low in stile,
> Makes Shepherds speak a Language base and vile:
> His Writings, flat and heavy, without Sound,
> Kissing the Earth, and creeping on the ground;

28   In the description of elegy immediately following (vv. 38–44) this genre is simply
     described as a woman with loose hair just like Ovid's *elegeia* (without the signaling
     telle que). On the reference to Ovid in the case of elegy, see Boudhors (1939) 274.
29   Picot (1963) 58 and Boudhors (1939) 273.
30   "Telle que se fait voir de fleurs couvrant sa tête, / Une blonde jeunesse au beau jour
     d'une fête"; see Gidel (1872) 2.310 and Delaporte (1970) 1.

You'd swear that *Randal*, in his Rustick Strains,
Again was quav'ring to the Country Swains,
And changing, without care of Sound or Dress,
Strephon and *Phyllis*, into *Tom* and *Bess*.)

These examples of excess are more or less disguised references to postclassical poets. For sounding too "high" (vv. 11–16) the two contemporary French poets Gilles Ménage and François Charpentier are identified as prime targets in the secondary literature. As for being too "base," Boileau even names his prime villain, Ronsard, who did not even bother to use the classical names. As in Sannazaro's tale, musical instruments have an important role to play, but here mostly as representative of the different levels of style.[31] Also the English translation refers to a contemporary poet here.[32] Boileau makes clear how unsuitable the first excess is through describing the discomfort of the pastoral landscape itself; Pan hides in the bushes and the Nymphs throw themselves into the water (vv. 15–16). We are back in the realm of the shepherdess on her way to the fête. In case of the second excess, that of being too low, Boileau considers this such a self-evident fault that no further comment is necessary.

To navigate between this Scylla and Charybdis of pastoral poetry is hard, but the prospective poet should take the ancients as guides (vv. 25–8):

Entre ces deux excès la route est difficile.   25
Suivez, pour la trouver, THÉOCRITE et VIRGILE
Que leurs tendres écrits, par les Grâces dictés,
Ne quittent point vos mains, jour et nuit feuilletés.

(Twixt these extreams 'tis hard to keep the right;
For Guides take *Virgil*, and read *Theocrite*:
Be their just Writings, by the Gods inspir'd;
Your constant Pattern, practis'd and admir'd.)

Virgil and Theocritus are here put on a similar level as guides, but the description of their poetry ("tendres écrits, par les Grâces dictés") is clearly biased towards Virgil, as this phrasing seems to correspond neatly with Horace's judgment of the *Eclogues* in Satire 1.10.44–5: "molle atque facetum / Vergilio adnuerunt gaudentes rure Camenae" (to Virgil the Muses rejoicing in rural life have granted delicacy and elegance). *Tendre* could be said to take care of the aspect of *mollis*

---

31 There is of course an important stylistic element in the choice of instrument (and the size of it) in Sannazaro as well. There is a contrast between the pastoral *sampogna* (bagpipe) and the epic *tromba* (trumpet) in ch. 10.

32 Soame/Dryden substitutes Ronsard with Randal, generally supposed to be Thomas Randolph (1605–35) – although the description does not quite fit Randolph's pastoral poetry; see Kinsley (1958) 4.1942 or Swedenberg (1972) 2.372.

and the *Grâces* seem very close to the *Camenae*. A Horatian link is further supported by the next verse where Boileau clearly imitates Horace's *Ars Poetica* (268–9): "vos exemplaria Graeca / nocturna versate manu, versate diurna" (Turn with your hand, turn the pages of Greek books night and day).[33] Finally, Boileau offers some examples of this route (vv. 29–37):

> Seuls, dans leurs doctes vers, ils pourront vous apprendre
> Par quel art, sans bassesse un auteur peut descendre; 30
> Chanter Flore, les champs, Pomone, les vergers;
> Au combat de la flûte animer deux bergers;
> Des plaisirs de l'amour vanter la douce amorce;
> Changer Narcisse en fleur, couvrir Daphné d'écorce;
> Et par quel art encor l'églogue, quelquefois, 35
> Rend dignes d'un consul la campagne et les bois.
> Telle est de ce poème et la force et la grâce.

> (By them alone you'l easily comprehend
> How Poets, without shame, may condescend
> To sing of Gardens, Fields, of Flow'rs, and Fruit,
> To stir up Shepherds, and to tune the Flute,
> Of Love's rewards to tell the happy hour,
> *Daphne* a Tree, *Narcissus* made a Flower,
> And by what means the Eclogue yet has pow'r
> To make the Woods worthy a Conqueror:
> This of their Writings is the grace and flight;
> Their risings lofty, yet not out of Sight.)[34]

In this passage the reader would expect examples from the pastoral poetry of Virgil and Theocritus ("Seuls, dans *leurs* doctes vers, ils pourront vous apprendre"). The way the effect of following the two poets is described as a possibility of rendering woods worthy of a consul in v. 36 is lifted from *Ecl.* 4.3 ("silvae sint consule dignae"), which in itself is such an elevation of the genre. Theocritus, however, seems completely eradicated and all the specific examples in vv. 31–4 are drawn from a third poet, namely Ovid. The stories of Flora, Pomona, Narcissus, and Daphne alluded to here are nowhere described in the pastoral poetry of Theocritus or Virgil, rather they are lifted from Ovid's elegiac calendar and epic,

---

33 Soame/Dryden's use of "just" here does not seem to hit the right nuance in its sole emphasis on the normative aspect. It also misses the Horatian flavor.

34 The final line in the Soame/Dryden version should rather be the first verse of the description of elegy: "D'un ton un peu plus haut, mais pourtant sans audace / La plaintive Elegie, en longs habits de deuil, / Sait, les cheveux épars, gémir sur un cercueil" (vv. 38–40).

the *Fasti* and *Metamorphoses*.[35] The description of the amoebean form (v. 32) could of course be a reference to either Virgil or Theocritus, but it is so general that it might as well be attributed to any of their successors. Thus it is by following examples from Ovid that pastoral poetry can have both grace and power.[36]

Boileau's elegant pastoral verse reveals precepts for pastoral poetry mainly through description. We get some explicit clues in the description of his allegorical shepherdess in the first third of the episode (vv. 1–10), but the main part (vv. 11–37) is made up of judgments of the pastoral practice of specific poets. By far the strongest imperative is accordingly a reference to the two models, Theocritus and Virgil (v. 26). This strategy of combining the normative and the empirical in the pastoral wilderness of the seventeenth century is, however, possible only through a tough process of selection. Most notably, Boileau leaves out the very popular Spanish and Italian traditions. This could partly be explained through the transgression of strict genres in the most popular of these works, for example, the pastoral romances of Montemayor and Sannazaro. However, one of Boileau's predecessors, Vauquelin de la Fresnaye, explicitly mentions Sannazaro in the line of succession from Apollo (*sic*), Theocritus, and Virgil.[37] Furthermore, Boileau in reality excludes Theocritus, or at least appeals to him only as mediated through Virgil. And the modern poets Ménage and Ronsard who both wrote "pure" pastoral verse are excluded on grounds of their inappropriate stylistic levels.

On the other hand, we have noticed that Boileau also includes "non-pastoral" poetry, the poetry of Ovid. And the opening lines alluding to the contemporary poet Segrais clearly supplement the ancient models. Furthermore, the references to the *Metamorphoses* might also be specifically colored by the modern horizon: most instances involve nymphs in beautiful surroundings, while there is little actual herding or amoebic song. This might be one way to bow tacitly to the romance tradition where the nymphs play a much more prominent part than in Virgil and Theocritus.[38] Thus we see that Boileau's neoclassical poetics is far from a simple return to the ancient rules. Rather we observe the same tendency as described in the case of the poets, that is, an identification and description of the pastoral genre as an appropriation of texts from both within and outside the pastoral realm depending on a contemporary perspective, in other words an eclectic process of reception.

---

35   Flora, *Fasti* 5.195ff.; Pomona, *Met.* 14.623–73; Narcissus, *Met.* 3.402–510; Daphne, *Met.* 1.452–567.

36   This is rather neat as Ovid, though not writing strictly in the pastoral genre, is an important factor in the pastoralizing of the Theocritean and Virgilian traditions, see n. 3 above.

37   Fresnaye, *Art Poétique* (1605).

38   The reference to Pomona might furthermore be a specific allusion to the contemporary debates as she was at the heart of a literary *querelle* about paganism in literature; cf. Delaporte (1970) 25.

Genre as a Process of Reception

In his article on pastoral and fictionality one of the founders of German reception theory, Wolfgang Iser, describes pastoral poetry in terms of a process of reception: "pastoral poetry unfolds itself as a process of reception which gains its own history from its continual reworking of the pastoral world."[39] However, at the same time as he makes this claim, he seems to give up the concept of pastoral as a generically definable entity: "In this respect one cannot talk about pastoral literature as a generically defined entity – after all, the pastoral transcends generic boundaries – but is, rather, a process of reception."[40] However, does the concept of genre have to go once it is recognized as a process of reception? Rather, given the thematization of the pastoral relay within pastoral poetry itself and the place played by eclectic reception in even the presumably most normative and generically oriented poetics of them all, Boileau's *Art Poétique*, the completely opposite claim might be made: that reception is crucial to the definition of the pastoral genre. There might therefore be a case for promoting a more "hard core receptionist" working hypothesis of genre than Iser does. And this is indeed what another founding figure within reception theory Hans Robert Jauss suggests when he regards genre as a succession of texts within a continuous process of horizon-setting and horizon-changing: "The new text evokes for the reader (listener) the horizon of expectations and rules familiar from earlier texts, which are then varied, corrected, changed or just reproduced."[41] Thus Jauss incorporates the transcendence of boundaries which Iser finds problematic by including a "legitimate transitoriness" in his concept of literary genres.[42]

Much depends on the object through which a theory is exemplified, and such a self-conscious genre as pastoral with its lack of ancient theory might be regarded as a particularly easy case for showing that genre is a process of reception. Jauss has, however, shown the value of a similar receptionist approach in the case of the medieval epic, romance, and novella.[43] Although there has often been a perceived conflict between an empirical and a theoretical approach to genre,[44] my reading of Boileau might show that in some cases this is a discursive rather than an ontological conflict. Even Boileau's apparently essentializing and normative poetics might, as we have seen, be regarded as offering a definition based on a process of reception. One way to mediate between empirical and theoretical approaches to genre might therefore be to look at genre as a process. Furthermore,

---

39   Iser (1993a) 25.
40   Iser (1993a) 27.
41   Jauss (1970) 13.
42   Jauss (1999) 79.
43   Jauss (1999).
44   See e.g. Conte (1994).

regarding this process as eclectic rather than simply selective makes it possible to take added impulses from new contexts into account. Such a model of genre might potentially be able to grasp both the stable and the varied, as well as the different contexts governing them, or to return to the pastoral world, to study the interaction between the piper and the pipe. For, after all, who can tell the dancer from the dance?

9

True Histories

Lucian, Bakhtin, and the Pragmatics of Reception

Tim Whitmarsh

History is dead – long live history.

Martindale[1]

This chapter focuses upon the relationship between reception and historicism.[2] It is a widespread, but misguided, assumption that reception is fundamentally anti-historicist. So far from espousing a kind of postmodern free play with textual connections, as their detractors sometimes assume, reception theorists often promote a distinctive and coherent philosophy of historical change. In particular, reception theory insists on the historical contingency of the interpreter's position: no longer the agent of timeless, disinterested positivism, the scholar is now disclosed as a cultural and historical *subject*. The practice of reception history throws this into the sharpest relief: an increased awareness of the range of different ideological positions on an aspect of ancient culture not only thickens our understanding (temporally and geographically) of other societies,[3] but also highlights,

I am most grateful to the interlocutors in Bristol for the opportunity to discuss the theoretical aspects of this chapter, particularly to Miriam Leonard and the editors of this volume. The Lucianic material was worked over in an Anglo-French colloquium on imperial elites in Cambridge: again, my thanks to participants for their improving comments.

1 Martindale (1993) 23.
2 The issue has crystallized, in recent years, particularly around the discussion of Virgil. For varying positions on the reception side, see esp. Martindale (1993) 35–54, (1997b); Fowler (2000); Thomas (2000), (2001); Laird (2003); for historicist counter-responses, see esp. Galinsky (1993–4); also West (1995).
3 On postcolonialist reception, see Hardwick (2000a), (2003a); Budelmann (2004); Goff (2005); forthcoming work by Phiroze Vasunia will further develop this fascinating field.

through the play of similarity and difference, the more or less hidden ideologies of modern Western scholarship.[4]

Reception is thus a historicist operation insofar as it exposes the secret history of ideological complicities. There remains, however, a nagging ambiguity around the value of historicism to reception. On the one hand, traditional historical epistemologies are routinely rejected: there is no "truth" about the past, only a potentially infinite proliferation of narratives. On the other hand, in order to validate the very project, the narrative of reception history is often presented as real, solid, and necessary, even by the most otherwise epistemologically skeptical of critics. Put simply, there is a strange double standard: the project of classical history is fundamentally misguided, that of postclassical history urgent and necessary.

Charles Martindale's *Redeeming the Text* presents the epistemologically skeptical position in its most radical form: "our interpretations of texts, whether or not we are aware of it, are, in complex ways, constructed by the chain of receptions through which their continued readability has been effected . . . we cannot get back to any originary meaning wholly free of subsequent accretions."[5] The paradox is evident. On the one hand, the originary meanings of classical texts are irrevocable, reading is always recursive. On the other hand, the postclassical reception is presented as real, solid, material, a "chain" binding modern subjects to their past ("whether or not we are aware of it"). In this guise, reception is certainly not an ahistorical venture; but it is certainly self-serving in its use of history. We could easily imagine a critique of the catenary model of reception history as a throwback to positivistic literary-historical realism. Is each community – each reader, even – in a culturally diverse modern state bound by the same chain? How binding is the chain, and what are the possibilities for emancipation? We might wish to think instead of reception as an infinite plurality of interpretative *potentialities* (along the carefully nuanced lines of Stephen Hinds's model of intertextuality in Roman poetry[6]), rather than a solid, immanent historical presence. And yet if we acknowledge this kind of thoroughgoing relativism within reception history then much of reception's claim to intellectual urgency is undermined. What is the argument for reading Virgil through Dante if Dante is only one of myriad possible routes to Virgil?

In this chapter, I suggest that reception has unnecessarily tied itself up with such anti-originarist critiques of conventional epistemology. Such issues have been inspired principally by the familiar Anglo-American distillation of Derrida's

4 E.g. Martindale (1993) 35: "all readings of texts are *situated*, contingent upon their historical moment . . . *to understand is always to understand historically*" (emphasis in original). Cf. Fowler (2000) 130: "Are our views of the opposition between rationality and emotion really the same after Captain Kirk and Mr Spock?"

5 Martindale (1993) 7.

6 Hinds (1998).

well-known writings on the supplement and *différance* from the 1970s: the traditional occidental preoccupation (it is held) with the self-presence of the originary voice is rejected, in favour of the proposition that meaning is deferred along an infinite chain of supplementation.[7] This is a position, however, that it is in practice difficult to maintain consistently (as Jonathan Culler had already observed in 1975[8]). Meaning is, surely, not determined *solely* at the point of reception;[9] it is the product of a complex dialogue between producer and receiver, and certainly also refracted through intermediaries. It is this sense of *reciprocal dialogue* – bilateral, shading into multilateral – that I wish to reinstate in this chapter. Reception cannot do without a serious engagement with history: it must give full weight to the past.

True Histories: Bakhtin, Dialogism, and History

In what follows, I argue against the epistemological-skeptical position, in favour of a pragmatics of reception. There is little to be feared and much to be gained from a judiciously pragmatic approach to historicism within the wider framework of reception. At one level, certainly, it is right that historicists have been too cavalier in their rhetoric of "facts" and "what we know." Yet, as we have seen, it is misguided to assume that reception can do without history: indeed, it relies on more or less evident historical models, its implicit assumptions about the means by which knowledge is transmitted and transformed (and indeed presumes also the intelligibility of those means). It behoves reception theorists not to renounce the practice of history, but to proceed to it with as much care and nuance as possible: to reject, in other words, not history itself but *bad* (that is, naive, unreflective) history.

My title, "True Histories," is of course at one level ironic. I take it as self-evident that there are no absolute truths outside of the axioms of mathematics and physics (and that even their truths cannot be represented neutrally within discourse). But I do also want to conjure a utopian intellectual practice that integrates the self-aware sophistication of reception with a commitment to the historical project of understanding the past: if not "true" in the particular (viz. absolutist) sense critiqued by skeptical epistemology, this historicism at least promises a more nuanced disclosure of the dialogism between past and present. In short, I propose a "pragmatics" of reception, whereby the Platonist language of knowledge and truth is replaced by an emphasis upon the *provisional* status of historical knowledge. This

---

7　I do not mean to imply that this is a wrong reading of Derrida's works of this period, merely that these rich and complex texts are about much more too.

8　Culler (1975) 249.

9　See Batstone's contribution to this volume (ch. 1).

"provisionality," indeed, is a complex phenomenon: for not only do we not "know" the past, we also do not "know" what we are doing with it in the present. Yet the process of exploring the past – of identifying, provisionally, its similarities and differences, its logics and opacities, and its modal contingencies (that is, its "might have beens") – does enrich our understanding of both ancient and modern societies. The study of an ancient culture is not a monologue but a dialogue, between – at least – two full and equal partners.

With dialogism, we approach the work of Mikhail Bakhtin (a critic who is, arguably, to the early twenty-first century what Derrida was to the late twentieth).[10] At this point, I wish to turn to the narrower matter of the study of literary texts. Bakhtin's value to reception studies has already been highlighted by Charles Martindale,[11] though I read him in a different way – in part because I focus largely on his later writings. Martindale emphasizes (and indeed critiques) Bakhtin's emphasis, in some of his mid-period writings, upon unresolved openness in literary texts. Bakhtin, however, came to realize that no text is simply an unfinalizable mass of competing voices. Any literary form is an utterance, and as such represents an attempt on the author's part to communicate meaningfully. As with any utterance, though, the significance of a literary text is constituted through dialogue between transmitter and receiver: "the event of the life of the text, that is its true essence, always develops on the *boundary between two consciousnesses, two subjects.*"[12] The author is thus as vital a subjectivity as the reader. Indeed, already in his better-known mid-period writings on heteroglossia (which he of course sees as embodied in the form of the novel), careful attention is also given to the contrary processes of "centralisation and unification": heteroglossic elements are subsumed within "the unitary plane of the novel," "drawn in by the novelist for the orchestration of his themes and for the refracted (indirect) expression of his intentions and values."[13]

Bakhtin's author, is, then, a very real agent in the determining of meaning; but also a problematic figure, accessible only through "refracted" articulation. Among his final jottings, Bakhtin distinguished "primary" authors from "secondary" authors: the primary author is the real human being who consciously and physically composes the work, while the secondary is the controlling consciousness within the text.[14] The primary author is inaccessible, except insofar as the secondary author is a reflex of the primary. As readers, we engage with the secondary. Nevertheless, the interpretative process depends fundamentally upon the desire to reanimate

10 On Bakhtin's value to classicists, see esp. Branham (2002b) and (2004). The best introductions to Bakhtin are Holquist (1990) and esp. Morson and Emerson (1990).
11 Martindale (1993) 30–4.
12 Bakhtin (1986a) 106 (emphasis in original).
13 Bakhtin (1981) 272, 292.
14 Compiled and translated as "From Notes Made in 1970–71": see Bakhtin (1986c).

authors in all their fulness. In another late work ("The Problem of the Text in Linguistics, Philology, and the Human Sciences"), he writes as follows:

> We find the author (perceive, understand, sense, and feel him) in any work of art. For example, in a painting we always feel its author (artist), but we never *see* him in the way that we see the images he has depicted. We feel him in everything as a pure, depicting origin (depicting subject), but not as a depicted (visible) image.[15]

"The author's intention" has long been the subject of skepticism among literary critics, but there are signs of renewal of interest in this maligned figure.[16] Bakhtin is surely right that any literary reading involves a kind of commerce with the absent author, even if that author is a figment of our own conjuring, created through "a special kind of dialogue: the complex interrelations between the text and the created, framing *context* (questioning, refuting and so forth)."[17] The author is thus not simply an invention of the reader, any more than the reader is invented by the author; meaning, rather, emerges from the conversation between the two. Created neither at the point of transmission nor at the point of reception, it emerges provisionally through the ongoing cognitive process of shuttling back and forth between subjective consciousnesses. This is not the end of it: Bakhtin's model rather simplifies by limiting the process to two interpretations, whereas we should, in fact, allow for polygonal relationships with intermediary interpreters too (namely, the *Rezeptionsgeschichte*).

Historicism plays a crucial role in this process of meaning-making. For Bakhtin and his circle, reacting vigorously to what he saw as the apolitical abscIsion of the formalists, this point was non-negotiable: "The theme of an utterance is concrete – as concrete as the historical instant to which it belongs. *Only an utterance taken in its full, concrete scope as an historical phenomenon possesses a theme.*"[18] History, understood as the very matrix of articulation within which a voice speaks, is the precondition for subjectivity: "It is precisely in the process of living interaction with this specific environment that the word may be individualised and given stylistic shape."[19] For sure, the familiar caveats apply: any analysis of historical circumstances can offer only an intersubjective interpretation, not a final truth. But if we accept that any utterance (whether that of an ancient author or that of any one of its subsequent interpreters, including the modern scholar) is

---

15 Bakhtin (1986a) 109.
16 Particularly in feminist, postcolonial, and Marxist theory: see esp. Burke (1992).
17 Bakhtin (1986a) 106.
18 Volosinov (1973) 100 (emphasis in original); many scholars consider this to be largely the work of Bakhtin himself. For Bakhtin's views on the formalists, see Medvedev (1985), another work that scholars believe to be largely Bakhtinian. On the disputed texts, see Morson and Emerson (1990) 101–19, a skeptical account.
19 Bakhtin (1981) 276.

an attempt to communicate within a given *Erwartungshorizont*, then historical context, both modern and ancient, becomes an integral part of the communicative act itself. Communication fundamentally involves the creation of an (historically and culturally circumscribed) identity, both for oneself and for one's addressee.

True Stories: Lucian and the History of Fiction

I wish now to turn to a paradigm for this process of dialogic communication at work in practice. As we shall see, my paradigm is not merely illustrative. Scholarship on ancient fiction deserves to be a privileged site for reflection upon these issues. Not so much because Bakhtin himself wrote upon the history of prose fiction, stretching his analysis into antiquity (his analysis is flawed,[20] and only tangentially relevant to our project anyhow). The more important reason is that, of all forms of ancient literature, the novel is the least dissociable from its subsequent reception. As is well known, neither the Greeks nor the Romans had a word to denote the genre; there is, indeed, a lively discussion as to whether the novel was a genre at all, and if so where its limits lie.[21] Does the modern novel have its roots in antiquity, or is it a product of the last three centuries? Is "novel," indeed, the right word to use for these texts? What do we gain, what do we lose, by styling them in this way?

This complex of questions is the subject of Margaret Anne Doody's recent "true story of the novel," where she argues for a series of master-tropes (culminating in the new-age figure of the "goddess") that underlie all narrative fiction, from antiquity to modernity.[22] A controversial argument, to be sure – but the ancient novels seem to raise such issues of cultural genealogy with insistent regularity. My present interest lies not so much in the actual construction of narrative histories of the novel as in the strategies appropriate to such a venture. In this context, it is particularly intriguing to find the boldest attempt at this project recurring to ancient paradigms. Indeed, Doody's very title (like mine) alludes to Lucian's celebrated two-book narrative, *True Stories* (in Greek, *alêthê diêgêmata*); and although at the level of explicit rhetoric, every word of her discussion projects a confidence in the veracity of her account, the allusion mobilizes a knowing awareness of the epistemological slipperiness of that particular text. In his prologue, Lucian famously writes that "I tell one truth, namely that I tell lies . . . for that reason, my readers should on no account believe in what they read" (*True*

---

20 In my view, at any rate: Whitmarsh (2004a). For a more sympathetic account of Bakhtin's usefulness to modern critics of the novel, see Branham (2002a).

21 For discussion and further references, see Whitmarsh (2005) and Goldhill (forthcoming).

22 Doody (1997); see also the "truer story" of Branham (2002a), with the analysis of the issues of generic genealogy at pp. 161–5. For the new-age elements of Doody's thesis (and a critique of them), see Morales (2004) 75–6, 163.

Stories 1.4). A "true story" of the novel rests, surely, on what scholars would conventionally take as a heterodox understanding of "truth." Doody, indeed, made her name as a novelist, and this scholarly publication itself has many of the qualities of a novel: it is by turns episodic, dramatic, ludic, elusive, heteroglossic. (Some would no doubt add "fictitious" too.)

Doody's strategy raises an intriguing question: does turning to ancient novels help us understand their subsequent reception? One of the most radical and alluring tropes of reception theory is the reversal of chronology, privileging Eliot's influence on Shakespeare. To propose a return to ancient texts, in this connection, might look at first sight like intellectual recidivism. Lucian was certainly an influential writer, in the conventional sense;[23] my aim here is, however, to do something that is (I think) altogether more disquieting. In reverting to Lucian and his cultural context, I aim to show how the subsequent literary reception of ancient fiction is, in a sense, already enfolded into a founding text.[24] This narrative history will thus re-reverse chronology; reception's familiar trope of chronological reversal will be invaginated. It will also instantiate Bakhtin's argument about the dialogic nature of communication, in that reading Lucian will be understood as the actualization of the primary author's will-to-literary-history.

Receiving True Stories

Lucian's texts focus obsessively upon the process of reception of literary and artistic product.[25] These highly mobile satires portray a dynamic cultural environment in which the aesthetic work is not a sealed monument, but the object of debate. In three cases, Lucian composes separate epilogues to earlier texts of his, describing and countering reactions to the latter.[26] Elsewhere, he differentiates between possible responses in sociocultural terms: in an ornate hall, for example, the common man gawps mutely, the educated speak eloquently (*On the Hall* 2);[27] on hearing the rare word *thumalôps* ("lump of charcoal"), the common folk stand agape, the educated laugh mockingly (*Lexiphanes* 24). Both these examples, clearly, contain an implicit metaliterary challenge to the reader of the text, upping the stakes for our own interpretative strategies. In his prologue speeches,[28] Lucian becomes explicit, and addresses the specific question of the reception of his own work. In

---

23 Robinson (1979) 65–238; Holzberg (1988); Baumbach (2002); Goldhill (2002) 43–54, 60–107.

24 See further Porter (2005a).

25 See the full discussion of this phenomenon at Camerotto (1998) 261–302, focusing upon Lucian's mobilization of *paideia* as a resource for intertextual play.

26 *Defence of "Portraits," Apology, Fisherman.* See further Whitmarsh (2001) 291–2.

27 Equally explicit at *Lexiphanes* 24.

28 On these *prolaliai* see Branham (1985); Nesselrath (1990).

Zeuxis, notably, he begins by protesting that he has been too readily misunderstood by fickle audiences who praise only his innovation. After two parables exemplifying the point, he concludes by telling his audience that "you are connoisseurs [*graphikoi*], and you look at everything artfully [*meta tekhnês*]; I only hope it is all worthy to be shown in the theatre" (12).[29] Clearly, Lucian is playfully attempting to steer his audience towards an approbative reading of his performance, by first telling them what a sophisticated interpretation of a text or work of art looks like, and then challenging them to live up to it.

The prologue of the *True Histories* reproduces this strategy, with an interesting twist:

> Just as athletes and those who work hard on bodily exercise do not merely concern themselves with health and exercises, but also with appropriate relaxation – for they consider it the greatest part of training – so also those who are serious about language [*tois peri tous logous espoudakosin*], I think, should relax their mind after much reading of more serious matter [*tôn spoudaioterôn*] and prepare it so that it is in the best condition for the next test. (1.1)

In this crucial passage, Lucian carefully brands his work as a recreational pastime for the cultivated class. This author's attempts to control the reception of his work (as with the passages we have already seen) demands contextualization within his contemporary cultural and historical climate, where *paideia* (education, civilized values) is seen as the central cultural mechanism for class differentiation.[30] Lucian's reception management is not just ludic; or, rather, the stakes of the game are determined by the nasty politics of second-century elitism, the marginalization of women, slaves, and the poor through cultural silencing.[31] History *matters* here: to slice away the embarrassing, but fundamental, power-play would be an act of abrogation.

I want to turn now to the *Rezeptionsgeschichte* of this passage. It is beyond my scope to analyse anything like the immense variety of readings, which extends from More's *Utopia* and Rabelais's *Gargantua* through Swift's *Gulliver's Travels* to Raspe's *The Adventures of Baron Munchhausen*.[32] Instead, I want to focus upon the most recent phase, namely the rash of attempts over the last 10 years to identify the text's interpretive community,[33] "those who are serious about language." For Georgiadou and Larmour, these are readers who can decode the text as a

---

29 See Camerotto (1998) 271–2, with 272 n. 56 on the term *graphikos* as a cultural affiliative of *pepaideumenos*.

30 On Lucian's satires on Greek *paideia*, see Swain (1996) 308–29; Whitmarsh (2001) 247–94, both with further references. For the broader context, see further Gleason (1995); Schmitz (1997).

31 See esp. Schmitz (1997) 91–6.

32 See n. 23, and esp. Robinson (1979) 129–44.

33 See esp. Fish (1980).

philosophical allegory.[34] For Alberto Camerotto, who reads Lucian primarily as a parodist of earlier texts, the text signals the "importanza per la composizione e per la recezione" of the raft of intertextual allusions underpinning it.[35] For von Möllendorff – whose Lucian is a theorist of fiction and style, forging a new genre of metaliterary pastiche – the text engages the reader specifically qua educated Greek: the *pepaideumenos* is a "Modell-Leser" (12),[36] capable of decoding the theoretical apparatus underlying the narrative.

Three different readings, then, implying three different conceptions of the text's "serious" content: philosophical commentary, intertextual allusion, meta-literary programmatics. If we take the conventional reception-theoretical position, then each of these has its own validity, and implies its own cultural and intellectual genealogy (and, to be sure, each of these interpretations does spring from an identifiable tradition). I have argued, however, for a more mobile, dialogic relationship between originary text and reception. If we reroute these interpretations back through Lucian, a different effect is created: each of these attempts to identify the "serious readership" exclusively becomes a bid for the elitist cultural capital of *paideia*. Modern scholars are still playing out the cut-and-thrust of Lucianic academic politics: the struggle to determine the reception of this text is recognizably the high-stakes game of the arrogation of intellectual and cultural privilege orchestrated so knowingly by Lucian in the second century.

And yet if we look closer at the passage, it becomes highly questionable whether there is a single, "proper" way of reading it. That the readership is described as "serious" (*espoudakosin*), and not (for example) "educated," is crucial. To begin with, it draws the text into the orbit of the familiar Lucianic rhetoric of "serious play" (*to spoudogeloion*).[37] But more pertinently: is a "serious" reader of a comic text the ideal interpreter? The question is immediately redoubled: the narrator defines the text we are reading as a relaxation from "serious matter" (*tón spoudaioterón*): which is to say, the *True Stories* will be, pointedly, a renunciation of the serious. Will serious readers be able to handle a text that defines itself as non-serious? If we self-select as the *spoudaioi*, the educated readership, will we be laughing with Lucian, or is the joke on us?

These teasing games with the reception of the text continue. The text offers, we read, not just entertainment (*psykhagôgia*), but also a "not uncultivated reflection" (*theôrian ouk amouson*) – an elegant litotes that enacts, even as it describes, a certain civilized sophistication. The reason for this *theôria*, we learn, is that the text does not just present exotic fiction, but also, most famously of all,

---

34 Georgiadou and Larmour (1998) 5–22.

35 Camerotto (1998) 33–4.

36 Möllendorff (2000): 11, 12, 17, 22, 26–7. For the *True Stories* as pastiche, see also Fusillo (1988). Fusillo also takes the text as parodying earlier narratives, but parodying their techniques rather than details; cf. also Rütten (1997) 47–62.

37 See esp. Branham (1989) 26–8.

each of the events described contains a not uncomical riddle [*ouk akômôdôtôs êiniktai*], aiming at some of the ancient poets, historians and philosophers who have written many ridiculous and mythical things. I would give their names, if it were not that they would be evident to you from your reading. (1.2)

This is the text's claim to high-level theory: that it contains intertextual riddles that will be self-evident to an informed reader. For the scholars discussed above, this is a straightforwardly programmatic statement. Yet when it comes to identification of the hypotexts for the various elements within the narrative, it proves surprisingly difficult to find prior literary references within the Greek tradition to cork-feet, whale-swallowings, and voyages to the moon. For sure, we have lost, largely or completely, a number of crucial texts, such as those of Ctesias, Antiphanes of Berge, and Antonius Diogenes; but it seems implausible to conclude from this absence that the hypotextual repertoire would have been instantaneously transparent to a second-century readership.[38] It will be clear that my position is very different: rather than telling us about his plans for intertextual motifs, Lucian is inviting us to chase the hares. A riddle (*ainigma*) does not necessarily have a single, final solution: witness, for example, the elusiveness of the riddle of the hawk and the nightingale in Hesiod.[39] Lucian's conception of the literary enigma is, I think, closer to James Joyce's, who wrote of *Ulysses* that "I've put in so many enigmas and puzzles that it will keep the professors busy for centuries arguing over what I meant."[40] When an author highly practiced elsewhere in the dissimulation of identities[41] scripts a narrator claiming deliberately to have withheld the identities of the authors of his hypotexts, it would be naive in the extreme to expect transparency.

The paradigm case of the mischievous narrator, according to Lucian, is Odysseus, who dazzled "those idiot [*idiôtas*] Phaeacians" with his mumbo-jumbo (1.4). Once again, the issue of audience response is foregrounded. Can we relax now, safe that we know what an unreliable narrator and a gullible audience looks like? Perhaps. For sure, Lucian insists that we will not be taken in by his tales: "the one true thing I will say is that I am a liar . . . you must not believe anything I say," he famously (and quasi-Socratically)[42] says (1.4). But this statement is far from straightforward. Is *everything* a lie? Does that include the statement that everything is intertextually modelled? Or that this is a text for

38 "[C]ertamente doveva essere più marcatamente percepibile per un lettore del II sec. d.C. che per un filologo moderno" (Camerotto (1998) 34).

39 Hesiod, *Works and Days*, 202–11. For the distinction between *griphoi* (which necessarily do have an ultimate solution) and *ainoi/ainigmata* (which need not), see Whitmarsh (2004b) 397–8.

40 Ellmann (1983) 521.

41 Whitmarsh (2001) 252–3.

42 Whitmarsh (2001) 252, with references.

relaxing with? Or indeed the suggestion that we, the readership, are substantively different from the idiot Phaeacians? Is this all a lie too?

I hope to have shown that the preface to the *True Stories* addresses itself to a readership who are not card-carrying, self-evidently educated readers, but whose identity as such is specifically being tested by this text. We do not read a text like this simply *because* we are educated (although to be sure, it would be tough going for one without a certain level of education); we read it for the *challenge* to our intellectual status within society. This is a narrative in which the failure of reference allows the text to become a dynamic satire on readers' own aspirations. In that it engages with *paideia*, the central medium of elite self-definition in the imperial period, it also demands a certain historical contextualization: it preys (like others of his works) upon the mechanisms of social distinction current in Lucian's contemporary world.

The reception of this text shows a marked desire to refashion it so that it *refers*, becomes *about something*. As I hope to have shown, that desire is provoked by the strategies of the prologue, which challenges the reader to locate the under-lying *theôria*, its "theory." In this sense, the true story of Western fiction is indeed a series of supplements receding back to an originary absence, since Lucian's text is built around a net of referential holes. Yet this does not imply that the originary text is pure absence, having no voice of its own. On the contrary, it can be argued that Lucian has always-already pre-written the history of fiction. When we read the *True Histories*, we are hailed as intellectuals, interpellated into the community of the knowing, cultivated elite who understand the meaning and value of literature; and at the same time mercilessly mocked for our failure to make sense of this madness, our inability to grapple with the radical alterity of fan-tastic fiction (what Lucian's narrator calls *to xenon tês hupotheseôs*, "the alien quality of the plot"; 1.2). Lucian's is a real (if evasive) subjectivity in the history of fiction, this ever elusive, self-renewing dialogue between modernity and antiquity (even if there can be no finalized description of that subjectivity). Not only this: we can also see how Lucian's satirical programme is historically embedded, rooted in his contemporary culture of elite *paideia*. Understanding Lucian "historically" (and, to reemphasize, I am speaking of a pragmatic not an absolutist historicism) is a crucial point of entry into the later reception of this text, with its competitive (but non-consumable) desire to supplement all of its gaps with "civilized" or "in-tellectual" responses. The *True Stories*, for historically identifiable reasons, demands that we invest our own identities in the production of meaning.

I have argued in this chapter that reception should not be seen simply as the prerogative of the chronologically latest interpreter. To the contrary, a historicist reading of an "originary" text can illuminate much of the subsequent interpreta-tion. In arguing this, I am not (of course) denying the productive role of the later receiver in the dialogue between antiquity and modernity: it takes two to tango, and no doubt many more to produce literary meaning. By focusing upon the originary text in the example of Lucian and the history of fiction (within the necessarily brief compass of this chapter), I have not sought to return to the idealization of the text-in-itself, so pertinently critiqued by reception theorists. My aim, rather, has been to represent the process of reading and interpretation as a dialogue in the fuller, Bakhtinian sense, instead of a straightforward process of one-way transmission. "Reception," indeed, is an unfortunate word for this process: it implies too simplistic a model of departure and arrival. What is needed is a richer sense of the constant shuttling back and forth between text, interpreter and intermediaries. Interpretation, we might conclude, is predicated upon not reception (an achieved state) but *recipience* (an ongoing process).

10

The Uses of Reception

Derrida and the Historical Imperative

Miriam Leonard

If the word "history" did not carry with it the theme of a final repression of difference, we could say that differences alone could be "historical" through and through
and from the start.

Derrida[1]

"Always historicize!"[2] When Fredric Jameson encapsulated his new vision of a
Marxist-inflected criticism in this categorical imperative it seems unlikely that he
had classicists in mind as his primary audience. Classicists have hardly needed
Marxism, let alone Jameson, to convince themselves of the necessity of electing the
historical as a foundation of their discipline. This is not to say that the relationship
between classics and historicism is a natural one, but rather that classicists'
predilection for the historical can be explained by a whole set of (historical)
reasons which are only marginally related to the development of Marxism and
its commitment to historical materialism. Indeed, the relationship between
classics and history has been continually renegotiated from the development
of *Altertumswissenschaft* to the advent of Foucauldian new historicism. The
theoretical underpinnings of historicism may be constantly evolving, but the
injunction to "historicize" is, in Jameson's words "the one absolute, we may even
say 'transhistorical,' imperative."[3]

In this chapter I want to argue that reception studies provide the opportunity
for a rigorous analysis of the "historical unconscious" of classical studies – an

My thanks to Tim Whitmarsh, Simon Goldhill, and the editors of this volume for their
helpful comments. Thanks also to my audiences at Royal Holloway and the Institute of
Classical Studies.

1   Derrida (1973) 141.
2   Jameson (1981) 9.
3   Jameson (1981) 9.

analysis which I hope will orient it to a more political horizon. Jameson's vision offers an agenda uncannily close to the professed remit of reception studies:

> *The Political Unconscious* accordingly turns on the dynamics of the act of inter-pretation and presupposes, as its organizational fiction, that we never really confront a text immediately, in all its freshness as a thing-in-itself. Rather, texts come before us as the always-already read; we apprehend them through sedimented layers of previous interpretations, or – if the text is brand-new – through the sedimented reading habits and categories developed by those inherited interpretative traditions.[4]

Is this not precisely the "organizational fiction" of a certain theory of reception? Jameson's delineation of the "socially symbolic act" of narrative, however, per-forms the same potentially contradictory double gesture which Ellen O'Gorman has identified amongst historicist classicists. Jameson combines an appeal to the specificity of the historical moment with a reference to a more transhistorical notion of "tradition." As O'Gorman argues: "This combination of reading texts within both "their" historical context and the literary tradition . . . creates a hybrid form of historicism, where time is alternately filled with and emptied of meaning."[5] And if this tendency is true of classics it is a fortiori true of reception studies. Jameson's formulation, in fact, uncannily teases out an ambivalence within the very hermeneutic tradition which has played such an important role in the develop-ment of reception studies. Gadamer has argued that the relationship between antiquity and modernity constructed in the humanist tradition cannot avoid con-fronting the fact that we moderns are not the natural and direct descendants of the Greco-Roman tradition, but are rather condemned to look upon it with the eyes of strangers. And yet, it is this tension between the historical situatedness of the modern reader and the inescapable power of the tradition which seems to transcend historical horizons which Gadamer reveals. This tension at the heart of hermeneutics represents the conceptual space within which much of the work in reception studies is conducted today. So while few studies eschew historicism com-pletely, often either the historical specificity of the past is sacrificed to a height-ened awareness of the situatedness of the present, or conversely the insistence on the historical specificity of the past cloaks the present's investment in its own situation. The historical moment is, thus, shunted both backwards and forwards between the past and the present.

This methodological fault-line within hermeneutics has a concomitant in the practice of classicists currently working in the field of reception studies. Charles Martindale's *Redeeming the Text*, for instance, which explicitly announces its debt to hermeneutics, rejoices in a free play of associations between classical text and (more) modern appropriation. His is a vision of an echoing of the past in the

---

4 Jameson (1981) 9.
5 O'Gorman (2002) 83.

present where the boundary between the two has been all but erased. Thus, putting what he calls an Eliotic spin on Gadamer's notion of the "fusion of horizons," Martindale writes "we have learnt to respect not only the presentness of the past but also its pastness, and not only the pastness of the past but also its present-ness."[6] Martindale's celebration of the afterlife of the classics, although distinctly heterodox in its conclusions, is paradigmatic of a branch of reception which sees the relationship between classical literature and its *Nachleben* as a dialogue between free-floating *texts*.

But the textual reception of antiquity is matched by a history of institutions, a story of intellectual, political, and personal ties which give rise to these invest-ments in antiquity. Recent works have tended to keep these stories separate. One could think of Christopher Stray's study of the development of classics in the nineteenth and twentieth centuries, *Classics Transformed*.[7] Stray's is a masterful, almost empirical, analysis of the academy stricto sensu, a narrative of curricula, examination papers, and professorial appointments, of Senior Common Room anecdotes and fierce personal rivalries. But Stray pays little or no attention to the interpretations of antiquity which emerged from this turbulent institutional history. Conversely those who have devoted themselves to the textual reception of antiquity have given short shrift to the historical logistics which Stray and others have insisted upon.

This essay argues for a relegitimation of the very "hybrid form of histor-icism" which O'Gorman has so skillfully critiqued. It argues from an ethical-political perspective that, although the historical can never stand entirely outside its present, the "trace" of the past should be celebrated rather than erased in the encounter between modern reader and classical text. My central example in defense of this thesis will come from Derrida's reading of the *Antigone* in *Glas*. Or more precisely, from Derrida's reading of Hegel's reading of the *Antigone*.

The figure of Derrida also acts as a sort of hero in *Redeeming the Text*. In Martindale's argument Derrida's notion of *différance* is enlisted to lay to rest the implicit recourse to historical positivism and "metaphysics of the text" which lurks behind the hermeneutic tradition of reception theory. As Martindale argues:

> In this book . . . I shall explore a historicized version of reception theory, associated above all with Hans Robert Jauss; but it will be one of a less positivistic character, which will concede rather more than he does to the operations of *différance*, the key term of Derrida's, which combines the idea of difference (meaning is an effect of the contrast between signs) and deferral (meaning always resists closure, a final – or originary – meaning, because signs never stand still).[8]

6   Martindale (1993) 7.
7   Stray (1998).
8   Martindale (1993) 6–7.

Martindale's recourse to Derrida, as I understand it, performs two functions. On the one hand the operation of *différance* makes any return to an "originary meaning" distanced from its reception impossible. Thus as he convincingly argues (echoing Jameson), "What else indeed could (say) 'Virgil' be other than what readers have made of him over the centuries?" (p. 10). On the other hand, in the Martindale reading *différance* also acts to destabilize the possibility of establishing any secure understanding of the historical context of this reception. In other words, not only is it impossible for us to establish a historical context for understanding an "original" Horace, it is equally impossible for us to establish a historical reading of Marvell's reading of Horace. In this proliferation of uncertainties the historical distance which separates the Horatian composition from its Marvellian reading, like the historical distance which separates the Marvellian Horace from his later reinterpretation by T. S. Eliot, is collapsed. The reception of the classical text becomes a conversation between poets across the ages. This is ultimately an aesthetic reaction to the Horatian oeuvre across the boundaries of history, society, and politics. It is my contention that this second reading of Derridean *différance* not only can be challenged by an alternative understanding of Derrida's notion of reception, but is also potentially damaging for understanding the uses of reception for classical scholars today.

I want to make the claim that Derrida's own practice of reading the texts of the past from the perspective of the present can give us a radical and innovative way of approaching the uses of reception by providing a model for bypassing the impasse between historicist and "traditionalist" readings of classical texts. In its passage through Hegel, Derrida's reading of *Antigone* in *Glas* emphatically parades the myth of an unmediated return to an "originary" classical text. Derrida's "Antigone" cannot be separated from Hegel's "Antigone." Not merely because Derrida is writing a commentary on Hegel and not Sophocles, but rather because, for Derrida, Hegel fundamentally changes the Sophoclean text itself. Derrida's critique of Hegel, then, will never pledge a return to Sophocles in order to discredit Hegel. Rather Derrida's "deconstruction" of Hegel's *Antigone* takes place within the Hegelian text itself. Derrida thus rules out any simple return to the Greeks. To paraphrase Martindale, *Glas* asks: "What else indeed could 'Antigone' be other than what readers have made of her over the centuries?"

But Derrida's dialogue with Hegel's *Antigone* does not merely show us that we can no longer read the Greeks naively – that is to say, without acknowledging the whole tradition of "modernist" thought in which they have become embedded. He also insists that there is no way of reading them without complicity. We cannot innocently reread Greek texts and the history of their reception without buying into a certain ideological appropriation. Hegel's reading of the Greeks is placed within a whole system of moral and political theory. Hegel's Greeks are not, in other words, "empty signifiers" of philosophical meaning: they come loaded with a series of associations and functions within nineteenth-century German thought.

And so it is precisely by insisting on this historical dimension of Hegel's appropriation that Derrida is able to perform his deconstructive commentary.

For Derrida becomes concerned with Antigone's exemplary function in the Hegelian text. Hegel's seminal interpretation of Sophocles in the *Phenomenology of Spirit* dramatizes a clash between family and state, the individual and the city. In *Glas* Derrida reveals how Hegel's reflection on Antigone's ethical consciousness is fully implicated in his vision of sexual difference. For Hegel denies Antigone full ethical consciousness which aims at the universal. And it is Antigone's role as a sister which is especially important to Hegel's elaboration of the relationship between sexual difference and ethical choice. But as Derrida points out, for Hegel, Antigone is exemplary precisely because she can support his argument, even – especially? – when she is not present. For as Derrida comments:

> Antigone is not specifically named in the [*Phenomenology*], but the whole analysis is fascinated by the essential figure of this sister who never becomes a citizen, or wife, or mother. Dead before being able to get married, she fixes, she grasps, transfixes, transfigures herself in this character of eternal sister taking away with her her womanly, wifely desire.[9]

Derrida ironically comments: "Hegel finds this very good, very appeasing."[10] Antigone becomes a figure of awe, of admiration, because her contradiction keeps the contradiction of Hegel's ethical system, of sexual difference in place. So "appeasing" it would seem that Hegel can write in the *Aesthetics*: "Of all the masterpieces of the classical and modern world – and I know nearly all of them and you should and can – the *Antigone* seems to me from this viewpoint to be the most magnificent and appeasing [*befriedigendste*] of all works of art."[11] As Hegel puts it elsewhere: "[*Antigone* ist] das absolute Exempel der Tragödie" ([*Antigone* is] the absolute example of tragedy). But what is the price of all this hyperbolic effusion, this exemplification? Antigone, as Derrida reminds us, is not even explicitly mentioned in Hegel's discussion of the family. When "Hegel introduces Antigone without naming her"[12] she disappears from the system, so Derrida writes:

> The effect of focusing, in a text, around an impossible place. Fascination by a figure inadmissible in the system. Vertiginous insistence on the unclassable. And what if the what cannot be assimilated, the absolute, indigestible, played a fundamental role in

9   Derrida (1986) 150.
10 Derrida (1986) 150.
11 Quoted in Derrida (1986) 150. Hegel (1986) 550. It looks as if Derrida might be confounding the German for appeasing *befrieden* with the word for satisfying *befriedigen*. The space between these two (mis)translations encapsulates many of the themes of this piece. I have followed Derrida's practice of highlighting certain words in German.
12 Butler (2000) 31.

the system, an abyssal role rather, the abyss playing a transcendental role and allowing to be formed above it, as a kind of effluvium, a dream of appeasement?[13]

For Derrida, Hegel's "dream of appeasement" is, thus, precisely the exemplarity of Antigone. But making an example of Antigone paradoxically results in making her the exile of the Hegelian text. Antigone – in the most literal sense – exceeds Hegel's text. Antigone's case is at the very centre of Hegel's argument, and yet, her presence, her name, is denied. But as Derrida suggests, the very logic of exemplarity is based on this logic of excess, this process of exclusion. The example must always at some level *exceed* the system it is called upon to support. Hegel's Antigone illustrates in the most extreme way how the example can always undermine as well as reinforce the general case, the universal law.

It is at this point that Derrida interjects: "Could one not say that Hegel has transformed into a paradigmatic and structural legality an empiric situation described in a particular text in the history of tragedy?"[14] Derrida's charge is all the more provocative given Hegel's self-identification as a great historicist. But what Derrida wants to show is how Antigone's exemplarity has become an ideological appropriation of the Hegelian text. By making an example of Antigone, by denying her her specificity and removing her from "the *history* of tragedy," Hegel has performed a domesticating gesture – a gesture whose ideological consequences for women, for our notions of political subjectivity, are still being felt today. For Antigone has been transfigured "into the character of eternal sister," removed from history, society, and politics. By transforming the Sophoclean text – that specific moment in the "history of tragedy" – into a paradigmatic and universal "truth" for modernity, Hegel puts a stop to the possibilities of *difference* which her historical specificity could have kept in play. By forcing Antigone into a universal, Hegel makes explicit the violence of the denial of specificity which the ahistorical reading necessitates. To put it in Benjamin's terms: "In this structure" Derrida "recognizes the sign of a Messianic cessation of happening, or, put differently, a revolutionary chance in the fight for the oppressed past. He takes cognizance of it in order to blast a specific era out of the homogenous course of history – blasting a specific life out of the era or a specific work out of the lifework."[15]

Furthermore, Derrida places his reading of *Antigone* in the context of Hegel's other writings about the Greeks. Derrida shows how Hegel's philhellenism is predicated on a radical anti-Semitism. Hegel's Greeks are in their very essence anti-Jews. For Hegel's engagement with the Greeks forms part of a much wider interest in the philosophy of history where the Greeks find their place in the

---

13   Derrida (1986) 171, 183. Between the two halves of this final sentence Derrida breaks
     off mid-sentence to insert 12 pages of correspondence between Hegel and his sisters.
14   Derrida (1986) 165.
15   Benjamin (1992) 254.

development of Western thought. More specifically in the context of *Glas*, it is crucially against the background of a discussion of the *Christian* family that Hegel will turn to *Antigone*. In his genealogy of Hegel's thinking on the family Derrida turns to an analysis of Hegel's early text *The Spirit of Christianity and Its Fate*. Derrida argues that in this text Hegel is committed to proving that there is no love, no true concept of the family, before Christianity. As Hegel's most outspoken attack on Judaism, this text has become the source of great controversy; by systematically opposing Judaism to Hellenism Hegel sets out to prove the infinite superiority of Greeks in all respects.

This conception of the Greek/Jew antithesis is fundamental to understanding Hegel's phillhellenism. In particular, it is the notion of citizenship which Hegel explores in the *Antigone* which comes into particular focus in this early text. For Hegel sets out to show that, unlike the Greeks, the Jews in their servitude were unable to form a notion of citizenship. Hegel quotes Leviticus 25.23ff.: "They could alienate nothing, for the land is mine and ye with me are strangers and sojourners from a foreign land."[16] And he goes on to say:

> Among the Jews, in the fact they had no freedom and no rights, since they held their possessions only on loan and not as property, since as citizens they were nothing at all. The Greeks were to be equal because all were free, self-subsistent; the Jews equal because all were incapable of self-subsistence.[17]

Nor is Hegel capable of restricting his commentary to theological history – it is not long before we have the necessary concomitant social theory.

> All the subsequent circumstances of the Jewish people up to the mean, abject, wretched circumstances in which they still are today, have all of them been simply consequences and elaborations of their original fate. By this fate – an infinite power which they set over against themselves and could never conquer – they have been maltreated and will be continually maltreated until they appease it by the spirit of beauty and so annul it by reconciliation [*aufheben*].[18]

The question of who the Greeks are to Hegel must always be bound up in the question of who they are not. As we have seen, in the Hegelian system the Greeks function precisely as the anti-Jews in his narrative of history.

> The great tragedy of the Jewish people is no Greek tragedy; it can rouse neither terror nor pity, for both these arise only out of the fate which follows from the inevitable slip of a beautiful character; it can arouse horror alone. The fate of the Jewish people is the fate of Macbeth who stepped out of nature itself, clung to alien beings, and so in their service had to trample and slay everything holy in human nature, had

16 Hegel (1948) 197.
17 Hegel (1948) 197–8.
18 Hegel (1948) 199. *Aufheben* here carries its technical sense in Hegel's dialectics.

at last to be forsaken by his gods (since these were objects and he their slave) and be dashed to pieces on his faith itself.[19]

Perhaps *this* is a passage we should keep in mind when we question why Hegel was to turn to Greek tragedy, why he chose *Antigone*. But what are the implications of this excursus into Hegelian theological history? If every time Hegel mentions the word "Griechen" what we should actually hear is "anti-Jews, proto-Christians" we may have to rethink our understanding of a certain classical tradition. Just as the exemplarity of Antigone becomes part of Hegel's political program, so too Hegel's privileging of Greek culture is based on violent prejudice.

"What do the Jews make of Hegel?"[20] asks Derrida, and well he might. One could be tempted to ask what *this* Jew should make of Hegel. How should one understand Derrida's relationship to Hegel? For Derrida explicitly, if characteristically ambiguously, identifies himself as a Jew in *Glas* when writing about his Jewish upbringing in Algeria. Derrida relates a seemingly autobiographical scene "in Algeria in the middle of a mosque which the colonists had transformed into a synagogue." Moreover Derrida's long, ornate description of the "double-banded" Torah scroll, "its two rolls spread apart like two legs,"[21] is undoubtedly meant to call to mind the typography of *Glas* itself – a book which famously juxtaposes two columns on each page itself recalling, for instance, the complex typography of the Talmud. At the end of this passage, however, Derrida unsettlingly interjects: "What am I doing here?"[22] Can Derrida stand aside from the power of the Hegelian reading? Can Derrida's Antigone ever truly escape her Hegelian genealogy? When Derrida goes back to the Greeks, when he makes an example of their culture, of their philosophy, can he ever really make them *his* Greeks? Or is his appropriation of the Greek always going to be caught up in the politics of its nineteenth-century predecessor? Can one, in short, make an example of Antigone without unwittingly becoming Hegel?

In the Derridean reading, then, Hegel's textual appropriation of Sophocles cannot be kept separate from the political histories of antiquity and modernity. Even this most theoretically imbued of studies insists on the ethical and political imperative of remembering history in the encounter between modern reading and ancient text. This version is no more committed to predicating an "original text" than even the most revisionist of literary histories; it rather reveals the necessity of coming clean about the ideological drive of the moment of reception. In *Glas* the historical specificity of *both* the Sophoclean text and its Hegelian and Derridean rereadings reveal how history can provide an oblique commentary on the practices of the present.

19 Hegel (1948) 205.
20 Derrida (1986) 84.
21 Derrida (1986) 240b.
22 Derrida (1986) 241b.

But can historicism and the political really be so confidently equated? From Jameson to Derrida the question of the historical has repeatedly been troped as an ethical if not a political one. The dangers of negationism have undoubtedly played their role in making history so sacrosanct to the Left. The notion of a Marxist criticism which eschews historicism is unimaginable. But it hardly needs stating that history has equally animated the ideological battles of the Right. The same appeal to history has not only been used to uphold strikingly different political causes but a championing of history has often gone hand in hand with stubborn apoliticism. Indeed, the dangers of a too easy conflation of historicism and political engagement are exposed in a debate between the classicists Jean-Pierre Vernant and Nicole Loraux. Vernant's work has appealed to many classicists because it seemed to contrast sharply with other "theoretical" writings on antiquity which were seen as forcing classical texts into a conceptual framework entirely alien to ancient problematics. His hallmark has been to make his own theoretical insights emerge, as it were, "organically" from the ancient texts. Far from a superimposed grid, the conceptual apparatus he uses is intricately interwoven in the internal dynamics of Greek writings. Vernant's strategy went hand in hand with the historicist injunction to "other" the Greeks. In an attempt to debunk the humanist vision of universal man, Vernant created what he called a "historical anthropology" of Greece. Historical anthropology's desire to respect the alterity of the Greeks led to the creation of a whole new vocabulary. As Loraux recounts, "in order not to betray the Greeks in their difference, we went as far as to borrow their words and so to evoke the concepts of 'middle,' 'persuasion' or 'wily intelligence' we, we too, talked of *meson, peitho* and *metis.*"[23] By refusing to translate these terms Vernant gave voice to the foreignizing imperative of his historicist programme. And yet, with its emphasis on structures of thought, binary oppositions, and the priority of language, Vernant's Greece looked more and more like the fantasy world of the Lévi-Straussian anthropologist. Vernant's trick, as it were, was to make structuralism speak Greek.

Nicole Loraux, however, has exposed the ruse of the Vernantian methodology. In an article polemically entitled "Éloge de l'anachronisme en histoire," she casts a retrospective critical gaze on the early Vernantian project "to return the Greeks to their own discourse."[24] She writes, "I began to ask myself *from where do we speak*, we who want to return the Greeks to their own discourse; how are we able to put ourselves, as it were, in parenthesis in order to make statements such as 'the Greek city is x' or 'The Greeks thought y'; by what miracle – us who had aimed to debunk the myth of a Greek miracle – were we able to gain such a direct access without mediation or distortion to Greek thought?"[25] It is not enough, Loraux argues, to place a term in transliterated Greek rather than in translation

23 Loraux (1996) 282.
24 Loraux (1993) 26.
25 Loraux (1993) 26.

to gain an unmediated access to a historically specific Greek preoccupation. For Loraux, it is impossible to gauge with any historical certainty whether the similarity between our own theoretical preoccupations and those of the Greeks is anything more than superficial. Vernant's practice of appealing to "genuine" Greek concepts, she argues, was a disingenuous attempt to "other" the Greeks which was all along dependent on a shared set of modern sensibilities. In other words, Vernant's Greeks were at their most Vernantian at the very moment he insisted on their radical otherness. In Loraux's eyes, Vernant's historicism had paradoxically resulted in the repression of difference.

Loraux insists that it is important to historicize Vernant's own practice of historicizing the Greeks. For Loraux, Vernant's longing to return to another Greece was the expression of his own dissatisfaction with the communist orthodoxy of his day. As she argues, in his early works Vernant returned to ancient democracy "to explain to Marxist intellectuals in the French Communist Party, and in particular to explain to himself, that democracy had emerged in Greece under the sign of debate and the free exchange of opposing views."[26] Moreover, the experience of the Algerian and Vietnam wars had made alterity a politically charged word for left-wing intellectuals. Vernant's other Greeks are marked to the core by the philosophy of difference which emerged from this period of political turbulence. But for Loraux, Vernant's purported project of historicizing the Greeks was not only self-defeating; it was also, in the final analysis, politically dubious. By making the Greeks other, one refused to allow them to speak to the concerns of the day. If Greek politics, for instance, were so radically different, how could they act as a critique of today's political practices? How could Vernant's Greeks have anything to say to the members of the French Communist Party? Loraux, in other words, exposes the dangers of refusing to translate the word *demokratia* with the word "democracy."

Loraux's eulogy of anachronism is written in the name of a more politically orientated approach to the reception of Greece. Where Derrida and Vernant in their respective ways have argued for the ethical benefits of disappropriating the Greeks, Loraux argues for the political merits of a self-conscious appropriation of the past. She thus relocates the political in a domesticating rather than a foreignizing gesture. And yet, Loraux's political model still relies to some extent on the injunction to historicize. She herself acknowledges the crucial importance of that "moment when one tries to suspend one's own categories in order to understand those of that 'other,' which, through a hypothesis, we call the Greeks." That other will always be, as Loraux argues so convincingly, a fantasm of the "other," but it is no less important for being so. What she highlights is the structural, or should one say the strategic importance of the historical. So, while Loraux is right to point out the pitfalls of fetishizing the past, I would like to resist the equally prevalent practice of collapsing the study of other cultures into a form of unthinking

26 Loraux (1993) 25.

presentism. We need to move beyond what Derrida has called the "tyranny of the same" that is precisely the inability of conceptualizing difference, or indeed *différance*.

Challenging Vernant, Loraux's "hybrid historicism" echoes both Heidegger's critique and his ultimate recuperation of the historical:

> Every report of the past . . . is concerned with something that is static. This kind of historical reporting is an explicit shutting down of history, whereas it is, after all, a happening. We question historically, if we ask what is still happening, even if it seems to be past. We ask what is still happening and whether we remain equal to this happening so it can really develop.[27]

Heidegger and Loraux articulate how the historical can and should act to disrupt the "final repression" of history. If *différance* "alone is historical through and through and from the start" it is also crucially able to resist the foreclosure of history. Through its very name the institution of classics has embodied this double character of the historical: classics is both final repression and endless deferral. The dialectic between presentism and historicity structurally embedded in the notion of reception has the potential to make classics a dynamic political force with a stake in "what is still happening."

---

27 Heidegger (1967) 43.

11

The Use and Abuse of Antiquity

The Politics and Morality of Appropriation

Katie Fleming

I [am] not at all sure whether the trendies do [*Rezeptionsgeschichte*] and the fuddy-duddies not or the reverse, or whether some phases of it, like those that involve Mussolini or *Spartacus*, reveal more than others . . .

M. D. Reeve[1]

Despite the diversity of subject reflected in these twelve essays [*The Use and Abuse of History*], there is a common concern: the place (or uses) of the past, not only in the academy but also in cultural life, past and present, and in the narrower field of politics and political argument. The echo in my title of the second essay in Nietzsche's *Thoughts Out of Season* is not accidental. Though neither my language nor my thinking is Nietzschean, I agree – and believe it important to argue – that what he called "monumental history" quickly slides into "mythical fiction"; that with the "antiquarian" and the "critical" methods of studying the past, "the past itself suffers wrong" and history then "annihilates and degrades life."

M. Finley[2]

Siamo tutti in periodo di decolonizzazione.

A. Momigliano[3]

The title of Nietzsche's essay is, of course, no longer widely translated in this convenient manner:[4] most editions would appear now to render "Vom Nutzen und Nachteil der Historie für das Leben" more knowingly as "On the Uses and

During the writing of this essay I received valuable help from both Charles Martindale and Richard Thomas. My thanks to them. Any shortcomings in the piece are, of course, my own.

1 Reeve (2001) 251.
2 Finley (1975) 9.
3 Momigliano (1969) 43.
4 For the attractiveness of the formula see e.g. Barzun (1974), Wyke and Biddiss (1999).

Disadvantages of History for Life."[5] Nonetheless, wherever one stands in the debate over the translation of Nietzschean idiom, Nietzsche's observations about the worth and place of history seem never to have been timelier. And not least in the field of classical scholarship loosely and sometimes contentiously described as "reception studies."[6]

The frequently polarized appearance of these "reception studies" – on the one hand, reception *theory*, genealogically linked to the work of Hans Robert Jauss, Wolfgang Iser, and so on;[7] on the other, reception *history*, more straightforwardly using the (frequently descriptive) methodology of what has been the established domain of "the classical tradition" – has led to a certain amount of anxiety about the categorizing and validity of such work. Notwithstanding this definitional dilemma, and perhaps inevitably, the majority of studies fall into the latter camp, namely the manner in which the ancient world has (re)emerged in the literature, politics, and cultural realms of the postclassical world. Such historico-descriptive work has occupied an increasing number of classical scholars and university syllabuses (despite the occasional portrayal of such studies as either a scholarly fifth column or mere dilettantism.[8]) The methodology derived from reception theory has, on the whole, been applied, albeit not uncontroversially, to the sphere of ancient literary studies. It is not my concern, however, to revisit these areas of discussion and debate: other essays in this volume deal in greater and more eloquent detail with these issues. Rather – as my title would suggest – I wish to discuss one aspect of the vocabulary used in the growing bibliography on the modern reception of antiquity. As such this essay is concerned, in the main, with reception *history*: however, as I hope to imply, it is – ultimately – impossible to separate the two strands of "reception studies" so neatly.

Of this work a significant proportion has, in recent years, concerned itself with the appropriations of antiquity – architectural, literary, ideological, and so on – made by the regimes of Mussolini and Hitler. Such scholars as Richard Thomas, Theodore Ziolkowski, and Maria Wyke, to name but a few, have written thoughtfully on this period of history and its relationship to the classical world and the classical tradition.[9] As an indication of its topicality, at the 2003 meeting of the American Philological Association in New Orleans, a panel was devoted to the misappropriation of antiquity by (specifically Italian) fascism. A 2000 volume of *Classical Bulletin* was (almost entirely) devoted to the role of the ancient world

---

5   See, for instance, Hollingdale's translation in the Cambridge Texts in the History of Philosophy series, Nietzsche (1997). However, Kaufmann (1950) also gave the title as "On the Use and Disadvantage of History for Life."

6   See Martindale (1993), Hardwick (2003a).

7   See Holub (1984) for a convenient introduction.

8   Although it would be unwise to suggest that such studies are entirely novel, as Reeve's wry article implies.

9   Thomas (2001), Wyke (1997), Ziolkowski (1993).

in Italian Fascism and Nazism, with the individual contributors signaling clearly their distaste for the subject matter in hand. It is clear then that, in the Anglophone academy at least, the abuse of the ancient world by twentieth-century totalitarian regimes is a popular area of research.

The prominence of such work in the field of reception studies is inevitable, not least because of both the continuing fascination with twentieth-century fascism and the prominence of World War II in (not only) Anglo-American life. That this conflict continues to cast a shadow over political, intellectual, and cultural life in Europe and the USA is resoundingly obvious (as demonstrated, for instance, by the striking lack of confusion surrounding the frequent epithet "postwar"). The period 1939–1945, philosophically at least, is now perceived as either the tragic culmination or rupture of centuries of European *Kultur*. The epoch-defining event, furthermore, of the Holocaust – "la césure historiale de notre temps"[10] – means that we will always live in a *postwar* world.

It is no doubt for this reason that intellectual and moral condemnation of such appropriations as, for example, Mussolini's Augustan pretensions and the imperial fantasies enacted in Speer and Hitler's architecture, remains central and necessary to the trajectory and conclusions of many of these scholarly accounts of Fascist and Nazi returns to antiquity. The horrors of this period of European history force the use of the idea of "*mis*appropriation" and abuse, and the surety of the postwar moral consensus against fascism renders it fairly secure. To criticize fascist uses of the past as misappropriation is, at first sight, a straightforward affair: we are none of us, surely, fascists. This notion, however, while consistently assumed, remains underexamined. After all, as Harry Schnur suggested in 1970, "Hitler was an evil genius, but not a stupid country bumpkin . . . His murderous hates, his racial fantasies, his calculated genocides make him an object of detestation; but do they invalidate his observations on the Pantheon and the Parthenon?"[11] It is thus precisely the terminology of use, but more particularly of *abuse* which I would like to examine in this essay. In so doing I hope to raise some wider issues about the place and importance of "reception studies" within the study of classical antiquity.

It is necessary, then, first to discuss – if not to define – the very notion of "abuse." We are, I would argue, on far from stable ground. "Abuse," like Chief Justice Potter Stewart's pornography, is something we seem to know only when we see it.[12] Yet to single out what, intuitively, we disagree with, or find distasteful, in the usage of ancient sources, figures, images, and so on surely does not get us very far. Of course, context might help, and within the narrower framework of classical scholarship the exposure of inaccuracies, misunderstandings (willful or not),

---

10   Lacoue-Labarthe (1987) 72.
11   Schnur (1970) 71.
12   Jacobellis v. Ohio, 378 U.S. 184, 197 (1964).

or outright fabrications might perhaps provide more solid definitional parameters.[13] Nevertheless, while most are comfortable with the contention that there are no "right" readings of, for instance, Virgil, we can perhaps agree that some are simply "wrong," and for a variety of reasons (although the level at which this can be stated comfortably might, in fact, be theoretically and intellectually banal). Such criteria might enable us to identify a "misuse" in fascist scholarship. Along these lines, much important work has been done in the latter half of the twentieth century, particularly by German and Italian scholars, to expose the extent to which the academy colluded with the ideological agendas of Italian Fascism and Nazism.[14] It is perhaps not difficult then to label, for instance, Helmut Berve's "politicized" historical scholarship as an *abuse* of ancient sources.[15] Although the Enlightenment ideal of scholarly objectivity has long since faded, it would seem rather (although arguably not entirely) less contentious to assert that certain practices and methodologies have no place in scholarly activity at least. Certainly, such a position seems defensible – particularly in historical studies. Deborah Lipstadt, for one, has shown in her study of Holocaust denial that there is a need to nuance the increasingly skeptical "atmosphere of permissiveness" in scholarship when approaching historical fact.[16]

However, once outside the less elusive confines of scholarship (even supposing that such a division exists), the issue becomes distinctly complex. The reach of "the classical" in all its forms – the bread and butter of many works of "reception" – is long and wide. It is now beyond cliché to admit that, from Dryden to Disney, Venice to Vegas, the "modern," usually Western, world has always been in dialogue with the ancient. Fascism and Nazism, then, can hardly be seen as unique in this respect. Moral and intellectual condemnation of their returns to antiquity, then, may become politically necessary, but will always be theoretically gratuitous. Other periods of history, other political and intellectual structures are also "guilty," to lesser and greater extents, of (frequently opportunistic) appropriations of antiquity, with all their concurrent distortions, exaggerations, and suppressions: recently, for instance, Christopher Stray has shown the prominent place of classics in nineteenth- and twentieth-century Britain, and Caroline Winterer's study of ancient Greece and Rome in American intellectual life from the eighteenth to the early twentieth centuries narrates the centrality of classicism in the USA; both have demonstrated the value of the flexibility of the classical to contemporary political and cultural agendas.[17] Of course, both these examples also

---

13 However, to remove classical scholarship from the wider discussion of "the classical" in culture more generally is, perhaps, to fall prey to the kind of lack of historical perspective which Leonard criticizes in this volume.

14 See e.g. Losemann (1977).

15 See e.g. Berve (1993 [1934]).

16 Lipstadt (1994) 18.

17 Stray (1998), Winterer (2002).

illustrate all too well the fact that "classical antiquity, however protean in its modern manifestations, has been most regularly deployed to bolster a supposed cultural elite of white males."[18]

It is perhaps in this latter arena, then, that the ideas gathered around notions of "abuse" begin to become clearer, for it is evident that, alongside the moral disgust felt at the activities of various fascisms, crucial issues concerning the ownership of "culture" are at stake. The prominence of classical antiquity – so central to the Western grand narrative – in European fascism illustrates precisely the perceived nature of the fragility (and value) of culture more widely. This is illustrated by the inclination to remove fascism, particularly National Socialism, from the discussion of Western "culture," absolutely speaking. It is this aspect which I shall examine now.

Of course, all studies dealing with any aspect of fascism must first address, to some extent, the almost insurmountable problem of its definition.[19] That this term is used to describe Nazism, Italian Fascism, the government of Vichy France, Franco's Spain, Salazar's Portugal, and virtually any other authoritarian regime, or politics, that is antithetic to democracy,[20] indicates the impossibility of deciding on any simple description of it. Moreover, beyond the confusing diversity of political systems that have been filed under the rubric of "fascism," there is the further complication that even within one specific regime, contradictory and diverse political and cultural aspirations can supersede each other or indeed coexist. Even when we focus specifically on Italian Fascism and German Nazism the generic use of "fascism" to embrace both these regimes seems unhelpfully vague. From even the most cursory of glances it is evident that the two regimes were different in many respects. Nonetheless, to insist that fascism is intrinsically indefinable risks becoming as much of a scholarly cliché as the assertion that fascism is "contradictory in its very essences."[21] Directly to engage with the debate on the definitions of fascism is obviously outside the scope of this essay. I will, however, examine one particular aspect of fascism which might, I believe, offer the possibility of better understanding the whole, by reference to a part. Moreover, such an approach engages directly with the centrifugal issues of culture and value in which "the classical" plays so central a role. The possibility of suggesting a definitional core for fascism becomes more realistic when approached from the point of view of its cultural politics and aesthetics.

18 Wyke and Biddiss (1999) 13.

19 See e.g. de Felice (1996) for fascism "come problema interpretativo" and Kershaw (2000) 20–46 for a useful account of the differing interpretations of Nazism.

20 Except communism, which has, nonetheless, joined Nazism and Italian Fascism under the banner of "totalitarianism." While these political systems do perhaps share this title, and participate in similar forms of cultural politics, nonetheless, communism has a radically different form of charter myth from those of fascism.

21 Golsan (1992) xi.

Not, however, in the more conspicuous areas of the relationship between fascism, Nazism, and (modern) culture. Prima facie, the two regimes displayed very different attitudes.[22] As Roger Griffin notes, for example, Italian Fascism "not only engaged in the conspicuous consumption of modernity and technology, but for twenty years staged a continuous firework display of different aesthetics, some of which, such as futurism, cubism and Novecento, were exuberantly modernist."[23] By comparison, Nazism utterly rejected artistic modernism of any kind, and evoked instead "nostalgia for the pre-modern certainties of classical pasts and Romantic idylls."[24]

Yet even this dichotomy may, at first sight, seem inaccurate and partial when one considers that Italian Fascism, like Nazism – as mentioned above – engaged heavily with antiquity, particularly in the constant association of Mussolini with Caesar and Augustus, and of modern and ancient (imperial) Rome. Furthermore, while rejecting modernism, National Socialism did not eschew modernity, not least in the realm of technology. Indeed, like Italian Fascism, it also advertised its avowedly modern nature and its assertion of a "new order."[25] However, it remains the case that the two regimes approached antiquity in distinctly disparate, and consequently revealing, ways, although often for the same reasons or ends (namely political, social, and historical justification and example).[26] Mussolini's turn to imperial Rome was probably as much a consequence of political precedent as of personal choice. Previous Italian statesmen and governments, particularly since the nineteenth-century reunification of Italy, had turned to ancient Rome as an appropriate model of a strong, unified state.[27]

22 That there was no Italian equivalent of the intimate relationship between Hitler and Albert Speer is perhaps indicative of some of the differences between Nazism and Fascism. Furthermore, that a great deal of art produced in Italy in the 1920s and 1930s (such as the work of some futurists), while approved of and indeed encouraged by the Fascist government, is not now held as taboo within the artistic canon, hints at the complicated relationship between the past and the present. A recent exhibition at the Henry Moore Institute in Leeds, *Scultura Lingua Morta – Sculpture from Fascist Italy*, May 31–August 31, 2003, demonstrated the stylistic diversity of the art produced under the banner of Italian Fascism and also its complex and often ambiguous relationship to ideology. See Campiglio et al. (2003).
23 Griffin (2001) 97.
24 Griffin (2001) 97.
25 Of course, this was already an Augustan notion.
26 The bibliography on fascism's engagement with antiquity is enormous. See e.g. Canfora (1980, 1989), Aicher (2000), Bondanella (1987), Edwards (1999), Kopff (2000), Kostof (1978), Stone (1999), Thomas (2001), Wyke and Biddiss (1999), Ziolkowski (1993). For a recent account see Näf (2001), which includes a comprehensive bibliography on the subject.
27 See Bondanella (1987), Edwards (1999).

However, Hitler's engagement with the classical past and the central part it played in his political *imaginaire* is more difficult to plot, and is indicative of a much more genealogically complex (national) relationship with the classical world. This eighteenth- and nineteenth-century "tyranny of Greece over Germany"[28] has been extensively documented and I cannot revisit it at any length here.[29] Debate continues over the role of this tradition, and its powerful manifestations in the German social and educational systems, in shaping the dramatic political landscape of the early twentieth century and contributing to the decline of liberal democracy and the concurrent descent into totalitarianism.[30] Hitler himself, however, famously displayed an interest in particular aspects of the Greek world. Greek and, more often, Doric or Spartan precedents and influence are invoked frequently in *Mein Kampf* and his "Table Talk." For instance, in 1942 he insisted that "[w]hen we are asked about our ancestors, we should always point to the Greeks."[31] Of course the association of the Spartans and Doric Greeks with Aryanism and racial and national purity was not, as any study of nineteenth-century classicism would reveal,[32] his own invention, and was widespread in the racial ideology of the time.[33] Despite these allusions, however, Hitler's obsession with monumentality and the concept of the ruin value of major buildings, as well as his architectural fantasies for Berlin and Germany, all point to Rome as his most visible ancient paradigm.[34]

On a wider level, the interfaces between fascism, Nazism, art, and the aesthetic (and consequently their impact on the cultural) are a controversial area of scholarship.[35] While many studies are prepared to explore and highlight ways in which Italian Fascism and Nazism engaged with, manipulated, and controlled the artistic and wider cultural world for their own ideological ends,[36] the idea that these regimes approached the artistic and the aesthetic in any other respect than political and ideological opportunism was, and for many remains, an anathema.[37]

Obviously this perspective has been heavily influenced by the human cost of these regimes. As Adam writes, with specific reference to the cultural production of Nazism:

28 Butler (1935).
29 See e.g. Christ (1986), Gildenhard and Ruehl (2003), Marchand (1996), Rawson (1969).
30 See e.g. Gildenhard and Ruehl (2003), Marchand (1996), Näf (1986), Sontheimer (1968).
31 See Trevor-Roper (1953).
32 See e.g. Leoussi (1998).
33 See e.g. Günther (1929).
34 See Scobie (1990), Losemann (1999).
35 See Griffin (2001).
36 See e.g. Brenner (1963), Cannistraro (1975), Thomae (1978), Malvano (1988).
37 See e.g. Poggioli (1968), Glaser (1978).

> The art of the Third Reich is difficult, complex, and controversial. Whether it be in
> the form of fine arts, architecture, film, literature, or music, it cannot be considered
> in the same way as the art of other periods. It must be seen as the artistic expres-
> sion of a barbaric ideology. One can only look at the art of the Third Reich through
> the lens of Auschwitz.[38]

As this statement makes clear, the specificity and enormity of the horrors of Nazism
mark it off from "normal" scholarly analysis. The very barbarism of European fascism
prohibits any notion of a Nazi "culture." If anything, both in its historically patent
negation of any moral norm associated with the notion of culture and its openly
hostile approach to those artistic expressions which it labelled as degenerate,[39] Nazism
could more easily be associated with the notion of "anti-culture."[40] The implications and consequences of Nazism bring out starkly the deep associations felt, if
not always explicitly expressed, between culture as a realm of life – art, literature,
and so on – and the normative idea of culture as describing civilized, moral life.
To talk of Nazi or fascist culture seems to be a reckless oxymoron.

However, more recent studies, the prophetic precursor of which is Walter
Benjamin's essay, "Das Kunstwerk im Zeitalter seiner technischen Reproduzier-
barkeit" (1936), contend not only that twentieth-century fascisms engaged
enthusiastically, if viciously and superficially, with the artistic and cultural world,
but also that the aesthetic and culture are necessarily embedded in the very fabric
of fascism.[41] If anything, fascism must be seen less in terms of the straightforward
political and ideological programs or governments in which it was embodied, than
as a complex social and political culture, which affected and shaped all aspects of life.

The desire to isolate and defend some kind of "authentic" national culture dominates the rhetoric of fascist literature and politics.[42] Invariably, this was to be achieved
through some kind of "rebirth," a palingenetic process that, by recourse to either
ancient or modern models (or both), should reinvigorate the national spirit in its
true nature. Thus fascism is posited as the spiritual, cultural, and political means
of rescuing society, at every level, from decline. In the "new order" thus brought
about, culture and politics would entirely merge.

38   Adam (1992) 9.
39   This condemnation by Nazism extended over the dual signification of "culture." In
     1937, a huge exhibition of "Degenerate Art" (*Entartete Kunst*) was held in Munich.
     In it several styles of art *and* the ethnicity or political orientation of their exponents
     were labelled "degenerate" and "non-German." The work of such artists as Beckmann,
     Klee, Dix, Kandinsky, and Picasso were all exhibited. See e.g. Barron (1991), Nicholas
     (1994), Petropoulos (1996).
40   Griffin (2001) 95.
41   Adam (1992), Spotts (2002). Like Benjamin, Adorno and Horkheimer, in their influ-
     ential work *Dialektik der Aufklärung* (1944/1947/1969), identified the effects and
     control of fascism over (cultural) life.
42   See e.g. Carroll (1995), Griffin (1991, 1996).

It is this, I would argue, that most often could serve to distinguish and unite the political systems that are collected under the banner of "fascism," and provide the means for some general definition. Fascism is not simply a political doctrine, but a cultural imperative. The studies of Roger Griffin (for instance, *The Nature of Fascism*, 1991) provide a useful model.[43] His succinct description of the elusive "fascist minimum" is the most helpful attempt at such a definition: "Fascism is a political ideology whose mythic core in its various permutations is a palingenetic form of populist ultra-nationalism."[44] The identification of this "mythical" element and the corresponding revelation of its associations with the aesthetic offer the most convincing route, I believe, towards a coherent discussion of fascism. Such an approach emphasizes the central importance of the (domination of the) aesthetic to fascism and its attempts at the totalization of society,[45] where no difference is to be found between politics and culture.[46] These studies are invaluable for the understanding of how fascism "could have appeared as an attractive alternative to democracy to political theorists, writers, and intellectuals who were not irrational nihilists but in fact were deeply committed to traditional values, art, and culture."[47] Moreover, any analysis of a fascist aestheticizing of culture has also the merit of uncovering the alarmingly deep roots of European fascism.[48] Far from it being simply a historically isolated phenomenon and an "aberration within or radical departure from the dominant Western political tradition,"[49] fascistic thinking can be identified as worryingly consistent with many long-standing mainstream European intellectual trends.[50]

43   Griffin is himself heavily influenced by George Mosse, whose seminal work on fascism and fascist culture, despite some initial lack of response, has recently been enjoying wider support. See Mosse (1964, 1966, 1980, 1999).

44   Griffin (2003) 5. This essay provides both a defence of his definition and an explanation of its terms.

45   See Gentile (1993).

46   See e.g. Griffin (1996), Kühnl (1996), Affron and Antliff (1997), Falasca-Zamponi (1997), Ben-Ghiat (2001).

47   Carroll (1995) 3. See also Sartre (1976).

48   See e.g. Sternhell (1986), Sternhell et al. (1994).

49   Carroll (1995) 3.

50   Of special interest to classical scholars must be the intimate connection between the origins of fascism and the classical world. Key figures of proto- and early fascism continually turned to the ancient world to formulate their anti-democratic theories. The thought of the radical syndicalist Georges Sorel was crucial to the formation of fascism. His work, *Réflexions sur la violence* (1908), with its call for violence as a political tool and assertion of the need of some kind of mythology to encourage revolt, was seminal for the intellectual development of fascism. Prior to this he had engaged at length with antiquity in a number of works, including *Le Procès de Socrate* (1889), *D'Aristote à Marx: L'ancienne et la nouvelle métaphysique* (1894), and *La ruine du monde antique: Concéption matérialiste de l'histoire* (1902). See Sternhell et al. (1994).

It is at this crossroad between postwar distaste for and anxiety over the place of fascism in European intellectual and cultural history, and the realization that culture and civilization go hand in hand with barbarism,[51] that the vocabulary of abuse emerges in the scholarship on fascism's engagement with the ancient world. And it is in this respect that the fault-lines between the "textual" and the "historical" approaches to "reception studies" become, paradoxically, more visible and also less easily demarcated. If our "uses" of antiquity are themselves always subject to moral and political (no less than intellectual) frames of reference, categories, and judgment – as any study of fascism's appropriation of the ancient world makes patently obvious that they are – then the issues of the aesthetics of reception which inform the work of more textually minded "receptionists,"[52] of the dialectic between production and consumption of texts, images, ideas, and so on, become critical. It thus seems rather obvious, then, to suggest not only that our interpretations of antiquity "in itself" are not objective, but that our interpretations of that antiquity's dialogue with modernity are also subject to the same dynamics of reading.

This is not, however, to admit a relativistic free-for-all, but to acknowledge, perhaps, the forceful evaluation of the dynamics of tradition made by T. S. Eliot in 1919:

> No poet, no artist of any art, has his complete meaning alone. His significance, his appreciation is the appreciation of his relation to the dead poets and artists. You cannot value him alone; you must set him, for contrast and comparison, among the dead. I mean this as a principle of aesthetic, not merely historical, criticism. The necessity that he shall conform, that he shall cohere, is not onesided; what happens when a new work of art is created is something that happens simultaneously to all the works of art which preceded it. The existing monuments form an ideal order among themselves, which is modified by the introduction of the new (the really new) work of art among them. The existing order is complete before the new work arrives; for order to persist after the supervention of novelty, the *whole* existing order must be, if ever so slightly, altered; and so the relations, proportions, values of each work of art toward the whole are readjusted; and this is conformity between the old and the new. Whoever has approved this idea of order, of the form of European, of English literature will not find it preposterous that the past should be altered by the present as much as the present is directed by the past.[53]

As the (evidently sardonic) quotation by Michael Reeve selected to begin this piece would seem to indicate, certain moments in the reception history of the ancient

---

51   See e.g. Benjamin (1992).
52   "Hans Robert Jauss [. . .] noted humorously in 1979, to the foreign ear questions of 'reception' may seem more appropriate to hotel management than to literature" (Holub (1984) xi).
53   Eliot (1951) 15.

world seem to hold our attention rather more keenly than others. I have already suggested that a portion of this is attributable to the long-standing "voyeurism" in Anglophone culture for World War II. No less important, however, must be the sense of anxiety felt over the fascist appropriation of culture – and its most significant standard-bearer, the ancient world. As I hope to have shown, however, the use of a vocabulary of "misappropriation" and "abuse," while still seen as politically and morally necessary, might nevertheless be theoretically and intellectually unnecessary. The challenge posed by fascism's use of the past, then, lies in our engagement with it: simply to dismiss, explicitly or implicitly, the appropriation of antiquity in the fascist regimes of the twentieth century as abuse is to understand neither the dynamics of that appropriation nor, ultimately, the regime that made it.

Part II
Studies in Reception

12

The Homeric Moment?

Translation, Historicity, and the Meaning of the Classics

Alexandra Lianeri

In 1932 Jorge Luis Borges engaged with a theme that had long played a key role in the modern encounter with antiquity: the translation of Homer. In his essay "La versiones homéricas"[1] the Argentinian writer set the problem of Homeric translation against the background of translating classical texts and began his reflection with a comparison between Homer and Cervantes. In this context, Borges confessed what he himself described as a "frivolous superstition": that he would reject any form of divergence from the *Don Quixote* brought about by translation. As he wrote:

> But how can we know now whether the statement "In a place of La Mancha, whose name I don't care to remember . . ." actually proceeded from divine inspiration? I only know that any modifications would be sacrilegious and that I could not conceive of another beginning for *Don Quixote*.[2]

The canonization of the *Quixote* in the Spanish tradition, Borges explains, has established the text as a monument that accepts no possible variations. It has thus sustained the superstition that any translations would be inferior to it, that the *Quixote*, like all great works of literature, is itself "unalterable and definitive."

This attitude towards the Spanish classic stood in sharp contrast to Borges' perception of the Homeric epics, which existed for him only in translation:

I would like to thank Yorgos Avgoustis, David Hopkins, Robin Osborne, Jim Porter, and the editors of this volume for invaluable comments and suggestions. I also want to thank Kostas Vlassopoulos for a discussion about democracy which gave me the idea for this essay's title.

1 Borges (1992) 1136.
2 Borges (1992) 1136. It is of course, paradoxical, that I have to read and quote this passage in translation.

> [T]he *Odyssey*, thanks to my opportune ignorance of Greek, is a library of works in prose and verse, from Chapman's couplets to Andrew Lang's "authorised version" or from Bérard's classic French drama and Morris's lively saga to Samuel Butler's ironic bourgeois novel.

The key to this statement lies in Borges' description of his ignorance as fitting and appropriate, an opportune condition that allowed him to apprehend his prejudice. Homer was not for him a finite text, an already achieved possibility. It rather manifested the incalculable repercussions of texts, the unending variability of words documented in translation: "What are the many renderings of the *Iliad*," he asked, "if not different perspectives of a mutable fact, if not a long experimental lottery of omissions and emphases?"

Borges was among the first thinkers who deployed translation to challenge the binary opposition between author and reader, and shift the attention from the production to the reception of a work. His essay on Homer's translations and his short story "Pierre Menard, Author of the *Quixote*,"[3] written in 1939, prefigured reception theory in developing a radical conception of the "reader as writer" and exploring translation as a model for the reading–writing process.[4] What is important for our discussion, however, is not so much Borges' repudiation of the ideas of "authorship" and "originality," as his confession that, despite his encounter with other literatures, outside the Spanish one, and despite his critique of the presumed permanence of the classics, he never fully dismissed the peculiar finality that sustains the classical tradition. Indeed, Borges' juxtaposition of Homer and Cervantes capitalized on the unavoidable persistence of this tradition. It identified a fundamental need for immortalizing the past at the very moment this past displays its historicity and its distance from the now.

The ensuing paradox of grounding tradition and continuity on the basis of rupture and discontinuity is the main theme of this essay, which examines the classics in relation to modern conceptions of historicity that both unite and separate past and present. This peculiar link which defines classicalness in terms of our links to past meaning, while simultaneously revealing the alienness and, indeed, the meaninglessness of classical texts, finds its paradigmatic expression in the form of translation, which both affirms and negates the possibility of the classics being meaningful to us. By focusing on Alexander Pope's conception and practice of translation, the essay explores this dialectic of the meaningful and the meaningless, the eternal and the historical, the true and the real, to interrogate definitions of the classic in terms of "surviving" or "accepted" meaning and to discuss the classical tradition as founded on the problematization of meaningfulness and the contestability of the relation between past and present.

---

3   Borges (1998).
4   See Levine (1992).

I Classics in Time: Encountering the Meaningless

What is the use of being known, if we have not been so to this sage or that mad-man, to a Marcus Aurelius or to a Nero? We shall never have existed for so many of our idols, our name will have troubled none of the centuries *before* us.

Emile Cioran, *History and Utopia*

At the most immediate level, Cioran's statement seems indisputable: our names will have meant nothing to the eras against which we measure ourselves. Yet equally manifest is the author's agony about this state of affairs, the despair over the limitations of the present and the need to mediate the past's distance from us. It is precisely this need to confront time, to pursue an infatuation with eternity, as Cioran puts it,[5] that sustains the category of classicalness. This means that the classics always entertain a certain relation to time, or, what is ultimately the same thing, a certain relation to death, to silenced meaning or meaninglessness. In the Western tradition this relation has taken the form of a struggle against death (yet a struggle which also puts death at the centre of human existence),[6] an obsession with immortality, which European modernity crystallized in the simultaneous imposition and denial of a break with past meaning. The classics, I would suggest, served as the privileged site for performing this dual gesture. Their "recognition" as classics confirmed the silence of the past; it brought about a rupture of any meaningful relation to what is no more. Yet it concomitantly contradicted this fissure by bestowing on the present the exclusive authority to resurrect the past as what had already anticipated the future, what defied death by being able to resist (its) time.

This paradoxical move must be distinguished from both the nostalgic return to antiquity and the pragmatic appropriation that reduces the past to the norms and aims of a self-enclosed present. By evoking an idealized past, nostalgia claims to repeat what is essentially unrepeatable, a past that was never present in the first place. As Susan Stewart writes in her essay *On Longing*,[7] nostalgic returning actualizes a "repetition that mourns the inauthenticity of all repetition." It sets up a realm of authenticity, the past, against the figure of a decayed, postlapsarian present, only to confirm the latter's inevitable fall from grace, its incapacity to recover its ideal. Conversely, pragmatic appropriation, in the sense of an instrumentalist seizure of tradition, seeks to subsume both the past and the present's relation to it into a fixed horizon of contemporary meaning. The argument that aspects of antiquity can be merely *used* to advance present aims implies precisely this act of appropriation and possession. It posits the past as a forceless relic, an object to be taken over and controlled by the interpreting subject. The classic,

5   Cioran (1987) 5.
6   See de Certeau (1999) 27.
7   Stewart (1984) 23.

by contrast, does not merely stem from a victorious conquest of the past in the name of the future; it also exposes the inevitable precariousness of all victories over what is gone. In other words, classicalness calls for a less coercive and more ambiguous mode of appropriation. The captors, by confronting the past's otherness, also encounter their own limits, and thus lay themselves open to transformation, exposed to their own imminent death. In this sense appropriation, as Paul Ricoeur has described it,[8] does not involve a subject who already masters her own being-in-the-world. Nor does it evoke a projection by this subject of the a priori of her own understanding onto the (textual) remains of the past. Appropriation is rather "the process by which the revelation of new modes of being . . . *gives* the subject new capacities for knowing himself." Far from being a way of claiming the past and taking hold of it, it implies instead "a moment of dispossession" of the present, a form of *self*-distancing that allows the creation of a new "*self*-understanding" and contrasts the *self* to the *ego* that purports to precede understanding.

It is this *self* which merges with and endeavours to reemerge from within the past that informs the concept of the classic. This means that the classic performs a peculiar form of appropriation, which substitutes the experience of the loss of meaning for the certitude of meaningfulness, and simultaneously demonstrates the impossibility of endorsing this loss and drawing the limits of the present. By enabling the reader to transform self-understanding through the potential for a new mode of being and a new capacity to project herself, the classic implies that meaning, as a positive entity which remains identical with itself within time, becomes problematized. What is more, this problematization points to the possibility that the construction of classicalness might involve the loss of all temporal contexts for defining meaning and the absence of a moment within which meaning acquires a fixed identity. The classic may thus be seen as arising from the confrontation of what the Czech philosopher Jan Patočka has aptly called "the meaning's point zero."[9] In other words, the classic may be born not out of certainty, but out of the despair Cioran ascribes to the relationship of modernity with tradition: the experience of the absence of meaning that characterizes a radical alienation from the past and the process of questioning whether there is something in our heritage that is still meaningful for us.

While this condition pertains, as we shall see, to the modern engagement with the past, one can trace its roots back to the link between classics and time drawn by Roman criticism. This is not to say that the concept of the classic can be traced back to antiquity. As James Porter[10] rightly observes, the categories of classicism and the classic in ancient criticism are constantly in search of a name, and the absence of that name points to the fundamental incoherence of these two

8   Ricoeur (1981) 192–3.
9   Patočka (1996) 56.
10   Porter (2005b).

concepts even more than the modern terms do. Indeed, in one of the earliest definitions of the classic in Western thought Horace deployed the concept, but not the word *classicus*, which he directly linked to the category of time: "est vetus atque probus, centum qui perficit annos" (*Epistles* 2.1.39). The classic is that which lives on, which continues to be read beyond its own age, which acquires an afterlife. Time is not therefore external to the canonization of the classics. It is constitutive of the category of classicalness.

The concept was, however, to be reformulated and linked to authority perceived as atemporality. The term *classicus*, introduced into Latin by Aulus Gellius, signified a supreme and distinguished order claiming to be unaffected by history. The opposition between the *scriptor classicus* and the *scriptor proletarius* (*Noctes Atticae* 19.8.15), which Aulus Gellius borrowed from political language,[11] alluded to a hierarchy that presented itself as accomplished and unchangeable. Gellius' classics utilized the imaginary of a social order that relocated socioeconomic divisions beyond the dynamics and contingencies of time. The classic confirmed its authority by obliterating temporality, by suppressing the threat posed to it by the changing criteria of authorization. It wiped out contention by moving itself outside time, by effacing the possible under the established, the alternative under the dominant, the historical under the permanent. Yet Gellius' definition contained a caveat that challenged this permanence and lodged the classic back in the realm of time. Their extrahistorical value notwithstanding, classics, he wrote, are ultimately the ancient writers (*cohors antiquior vel oratorum vel poetarum*). The classic appears to us as a standard of measurement, an immutable model. But when it is recognized as such, it reveals more than its permanence. It lays claim to a genealogy, and thus an order that was itself attained and imposed, an authority that had to confirm its dominance, a privilege reached by conquest and defeat, and thus subject to overthrow. The classic's resistance to time is no mere sign of its timelessness; it is also a reduction of its status to rules produced by historical and contingent standards.

This conflictual meaning was crystallized with the introduction of the term "classic" into the vernaculars in the mid sixteenth century, a period when the *Ars historica*, as Anthony Grafton suggests, began to reflect on the inaccessibility of past eras by thematizing the category of "historical times."[12] While the first recorded occurrence of the word *classique* in French, in 1548, designated a timeless paradigm,[13] the term soon became associated with antiquity, and the Greek and Roman writers in particular. Far from shaping an immutable paradigm that united ancient and modern times, this move implied, instead, the foundation of unity on the division between Greek and Latin classics, which was, in turn, reflected on the fundamental rift between Greece and early modern Europe. The history

---

11 See Kermode (1983) 15.
12 Grafton (2005).
13 See Wellek (1973).

of classical scholarship testifies to this divide. As M. L. Clarke has argued, the Renaissance use of Greek in education hardly changed the fact that European thinkers continued to evoke a Latin heritage, while viewing themselves as separated from the Greeks.[14] One can further recall the extensive body of Latin translations from the Greek, by scholars such as Leonardo Bruni, Giannozzo Manetti, and Desiderius Erasmus,[15] to conclude that, despite the eagerness for the promotion of Greek studies by certain Renaissance writers, the classical tradition was perceived as divided, split from within by the conflict attributed to its originating moment.

The subsequent *querelle* between the ancients and the moderns heightened the force of this division without, however, precluding assumptions of continuity and coherence that linked the conflicting parties. It would be mistaken, in my view, to read the *querelle* as a struggle against the ancients, a protest against the limits and limitations of tradition. If, as Heraclitus said (*fr.* 80), war is what is common, what brings together the battling enemies, then a struggle is an act of unity as much as it is an act of separation. The eighteenth-century battle with antiquity, as I argue in the next section, was not formed as a mere break with the ancient past, but as the denial of this past's unity as an inaugural moment. When Alexander Pope famously turned to Homer to bring ancient and modern writing onto the field of battle he implicitly recognized the epics' privileged link to modernity by choosing Homer as the paradigmatic enemy and by bestowing on European civilization – a category that legitimized its unity through its link to "modern" times – the unique right to perform this encounter. By the same token Pope pronounced an unassailable divide between the ancients and the moderns, articulated, as we shall see, not as a direct break, but as a form of discontinuity, a tension between the meaningful and the meaningless, within the originary moment of the classical.

The premise of Pope's *Iliad*, as he explained in his Preface, was that the Greek and Roman worlds "are now no more" and that readers of classical literature "are stepping . . . backward into the remotest Antiquity, and entertaining themselves with a . . . surprising Vision of Things."[16] Yet this premise did not entail a view of the *Iliad* as the mere voice of what is gone. It did not insinuate a rejection of Homer's paradigmatic, or, indeed, classical status for modernity, but, contrari-wise, involved the (re)definition of this status as the quality that brings together and unifies the temporal and the surviving, the odd and the familiar, the past and the present, the meaningless and the meaningful. This is the reason why clas-sicalness, as I shall argue in what follows, became inextricably bound to the notion of translation. As a quest for foundations that saw origin as an elusive and per-ishable moment, and a promise of survival that questioned both the attainment of eternity and the links between past and present, the classic found its privileged

14 Clarke (1945) 15; see also Clarke (1959).
15 See Botley (2004).
16 Pope (1967) 7.14.

site not in the acclaimed positivity of original expression, but in the fleeting, in-between moment of the practice of translation.

II Theorizing Translation: Pope's Homer

> Homer . . . seems to have taken upon him the character of an Historian, Antiquary, Divine, and Professor of Arts and Sciences; as well as a Poet . . . All these ought to be preserv'd by a faithful Translator, who in some measure takes the place of Homer.
> Alexander Pope, Postscript to the *Odyssey*

The translator's ambition to achieve faithfulness by transposing himself into the place of the author points to the key paradox of translation: that the act of translating can never succeed in achieving its goal, that the task of the translator implies a fundamental impossibility and failure. Pope appeared conscious of his predicament. "Upon the whole," he wrote in the Preface to his *Iliad*, "I must confess myself utterly incapable of doing justice to Homer. I attempt him in no other hope but that . . . of giving a more tolerable copy of him than any entire translation in verse has yet done."[17] It is significant that, despite the intense controversy over Pope's linguistic and scholarly competence, no critic of his *Iliad* offered a solution to the quest for "becoming" Homer. On the contrary all reviewers of the work pronounced the insolubility of the translator's dilemma. As John Dennis, Pope's most outspoken and rigorous opponent, put it, it is impossible for anyone to express in a translation the poetical language of Homer.[18]

But why would Homer be impossible to translate? Why should the *Iliad* posit the question of translatability in a more serious or irrevocable manner than other, non-classical writings? Or, from a different viewpoint, what does the problem of translation suggest about the attributes of Homer as a classic? Is what Porter describes as the basis of Homer's classicalness, the "utter mystery and unreachability," the very indeterminateness of "the idea of Homer,"[19] linked to the field of ceaseless conflict, contest, and redefinition formed by translation?

Pope begins to reflect on Homer's translatability by invoking the technical dilemma of literal versus free translation. He quickly rejects literalness as unable to produce translations that would "be just to an excellent original in a superior language." Yet he also warns us against the great mistake of "a rash paraphrase . . . which is no less in danger to lose the spirit of an ancient, by deviating into the modern manners of expression."[20] A consistency of the two modes seems to be the only viable option, but the criteria for choosing the one over the other move

---

17   Pope (1967) 7.21.
18   Dennis (1943) 123.
19   Porter (2002) 58.
20   Pope (1967) 7.17.

beyond the translator's technical language. Instead, the main reason for deciding whether to follow Homer literally or to rewrite him is the source text's consistence with the classical ideal. When the author departs from this ideal, then the proper mode of translation is a refining paraphrase. As Pope writes in his "Essay on Criticism": "Homer's thoughts refine, / And call new beauties forth from every line!"[21] Yet when the source text reflects the immortal light of classicalness, then the choice is literal translation: "If there be sometimes a *darkness*, there is often a *light* in antiquity, which nothing better preserves than a version almost literal."[22]

The technique would have implied a pragmatic appropriation, by acting to subjugate Homer to contemporary literary paradigms, had Pope not added an important proviso: that Homer embodied himself the inaugurating move of classicalness. He was the poet par excellence "who most excelled in that which is the very foundation of poetry": the "invention that, in different degrees, distinguishes all great geniuses."[23] The contention stood within the lineage of Longinus' emphasis on poetical genius rather than the concrete qualities of a work and the critic's view of the sublime as an inspired product of passion rather than technique.[24] Yet, unlike Longinus, who envisioned a division between a sublime and an ordinary Homer, Pope deployed the notion of genius to bring together what he saw as the conflictual attributes of the Homeric epics. His claim was not therefore that parts of Homer's poetry were in some way more classical than others, but, more radically, that Homer's apparent departures from classicalness were directly linked to his classical qualities. They were products of the same genius, as Pope put it, that gave rise to Homer's virtues, proceeding "from so noble a Cause as the Excess of this Faculty."[25]

One must not understand this pronouncement as an unqualified praise of Homer. Unlike his model and predecessor in France, Madame Dacier, Pope would never contend that the *Iliad* offers a model for all kinds of poetry. Nor would he endorse Madame Dacier's conviction that the Homeric times and manners were so much the better the less they were like the present time.[26] Pope not only recognized a non-perennial quality in Homer's writings, but also rejected the vocabulary of difference to describe this quality as a threatening alterity, a moment of incomprehensibility: the "darkness" of Homer (see above). His position thus allowed for

21 Pope (1961) 1.315–16.
22 Pope (1967) 7.17.
23 Pope (1967) 7.3.
24 See e.g. Longinus' (8.4) praise of the tone of "genuine passion, in its right place, when it bursts out in a wild gust of mad enthusiasm and as it were fills the speaker's words with frenzy" (Longinus (1907)). On the role of Longinus in shaping eighteenth-century literary criticism via the numerous editions of Boileau's translation of 1674 see Hopkins (2004) and Monk (1935).
25 Pope (1967) 7.13.
26 Pope (1967) 10.394.

the possibility of the classic embodying this threat, of the eternal and the meaningful being in conflict with themselves.

This contention was closely linked to the Quarrel between the Ancients and the Moderns as the articulation of a radical break with the past, which Pope both performed and refused to accept. As Joseph M. Levine has remarked, "no one touching Homer in 1714 could avoid the *querelle* or fail to take a stand." Pope had to "declare himself."[27] Yet Pope's *Iliad* did not quite *declare* a position. On the contrary the translator resolutely dismissed the foundations of the battle by substituting the inquiry into the division between the true and the false for the opposition between ancients and moderns. As he wrote in his "Essay on Criticism":

> Some, foreign writers, some, our own despise;
> The ancients only, or the moderns prize.
> Thus wit, like faith, by each man is applied
> To one small sect, and all are damn'd beside.
> . . .
> Regard not then if wit be old or new,
> But blame the false, and value still the true. (394–7, 406–7)

Pope's evaluative criterion – the true – does not offer a unified measure for taking sides. On the contrary, it denotes the impossibility of choosing by pointing to the peculiar temporal status of "the true" and its other. The issue at stake is the conception of "the true" against the fundamental relation animating the quarrel: that between *archê* (defined here as beginning, principle, and power) and progress. In this relation each party laboured for and struggled against the other. As the moment of *archê*, "classical" antiquity enabled the designation of modern times as a qualitative category, rather than a categorization of time, the end-product of a teleological process that confirmed the paradigmatic – that is, classical – status of European civilization against its others. Europe's acclaimed origin thus authorized "European" classical principles and destiny. At the same time, however, this destiny was realized in Europe's departure from its "beginning," in the move of progress affirming the incontrovertible breach of unity between the ancients and the moderns.

The interplay of Homeric "darkness" and "light" was defined through this paradoxical temporality. The designation of *archê* imposed both the principles and the limits of classicalness. It drew up a frontier that defined the classic by declaring the meaningless of what was taken to exist outside of it, by silencing the classic's other. By the same move, this other reached the classic as the arbitrary moment of split, the *archê* which, as de Certeau wrote, "is *nothing* that can be said,"[28] as

---

27 Levine (1991) 194.
28 de Certeau (1999) 35.

it itself designates the proper limits of speaking. This is why classicism, as Porter has argued, demonstrates a temporal logic which is less retrospective than it is consistently regressive: it cannot halt its backward-regarding search for the classic original. In other words, it cannot speak of its own *archê*. Hence Homer, Porter observes, is the archetypal classic that interrogates classicism by coming as he does either too early or too late to supply a classic original. Paradoxically Homer has always been felt to be more or less classical than the classical authors of the fifth century: either too primitive or too perfect, but most often a conflictual combination of both.[29]

In discussing Homer's morality, Pope observed not merely the specificity, but also the darkness of Greek morals, the incomprehensibility of the "boasting temper and unmanag'd roughness," the unreasonable "pride, anger, or cruelty"[30] as a form of morality. Yet Pope also denied this lack of continuity and followed Horace's description of the poet as "a master of morality."[31] As a beginning, *archê* exceeded meaning; and yet it was its presence as a void within meaning (the non-moral principles of morality) that sustained the rules of meaningfulness in modern ethical discourse. In this sense Pope acknowledged that any comparison between the ancients and the moderns must recognize the latter's fundamental disadvantage: the lack of this afterlife, which amounts to nothing less than the lack of classical status. Even if we used the same industry and took the same care with the ancients, he wrote, "we should still lie under a . . . misfortune: they writ in languages that became universal and everlasting, while ours are extremely limited both in extent and in duration."[32] This means that the ancients wrote in languages that were not, but became, classical through their connection to the modern.

It follows that the *archê*, in its role as a principle and a source of power, is predicated on the link between the beginning and the end, between the ancients and the moderns. This condition brings the processes of reception and translation to the centre of the category of classicalness. For the classic, as I argued, does not express a unique moment in time (since this moment is always internally divided as an *archê*) but the travel between the *archê* and the future, between the untraceable beginning and the principle that defines the destination and animates the act of traveling. In this sense, Pope locates the criterion of the true neither in the ancients nor in the moderns, but in the latter's encounter with antiquity. "All that is left to us," he writes, "is to recommend our productions by the imitation of the Ancients: and it will be found true, that in every Age, the highest character for sense and learning has been obtain'd by those who have been most indebted to them."[33]

29   Porter (2005b).
30   Pope (1967) 7.72; see also Pope (1967) 10.394.
31   Pope (1967) 7.73.
32   Pope (1961) 7.
33   Pope (1961) 7.

Pope's translation of Homer offers therefore the paradigmatic site for the realization of the classical principle: the text in which Homer's darkness appears as a void in meaning that sustains Homer's classicalness. This void, a sign of the tension underlying Homer's fundamental contradiction as a classic, enters the translated text and shapes its antinomies. At the opening of the *Iliad* Pope writes:

> Achilles' wrath, to Greece the direful spring
> Of woes unnumber'd, heav'nly goddess, sing!
> That wrath which hurl'd to Pluto's gloomy reign
> The souls of mighty chiefs untimely slain;
> . . .
> Since great Achilles and Atrides strove,
> Such was the sovereign doom, and such the will of Jove! (1–4, 7–8)

The passage brings together within the same discourse the darkness of antiquity and the line of continuity between ancient and modern times. In his comments on the translation Pope expresses his "surprise" over Homer's call to the muse to tell him the story he was meant to have invented. So is "a Poet to be imagin'ed intirely ignorant of his Subject[?]" Pope asks, deploying an argument previously outlined by other critics. "May not Homer be allow'd the knowledge of so plain a truth, as that the will of God is fulfill'd in all things?"[34] Is Homer, in other words, unfit for being credited as the first classical author? The threat posed by the muse is twofold. On the one hand, the poet's invocation of the muse negates the modern idea of authorship as the product of individual inspiration (what Pope called Homer's power of invention). On the other hand, the role of the muse as goddess and her privileged positioning at the beginning of the poem challenges the assumed nature of the divine, which must display continuity between Homeric religion and eighteenth-century Christianity. If "nature and Homer," Pope wrote, "were the same," and thus "to copy nature is to copy [the ancients],"[35] then Homer's gods must also express the power of divinity represented by Christianity. A muse that takes the place of the author and comes to be prior to God is meaningless, Pope suggests, in terms of modern literary and Christian discourses. Hence, in the footnotes accompanying his text, Pope shakes off both threats by de-classicizing the muse's status and presenting her as perishable: she becomes the product of the distinct modes and beliefs of Homer's time. The practice of translation displays a similar tension. The use of the adjective "heavenly," the choice of the phrase "sovereign doom" to describe "the will of Jove," and the emphasis on Zeus' power effected by putting his name at the end of the passage, all assimilate the muse to Christianity. Yet the name of the muse remains in the translation as an absent voice, a lack marking the silencing of the other through which

34 Pope (1961) 84.
35 Pope (1961) 255.

modern conceptions of authorship and Christian ideas of the divine acquire their authority.

This fundamental lack, the name of the other, that makes Homer intelligible to us, brings to light a crucial link between translation and the theorization of Homer's classical status. As a practice, Pope's translation articulates what his theoretical reflection on Homer points to but never quite reaches: the absence of the moment that could designate Homer's meaning as a classic and the subsequent centrality of this absence within the discourse of classicism. As a conceptual category, translation, by occupying the in-between space between the point of origin and the point of reception, indicates the link between the *archê* of classicalness and the present this *archê* seeks to authorize. As a form of writing, the text of translation, as the analysis of Pope suggested, voices the friction between the imagined vision of the classic and the other which enters this vision as a lack that evokes classicism's struggle with its other. As a turn towards the past that unavoidably fails to reach its goal, translation finally negates an original Homeric moment outside the burden of the classical tradition. The impossible task of the translator illustrates how the experience of the loss of continuity – the modern break with antiquity – was not a means to transcend classicism, but, as this essay has argued, the foundation of Homer's classical status. Finally, as the means of designating not only the displaced moment of the classic but also the foreclosures and possibilities this moment predicated, translation becomes the paradigmatic metaphor for a reflexive reading of the Greek and Roman traditions, a history of antiquity that seeks to encounter the meaningless which it incorporates within its practice. Such a history could play a crucial role in what Patočka designated as the shaking of accepted meaning and the unfolding of embryonic possibilities[36] this shaking presents for the ethical and political role of the classics.

36 Patočka (1996) 62, 77.

13

Looking for Ligurinus

An Italian Poet in the
Nineteenth Century

Richard F. Thomas

> Tragedy can be useful; the lyric poets too are wholesome, but only if you pick out
> not just the authors but also the parts of the work: for much Greek lyric is obscene,
> and there are bits of Horace I would not want to go through in class.
>
> Quintilian 1.8.6

> I have passed over in silence those that could contribute nothing to the instruction
> or delight of the reader, and nothing to the credit of the author. Not a few are
> omitted as being repetitious, and others because they are stained by the base con-
> ditions of social life in Rome.
>
> Sir Stephen De Vere[1]

Here are two Horatian readers, having more or less the same thought, though
greatly separated in time, culture, and place. Quintilian and De Vere, whose task
it was to explain the moral uses of Latin poetry, express negative aesthetic reactions to parts of the (same) texts that form their laboratory.[2] On the other hand,
this reaction was presumably not shared by Maecenas, Augustus, Propertius, or
any number of Horace's, or Quintilian's, contemporaries, any more than it is shared
by many of us. De Vere's contemporaries, however, are a different matter, which
is why my major focus will be on nineteenth-century, ethically fastidious, reception.[3]
The coincidences and failures to coincide among these three groups (urbane ancients,

1 Explaining his omission of almost one half of the *Odes*.
2 Newman thought Horace "perhaps weaker in his own line than his immediate predecessor Catullus, a man whose disgusting impurity has marred half his poems, and who
   probably did not live to attain his full perfection" (Newman (1853) v). It is because
   of such aesthetics, and particularly the aesthetics of the erotic, that we have literally
   scores of Horace translations into English alone from 1860 to 1910, and not even a
   handful of Catulluses.
3 We must be sure not to generalize about the deadness of the nineteenth century, as
   Hardwick shows (2000a) 23–42.

fastidious ancients and moderns, tolerant contemporaries) allow a variety of intellectual processes to take place at the synchronic and diachronic level. If meaning is activated at the point of reception, then my own reading, by taking into account those of others, can through affirmation, reflection, modification, rejection, perhaps detect in the various reactions what is familiar, unfamiliar, or strange in the source text. My own interests in reception, then, are historicist, consisting in a recovery of the cultural conditions that combine with aesthetics and subjectivities, as observed in very marked readings of literature. In recovering those readings we also and necessarily focus on the gaps and on difference between our own readings and those of others, and may in the process be able to go some way towards objectifying our subjectivities.

Here translation seems to me to provide particularly productive material in that it requires the reader/translator to put into words the actual process of reading, and so calls for a fuller representation and testament of that reading than might other forms of reading and writing. If for instance we look to Dryden's Virgil, there can thus come into focus not just the gap between our own reading and that of seventeenth-century translation, but also the gap and space between the source text and the translation text, the Roman Augustan text and the English Augustan text. Such multiplication of the moments of reception in turn brings out complexities both in the text and in its tradition.

Our ability to evaluate these cultural gaps will nowhere be clearer than when the subject has become socially taboo for the world of the translating text. The tolerance of the sexually explicit that is now permitted at least in secularized corners of contemporary Western societies (is it?) creates useful reception conditions. We might look at the opening of Catullus 16 under the assumptions that (1) there is the possibility of a shared cultural outlook between (such secularized corners of) twenty-first-century translation culture and the source cultures of, say, Catullus or Horace, and that (2) there is a huge gap between these two cultures on the one hand, and that of Victorian England (at its most prudish) on the other. So, exemplifying (1) we have the opening of Catullus 16, whose delight in the obscene insult is evident in the original ("Pedicabo ego vos et irrumabo, / Aureli pathice et cinaede Furi"), as in Dorothea Wender's 1980 translation ("I'll bugger you, Aurelius Swishy-tail, / I'll shove it down your throat, Queen Furius"). I am not sure about "Swishy-tail," though the connotation is clear. At first sight we might feel a sense of enlightenment inherent in Wender's version, as compared to evasions of the actual meaning of the two verbs that characterize earlier translations, commentaries, and lexica. But that sense may also be fleeting. Perhaps something has happened (whether we call it "political correctness" or tolerance) between 1980 and 2006 that in fact makes the abusive use of "bugger" and "shove it down your throat," even in the context of a literary joke, more problematic. Or more problematic in certain "enlightened" parts of contemporary culture, while less so elsewhere? In other words the apparent urbanity of a poem such as Catullus 16 can come back to bite the hand of the reader open to its apparent urbanity.[4]

As for the gap referred to in (2) it is certainly wide, but perhaps not unbridgeable since there are exceptions, and even these are themselves subject to interference. Sir Richard Burton, translator of *Arabian Nights* and *Kama Sutra*, was an apparent exception, although even he was posthumously thwarted at least in part by the taboos of the culture against whose grain much of his work had gone. Leonard Smithers had Burton's Catullus published in 1894 (Burton died in 1890), including an opening of Poem 16 whose obscenities had been removed by Burton's wife, with the elliptical result: "I'll . . . you twain and . . ."[5] But ellipsis, editorially or otherwise supplied, like aposiopesis or other forms of euphemism, only removes obscenity from the immediate text, not from the imagination of the reader. Once we identify the masculine gender of Aurelius and Furius, it is clear, with only a pair of options as to specifics, what the speaker is threatening. The words are kept off the page but they are still made available.

The process of ellipsis is really no different from what we find in ancient reception, that is in dealing with intertextuality and allusion. The shepherds of Theocritus could occasionally be refined, and speak euphemistically.[6] But they also knew how to call a spade a spade. "When can I recall learning and hearing anything good from you?" asks Lacon at *Idyll* 5.39–40. "When I was buggering you and you were hurting; and these she-goats were bleating away as the billygoat poked them." The Virgilian reception of this insult, although contextually referring to this locus, opts for ellipsis: Damoetas: "we know both who was . . . you, goats looking sidelong, and in what chapel, with the easy-going Nymphs getting a laugh out of it" ("novimus et qui te, transversa tuentibus hircis / et quo, set faciles Nymphae risere, sacello"; *Eclogue* 3.8–9). Virgil's modification caused a refinement in the genre, but we still have no doubt about what Damoetas saw or says he saw.

---

4   Robinson (1997) 136 captures the cultural gap that may be seen between, e.g., "enlightened" baby boomer tolerance for abusive obscenity and "Gen-X" cultural deconstruction of the same. He is reacting to the praise by Venuti (1994) 88 of the version of John Nott's seventeenth-century translation of Catullus' poem. Venuti had noted that that version's "abusiveness (even if homophobic by late twentieth century standards) conveyed Catullus' Roman assumption that a male who submitted to anal or oral intercourse – whether willingly or not – was humiliated whereas 'the perpetrator himself was neither demeaned nor disgraced.'" If we do not share that Roman assumption, how can we translate, or even read, Catullus 16, except as a museum piece perhaps?

5   Gaisser (2001) 136–7.

6   On pastoral euphemism, and the lack of it, see Clausen (1994) 94–5, also with reference to Adams (1981).

It is really only full omission that works, complete omission of the entire poem, or sufficient parts of it, as in F. W. Cornish's 1912 Loeb translation, which prints only the opening six of Catullus' fourteen lines (the lemma reads "XVI (a fragment)"), but similarly substitutes the three dots (rather than Burton's pronouns, future tense, and addresses with appropriate epithet) and for their opening: ". . . who have supposed me to be immodest, on account of my verses, because they are rather voluptuous. For the sacred poet ought to be chaste himself, his verses need not be." For the Latinless the obscenity is gone but at the same time Cornish's poem has truly become a fragment, incomprehensible.

This chapter, then, will examine the ways translation functions across cultures with radically differing expectations and tolerances regarding sexual license and sexual taboos. As for theoretical models, on one, by applying the concepts and terminology of Lawrence Venuti and others, we might seek to explore this aspect of translation on the axis between the two poles of domestication and foreignization. The former wrenches the source text into the contemporary culture of the translation language, and in the process carries over, represents, and renews the original, even though we may be less happy calling it "Catullus" or "Martial," and it is perhaps a preferable mode from an aesthetic point of view. Foreignizing translation somehow tries to bring the contemporary reader back to the culture of the original – a process that is often neither possible nor desirable if our eye is on poetry and poetic meanings. How, for instance, does one represent the relative archaism of Aeschylus vis-à-vis Euripides without implying that the latter is a part of contemporary Anglophone culture, the former resident somehow in an earlier Anglophone culture? It is likely that a foreignizing translation of Aeschylus – whose linguistic register necessarily implies the existence of Sophocles or Euripides, even when we are not talking or thinking of Sophocles or Euripides – will never take us back to an actual Aeschylean cultural context, precisely because that context was dismantled by what happened to Athenian culture, and with it to the language of Attic tragedy, in the course of the fifth century. On this model foreign or domestic translation of Aeschylus may never be fully possible.

And what happens with domestication when differing codes of morality, particularly differing sexual mores, come into play? In such circumstances domestication may first of all be an impossibility. So for instance in nineteenth-century translation of some of the *Epodes*, one can practice domestication only by euphemism or even bowdlerizing ("in which those words and expressions are omitted which cannot with propriety be read aloud in a family," as Dr. Bowdler put it in 1818). Here a domesticating reception would function as a severely violent hermeneutic act, precisely by denying that hermeneutics, and even reading, is possible. The result would be nothing. On the other hand a foreignizing of what is morally problematic will be confronted by the same problems as its apparent opposite, domestication. Sometimes such foreignizing is literally achieved, as when obscene Greek is represented by literally precise obscene Latin (so Gow's Theocritus or the Loeb of the Greek Anthology), so that only the Latin-reading contemporary reader, for whom the foreign is assumed to be familiar (or domestic), is capable of comprehension.[7]

A second way into this topic, and still fruitful in my view, looks to John Dryden's tripartite division of translation: metaphrase, paraphrase, and free imitation. Metaphrase involves "turning an author word by word, and line by line, from one language into another"; paraphrase is defined as "translation with latitude, where the author is kept in view by the translator, so as never to be lost, and his words are not so strictly followed as his sense; and that too is admitted to be amplified, but not altered" (*Preface to Ovid's Epistles* (1680)); in the third mode, that of imitation, "the translator (if now he has not lost that name) assumes the liberty, not only to vary from the words and sense, but to forsake them both as he sees occasion; and taking only some general hints from the original, to run division on the groundwork, as he pleases."[8] Dryden's own preference was for the middle way, although I have argued that he so mistakes, so *alters*, the sense of Virgil in his 1697 *Aeneis* that he is often a de facto free imitator rather than a paraphraser.[9] Charles Martindale, who has well expressed the problematic relationship between paraphrase and imitation, also argues for the superiority of metaphrase, and specifically in a Horatian context.[10] He takes as his test cases *Odes* 1.5, the Pyrrha Ode, specifically preferring the metaphrastic version of Milton, to the "imitation" of Cowley and "paraphrase" of Fanshawe: "I find it difficult to be altogether temperate in my admiration for Milton's version."[11] I would agree, but there is something very marked about that version, with its explanatory note which, to anticipate Dryden, announces "I am a metaphrase":

> *The Fifth Ode of Horace, Lib. I*
>   *Quis multa gracilis te puer in Rosa,*
> Rendred almost word for word without Rhyme according to the
> Latin Measure, as near as the Language will permit.

The problem, it seems to me, is that such metaphrastic versions are and always will be few and far between. We will in due course come to another, also mentioned by Martindale, Ben Jonson's version of *Odes* 4.1. But first I would ask, under what circumstances can a linguistic metaphrase be culturally impossible, and when it is impossible can paraphrase or imitation come to the rescue, or will these

---

7 For a good treatment of some of these issues see Venuti (1998) ch. 4, "The Formation of Cultural Identities," 67–87, a nuancing of his earlier writing on domestication and foreignization.

8 The essay is now quite familiar, and anthologized, for instance by Schulte and Biguenet (1992) 17–31; see 17 for the general definition.

9 Thomas (2001) 122–89.

10 Martindale (1984a); also (1993) 76–84.

11 Martindale (1984a) 54.

too be impossible? An examination of this question in the context of the nineteenth-century reception of *Odes* 4.1 and 4.10 is revealing from the diachronic perspective of the history of scholarship, but it may also lead us back to the synchronic reading of Horatian poetry, with reception indistinguishable (as often) from interpretation.

The delicately erotic Horatian lyric (such as the ending of *Odes* 1.9) will generally survive even in a culturally severe setting, while the truly obscene will simply disappear. So *Epodes* 8 and 11 are simply omitted from the translations of Sewell (1850), Martin (1860), and Lytton (1869). It was not always so, and Christopher Smart's 1767 translation in fact gives access (albeit euphemistically) to Horace's attacks on these sexually aggressive old women, although he goes beyond euphemism into obscurity at the end of *Epode* 8: "quod ut superbo provoces ab inguine / ore allaborandum est tibi" ("but for you to raise an appetite, in a stomach that is nice, it is necessary that you exert every art of language"). Precisely in the years Horace was writing these epodes the future ruler of the world, Gaius Octavian, produced his obscene and cruelly witty attack on Antony's wife Fulvia (ap. Martial 11.20), a poem as obscene as any in its age. Such material is culturally untranslatable, and the gap between pre-Christian Rome and Victorian England (as well as many other cultures, our own included) results in the silencing of the former.

The *Epodes* are in fact not much translated in the nineteenth century, while English versions of the *Odes* proliferate, sometimes more than two per year. Horace the lyricist was beloved, in part because of the ethical odes; so Newman (1853) in the preface to his translation: "I hardly know that it is a recommendation of his poetry to remark, that in past generations the sermons of half our divines might seem to have been borrowed from it."[12] It is therefore interesting to observe the few instances in which the generally translatable lyric voice "lapses." Let us consider *Odes* 1.6.17–32. Between reflection on the gods' demonstrated displeasure at Roman neglect of religion (1–16) and contemplation of the old, now lost, Roman virtues that were once her strength (33–48), Horace pinpoints the problem; moral values have been torn to shreds:

> fecunda culpae saecula nuptias
> primum inquinavere et genus et domos:
>   hoc fonte derivata clades
>   in patriam populumque fluxit.   20
> motus doceri gaudet Ionicos
> matura virgo et fingitur artibus
>   iam nunc et incestos amores
>   de tenero meditatur ungui.
> mox iuniores quaerit adulteros   25

---

12 Newman (1853) vi.

> inter mariti vina neque eligit
> cui donet impermissa raptim
> gaudia luminibus remotis,
> sed iussa coram non sine conscio
> surgit marito, seu vocat institor   30
> seu navis Hispanae magister,
> dedecorum pretiosus emptor.
> non his iuventus orta parentibus
> infecit aequor sanguine Punico
> Pyrrhumque et ingentem cecidit   35
> Antiochum Hannibalemque dirum . . .
>
> *Odes* 3.6.17–36

The central three stanzas become quite explicit as the Roman *virgo* begins her downhill slide by learning morally corrupting Ionian (that is, eastern) dance steps (21–2), then contemplates love affairs (23–4), graduating after her marriage to adulterous affairs with younger men behind the back of her drunk husband (25–6), and finally offers herself indiscriminately, her husband complicit, to any shopkeeper or Spanish skipper (26–32). Not a single word is offensive, and everything is more or less euphemistic or paraphrastic. But clearly the bride's extramarital activity, the husband's complicity, the lower class and racially defined status of the adulterers ("institor . . . navis Hispanae magister"), all of these details constituted an assault on the male Victorian mind. Conington (1863) responded by omitting all twelve lines, and covering up the gap, reducing twenty lines to six:

> An evil age erewhile debased
> The marriage bed, the race, the home;
> Thence rose the flood whose waters waste
> The nation and the name of Rome.
> Not such their birth, who stain'd for us
> The sea with Punic carnage red.

Staining the sea with Punic blood is acceptable, for Conington's is an age of empire, but the destruction of family values is another matter. Conington is followed in this procedure by De Vere (1888) and Aglen (1896). One interesting phenomenon in translation of this period has to do with the traces of the offending matter: while Conington presents a seamless translation which suppresses the offending and omitted material, other versions at least give us a lacuna, similar to the ellipsis we noted in the treatment of bucolic obscenity. So for instance Sewell (1850):[13]

---

13 Likewise the translation of Du Faur (1906).

> Teeming with crime, hath age on age
> Our bridals first, and lineage,
> And household hearths been sullying:
> And, streaming down from this well-spring,
> Swept like a flood hath desolation
> In our fathers' land and nation
>
> . . . .
> . . . .
> . . . .
>
> Not from such parents sprung as these
> Did our young manhood stain the seas
> With Punic blood, and slew for us
> Pyrrhus and huge Antiochus,
> And Hannibal cursed.

What is lost here is the poem itself, gone along with the four-step progressive decline of the *virgo*. This decline is essential to the meaning of the poem, which ends with the famous recapitulation: "aetas parentum peior avis tulit / nos nequiores, mox daturos / progeniem vitiosiorem" ("the age of our parents, worse than our grandparents', has produced a more worthless group in us, soon to deliver a still more depraved progeny").

Others were able to confront our corrupted Roman woman; Newman and Lytton translate the lines quite openly. For them the issue has to do with sexual orientation, a very different matter, and one that brings us to *Odes* 4.1. Horace there returns to lyric, having for a few years eschewed the genre in favor of the general ethics of the first book of *Epistles*. Now some 50 years old, the poet resists the advances of Venus, so coupling a *recusatio* of erotic lyric with an entry back into a genre that is now to be infiltrated by the mature Augustus and the Julio-Claudian princes. The ode ends with a surprise ending, with the poet in his dreams pursuing not Cinara or the women of his earlier lyric, but the male Ligurinus.

> me nec femina nec puer
>   iam nec spes animi credula mutui   30
> nec certare iuvat mero
>   nec vincire novis tempora floribus.
> sed cur heu, Ligurine, cur
>   manat rara meas lacrima per genas?
> cur facunda parum decoro   35
>   inter verba cadit lingua silentio?
> nocturnis ego somniis
>   iam captum teneo, iam volucrem sequor
> te per gramina Martii
>   campi, te per aquas, dure, volubilis.   40

My interests here are first in observing the way the surprise ending is received and treated in a culture that loves Horace but cannot easily have him dreaming of Ligurinus; in addition this scrutiny of the translation reception may point the way to other hermeneutical ventures, including reconstructing a point of reception coinciding in time with Horace's composition.

Charles Martindale has referred to Ben Jonson's metaphrastic version of this poem.[14] Let us see how his version deals with the close:

> Me now nor wench, nor wanton boy,
> Delights, nor credulous hope of mutual joy,
>   Nor care I now healths to propound;
> Or with fresh flowers to girt my temple round.
>   But why, o why, my Ligurine,
> Flow my thin tears, down these pale cheeks of mine?
>   Or why my well-graced words among,
> With an uncomely silence fails my tongue?
>   Hard-hearted, I dream every night
> I hold thee fast! But fled hence, with the light,
>   Whether in Mars his field thou be,
> Or Tiber's winding streams, I follow thee.
>   Ben Jonson, *Underwoods 86 (Horace)*

The Latin of Horace's poem has two gender-markers (in addition to the comprehensive opening "me nec femina nec puer"): the short final -e of the masculine vocative *Ligurine* (that is, not a parallel to Chloe, Lyce, etc.), and the inflexion of *captum*. While the gender of Jonson's Ligurine (rhymes with "mine") is not really in doubt (and he is preceded by "wanton boy") the way is shown to others, who would be able to transform or at least leave the gender ambiguous:

> Sewell (1850)
>   Me neither **damsel** now,
>   Nor the trustful hope of responsive love . . .
>   But why, Alas!
>   Why, **Ligurine**, o'er my cheeks is welling
>   The slow intermitting tear?

> Newman (1853)
>   Me no longer **sex or youth**
>   Moves, . . .
>   Ah! But why? say, **Ligurine**, why
>   Trickles down my cheeks the stealthy tear?

---

14 Martindale (1984a) 54.

Conington (1863)
> I can relish **love** no more . . .
> Ah! But why, my **Ligurine**,
> Steal trickling tear-drops down my wasted cheek?

So in all three cases the gender certainty of *puer* has been lost or obscured, while the name Ligurinus has become trisyllabic "Ligurine" but visually it is like Chloe, Lyce, Lalage, et al., and the gender of *captum* can be blurred in translation.

The most violent way of proceeding is excision, particularly at poem's end, since (unlike the case of 3.6) we do not return to the story. Lytton (1869) is a case in point:

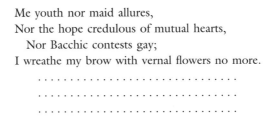

> Me youth nor maid allures,
> Nor the hope credulous of mutual hearts,
>   Nor Bacchic contests gay;
> I wreathe my brow with vernal flowers no more.
>
> . . . .
> . . . .
> . . . .

"Youth" is slightly ambiguous, though coupled with "maid" points towards a male individual (unlike Newman's "sex or youth"), but since the poem ends with disavowal of interest, even a gendered "youth" can stay in there, and we note that *iam* which came right after *puer*, belongs now to the wreathing of the final line ("no more"), so perhaps Horace is saying he never was interested in the male. More importantly Ligurinus, along with Horace's erotic dream (and the reversal it brings), are gone, so the recusational attitude of the first part is all that is left – which ruins the poem of course. William Gladstone, who on retiring from office in 1894 found solace in translating Horace, followed the practice of Lytton:

Gladstone (1894)
> Me nothing moves; nor maid nor boy,
> Nor hope of friendship's mutual joy;
> In bouts of wine I count not now,
> Nor bind with fresh-cut flowers my brow.

"Nor maid nor boy" keeps the possibility in, but Ligurinus and the dream are gone from his ending too, replaced by a footnote that draws attention to the omission: "The concluding lines of the Ode are purposely omitted" – which doubtless sent his readers scurrying to locate them elsewhere. Moving into the twentieth century we find the Australian Du Faur (1906) ending with unambiguously non-gendered "youth" representing *puer* (while *femina* has become "pleasure," also avoiding gender), and similar excision, but no asterisks, and no footnote:

> Me no more pleasure now
>   Youth, or fond hopes of mutual sympathy,
>   Can give, – nor strife in cups, and rivalry,
> Nor fresh flowers on my brow.

Otherwise, following the First World War the poem is generally allowed to end as Horace ended it, with the notable exception of Dunsany (1947) who ends oddly:

> But me no woman pleases now
>   Nor boy, nor hope of mutual trust,
> Nor to bind roses on my brow
> Where wine and women are discussed.

He cannot resist a parenthesis: "(*As a convinced Unionist and, usually, an admirer of Horace, I am very reluctant to prefer Mr. Gladstone to him, but I do so on this occasion, and I follow Mr. Gladstone in not translating the unpleasant last lines of this ode*)."

Two issues complicate this particular example, having to do with intertextual aspects of reception-translation. First of all, in other cases translators could just omit the offending poem, but 4.1 is not just any poem, for the book can scarcely begin without it.[15] There is, moreover, that other poem, 4.10, projecting forward to the time when Ligurinus has become less erotically appealing. This poem *can* be dispensed with, and that is the course taken by a number of translators (Conington, Lytton, Du Faur, and Aglen, for instance). Alternatively, the gender of Ligurinus can be obscured in that poem too, as occurs in the brilliantly violent version of Martin (1860):

> To a Cruel Beauty
> Ah, cruel, cruel still,
>   And yet divinely fair,
> When Time with fingers chill
>   Shall thin the wavy hair,
> Which now in many a wanton freak
> Around thy shoulders flows,
> When fades the bloom, which on thy cheek
>   Now shames the blushing rose;
>
> Ah, then as in thy glass
>   Thou gazest in dismay,
> Thou'l't cry "Alas! Alas!
>   Why feel I not today,

---

15 See Murray (1985) for the (unlikely) view that the book was intended to begin with the more "Augustan" ode, 4.15.

> As in my maiden bloom, when I
>   Unmoved heard lovers moan;
> Or, now that I would win them, why
>   Is all my beauty flown?"

Thinning hair is generally but not necessarily a male attribute; the fading of the
bloom on the cheek, however, is a definite feminization, compared to the Latin,
where the aging Ligurinus will be distressed to look on the reflection of his "shaggy
face" ("faciem . . . hispidam"), while "in my maiden bloom" is a violent regen-
dering. Martin alludes to the deliberate tampering in the preface to his second
edition: "In a few instances where, for obvious reasons, a literal reproduction was
not desirable, as in the 25th Ode of the First, and the 10th Ode of the Fourth
Books, and in occasional passages elsewhere, the translator has not hesitated to
make such deviations from the text as are required by the purer morals of the
present day."[16]

Likewise the name may be dropped (as occurs in Aglen (1896)), and so the
gender issue finessed. This had already been the recourse of Alexander Pope
(*Imitations of Horace*, 1737). Pope's version is strongly domesticating, for
instance replacing the Campus Martius with the Mall and the Canal, and both in
its essence and in the title he gives it, it is at the opposite pole from metaphrase,
that is, free imitation:[17]

> For me the vernal Garlands bloom no more.
>   Adieu! Fond hope of mutual fire,
> The still-believing, still-renew'd desire:
> Adieu! The heart-expanding bowl,
> And all the kind deceivers of the soul!
> – But why? ah tell me, ah too dear!
> Steals down my cheek th' involuntary Tear?
> Why words so flowing, thoughts so free,
> Stop, or turn nonsense at one glance of Thee?
> Thee, drest in Fancy's airy beam,
> Absent I follow thro' th' extended Dream,
> Now, now I seize, I clasp thy charms,
> And now you burst, (ah cruel!) from my arms,
> And swiftly shoot along the Mall,
> Or softly glide by the Canal.
> Now shown by Cynthia's silver Ray,
> And now, on rolling Waters snatch'd away.

---

16 Martin (1860) xxxiii.
17 As throughout: *sub regno Cinarae* becomes "As in the gentle reign of my Queen Anne,"
    while Paullus Maximus is "Murray."

This ultimate act of domestication is also an act of distortion and misrepresentation, and aesthetically appealing as it is, it can be considered a translation only if by that we mean an absolute cultural carrying over.

A peculiar form of free imitation is to be found in the doggerel of Kipling, who uses humor to defuse the cultural "difficulties" of Horace. He has "versions" of 4.1 and 4.10, which I include partly as curiosities, partly to show another way of dealing with the culturally problematic:

4.1

Venus moves me no more.
I can look without heat on a whore:
But I'm learning as most men of sin do,
That, when love flies out of the door,
Perversion comes in at the window.

4.10

Kipling (Charles Carrington)
This is the Knowledge that comes to us after –
   The Chance has been missed –
Filling Gehenna with populous laughter
   For Maidens unkissed.
Oh Worm that returns!
Oh Fire that burns!
Oh Folly that yearns!
Had I wist – had I wist – had I wist!

Affinity to Greek epigram also provides grounds for defence. The name of Ligurinus is not to be found in Lord Lytton's 1869 version, but he still feels the need to "defend" Horace: "This book, indeed, only contains two love poems besides the first [whose ending he curtailed] – viz. the tenth and the eleventh; and one is glad to think that the tenth (omitted in the translation) was merely an artistic imitation or translation of the Greek." So it is that John Marshall (1907), Rector of Royal High School in Edinburgh, does translate 4.1 and 4.10 almost metaphrastically, but he also writes in his introduction:

The omission by Conington and others of certain odes or parts of odes, which deal with an evil that is always with us, has given the impression, entirely erroneous and unjust, that Horace was a licentious poet. His voice, as those who choose to read will I think find for themselves, is practically invariable for virtue and clean living; where there appears to be here or there some falling away, as in the Ligurinus ode, this seems to me to be no more than a concession of an aesthetic kind to the standard in these matters left to him by his Greek exemplars. Such compositions, I believe, represent no real tendency to, or taste for, evil in the poet himself.[18]

18 Marshall (1907) viii.

And the most elaborate version of this rationalizing comes with the version of Garnsey (1907):

> "Ligurinus," like "Phyllis" (IV.11), etc., is pure *apparatus lyricus*. The subject intro-
> duced by this name may be dismissed in a few words. It was viewed in the same
> light as other irregular connection. Freely talked about but a scandal if indulged in
> openly . . . Horace's Greek models had long before familiarized the topic, and this
> fact probably explains its introduction, so strange to our ideas, in a prefatory Ode
> like the present. If we look back at I.32, this becomes clear . . . Had Alcaeus never
> celebrated Lycus of the dark eyes and hair, we should probably not have heard any-
> thing from Horace of "Ligurinus." . . .[19]

The translator is here transformed more fully into an interpreter, as reception, conditioned fundamentally by the translation culture's morality, nevertheless is enabled by hermeneutics to produce a metaphrase (the end of 4.1 is there in Garnsey, and in 4.10 Ligurinus looks at his "hirsute mask"). Horace is simply posing as Alcaeus, so the "love that dare not speak its name" does precisely that, since it does not belong to our sympathetic friend Horace, but is part of the "Greek" tradition.[20]

This focus and anxiety about the ode indeed take us back to the poem itself, and to the fact that it *is* an oddity, not in terms of value judgment, but in terms of Horatian practice. The nineteenth-century obsession with Ligurinus causes a scrutiny under which his actual identity becomes suspect, since his presence, regardless of Horace's lifestyle or orientation, is poetically un-Horatian. Cinara, with whom the poem begins, and Ligurinus here at the end, take us back to synchronic possibilities, to Horace the allusive, Callimachean poet signaling with these names his return to sympotic/erotic poetry. For *kinara* means "artichoke," and Gregson Davis suggests a sympotic nuance to the name since Alcaeus fr. 347[21] urges sympotic activity when "the artichoke is in bloom" (4: *anthei de skolumos*).[22] But the signification may be more erotic than sympotic, since at that time (in the heat of midsummer), as Alcaeus continues, "women are most lustful" (4: *nun de gunaikes miarotatai*), a condition shared by Cinara at *Epistles* 1.7.28 (*protervae*). Likewise Davis sees a sympotic significance in the name of Ligurinus, who may be related to *ligurrio* and *liguritio* ("fondness for dainties"), as is appropriate to the *convivium*.[23] I suggest Horace may have different "licking" in mind for Ligurinus: the line from the Atellan farce, applied to the proclivities of Tiberius (Suetonius,

19   Garnsey (1907) 23.
20   Shackleton Bailey (1982) 67–78 has well deconstructed this reading of 4.1, particu-
     larly the reading of Williams (1962).
21   Lobel and Page (1955).
22   Davis (1991) 69.
23   Davis (1991) 65–71.

Life of Tiberius 45: *hircum vetulum capreis naturam ligurire* ("the old goat licks the private parts of the does")) suggests the antiquity of the meaning, and may be supported by Catullus fr. 2: *de meo ligurrire libido est.*[24] Which would take us back to the world of the *Epodes*, and the younger Horace's instructions to the old woman: *ore allaborandum est tibi*. And at the risk of displaying my own Victorianism, that is a good place to stop.

---

24 See *Thesaurus Linguae Latinae* s.v. *ligurrio* 1396.79–81.

14

Foucault's Antiquity

James I. Porter

> The idea of the *bios* as a material for an aesthetic piece of art . . . is something which fascinates me.
>
> Foucault[1]

I   Introduction

The French philosopher and cultural historian Michel Foucault is not usually aligned with the classical tradition, an odd lapse if there ever was one: he is as much a part of the tradition as he is one of its more active interpreters – or, as Foucault would prefer to call himself, a "genealogist."[2] So, the questions of how Foucault received antiquity and how we should receive Foucault's antiquity are perhaps best addressed by reinserting Foucault into the classical tradition he uses for his own reception of the past. Foucault's grasp of Greece and Rome is not direct or immediate by any stretch of the imagination; it stands squarely in the grip of a number of traditions of classical reception. My interest in the present essay will be in recovering some of the strands of reception that seem to color Foucault's reading of one particular aspect of antiquity in his last decade of writing, namely, modern views of ancient subjectivity and subject-formation. One aim of this essay will be to underscore this dimension of Foucault's later thought, and to show how surprisingly close to pre-postmodern and classicizing readers of the past the presumed postmodern Foucault in fact stands. A suggestion of indebtedness will not lie far off. By contrast, contemporary readings of Foucault, whether critical or adulatory, tend to ignore this inheritance, and they do so at their peril. A

Many thanks to the editors of this volume, and especially to Charles Martindale, for comments on an earlier version of this essay, and also to Miriam Leonard.

1   Foucault (1983) 235.
2   For an exception, see n. 43 below.

further aim of this essay will be to reexamine the contours of Foucault's history of the self and to attempt to cast these in a new and different light.

Self-fashioning is the contemporary and attractive idea, most recently promoted by Foucault, that subjects are not found in the world but are invented, that they can take possession of their fabricated lives by becoming their own authors, which is to say by applying their own agency to themselves and by giving shape to their lives, thus affirming their (fictive, constructed, self-fashioned) selves through what is, in the final analysis, an aesthetic practice of self-making and sublimation. The body is one of the basic *loci* of this art of self-construction; the will to change is its instrument. And on the Foucauldian theory, the way forward to a new, daring, and postmodern form of subjectivity is by way of a return to what is held to be the classical model of self-production, the Greek and then Roman "art of life" (*technê tou biou*), which is the art of "exercising a perfect mastery over one-self" – in other words (which are Foucault's), an "aesthetics [and 'ascetics'] of existence," freely constructed within a system of relations of power that are enabling and constraining at one and the same time.

As this brief encapsulation ought to make plain, the promissory note of self-fashioning is a tall order indeed. It is also (I believe) a barely coherent concept that in Foucault's hands probably tries to explain too much all at once: pagan and postmodern subjectivities; the contingency of all history; historical change, conceived as rupture (by claiming that contingency somehow releases subjects from necessity); the artfulness of identity (which leaves wide open the question of how to decide *which kind or genre* of art identity is meant to embody); the history of sexuality *and* the history of subjectivity (while often leaving uncertain which of these two histories is in focus at any given moment); and so on. I want to expose some of the vagaries of Foucault's thinking in these areas by making three points.

First, Foucault's project of reclaiming subjecthood is indebted in various ways to the classical ideals of the modern Enlightenment, which advocated its own form of self-fashioning or self-cultivation (*Bildung* and *Selbstbildung*) modeled on an equally unfocused and *aestheticized* notion of "the Greeks" – one, in other words, that turned them into works of art, a notion to be explored in the third section below in connection with Humboldt, Winckelmann, and Nietzsche. Second, Foucault's self-advertised and much celebrated alignment with Nietzsche is para-doxical. (The French title to volume 1 contains an overtly Nietzschean echo: *La volonté de savoir*, while subsequent essays and interviews bring out the connec-tion even more explicitly.[3]) Nietzsche would have been at the very least thoroughly ambivalent towards, if not sharply critical of, Foucault's theoretical tendency, which is to treat self-making as the product of self-denial, in other words, of ascesis – in Foucault's terms, the product of "techniques of the self," which in pagan anti-quity were carried out through "harsh" yet "subtly" articulated regimes of rigor,

---

3   See, for instance, Foucault (1983) 237, and the whole of that essay ("On the Genea-logy of Ethics"), and Foucault (1988a) 250–1: "I am fundamentally Nietzschean."

abstention, austerity, renunciation, and the like (2.25, 253).[4] Third, the effect of Foucault's history is to render classical antiquity a latent form of *Christian asceticism*.

My questions, then, are these: Is Foucault practicing a form of *classical idealism*? (By this phrase I mean to label the modern worship of the classical ideal.) Can his project be said to be Nietzschean? Is his theory even coherent? In order to assess these questions, I will begin by narrating Foucault's history in its ideal lineaments (the story he wants to tell). Then I will consider the story that Foucault actually tells, at least on a different reconstruction of it (namely, my own). Finally, I will turn to some of the complicating modern sources of the Foucauldian self. I should mention that this essay is conceived as part of a larger reassessment of the role of the classical ideal in contemporary views of the classical world (a book-length study to be titled "What is 'Classical' about Classical Antiquity?"). But I hope it can also stand on its own as a first attempt to trace the modern genealogy of the ideal of self-fashioning modeled on antiquity and to help put in a clearer light some of the implications of this genealogy for Foucault and for others in his wake.

II   Genealogies of the Modern Self

When Foucault declared the (imminent) death of man[5] no one could have predicted "man's" resurrection in a theory of the cultivated self in the West. My interest is not in the self-refuting claim that the Subject is or is about to be dead, but in the obsessiveness with which Foucault's later writings, consistent with his earlier ones, pursue the study of the Subject's birth, formation, and transformation.[6] To help Foucault rhyme with himself, we might say that his writings trace nothing but the prolonged "death" of the Subject, or rather its mortification – ambivalently, to be sure, and with all the power of a riveting fascination. On the other hand, the Subject, for Foucault, just is born of a mortification – of the flesh, of desire, of its capacity to act freely without constraints of any kind (even if these things – the body, desire, freedom – are produced just in order to be constrained). And so his claim about the death of man is literal and paradoxically self-negating

---

4   References in the body of the text are to the English translation of Foucault's three-volume *History of Sexuality* (Foucault (1980, 1985, 1986)).

5   Foucault (1966), esp. 398.

6   For the equivalence of "the death of man" with "the death of the Subject," see Foucault (1989) 61. To be sure, Foucault remains hostile to the modern project of humanism and its attendant subjectivities. Nevertheless, by retaining the ideas of "subject" and "self," and indeed by providing a kind of "humanistic image of ancient thought" (Cambiano (1988) 144), Foucault's final project installs within itself an odd dissonance that deserves to be explored.

all in one. His final writings, especially his three-volume and never completed *History of Sexuality*, are proof of this. And the recently released Collège de France lectures, *L'Herméneutique du sujet* (2001), confirm this reading.

Listen to some of Foucault's most influential readers and you will hear a different story. *The History of Sexuality* has given credence, if not the full impetus, to a trend in scholarship that has celebrated the unqualified powers of self-making, self-fashioning, and self-performance. This "affirmationist" tendency celebrates the vital processes of the production of subjectivities ("subjectivation"), while eschewing its negative downsides ("subjection"). Its main exponents in philosophy are Judith Butler, Richard Rorty, and Alexander Nehamas – perhaps not coincidentally, all three of these American, possibly reflecting a prototypically American ideal of self-fulfillment and self-realization.[7] In literary studies its exponents are the New Historicists (starting with Stephen Greenblatt's *Renaissance Self-fashioning* (1980)). In history and anthropology, the examples are too numerous to name, but in classical circles Paul Veyne and David Halperin come to mind.[8] Thanks to these powerful interpreters of Foucault, the contemporary academy has given rise to a "Foucault-effect" that has taken on a life of its own – in different flavors, to be sure, but more or less reducible to the proposition, "subjects/sexuality are culturally constructed, not naturally given," but with the additional historical nuance, which shows that for Foucault cultural construction is (perhaps surprisingly) itself a *modern* construct, but by no means an inevitable one: "the modern subject is culturally constructed, while the ancient subject is self-constructed."

Foucault's genealogy of the modern self has more than a historical dimension: it also has a moral dimension. The contingency of sexual norms bespeaks vast freedoms, a kind of unheard-of malleability and plasticity of subjectivity, if not a complete emancipation from normativity. This line of approach is known among classicists as a mode of existence "before sexuality," when sexual behaviors were fluid, not essence-defining and not yet divided by desire and its repression, and among postmodern exponents as an emancipatory "self-fashioning," in which identities are contingent, fluid, "per/formative," and seemingly convertible at will (again). Outside of classics, we find statements like the following, some "sexed" and others not, in a quasi-Foucauldian spirit: identities can be signified not only through the conscious "marking" of performative boundaries (through "citation", theatrical miming, and "rendering [them] hyperbolic"), but also through "the resignification of norms," by "*establishing* a position where there was none" before;[9] "life is literature" and autobiographies are (optimally) a work of art representing "an

---

7   Many thanks to Charles Martindale for underscoring this last point.
8   See Veyne (1988a, 1988b); Veyne in Davidson (1997); Halperin (1990); also Halperin, Winkler, and Zeitlin (1990); for a second-wave response, see Larmour, Miller, and Platter (1998).
9   Butler (1993).

art of living";[10] subjects need to explore "the forms of ascesis, the spiritual exercises of ethical self-fashioning, by which modern subjects can achieve transcendence";[11] or finally, the "*Risiko-Gesellschaft*," or risk society, is redefining the very conditions of existence, with its heady vision of a global "post-work society" and its new subjective identities, whereby individuals are "*Lebensästheten*," "artists of and in their own life . . . who shape and stage themselves and their life as an aesthetic product" with a view to (indeed, tailored in response to) the new market dimensions – no longer mass markets but "niche- or mini-markets": here, in this last instance, self-realization is unabashedly (and frighteningly) a question of "self-*exploitation*."[12] Beck's vision gives a political contour to the Foucauldian dynamic, and possibly helps place it in a larger, global context, well beyond that of an academic fashion. Or else it marks the final global pretension of that postmodern fashion.

But surely there is something wrong with these extensions of the theory, whatever other attractions and virtues they may have to offer. Foucault, after all, was the first to decry the 'liberationist' theology of the Subject. The whole of *The History of Sexuality* volume 1 stridently warns against all such illusions, as do the parting words of that book: "The irony of th[e] deployment [of the modern regime of sexuality, with its 'austere monarchy of sex'] is in having us believe that our 'liberation' is in the balance" (1.159). The absolution from certain sexual normativities, Foucault seems to be saying, is pursued and paid for by forgetting about the concomitance of other enabling normativities – as if (it too often is made to appear) the absence of a code of sex in antiquity wasn't bought at the cost of a host of other constraints, codifications, regulations, and encumbrances that may have been, in their own way, just as dear or deplorable. To overlook these is to fall prey to historical blindness. It is also to fail to read Foucault, who later added, "and then I discovered . . . that this pagan ethics was *not* at all as liberal, tolerant, and so on, as it was supposed to be."[13] Subjects aren't freed by self-fashioning; they are subjected to severe and austere constraints, which are the conditions of their birth and existence as subjects.

It is true that on the surface and at times Foucault seems to point in the same direction as Butler, Rorty, Nehamas, and others go. Nevertheless, there are deep continuities between the first and the last two volumes, which is to say between the ancient and modern regimes of subjectivity that not even Foucault can deny. In the roughest of terms, Foucault is tracing the emergence of the Western Subject ("the genealogy of the subject"). What he would like to demonstrate is the

10 Nehamas (1985, 1998); "every human life [is] a poem" and a matter of "self-creation" (Rorty (1989)).
11 Halperin (1995) 102, but see 118 for a more politicized and plausible reading of Foucault's thesis.
12 Beck (1998).
13 Foucault (1983) 230; emphasis added.

existence of two distinct historical forms of subjection and "subjectivation" (*asujettisement*): modern prohibitory economies of behavioral norms contrast with ancient modes of "problematization," of "moral solicitude," that is, with a regulation (distribution, usage) of pleasures and anxieties; the Christian (and later) hermeneutics of the self (designed to locate the truth of desire, of a desiring self) contrasts with an organization of loosely knit practices and behaviors (of which desire is just one element). In a word, modern subjection contrasts with ancient self-subjection (2.5, 10, 15–20, 26). And yet, despite all, there is a tragic, teleo-logical impetus to this history. The roots of anxieties in antiquity are *not yet formed as prohibitions*, as history assures us they eventually will be. Meanwhile, adding to the melancholy of this history is the fact that the anxieties seem to be fundamentally of the same nature as their later counterparts. It remains to decide whether the tragedy consists in the formation of a *sexual* Subject, or in the formation of *a subject of prohibitions simpliciter*, of which the sexual Subject is but the most spectacular example.

The trouble is that Foucault's history, which would trace ruptures, in fact traces continuities.[14] On Foucault's vision classical antiquity does not merely lay the ground for the Christian ascetic Subject but anticipates it almost completely – in an ascetics of the self that gives birth to the modern Subject.[15] In the place of a lacunose history of seemingly random epistemes, what Foucault's history reveals instead is an inexorable "intensification," a continuity, a logic, and a "destined" neces-sity. And in the place of a history of sexuality, it reveals the history of the emergence of the ascetic, self-disciplining Subject, a Subject that results from the (self-)imposition of a "style," one that entails tremendous constraints, abnegations, denials, and abstentions, what Foucault calls "techniques of the self." The self models itself through practices of self-observation and self-surveillance, inner conversation, conversion, but also through abstinences of all kinds, literally worrying itself into new existence, most intensively of all in the Roman imperial era: "Fear of excess, economy of regimen, being on the alert for disturbances, detailed attention given to dysfunction, the taking into account of all the factors (season, climate, diet, mode of living) that can disturb the body and, through it, the soul" (3.57). We are in the realm of psychic hypochondriacs, or if you like, hysterics of the soul.[16] Neurosis, but also psychomachia, are the traits of the new and ever intensifying psychic life of power in antiquity: the agonism of public display becomes an agonism of virtue, and ultimately a private battle within; life is a tortuous "*askêsis*," an ongoing struggle for self-purification (for example, 3.136–7); sovereignty over the self is won at great cost, even if the goal is per-manent, and autarkic, serenity. The Subject is born of a permanent and ongoing "crisis," and may ultimately be nothing but a name for this crisis (3.95).

14   "We are not talking about a moral rupture" (Foucault (1983) 244).
15   See Porter (2005c).
16   Cf. Foucault (1988b) 29.

If pagan antiquity reveals "harsh" yet "subtly" articulated regimes of rigor, abstention, austerity, and renunciation, as volume 2 of *The History of Sexuality* claims,
it simultaneously reveals "*the harshest* [of such regimes] *known to the West*," *mon-
asticism included*.[17] And so, against all of Foucault's best expectations, his history
turns out to be fatally linear: "Continuities can be identified," he writes in the
third volume (3.143), practically bewildered at what he has discovered – or else
produced. He goes on to resist his own tentative conclusion, insisting upon the
"fundamental differences" between the two cultures, pagan and Christian. One
avenue of difference is to attribute a positivity to pagan asceticism and a negativity to the Christian and modern forms of the same.[18] But that is arguably to
misread the productivity of abstention in its later forms. It is also to underread
the negativity of the Platonic view of self-fashioning, which at least in the *Phaedo*
is geared not so much to producing a positive ethical substance through the use
of pleasures as to approximating to a condition of death in life as far as possible
(see *Phaedo* 67de: "practice for death," which gives content to *Phaedo* 115b: "take
good care of your own selves"). A second escape is the tactic of bait and switch,
as Foucault's history vacillates between a history of subjectivity and a history of
sexuality (leaving the reader ever uncertain as to which of these two histories is
in focus at any given moment). Nonetheless, as if by divine (or methodological)
decree, sexuality must, in the end, prove to be definitory of the Subject, the mark
of its final subjection (*passim*).

But this is strange and counterintuitive. It presents a logical bind for Foucault,
who is in effect repeating the reductive sexualization of the subject that is
abhorred in *History of Sexuality* volume 1. And he does so on two different
levels. He insists on sexuality (its presence or its absence), not only as an epochal
marker, but as fully determinative of "the forms of integration of [the] precepts
[about sex] in the subject's experience of himself" even in antiquity, and the last
two volumes of his *History* are drenched in sexual discourse – however much
Foucault may claim to find that "sex is boring," not to say "disgusting,"[19] which
perhaps helps to explain why his interest lies solely in *techniques*. Indeed, at the
end of Foucault's account it turns out that the ascesis and techniques of the self
that so intensify in the first two centuries CE, all this sexual "austerity" and its
attendant anxieties, have been a permanent feature of his *History* from the fourth
century BCE on, presciently forecasting ("announcing") "a future morality": "We
have encountered in Greek thought of the fourth century BC formulations ['principles of sexual austerity'] that were not much less demanding" – indeed, they
are "the harshest [such regimes] known to the West," as we saw earlier; the sexual
act was long considered "dangerous, difficult to master, and costly" (3.237); and

17   Foucault (2001) 14; emphasis added.
18   As in Foucault (2001) 15.
19   Foucault (1983) 229, 233; the latter phrase ("disgusting") pertains only to ancient
     Greek sexual practices.

so on. It is hard not to conclude that what Foucault has been narrating all along is not the alternative ethical substance of the classical period but the rise of Christian asceticism in the Mediterranean West.

III   *Souci de Soi* and *Selbstbildung*: Foucault's Enlightenment Project

Much more could be said here, but I now want to tie Foucault's final project more firmly to its roots in the modern tradition of *Bildung* and *Selbstbildung* (easily rendered by Foucault's hallmark phrase *souci de soi*, as Foucault is well aware).[20] A good point of departure is the architect of the modern classical ideal, Wilhelm von Humboldt (1767–1835), who gave philosophical depth to Winckelmann's aestheticization of the Greeks. Humboldt follows Winckelmann in all the essentials, starting with the aesthetic consistency of the classical ideal, its anchoring in a fantasy of beauty that is presumed not to be our own and yet incites us to identify with it, indeed to make it our own.[21] The body is the natural referent of this ideal, given "the value that the Greeks placed on the freely cultivated (*ausgebildeten*) body and its strength (*Stärke*)": for "the Greeks' particular sensibility to beauty was bound up with . . . the considerable attention [they gave] to the development of their personal powers, and above all their bodily ones, and with the inclination to sensuousness that the Greek climate worked rather strongly [upon them]."[22]

Humboldt admires the ideals of "self-cultivation" he finds literally embodied by the Greeks. Body-*Bildung* is an essential element of ethical self-realization, and that is his inheritance from Winckelmann.[23] To this picture Humboldt adds a few traits of his own, whether borrowed from contemporary organicist and vitalist philosophy or anticipating a future trend. Life and one's character, he says, are ideally to be conceived as "a work of art" that exhibits "a single unified style and spirit."[24] Constantly in search of themselves, Humboldt's Greeks must reinvent themselves at every moment, each time "more beautifully."[25] They are in this sense their own "work of art": for "life can be regarded as an art (*Kunst*), just as the character that is represented in life can be regarded as a work of art (*Kunstwerk*)," which is to say the product of its own vital activities.[26] (As Nietzsche would write

---

20 See Foucault (2001) 46, where he is unafraid to render "*culture de soi*" with "*Selbstbildung*," the motto of the German humanistic tradition.
21 Cf. Humboldt (1960–81) 2.18–19 (1793).
22 Humboldt (1960–81) 2.13; see Winckelmann (1985 [1755]) 32–4; Porter (2000) ch. 4.
23 Humboldt (1960–81) 2.49, 16.
24 Humboldt (1960–81) 2.66, 70.
25 Humboldt (1960–81) 2.68.
26 Humboldt (1960–81) 2.66; cf. 2.6, 8.

in his "Encyclopedia of Classical Philology" lectures from 1871, perpetuating the now faded tradition, "[The Greeks] have something of *Kunstwerke* in them."[27]) And in its purest form, the Greek character displays a certain *ascetic* beauty. The fabled "simplicity" of the Greeks, made into a slogan of classicism after Winckelmann, has this sense of ascetic reduction as well. As an example Humboldt cites Pindar, but the choice is determined by the German myth of racial purity, according to which the Dorian race is the purest and most essentially Greek race, and an Aryan precursor of the Teutonic race. In addition to his classicizing traits (the "tranquility" and "cheerfulness" of his poetry), and his penchant for homoerotic *Knabenliebe*, Pindar betrays signs of an "awkward gravity," an austerely religious and "almost Hebraic" "seriousness, dignity, and awe," in short, a "radiating sublimity": "reverence for heroes of the distant past," even "bitterness" and "severity."[28]

This aesthetic holism, which is a staple of classicism, is for Humboldt tied to a theory of power and energetics that is expressly opposed to the traditional metaphysics of substance and to a certain essentialism, notably an essentialism of the self. Classical idealism will have nothing to do with either of these things. What gives rise to ever renewed self-activity and self-identity on this theory are, in Humboldt's more speculative idiom, the unpredictable "excesses" that naturally occur among the drives and formations of the will.[29] Identity here is not a latency to be realized but an interplay of forms and forces, of sheer exertions and desires, that is *idealized* in an unanalyzable totality.[30] The self, on this view, is a work of art in the precise sense that it is a problematic and irrational ideal.[31] It is managed by an economy of drives (*Triebe*) that pulse energetically through the body and the soul (in question are "*Kraftenergien*" that subtend a process whose law reads: "something new can and must come into existence, forever and ever"), as it strives forwards, driven by "desire" and "yearning" (*Sehnsucht*), towards self-completion, and a unity of "style" (*Stil*): the classical self *just is* the inaccessibility of itself to its own ideal – or else, more aptly, it is the inaccessibility of its *ideal* to its self.

Nietzsche would later call this Goethean impulse to self-unity a will to power but also – in un-Foucauldian fashion – a process of "idealization" that ultimately rests upon deception and especially self-deception ("*We need lies . . . in order to live*").[32] "Goethe surrounded himself with nothing but closed horizons . . . What he aspired to was *totality*. He disciplined himself to a whole, he *created* himself."[33]

---

27 Nietzsche (1967–) 2, pt. 3, 437.
28 Humboldt (1903) 1.411–29 ("Pindar," 1795).
29 Humboldt (1960–81) 2.28–9.
30 Humboldt (1960–81) 2.34.
31 There are clear parallels in Winckelmann's aesthetics; see Potts (1994) 156–7.
32 Nietzsche (1988) 13.193.
33 Nietzsche (1990) 112.

This is a perfect echo of Humboldt's language. Their common denominator is a view of idealization *as* disavowal. Does Humboldt give us something like a *classical* theory of the will to power? His view, or vision, is full of intriguing complications. Humboldt was at least frank about the anachronism and ahistoricity of his conception; it is contrived so as to be intelligible, and seductive, to contemporary *Germans*.[34] Nietzsche would label all such idealism an expression of the ascetic ideal, which he both attacked and tragically bemoaned as a hapless necessity: "Apart from the ascetic ideal, man, the human *animal*, had no meaning so far. His existence on earth contained no goal . . . *This* is precisely what the ascetic ideal means: that something was *lacking*, that man was surrounded by a fearful *void* – he did not know how to justify, to account for, to affirm himself; he *suffered* from the problem of his meaning."[35] This is *Nietzsche's* version of "problematization." Hence, asceticism, the need and desire for self-affirmation, is co-extensive with the entire historical and imagined emergence of mankind; it is all that Nietzsche most "despises" in mankind, and ambivalently admires about it as well. Nietzsche's (supposed) counter-ideals of self-overcoming, of "resignifying" one's self, of an *Übermensch* who lives beyond the regimes by which subjects come to be formed in conventional culture, can be shown to be the ultimate *product*, indeed the *hallucination*, of the ascetic creature "man."[36] Nietzsche thus *ironizes* Foucault's project of self-formation, at least on this reading of both thinkers.

However we choose to read Nietzsche or Foucault, Foucault's conception obviously has roots in modern tradition: "The deliberate attitude of modernity is tied to an indispensable asceticism."[37] In point of fact, an entire history of modernity (or rather, of modern views about modern life) could, and probably should, be organized around the – plainly perverse – ideal of ascetic and aesthetic self-fashioning, with its fusion of pagan and Christian impulses, of which Foucault would be merely one of the more recent chapters.[38] After Nietzsche, its exemplars would include Matthew Arnold, who upheld an ideal of culture "as a general and harmonious perfection of human capacities," and later Walter Pater, who is even more specific: "The ideal of asceticism," Pater writes in *Marius the Epicurean* (1885), "represents moral effort as essentially a sacrifice, the sacrifice of one part of human nature to another, that it may live the more completely in what survives of it" (the ascetic practice he has in mind is one of self-cultivation).[39] Similar tendencies

---

34 ". . . nur Deutschen verständlich" (Humboldt (1960–81) 2.68).
35 Nietzsche (1967) 162.
36 See Porter (1998, 1999a).
37 Foucault (1984) 41. Obviously, other strands are at play here, in varying degrees, from Montaigne to Castiglione, Newman, Wilde, Genet, Proust, and even Barthes, apart from the peculiar blend of aesthetics and ascetics that looks back to a classical ideal for its sources of the self.
38 See Harpham (1987).
39 Quoted in Baldick (1983) 53.

are plainly and more relevantly in evidence in Pater's *Greek Studies*.[40] Behind these figures lies an entire tradition, or matrix, of Enlightenment ideology, once described by Norbert Elias as "the social compulsion to self-compulsion"[41] and later approved of by Foucault in his reading of Kant in the essay from 1978, "What is Enlightenment?"[42] And at the other end of the process lies Freud's (often Nietzschean-sounding) analysis of the role of ideals in the constitution of culture and of cultural subjects made good through the reciprocal processes of renunciation and sublimation. Foucault's Greeks and Romans are the projection of these Enlightenment ideals onto the past – when they are not merely proto-Christians rejecting their own pagan antiquity.[43]

Given this background, we would seem to be faced with a kind of theoretical astigmatism by Foucault: how can he fail to see the connections and his various indebtednesses? In fact, Foucault *is* well aware of the connection, as mentioned earlier; he simply chooses to ignore it when it suits his purposes. One example comes from an interview held in 1983: "*Q*: So Nietzsche, then, must be wrong, in *The Genealogy of Morals*, when he credits Christian asceticism for making us the kind of creatures that can make promises? *A*: Yes, I think he has given mistaken credit to Christianity, given what we know about the evolution of pagan ethics from the fourth century B.C.[E.] to the fourth century [C.E.]."[44] Foucault here shows himself seemingly willing to lay the blame for the modern ethical paradigm, which he would critique, at the doorstep of antiquity – indeed, willing to view the modern paradigm as the evolved form of the ancient practice. Ironically, historical determination penetrates a theory at the very moment when that theory claims to have found the key to transcending the past: self-fashioning, as Foucault conceives it, which is to say conceived as an exotic possibility, is itself plainly a *modern* cultural construct.

Coming to terms with Foucault's dilemma raises a more general problem for anyone involved in the reception of classical culture, namely the difficulty of "objectifying our objectifications" (Bourdieu), of determining to what extent the criteria we apply to social description are themselves conditioned by our own frames of reference.[45] The very exoticism that antiquity can present to us is just as often

---

40   See "The Marbles of Aegina," in Pater (1914 [1894]).

41   Elias (1969) 2.323.

42   Foucault (1984); and see Foucault (1983) 251 on another significant predecessor in the theory of "the famous aesthetics of existence," Jacob Burckhardt.

43   See Leonard (this volume) and Leonard (2005) for Foucault's earlier and more overtly politicized engagement with Enlightenment ideals in the wake of Lévi-Strauss and Jean-Pierre Vernant.

44   Foucault (1983) 248.

45   See Bourdieu (1990), esp. ch. 1. With Foucault's voluntarist notion of the self contrast Nietzsche's competing notion of unwilled and often unwanted activity (unconscious agency) at the heart of all volitional acts (on which, see Porter (1998)).

a reflex of our conditioned conceptions of "the exotic." Here, paradoxically, the very proof of "objectivity" may have the best chances of lying not in the realms of the strange or of the familiar, but in the shimmering moments of the *uncanny*: those moments when, to speak with Freud, we look into a reflective medium, catch an alienated glimpse of ourselves, and discover that we "are not at all pleased" with what we find there.[46] One of the methodological advantages of this kind of investigation into the uncanny is that it is not clear how it can be cultivated as a method, although as a criterial experience it is something at which investigations can be aimed or by which they can be adjudged successful. For an approach like this represents coming into contact with *unwanted identifications*. The truly exotic, on this model, may turn out to be not exotic at all, and not even uncannily similar, but merely banal, other (with a small *o*), incalculably different, or incalculably similar – inciting, or else resulting from, a narcissism of small differences. Antiquity (our "other" in the present case) can prove most alien when it alienates us from the models of comprehension by which we seek to grasp it. And that, in the end, may be Foucault's final achievement.

---

46   Freud (1953–74) 248 n. 1.

15

Fractured Understandings

Towards a History of Classical Reception among Non-Elite Groups

Siobhán McElduff

There are, no doubt, even among us, some few whose hearts are corrupted, and whose minds are perverted . . . whose whole education consists of a few scraps, taken from immoral or impious writers.

Edward Dillon, Bishop of Killamacduagh and Kilfenora,
Pastoral Letter (April 6, 1798)

The history of the book . . . must equally be a history of the reader.

K. Whelan[1]

In *Reception Studies* Lorna Hardwick writes that "reception studies have to be concerned with investigating the routes by which a text has moved and the cultural forces which shaped or filtered the ways in which the text was regarded."[2] This paper examines how classical texts moved amongst an unlikely set of readers, the non-elite of eighteenth- and nineteenth-century Ireland. Some might argue that those I discuss here are simply an interesting oddity, a footnote to the history of classics who have no place within a study of classics or of reception. Yet if one looks at Ireland it becomes clear that these readers represented the norm and not the exception in classical reception and in the study of classics; nor, I would argue, is Ireland an aberrant example in the history of classical reception.

By ignoring such groups we create a false history of reception and of classics itself. Few individuals have ever had complete access to classical texts even in translation and fewer still have read those texts with a complete (or even partial) education in classical culture and history; most readers instead operated, and still operate, from a fragmentary and fractured understanding of such texts. Thus my aim here is twofold: to describe an aspect of reception history which is likely to be unfamiliar to most classicists and to gesture to an alternate and more inclusive

---

1 Whelan (1996) 134.
2 Hardwick (2003a) 4.

model for understanding and discussing reception that would include those traditionally excluded from studies of reception: non-professional readers, the non-elite, all those who have limited (or no) access to traditional channels of education and transmission.

Problematically for studies like this, it is true that among the non-elite of the past "reading remains the most difficult stage to study in the circuit that books follow."[3] A lack of access to traditional means of publication meant that they were considerably less likely, to put it mildly, to issue slim volumes of poetry or to leave behind detailed accounts of their reading habits. In addition, their reading matter circulated in ephemeral and hard-to-track cheap print traditions,[4] not in the standard editions and texts which were more durable and which we are more familiar with. Although some might buy second-hand books,[5] normal reading fare for the poor consisted of chapbooks and broadside ballads. (Chapbooks were small,[6] illustrated, and often abbreviated books carried by traveling peddlers which cost anything from a penny to 6*d*.; broadsides were single-page printed ballads which sold for a fraction of a penny.) The subject matter of chapbooks varied wildly and anything that could conceivably sell was sold. In Ireland Ovid's *Art of Love* circulated as a chapbook, and it appeared thus in Irish schools, much to the disgust of observers. Each publisher issued his texts with cuts, variations, and additions as he saw fit; hence it is often impossible to know what version of a text was in circulation at any one time and which one any particular reader was in possession of.

The very poor might as a last resort learn even without books. The English working-class poet Ann Yearsley taught herself classical history from prints in shop windows,[7] knowledge she put on display in her satire *To Ignorance, Occasioned by a Gentleman's desiring the Author never to assume a Knowledge of the Ancients*. Material also circulated orally, in storytelling traditions (see below); such material was even more ephemeral than the chapbooks and is even harder to track. As a result of such situations one needs to adopt a flexible approach to the movement of information amongst the non-elite.

Even if some evidence is scanty, for Ireland of this period we are supplied with an abundance of travelers' accounts, government reports (especially those relating to education), and lists of books found in the hedge schools (the reading material of Irish peasants was a subject of particular fascination for the British and Anglo-Irish). We also have some first-hand accounts from readers; one of particular importance is William Carleton's *Autobiography*. Carleton, the son of a peasant farmer, both studied and taught in non-elite schools and, while one has

---

3 Darnton (1990) 122.
4 Pollard (1989) 218.
5 Altick (1998) 254.
6 Usually 24–36 pages, but they could be up to 144 pages in length.
7 Landry (1990) 163.

to approach his material with caution, he gives valuable insight into the trials of an Irish peasant education. We also possess numerous ballads and poems which circulated among the peasantry; much of their material originated on a folk level[8] or, if it originated elsewhere, had to appeal to the non-elite in order to sell; hence their subject matter can be seen as illustrative of non-elite tastes and interests. While not all of this material survives, enough does to give us an understanding of the circulation of classical *topoi* and figures in Irish popular culture.

One particular reason why eighteenth- and nineteenth-century Ireland is a particularly fruitful ground for investigating the reception of classical literature among the non-elite is its unusual and well-documented educational system. This system sprang up because of a sequence of seventeenth-century laws (the so-called Penal Laws) intended to restrict the access of elite Catholics to education. Initially these had little impact on the lower classes of Ireland; however, as the eighteenth century progressed, Irish society underwent a series of cultural and economic dislocations which inadvertently affected the education of the poor. One of the most significant was the collapse of the system of poetic patronage; poets, the traditional educators of the Irish Catholic elite, faced hard times under these laws as their patrons either lost their estates, saw them reduced greatly in size, or began to mold themselves after the pattern of English gentry. As their patronage evaporated so did their social status, leaving them more and more dependent upon the non-elite for support;[9] they became teachers without pupils who had to seek new students among the non-elite. This partially explains the presence of non-essential subjects like Latin, Greek, and even Hebrew[10] on the curricula of schools for the poor and the availability of teachers of these subjects. Teaching was a self-replicating profession, with ambitious poor students moving from region to region to seek out famous teachers and particular subjects. Students of classical languages, for example, when finished with their local schools might travel to Munster where tradition held that the best Latin schools were.[11] There they could become "poor scholars," students who aided the teacher in return for further instruction.

The schools they studied in are traditionally called hedge schools because in the early days of the Penal Laws restrictions on education were still enforced with a certain degree of enthusiasm, forcing some schools to be held in hedges or ditches – a supreme act of optimism given the Irish climate. Their numbers rose consistently until in 1824 of 11,823 schools recorded by the Second Commission for Irish Education, 9,352 pay schools (or hedge schools) were listed "which received no support of any kind; and of these the Hedge Schools formed the majority."[12]

---

 8   Wilgus (1977) 113.
 9   Cullen (1990) *passim*.
10   McManus (2002) 127.
11   Dowling (1968) 38–41.
12   Dowling (1968) 33.

In numerical terms this meant that out of 408,065 Catholics educated in Ireland, 377,007 were educated in pay or hedge schools.[13] Despite the progressive relaxation of these laws over the latter half of the eighteenth century,[14] this remained the situation up until 1831 when the Irish National Education System was established.

The fees in these schools varied considerably; however, on average students paid up to 1*s*. 8*d*. per quarter to learn spelling, 6*d*. to 2*s*. for reading, 2*s*. 2*d*. to 3*s*. 3*d*. for writing, and 4*s*. to 11*s*. for Latin.[15] These figures remained constant over the eighteenth and nineteenth centuries even as incomes rose.[16] Agricultural wages for laborers (the poorest section of Irish society) averaged 1–2 shillings a day, hence for the poorest a decision to have one's child taught an expensive subject like Latin could not be made lightly, and would be financially impossible for many. However, schoolteachers could be paid in goods and often had extreme problems getting any pay at all.[17] As a result their incomes were often extremely low, lower than that of many peasants[18] – a famous poet once complained he could earn more as a laborer than as a teacher[19] and his complaints were not unique.

With no authority to train them or even to weed out the obviously insane, the quality of schoolteachers could vary wildly. Carleton described one of his Latin teachers as "an individual who should have been closely confined in a lunatic asylum during his life."[20] Sometimes disreputable, and frequently peripatetic, teachers surfaced in multiple locations throughout the course of their careers and students had to be similarly mobile as schools had a habit of rapidly appearing and disappearing.

These schools were a continual source of unease for the authorities as they were almost impervious to outside control of their teachers and their curricula. As one member of parliament stated, "[in Ireland] the education of the poor was left to the poor; and no good education would possibly come from their educating each other."[21] Teachers of classics were seen as particularly dangerous. In 1749 Sir Richard Cox grumbled that "these are the men who lay the foundation of that lamentable ignorance in which the Irish papists are bred. They indeed teach a little bad Latin, but much superstition and more treason."[22] Frequently perceived to be the organizing forces behind rural unrest and peasant secret societies, many teachers were heavily involved in the United Irishmen's 1798 rebellion.[23]

13 *Parliamentary Debates* (1826) 18.
14 Dowling (1968) 24–5.
15 Dowling (1968) 82.
16 Adams (1998) 112.
17 Corcoran (1932) 59.
18 Connell (1995) 24–6.
19 O'Tuama (1981) 184.
20 Carleton (1896) 41.
21 *Parliamentary Debates* (1824) 1480.
22 Dowling (1971) 78.
23 See Anon. (1799) 19; Smyth (1998) 115; Beames (1983) 60–1.

Efforts were made to suppress classics in non-elite schools; Richard Edgeworth, one of the commissioners of Irish education, commented that "I have been told that in some [charity] schools the Greek and Roman histories have been forbidden; such abridgements of these as I have seen are certainly improper; to inculcate democracy and a foolish hankering after undefined liberty is particularly dangerous in Ireland."[24] He suggested that Irish peasants instead be made to read books "inculcating piety, and morality and industry."[25] From the perspective of the authorities, he had a point: given that Ireland during this period was beset with large-scale and well-organized rural unrest, Goldsmith's opinion in his *History of Rome* that the Gracchi and not the Roman Senate were in the right over Roman land reform could prove to be explosive (Goldsmith's histories of Greece and Rome were available as sixpenny chapbooks and are widely attested in hedge schools). But there was more to anxieties about classical education in hedge schools than simple fear of rural unrest, as can be seen in William Hickey's comments to the peasantry that:

> This is a bad unprofitable kind of education which you should avoid, such as a near neighbour of mine is giving to his boys . . . They are now far advanced in Greek and Latin! A school of this description is a nuisance among you. The master is wrapped up in the pride of classical knowledge, and despises the lower branches of instruction, which would be ten times more valuable to your children than all his Greek and Latin. The father, when I asked him why he sent his children to a Latin school, answered that he thought it a *brave* chance to hit upon one could *tache* it; for he was *tould* it was a fine thing to know the *dead languages*, and *to be through the authors* . . . I never could bear to hear of their reading a sentence in the books they are taught.[26]

The worry always was that, as William Peel argued "this was not the education which would best fit them for their usual purposes of life."[27] What was an acceptable education for the elite and increasingly, the middle classes of both Britain and Ireland was not acceptable for the Irish lower classes, who were to be broken "to the habit of docility" through a "limited curriculum."[28] There is the hint of fear that if Latin circulated freely amongst the non-elite, it might become devalued as a piece of elite intellectual merchandise and thus less useful as "a central resource for the self-recognition and social closure practiced by an assimilated

---

24 Edgeworth and Edgeworth (1820) 457.
25 There were several organizations dedicated to improving the moral quality of cheap literature in Ireland, chief among which was the Kildare Place Society; none were particularly successful.
26 Hickey (1833) 129.
27 *Parliamentary Debates* (1826) 18–19.
28 Fitzgibbon (1868) 87.

noble-bourgeois elite."[29] Other anxieties revolved around ethnicity; Latin was felt to be doubly inappropriate for Irish peasants, who were both poor *and* of a disreputable ethnicity. In Hickey's comments there is a visceral sense of repugnance to the idea of poor Irish reading and speaking Latin, as if it could become tainted by association. Given that these critiques were often addressed directly to Irish peasants and not just bruited about in parliament, it seems likely that they were not infrequently aware that learning a smattering of the classics might be a useful way of thumbing one's nose at the authorities.

The somewhat disreputable teacher and poet Donncha Rua McNamara, faced with questions in English from a group of drunken and upper-class ship passengers, pretended not to understand and proceeded to reply in Latin, trumping their imperial language with another more prestigious one.[30] Jonah Barrington relates the story of an aggrieved waiter in an inn in Kerry, who, having been rebuked by him for poor service, fixed him with a glare and muttered a threat in Latin. He was as good as his word: four miles down the road the wheels of Barrington's carriage fell off.[31] Within peasant society classical education could also be used to claim social distinction; when Carleton was forced to curtail his education because his family lost the small farm it rented, he determined to become an apprentice stone-cutter. He selected his master because during the interview "he got down a Justin and translated a portion . . . this bit of Latin told in his favour, and placed him out of the category of common stone-cutters."[32]

But were the authorities correct about revolutionary readings of classics in Irish schools? As mentioned above, rural Ireland in this period was in a constant state of unrest. In such circumstances classical history might be used to solidify a consciousness of national and economic oppression and may have given some disgruntled peasants "a convenient concept of despotic and arbitrary use of power which was useful and appropriate in assessing their problems."[33] There are some signs of this; one elaborate anonymous letter posted in Clonmel in 1819 used figures drawn from classical history – Nero, Caligula, and Xerxes – to describe the Prince Regent and the English authorities.[34] Perhaps some of these exempla were inspired by works such as the *History of the Emperors of Rome* or by Herodotus, both of which are attested in hedge schools.[35] On the other hand, the revolutionary ideology and rhetoric of the United Irishmen and biblical

29   Stray (1998) 29.
30   McNamara (1853) 24.
31   Barrington (1830) 157.
32   Carleton (1896) 103.
33   Beames (1983) 97–8.
34   Gibbons (2004) 101–2.
35   A sample list of books read in the hedge schools was issued by the Commissioners for Irish Education in 1825; these titles and others mentioned throughout this paper are drawn from this list.

exempla are more common in such letters and many just contain simple and unadorned threats.

For more elaborate use of classical imagery one needs to examine revolutionary ballads, such as *The New Bunch of Loughero* (c.1830), which elaborately parallels Telemachus' search for Odysseus with the contemporary search for Napoleon. There Ireland is figured as Penelope, who chastely awaits the return of Odysseus/ Napoleon, who will rid her of her current suitors, the English.[36] However, most ballads tend to be much more eclectic in their methods and assemble material from all periods and traditions. *The Grey Horse*, for example, traces the adventures of its titular character through Mediterranean and Irish history. After having been present with "Maccabeus the great" in Judea, this fabulous horse moves on into classical history:

> My horse got new shoes and pursued his journey to Troy;
> When the news came to Troy, with great joy my horse he was found,
> He crossed over the wall and he entered the city with joy I am told.
>
> The city being in flames by the means of Hector's sad fate,
> My horse took his leave and there no longer would wait
> I saw him again in Spain and he in full bloom,
> With Hannibal the great, and he crossing the Alps into Rome.[37]

The lack of attention to chronology is characteristic of Irish ballads and of the chapbooks, which had no problem tossing St. Patrick into the world of classical mythology;[38] writers felt free to mingle all sorts of material from various periods together, either from a blithe disregard for historical accuracy or because their own education had left them somewhat confused.

However we judge the quality of these ballads, we should realize that these writers had a serious aim in using classical parallels, which "was to arouse courage, indignation, confidence, hope, scorn, pity and a sense of kinship with the mighty dead."[39] In the context of elite disapproval of classics in hedge schools it was a neat move to interweave even a brief mention of classical heroes into the framework of a revolutionary ballad, as you could rely on offending the authorities twice. Thus, whoever wrote that "poor mamma would faint if *Spem Gregis* would glance at a firelock," in *Ireland's Glory* (a ballad from 1793 that celebrates the French Revolution and the demise of monarchy) may have intended this snippet from the *Eclogues* to be doubly shocking, by placing Virgil's words not only in a lowly ballad but in one written by an *Irishman*.

36   Zimmerman (1967) 188–90.
37   Zimmerman (1967) 211.
38   As in the extremely popular *Seven Champions of Christendom*.
39   Stanford (1976) 218.

Writers might claim they turned to classical poetry from a refusal to write Irish epic poetry in a downtrodden age; such is the case in Donncha Rua McNamara's *Eacthra Ghiolla an Amaráin* (*Adventures of a Luckless Boy*, *c.*1745), an elaborate but compressed parody of the *Aeneid*. After opening his poem with a *recusatio* of Irish epic and a rant on the miserable wages paid to school-teachers, he then relates a *catabasis* he experienced while in a drunken stupor (throughout the poem his less than sober state contrasts with the restraint and moderation of his heroic model). In his *catabasis* he journeys through the under-world under the direction of a *spéirbhean* (a fairy woman); throughout he con-tinually corrects the "errors" of the *Aeneid*, pointing out that the ferryman over the Styx is not Charon, but the Irish hero Conan, who speaks Latin and Irish (but refuses to speak English), and that the underworld is peopled not just by classical heroes and writers, but also by Irish heroes and poets. Written in Irish, this poem testifies to some interest in hearing quite elaborate parodies on clas-sical themes among the lower strata of society, who were more likely to speak Gaelic (though not all who spoke Irish were necessarily non-elite). Even though the *Eacthra* is a complicated and elaborate poem, like simpler forms of poetry such as ballads, it freely intermingles Irish and classical material all the while expressing the sedi-tious hope that English rule in Ireland will end soon. McNamara was a hedge-school teacher; one wonders if his students learned that "foolish hankering after liberty" which Richard Edgeworth so worried about.

However, it would be a mistake to see the hedge schools as smoothly func-tioning sites of revolution, turning out Latin scholars primed for rebellion. They were too chaotic to be that efficient, and their economic and social situation ensured that students usually had only a restricted access to any information. This is per-haps best illustrated by looking at the myriad types of books students used as read-ers, as in this 1808 list from a school in Clare:

In History, – Annals of Irish Rogues and Rapparees
In Biography, – Memoirs of Jack the Bachelor, a notorious smuggler, and of Freeny,
a celebrated highwayman.
In Theology, – Pastorini's Prophecies, and the Miracles of Prince Hohenloe.
In Poetry, – Ovid's Art of Love, and Paddy's Resource.
In Romance Reading, – Don Belianis of Greece, Moll Flanders, &c, &c.[40]

(*Paddy's Resource* was a collection of revolutionary ballads issued by the United Irishmen, somewhat unusual company for Ovid.) Such situations arose because pupils purchased or borrowed whatever reading material was available and used them as readers[41] with little regard for content or appropriateness as schoolbooks.[42]

---

40 Dutton (1808) 236–7.
41 Loeber and Stouthamer-Loeber (1999) 132.
42 Adams (1998) 103.

Hence it was entirely possible that a student might employ Ovid or Herodotus' *Histories* as a primer if a copy of that book was all he or she could find. Books were expensive commodities; if you were lucky enough to get your hands on one you did not quibble about its subject matter but used it as best you could.

The result of such a laissez-faire environment meant that students could easily go from reading *The Pleasant Art of Money Catching* to Lucian's *Dialogues of the Dead* or the *Iliad*, without pause for reflection on the differences between them. In addition, students were usually precluded from ever building upon the knowledge gained from one text in any consistent manner as they relied on chance to obtain their books.[43] All of this made for much variety in reading material but little consistency; readers in (and outside) school hence had a necessarily fractured understanding of the past and its literature even if they wished otherwise. Such situations, however, were not unique to Ireland: the poor elsewhere also read whatever they could get their hands on.[44]

The shortage of books meant that several students might also end up sharing the same text; this was particularly true of Latin and Greek texts which were hard to procure and expensive. One teacher told a visitor to his school that "this is the only Homer I have, and though seven boys read out of it daily, it never causes a moment's dispute"[45] and the same was true of his tattered edition of Virgil. Access to such books was a communal, not an individual experience – as was all education; most schools were held in one-room cabins, with all subjects taught side by side.

As a result it is not clear that students necessarily distinguished between types of texts, or that it initially even crossed their minds to do so. Carleton, for example, wrote that he read the classics as novels, reading for the narrative rather than the content without distinguishing between them and other fiction:

> I had gone before this beyond the fourth book of Virgil, and if ever a schoolboy was affected almost to tears, I was by the death of Dido. Even when a schoolboy, I did not read the classics as they are usually read by learners. I read them as novels – I looked to the story – the narrative – not to the grammatical or other difficulties . . . The truth is, I read the classics through the influence of my imagination, rather than of my judgment.[46]

This might explain why he also wept profusely when reading *Amanda; or, The Reformed Coquette*: with little idea that there were distinctions between these two texts, he reacted extravagantly to both. In his study of eighteenth- and nineteenth-century British working-class readers, Peter Rose noticed a similar trait; one

---

43   Loeber and Stouthamer-Loeber (1999) 133.
44   Cf. Altick (1998), chs. 2 & 3.
45   Owenson (1807) 211.
46   Carleton (1896) 71.

person told how he went from reading children's chapbooks to Homer "without being conscious of break or line of division . . . I found [Homer's works] to be quite as nice children's books as any of the others."[47] Such readers may have been unclear about distinctions drawn between high and low forms of literature because all books were valuable and rare objects and they were often forced to use quite complicated texts to learn basic literacy skills.

Further, as it "requires some training to distinguish fact from fiction, and still more training to distinguish fiction from lies,"[48] students left to their own devices did not necessarily immediately distinguish between fiction and other types of literature. In other words, readers with limited educations may have been unable to discriminate between works like Goldsmith's histories of Greece and Rome and Homer's *Odyssey*, thus it is possible that the author of the *Bonny Bunch of Loughero* thought of Odysseus and Napoleon equally as historical characters. Like the British working-class readers Rose discusses, Irish peasants might have believed much of what they read was equally true, equally valid: perhaps this is another reason why ballads and other folk poetry tend to collapse material drawn from classical, biblical, and Irish sources together without marking any distinctions between them. In a limited and chaotic education how could one necessarily tell the difference between genres, between a work like *Paddy's Resource* and Ovid's *Art of Love*, or distinguish between myth and history?

Such attitudes may have been encouraged by the way material circulated outside schools. Crofton Croker described a scene he viewed in the aftermath of the rebellion of 1798:

> In an evening assembly of village statesmen he [a schoolteacher] holds the most distinguished place, from his historical information, pompous eloquence, and Classical erudition. His principles verge very closely on the broadest republicanism; he delivers warm descriptions of the Grecian and Roman commonwealths; the ardent spirit of freedom and general equality of rights in former days – and then comes down to his own country, which is always the ultimate political subject of discussion . . . he is an enemy to royalty and English dominion.[49]

We hear elsewhere of classical stories circulating in oral culture; the one-time hedge-school teacher Eoghan O'Sullibhean told tales of Troy to entertain his fellow laborers.[50] In such cases we have little information on what version of the legend was told (presumably the most entertaining one possible) and it is hard to gauge the reception of such tales. However, what seems clear is that when classical stories were told they were frequently interwoven into a narrative that

---

47   Rose (2001) 95.
48   Rose (2001) 94.
49   Crofton Croker (1824) 328–9.
50   O'Tuama (1981) 185–6.

also included Irish grievances and non-classical material, without any distinctions
being drawn between these elements. In this they paralleled Irish education, which
presented students with a hodgepodge of information, which they then made sense
of on their own.

They made sense of it in innovative and creative ways, reflecting and exploit-
ing "the unevenness of knowledge which characterizes the colonized society."[51]
As omnivorous consumers and reusers of all the literary and historical traditions
they encountered, they were not just passive consumers of the scraps of knowledge that got tossed their way; like Menocchio, the heretical miller of Carlo
Ginzburg's *The Cheese and the Worms,* they "did not simply receive messages transmitted down the social order"[52] but creatively interpreted what they read and heard
to align it with their understanding of the world and connect it with their experiences. The Irish hedge-school master described by Crofton Croker (above) did not
passively absorb classical history, but reshaped it into a rebellious narrative which
would reflect his listeners' concerns and interests. While Irish peasants might have
been somewhat unusual in their relationship to the classics, they were by no means
unique; for example, the English metalworker V. W. Garratt also used his readings of classical literature to solidify his belief in the unfairness of the status quo.[53]

As the materials available for the study of non-elite readers have grown dramatically over recent years, making it easier to track the movement of all literature amongst the lower classes, we surely have an obligation to examine the reception
of the classics amongst these groups, for judged on sheer numbers alone how
they read and utilized classical texts was not abnormal, but eminently normal. After
all, in Ireland thousands more learned of Odysseus through *The New Bunch of
Loughero* than ever heard of him by any other means; to ignore such individuals
is to ignore a large part of reception history. However, there is another reason
why looking at groups like this is a useful practice; examining both the formal
and informal processes by which classical material filtered through Irish peasant
society and their creative responses to that material can help us understand the
multiple ways that classical texts and images are received within our own society.

Consider, for example, the case of Wolfgang Petersen's recent film *Troy.*
Despite its limited commercial success, this film has produced on the Internet
communities of fanfiction writers who rewrite or add elements to its version of
the Trojan War. Some have read the *Iliad,* many have not, fewer still are familiar with Homeric culture, yet this does not prevent them from producing their
own versions of the narrative, sometimes adding elements from other cultures and
myths to make the story more satisfying and intelligible for themselves and their
audience. Like the readers I discussed in this paper, these audiences do not

51   Lloyd (1994) 64.
52   Darnton (1990) 155.
53   Rose (2001) 43.

passively absorb a version of a classical text, but creatively rework that image to suit their tastes and needs. Nor are they an isolated case; there are fanfiction communities for rewriting other classical myths and literature. However, unless we develop a more expansive concept of reception we will continue to exclude these and similar groups from our discussions of classical reception. As Kevin Whelan's quotation which heads this paper points out, the history of the book must be a history of the reader: this means all readers, not just a select few.

16

Decolonizing the Postcolonial Colonizers

Helen in Derek Walcott's Omeros

Helen Kaufmann

I Introduction

There is no reception without a receiver, and there is no colonization without a colonizer. Although these two statements have no logical link, there is a sense in which receivers are also colonizers. Both in reception and in colonization an "other" is subjected to the all-defining points of view of the appropriators. To give just two examples, receivers will always characterize John Barth's *Menelaid* in terms of its relation to the fourth book of Homer's *Odyssey*, and colonizers will never learn the language of a North American Indian tribe. The receivers and colonizers are equally content with their points of view and do not mind subjecting the "others" concerned to them. Ironically, they will mostly feel free to explore (and exploit) their subjects at will while they are in fact locked up in their own necessarily limited frameworks of reference, be it classical literature or Western European culture. Thus, despite their positions of power as receivers and colonizers their minds are colonized even while colonizing. Whereas every reception, even every reading, can be described in terms of colonization so as to highlight the political nature of reception and reading, the terminology more obviously triggers ethical questions if the text is about the former colonized and the receiver is not one of them (either ethnically or by education). Can such receivers avoid recolonizing the characters of a postcolonial text at all? The answer seems to be yes and no. They cannot because they only have their own mental framework to make sense of the "other." So they will automatically gather all the references to the (fictitious) worlds familiar to themselves and define the new world in terms of differences from them. On the other hand, yes, even they can get beyond a simple appropriation of the "other" if they are willing to get involved in the alterity of the "other" or if they are forced to rethink their interpretation of the "other" because they cannot make the correspondences fit. Here, in encouraging the receivers to revise their interpretations of the obvious correspondences towards the differences, is a unique chance for reception studies to help decolonize the minds of the receivers.

A number of postcolonial texts containing classical correspondences have been described as working towards decolonization, for instance late twentieth-century African refigurations of Greek drama.[1] Derek Walcott's *Omeros* (1990), a narrative poem about the Caribbean island of St. Lucia and its people, is another such example. Decolonization in *Omeros* means a move towards hybridity, which in turn involves a caribbeanization of Western culture as well as of the African ethnic and cultural background. This affirmation of hybridity can be seen in the analysis of various aspects of the poem such as the title "Omeros," which, on the one hand, is the pronunciation of Homer's name as heard by the narrator from a (contemporary) Greek girl (II.iii, p. 14) and, on the other, is etymologized as the three Creole words "o" ("the conch-shell's invocation"), "mer" ("both mother and sea in our Antillean patois") and "os" ("a grey bone") (II.iii, 14) bringing together Homer and the primeval landscape of the Caribbean, or, to take another example, in the character of Achille, who in a vision finds out that he would be a stranger in his ancestors' African village (XXV–XXVIII, 133–52) and who marks his distance from Homer's Achilles by the French form of his name. The following study will concentrate on the character of Helen in *Omeros* and her perception and reception as "Helen of Troy." Helen, who seems to be the most beautiful woman on St. Lucia, works in the household of the English veteran Major Plunkett and of his Irish wife, Maud. After a quarrel with Achille, a fisherman and her lover, she moves in with Hector (XXII.i, 116), who has exchanged his traditional occupation of a fisherman for that of a taxi driver (XXII.ii, 117f.). Hector dies in a car accident (XLV.ii–iii, 226–31), and Helen is reunited with Achille (LIII.iii, 267).

Helen in *Omeros* is particularly suitable for a reception study because in addition to being subjected to any reader-receiver she is also perceived/received as "Helen of Troy" within *Omeros* both by Major Plunkett and by the narrator.[2] Since there are, at least potentially, as many receptions as there are receivers, I have decided to compare Major Plunkett's and the narrator's experiences with that of just one reader-receiver, a student of reception with an education in classics called H. Even though her biographical details do not matter, her reception of Helen strongly depends on them. If she was not a classicist and/or if she had a different name, her reading of *Omeros* and her reception of Helen would most probably have been different. Her reception then is as individual as those of Major Plunkett and the narrator. It has therefore seemed best to present the three personal reception stories without even trying to generalize the reader's experience. While the narrative arrangement of the argument allows for individuality, it has one major drawback: as a narrative about a series of hermeneutic steps it fails to

---

1   See Hardwick (2004) 233–9, and for the decolonizing function of classical correspondences in postcolonial literatures also Hardwick (2002), (2003a) 110f., and (2005a).
2   For an analogous treatment of readers of *Omeros* with Plunkett and the narrator with respect to the Homeric correspondences see Terada (1992) 191f.

show how the different images of Helen are at work simultaneously without re-placing each other.

When Major Plunkett, the narrator, and the reader H. associate Helen of St. Lucia, a representative of the former colonized, with Helen of Troy, they reflect a conscious desire to honor her. This may itself be a questionable idea since Helen of Troy has always been seen as a very ambivalent figure, famous for her beauty and for causing the Trojan War, but none of the three receivers seems to be aware of that. For them "Helen of Troy" is a positive figure because of her beauty and her ancient Greek origin. While integrating this exotic Helen into the Western cultural tradition, they also reveal an urge to pin her, the contemporary Caribbean woman and the embodiment of St. Lucia, down in familiar terms in order to make sense of her. This attempt to define her identity implies another, postcolonial, colonization. However, Helen eludes her new colonizers, and sub-sequently plays a major part in their decolonizations. What started out as an intellectual exercise, a study of the reception of the Homeric Helen in *Omeros*, has turned into a highly political process of attempted recolonization and suc-cessful decolonization.

II   Helen as Helen of Troy: Honor and Attempted Recolonization

Even though Major Plunkett, the narrator, and the reader H. all compare Walcott's Helen with Helen of Troy, their comparisons differ considerably. Let us first con-sider H.'s approach to Helen and her method of comparison. She sets out to invest-igate in what respects Helen in *Omeros* resembles the Helen of the *Iliad* and that of the *Odyssey* respectively. At first sight she has noticed that, like Helen of Troy, the Caribbean Helen is the object of a quarrel between two men. Achille and Hector fight for her on several occasions, for example:

> . . . The duel of these fishermen
> was over a shadow and its name was Helen. (III.i, 17)[3]

Or:

> . . . Hector
>
> would win, or Achille by a hair; but everyone
> knew as the crossing ovals of their thighs would soar
> in jumps down the cheering aisle, or their marathon

---

3   The references to *Omeros* indicate chapters and sections of the poem followed by page numbers of the Faber and Faber edition (Walcott (1990)).

six times round the village, that the true bounty was
Helen, not a shield nor the ham saved for Christmas. (V.iii, 32)

Helen in *Omeros* is the object of a fight also in another sense. She often stands for the island of St. Lucia called "Helen of the West Indies," which was the object of war between the colonial powers France and England at the end of the eighteenth century. At that time St. Lucia changed hands more than ten times. In addition to being an object of war both the Caribbean and Iliadic Helens provoke reactions of admiration to their appearance, as H. has found out. In the *Iliad* Helen's provocation is obvious from the admiring whispering of the old men when she walks to the city walls:

"Surely there is no blame on Trojans and strong-greaved Achaians
if for long time they suffer hardship for a woman like this one.
Terrible is the likeness of her face to immortal goddesses."
(Hom. *Il.* 3.156–8)[4]

In *Omeros*, Helen attracts the attention of the tourists:

I felt like standing in homage to a beauty

that left, like a ship, widening eyes in its wake.
"Who the hell is that?" a tourist near my table
asked a waitress. (IV.iii.23f.)

Moreover, both Helens are to some degree caught in their roles. In book 3 of the *Iliad*, there is an interesting expression of this when Helen is weaving a picture about the Trojan War. In doing so she acts as a narrator and can present her material as she likes, but at the same time she cannot avoid the war being fought for her sake, which means she cannot escape being "Helen of Troy":[5]

. . . she was weaving a great web,
a red folding robe, and working into it the numerous struggles
of Trojans, breakers of horses, and bronze-armoured Achaians,
struggles that they endured for her sake at the hands of the war god.
(Hom. *Il.* 3.125–8)

In *Omeros*, it is the lack of an interior perspective that reduces Helen to her role and makes her an icon. She is predominantly presented from outside, does not speak much, nor reveal her thoughts.[6] It is, for instance, not clear why she leaves

4   Translations of passages from the *Iliad* are Lattimore's (1951).
5   See Latacz (1987) 65f. and Suzuki (1989) 36–43.
6   See Terada (1992) 190f. and McClure (1993) 9f.

Achille for Hector (XXII.i, 116). Her move is all the more surprising since a number of details suggest that she would rather stay with Achille, for example when she, waiting for Achille's return in Hector's house, is compared to Penelope:

> . . . Not Helen now, but Penelope,
> in whom a single noon was as long as ten years. (XXIX.i, 153)

In fact, Helen's move from Achille to Hector seems to result from the role she inherited together with her name. For such a literary determinism in *Omeros* there are other examples such as Philoctete's suffering from his wound (I.i, 4), but also his eventual recovery (XLIX.i, 246f.).[7] For Helen, the consequence of her name appears to be that she has two rival lovers, but also that she prefers the first (Achille) to the second (Hector) since in the *Iliad* Helen also likes Menelaus better than Paris, at least when the former defeated the latter in the duel:

> . . . and [she] spoke to her lord in derision:
> "So you came back from fighting. Oh, how I wish you had died there
> beaten down by the stronger man, who was once my husband.
> There was a time before now you boasted that you were better
> than warlike Menelaos, in spear and hand and your own strength."
>   (Hom. *Il.* 3.427–31)

Moreover, she reproaches herself for leaving Sparta when she says to Priam:

> "[A]nd I wish bitter death had been what I wanted, when I came hither
> following your son, forsaking my chamber, my kinsmen."
>   (Hom. *Il.* 3.173f.)

Corresponding to both the Homeric Helens, but more strongly to the Helen of the *Odyssey*, Queen of Sparta, Helen in *Omeros* has a queenlike pride despite her low social position. This makes Maud complain:

> . . . Helen had kept the house
>
> as if it were her own, and that's when it all begins:
> when the maid turns into the mistress and destroys
> her own possibilities. They start to behave
>
> as if they owned you, Maud said. (XI.i, 64)

Given her position as a queen, Helen in the *Odyssey* is free to do what she wants. At some point, for instance, as she fears that an evening spent with Menelaus, Telemachus, and Peisistratus could end in sorrowful wartime memories, she quickly adds some magic drug to the wine to dispel the sadness of her guests:

---

7 See Hardwick (2000c) 105.

> Now Helen, who was descended of Zeus, thought of the next thing.
> Into the wine of which they were drinking she cast a medicine.[8]
>
> (Hom. *Od.* 4.219f.)

Walcott's Helen is equally free to make her own decisions. When she cannot find work, for example, she sets up a small business on the beach and takes care of her life in this way:

> . . . because they thought her moods uncontrollable,
> her tongue too tart for a waitress to take orders,
> she set up shop: beads, hair-pick, and trestle table. (VI.iii, 36)

At this point of her comparison the reader H. concludes that Walcott's Helen corresponds to her Homeric predecessors in a number of ways. In fact, she combines the most important characteristics of both – object of war and icon of beauty, her role inherited from the Iliadic Helen, but her pride and personal initiative derived from her Odyssean counterpart. Consequently, H. is pleased to award Helen the status of a true modern "Helen of Troy," which is meant as an honor for Helen and at the same time indicates H.'s goodwill towards her. Her sense of satisfaction, however, is not so much due to Helen as to her own success at having fitted Helen into the Homeric framework of her mind and having so reduced her to a familiar character.

Major Plunkett's attitude towards Helen is less lighthearted and more problematic. On the one hand, he is constantly aware that through his race and his British nationality he represents the former colonizers, which causes him to want to make up for the guilt of his ancestors by some personal contribution to the race of the formerly colonized. On the other hand, Plunkett is concerned to suppress his passion for Helen, who works as a maid in his house. For these two reasons he starts writing a history of St. Lucia, the "Helen of the West Indies," which should integrate the island into world history:

> So Plunkett decided that what the place needed
> was its true place in history, that he'd spend hours
> for Helen's sake on research. (XI.i, 64)

Such a history would also honor Helen, he thought:

> . . . she seemed to drift like a waif,
> not like the arrogant servant that ruled their house.
> It was at that moment that he felt a duty

---

8   This is Lattimore's (1965) translation.

> towards her hopelessness, something to redress
> (he punned relentlessly) that desolate beauty
> so like her island's. (V.iii, 29f.)

His project is centered on a description of the Battle of the Saints (1782), the sea battle in which England and France fought for the island. In his research Plunkett finds more allusions to the Trojan War. That a French frigate was called "Ville de Paris" (XV.ii, 85), for instance, makes him state:

> . . . Paris gives the golden apple, a war is
> fought for an island called Helen? (XIX.i, 100)

For a while Plunkett feels that by pointing out the Homeric background of the Battle of the Saints he helps to highlight the historical importance and beauty of the island and thus to integrate it (her) into the history of the Western world. Even though his intentions are contrary to those of a colonizer, his research is prone to recolonize Helen/St. Lucia. At the same time doing historical research is the only way for him to capture Helen, the local woman, without committing adultery. At this point one might wonder how far Plunkett represents the average receiver. Do we pursue and bury our hearts' desires in reception studies? A positive answer to this question would equal a call for psychoanalytic reception studies.

The narrator of *Omeros* is as infatuated with Helen as is Plunkett. He also sees in her the embodiment of her race and of St. Lucia, but unlike Plunkett he, the poet, decides to elevate the beauty of Helen/St. Lucia by literary means:

> But the name Helen had gripped my wrist in its vise
>
> to plunge it into the foaming page. For three years,
> phantom hearer, I kept wandering to a voice. (LXIV.ii, 323)

Homer is a suitable model for the narrator's glorifying description of the primeval beauty and life on St. Lucia because the Greek poet successfully adapted the traditional oral poetry to the needs of the society of his own time. Moreover, his stories have been famous ever since and he is now seen to stand at the beginning of a literary tradition. On the other hand, the narrator closely associates Homer (and Virgil) with the language and literature of the Western colonizers:

> I said: "Homer and Virg are New England farmers,
> and the winged horse guards their gas-station, you're right." (II.iii, 14)

This association of Greek culture with Western imperialism is also obvious from his reflections about slavery:

> . . . I thought of the Greek revival
>
> carried past the names of towns with columned porches,
> and how Greek it was, the necessary evil
> of slavery, in the catalogue of Georgia's
>
> marble past, the Jeffersonian ideal in
> plantations with its Hectors and Achilleses,
> its foam in the dogwood's spray, past towns named Helen,
>
> Athens, Sparta, Troy. (XXXV.i, 177)

Consequently, by using Homeric terms to raise Helen/St. Lucia to epic grandeur, the narrator robs her to some degree of her racial background and hands her over to the former colonizers just as her African ancestors had been delivered up to slavery. Here, the parallels between Helen and the Caribbean and between the Homerizing narrator and the imperial colonizer are obvious, even though Homer and the Western literary tradition, as much as the African cultural tradition, have become an integral part of the Caribbean.

The three comparisons by H., Major Plunkett, and the narrator respectively differ from each other in a number of points. For instance, only H. goes back to the Homeric texts and differentiates between the Helen of the *Iliad* and that of the *Odyssey*. Despite such differences, the receivers' motives behind their studies have points of similarity. They wish to dignify Helen and to elevate her above her low social status by associations with Helen of Troy. In this context it is worth noting that the same idea, that is to say the elevation of Walcott's characters by Homeric analogies, can be found in the back cover text of the Faber and Faber edition of *Omeros*: "though Derek Walcott's protagonists, Achille and Philoctete, are simple fishermen, they . . . take on the specific gravity and resonance of their mythic Greek namesakes." This quotation is remarkable for its direct appeal to a Western view of the world, but it cannot gloss over the fact that the Homeric associations also imply an attempt at recolonization by those who use them as the only basis for their understanding of *Omeros*. By framing Helen in familiar terms H. integrates her into the classical world of her imagination. Likewise, Major Plunkett and the narrator recolonize Helen/St. Lucia by including her in Western history and characterizing her as Helen of Troy in poetry respectively.

III   Helen without Helen of Troy: Resistance and Decolonization

Luckily, Helen resists her recolonization. She eludes H., Plunkett, and the narrator so that they cannot but notice their failures. In Plunkett's case, his historiography soon focuses on the conflict between the colonial nations France and Britain (see XIX.i, 100), and so increases his distance from Helen, the island, and the woman. Furthermore he loses his (fictitious) son, a midshipman called Plunkett, who died in the battle for St. Lucia.

> . . . Well, he had paid the debt.
> The breakers had threshed her name with the very sound
> the midshipman heard. He had given her a son. (XIX.iii, 103)

The ambiguity of the pronoun "her" in the last line (to the island or to Helen) points to Plunkett's awareness that he is deceiving his wife by his research: "the harder he worked, the more he betrayed his wife" (XIX.iii, 103). His infidelity is all the more distressing for him as Maud dies soon afterwards. Now he has to seek reconciliation with Maud's spirit through the local healing woman Ma Kilman before he can forget his historical project (LXI, 303–9). Accepting his failure he learns to meet the people of St. Lucia on equal terms and to view Helen just as a beautiful woman:

> . . . he began to speak to the workmen
> not as boys who worked with him, till every name
>
> somehow sounded different; when he thought of Helen
> she was not a cause or a cloud, only a name
> for a local wonder. (LXI.iii, 309)

Like Plunkett the narrator has to admit that Helen as Helen of Troy evades his attempts to capture her. He has long considered Plunkett's historiography as being wrong, but he can approach Helen without the Homeric associations dominating his image of her only when he acknowledges that his literary project differs from Plunkett's research in methodology only and is therefore equally wrong.

> . . . I despised any design
> that kept to a chart, that calculated the winds.
> My inspiration was impulse, but the Major's zeal
>
> to make her the pride of the Battle of the Saints,
> her yellow dress on its flagship, was an ideal
> no different from mine. (LIV.ii, 270)

Only then does he understand that Helen needs neither him nor Plunkett:

> . . . There, in her head of ebony,
> there was no real need for the historian's
> remorse, nor for literature's. Why not see Helen

> as the sun saw her, with no Homeric shadow,
> swinging her plastic sandals on that beach alone. (LIV.ii, 271)

However, the practical consequences of this insight are rather difficult to realize for the narrator since he has built his poetic career on a Western literary education which includes Homer. In his poetological struggle he is helped by Omeros, another Homer, who shows him that his, that is Homer's, poetry is mainly based on his personal experiences even if it has now come to be considered part of the Western cultural tradition:

> A girl smells better than a book. I remember Helen's
>
> smell. The sun on her flesh. The light's coins on my eyes.
> That ten years' war was nothing, an epic's excuse. (LVI.iii, 284)

The narrator is then led through the underworld by Omeros. There he understands that if he wants to serve St. Lucia he has to accept the independence of the Caribbean Helen and at the same time creatively use the Western literary tradition for his poetry. Another poetological advisor, the lizard, teaches him to differentiate between the ancient and the contemporary Helens:

> You were never in Troy, and, between two Helens,
>
> yours is here and alive; their classic features
> were turned into silhouettes from the lightning bolt
> of a glance. These Helens are different creatures,
>
> one marble, one ebony. (LXII.ii, 313)

Through her resistance to being captured in terms of Western literature Helen has helped the narrator to discover the hybrid culture of St. Lucia and to find a postcolonial poetic voice that is not colonizing. In this way he has also freed Homer from the close association with the colonizing West[9] to becoming a model for any poetry on the primeval beauty of people and land.

Finally, the reader H. has to concede that Helen subverts her Odyssean characteristics of a queen in various ways, for example by constantly using the local variety of English:

> . . . "Girl, I pregnant,
> but I don't know for who." (VI.i, 34)

---

9   See Thieme (1999) 154f. and Hardwick (2004a) 242.

> . . . "Is no sense at all
> spending change on transport." (VI.i, 34)

She even sings the Beatles song "Yesterday" in this linguistic variety (VI.ii, 34).
Furthermore, she uses slang rather frequently, for example:

> . . . What the white manager mean
> to say was she was too rude, 'cause she dint take no shit
> from white people. (VI.i, 33)

Moreover, her laughter is "loud ringing" (VII.i, 38) and "infuriating" (XXIII.iii,
123). Laughter is a general indication of subversion; for the interpretation of
Helen's laughter it is also remarkable that Walcott once described the Caribbean
laughter as "loud and ringing."[10] Consequently, Helen's laughter marks her as
thoroughly Caribbean and distinguishes her from her Greek namesakes. H. then
discovers that her comparison of Helen with the Helen of the *Iliad* is equally
inappropriate at a crucial point. For even if it is true that Achille and Hector repeatedly fight for Helen (III.i, 15–17 and V.iii, 32), Helen's decision to leave Achille
for Hector (XXII.i, 116) and later to come back to him (LIII.iii, 267) does not
depend on the outcome of her lovers' duels. What first seemed to result from
her inherited role, the fact that she changes her partner twice, can now be attributed to Helen's own will. This implies that she is less determined by her role
than the Helen of the *Iliad*. Helen's failure to fit with H.'s Homeric scheme makes
H. pay attention to Helen's Caribbean identity, and redeems her mind from the
narrow framework of classical literature.

Helen has succeeded in resisting the three attempts to reduce her to Helen of
Troy and to recolonize her. Her opposition to Plunkett and the narrator is important for the plot of *Omeros* since only after they give up describing her in terms
of Helen of Troy can she decolonize them, that is, help them to find their identities in the hybrid society of St. Lucia. H.'s decolonization, on the other hand,
takes place while H. is reading *Omeros* so that Helen's influence can even be said
to reach beyond the confines of the book. After their decolonization the three
receivers view St. Lucia and its inhabitants free from thoughts of recolonization.

IV   Conclusion

The three readings of Walcott's Helen as attempted recolonizations and successful decolonizations emphasize the role of the reader/receiver as a (potential) new
colonizer in the field of reception studies. Helen of Troy haunts her Caribbean
namesake not because they are alike, but because Plunkett, the narrator, and

10   In Sjöberg (1983) 27 (Baer (1996) 84).

H. desire to make her and the island of St. Lucia part of Western history, literature, and culture. Only through their failures are they able to escape their own
colonizing attitudes. This process of decolonization entails abandoning the categories "colonized" and "colonizer" in St. Lucia's postcolonial society. As a result,
the old wounds of Plunkett (LXI.iii, 309)[11] and of the narrator (LIX.i, 294f.) start
healing. This process of healing provides the closure to *Omeros.* H. as a reader is
excluded from this closure, but the healing power of reception has made her understand more of *Omeros* than most critics have done according to Walcott (1997)
232f.:[12]

> I . . . knew (and know) that nobody takes the last part of the book seriously . . . If
> you look (if you take the trouble to look) at *Omeros,* you will see that the last third
> of it is a total refutation of the efforts made by two characters. First, there is the
> effort by the historian, Plunkett . . . The second effort is made by the writer, or nar-
> rator . . . who composes a long poem in which he compares this island woman to
> Helen of Troy. The answer to both the historian and the poet/narrator . . . is that
> the woman doesn't need it.

At the moment it does not matter how (un)authoritative Walcott's statement
is. It is only important in as far as it suggests that readers of *Omeros* do not
necessarily have an experience similar to that of H. By saying so it reveals a low
awareness of the role of the receiver within reception studies and calls for further
research in this area. This has also been H.'s conclusion, for by now she has learnt
that reception depends entirely on a receiver's initiative and that, at the same time,
the receiver has to subject herself to the process of reception if she does not want
to miss its point.

This insight suggests a new interpretation of the function of the Homeric
correspondences and their denial in *Omeros.* The two-step narrative argument
of first the association with Homer's poetry and then the negation of any similarities has puzzled a number of critics. They have argued that this process is either
to be seen as a means to redefine epic (Davis), or to remind us of the true (oral,
non-authoritative) nature of epic (Farrell; Dougherty) on the one hand, or, on
the other, as an expression of the poet's later irritation with earlier parts of the
poem (Breslin).[13] However, according to H.'s experience, the double argument
itself is crucial for the reader's understanding of life on St. Lucia as described in
Omeros. This is probably true for most if not all the readers educated at a Western
institution. How the Homeric/non-Homeric argument of *Omeros* works for other
readers/receivers is someone else's story to tell.

11 For a more negative reading of Plunkett see Fumagalli (2001) 213–15.
12 Walcott's claim has been contested by Breslin (2001) 243, who names Terada
    ((1992) 185) as a critic among others who have taken the last part of *Omeros* ser-
    iously even before Walcott stressed its importance.
13 Davis (1997b) 327–30; Farrell (1997) 261–7 (Beissinger, Tylus, and Wofford (1999)
    283–7); Dougherty (1997) 337, 355f.; Breslin (2001) 271f.

17

Remodeling Receptions

Greek Drama as Diaspora in Performance

Lorna Hardwick

This discussion sets out a possible model for the situation, explanation, and criticism of very modern receptions of Greek drama. The vibrancy of Greek drama productions in the last third of the twentieth century and beyond has been associated with wider aesthetic, cultural, and political changes.[1] This has happened in a paradoxical situation in which it is claimed that Greek drama is revived at times of crisis and yet knowledge of ancient Greece and Rome and access to classical languages has long been displaced from the center of modern Western culture. Debates about translation and staging and the responses of audiences and critics are part of a contested cultural space. Examples of new stagings and revivals pile up, yet they need a better explanatory framework for analysis if they are not merely to represent a kind of presentist antiquarianism.[2] There have been two noteworthy recent discussions of what a stronger theoretical framework might involve. Edith Hall has examined the provenance of the theoretical approaches most commonly used in the performance analysis that underpins studies of receptions of Greek and Roman drama and locates these firmly within the European tradition.[3] Kevin J. Wetmore Jr. has explored types of interaction between Greek culture and African and African American receptions.[4] Wetmore has called attention to the importance of foundation myths in Greek culture and to their impact on reception and has noted the variety of interpretations and critiques that have been applied to the Athenian democratic culture that provided the context for the plays. Valuable

---

1 Hardwick (2000a) ch. 4.
2 The databases of the Oxford University Archive of Performances of Greek and Roman Drama <http://www.apgrd.ox.ac.uk> and the Open University Reception of Classical Texts Research Project <http://www2.open.ac.uk/ClassicalStudies/GreekPlays> both provide extensive documentation to support a broader research framework. The former provides a historical perspective, the latter focuses on the processes of creation of modern performance and its relationship with cultural realignments.
3 Hall (2004).
4 Wetmore (2002, 2003).

work has been done on particular aspects of performance history and staging.[5] Furthermore, it has been suggested that at some time in the twentieth century the plays ceased to "belong" to the European tradition.[6] Analysis of turning points in cultural history has emphasized interaction between innovation and renovation and the energizing impact of diaspora situations.[7] I suggest that provisional explanation and the framing of future research questions may be helped by the heuristic use of a model which frames the diasporic situations in which Greek plays have been staged in the late twentieth and early twenty-first centuries.

The term "diasporic situation" covers a variety of voluntary and involuntary conditions of displacement, migration, and exile of communities and individuals together with associated conceptions of origins, cultural memory, and the defining practices of identity.[8] The richness of the Greek plays as fields for working through these issues is enhanced by the fact that the play-texts are themselves diasporic, uprooted from their origins in time, place, and language and reread through the filters of subsequent cultural contexts.[9] Conceptualizing classical texts as in themselves diasporic requires ongoing review in the light of new evidence. Receptions may be perceived as continually reconstituting the ancient texts and/or as revealing previously hidden and marginalized facets (in itself an indicator of further appropriations). Interaction between the deracinated text and the changing contexts of reception provokes contests about genealogy and challenges foundation myths. A diasporic model of classical reception implies a dialogic relationship between ancient and modern and is inimical to models which see reception as relevant only to the receiving context. Moreover, since migrations involve continuity as well as change, mapping collisions and overlaps between different reconstitutions of the "same" ancient play text also challenges models which see each reconstituted reading as irretrievably alienated both from the ancient text and from other receptions.

The Dynamics of Cultural Engagement in Diaspora Situations

A threefold process of cultural and political engagement has been identified as a positive and dynamic characteristic of diaspora communities.[10] It is possible to track

---

5   Macintosh (1997, 2000); McDonald (1992, 2000, 2003); McDonald and Walton (2002); Taplin (1977, 1978); Macintosh et al. (2005); Walton (1987, 2002); Wiles (2000, 2003, 2004).

6   Foley (2001).

7   Burke (1998); Greig (2000) 27.

8   Barkan and Shelton (1998); Bery and Murray (2000); Brah (1996); Hall (1990); Mishra (1996); Safran (1991); Saïd (1993).

9   Martindale (1993). Discontinuity is evident even in the cultural and political contexts of Greece itself: see Van Steen (2001, 2002a, 2002b, 2002c).

10   Gilroy (1993); Hardwick (2004a).

this process through analysis of individual case studies of the translation, adaptation, and staging of Greek drama and through the comparison of the appropriation of particular source plays in different cultural and political contexts. The comparative element also enables a critical stance towards unilinear models of development and "progression." The first stage in political engagement involves what cultural critics have called *self-emancipation*. This self-emancipation may be from slavery, subjugation, or any kind of oppressed or victim status. It is not synonymous with the material act of liberation or independence. Rather, it is a drawn-out process that chronologically, morally, and intellectually may precede, accompany, or follow physical independence.[11] As exemplified in drama, this process of self-emancipation takes different forms according to the cultural politics of the theatrical context, the degree of overt or implicit censorship, and the immediate and longer-term aspirations of the writers, directors, actors, and audiences.

For example, in South Africa, Greek drama has been used in a variety of theatrical forms as a means of confronting apartheid and challenging restrictive assumptions about the aesthetic and cultural energies of marginalized groups. Workshop theater evolved in the townships which were themselves a space in which people who had been displaced from their land came together.[12] Workshop theater began as an art form of protest and consciousness-raising in which the actors initially improvised and then developed their work to share with audiences the moments of reversal, recognition, and aspiration that the cast themselves had experienced. At a time when most politically committed theater groups were repressed by the authorities, various township theater groups staged Greek plays. The themes of resistance and civil strife made *Antigone* the play of choice and groups such as TECON (The Theatre Council of Natal) and the Serpent Players staged free adaptations of Sophocles' play.[13] The Serpent Players production grew into the play-within-a-play that made Antigone the pivotal force in *The Island*, a collaboration between Athol Fugard, Winston Ntshona, and John Kani first performed in 1973. The play's influence extended far beyond its immediate impact. For actors and audiences, Antigone was perceived not only as freedom fighter but also as an icon of conscience. Creon was not only an oppressor but a man who had failed to think through the responsibilities of power.[14] So the production showed the way to other adaptations that reflected on the dilemmas of resistance. It also anticipated later developments in multilingual and intracultural theater by using everyday language, far removed from the formal language associated with canonical drama and mixing Xhosa, Afrikaans, and English, although some of these aspects were diluted as the play moved beyond Southern Africa. Its performance history exemplifies the move from protest play to canonical status, both within South Africa

11   Ngugi (1986).
12   Fleishman (1990); Walder (1993).
13   van Zyl Smit (2003).
14   Mandela (1994); Hardwick (2000a) ch. 4.

and beyond. Thirty years after the original samizdat performance there was a tri-umphant "final tour" in Europe with Kani and Ntshona in their original roles.

However, not all performances of Greek drama in South Africa in the apartheid period necessarily invited or even stimulated direct and radical critique of the regime. This variability is found in many cultural locations and suggests that the emergence of a transformative theatrical aesthetic is a problematic and irregular process involving reconfigurations of formal and traditional elements as well as audience expectations.[15]

Similarly, the process of self-emancipation is complex and prone to interruption, involving intracultural as well as cross-cultural aesthetics and cultural politics. These issues persist into the second aspect of the process of political engagement in diaspora situations – *the achievement of civic participation in new contexts.* Southern African research has again been prominent in opening up this field, and in particular has examined the ways in which workshop theater and its analogues has moved from being a protest and consciousness-raising art form to one that is actively reconstructing and revising cultural relationships in the new South Africa, including addressing controversial problems.

An example of this in practice is *The City of Paradise*, an adaptation of the Electra myth, staged at the University of Capetown in 1998 in a period when the post-apartheid democratic government of South Africa was facing a situation of strongly contested questions of revenge, retribution, and the possibility of forgiveness for the wrongs inflicted by apartheid. The Truth and Reconciliation Commission, established in 1995, provided a public space for the victims and perpetrators of apartheid to confront the past and create a more hopeful future. The director and actor Mark Fleishman, who had already in 1994–6 created a multilingual *Medea*, worked with students to make a new version of the Electra story, drawing on Aeschylus' *Choephoroi*, the *Electra* plays of Sophocles and Euripides, and Euripides' *Orestes*.[16] Analysis of the resulting production indicated that most of the characteristics of township workshop theater were present: specifically, the play was created by a group for performance; it had more to do with life experi-ence than with literary responses; it drew on traditional oral forms; the perform-ance style was characteristic of township culture – non-naturalistic, physical, musical, including narrative and dance within the performance; it displayed an ironic and comic vision; it represented an urban form of cultural expression in which the emphasis was on the collective and the regenerative and transformative potential of drama.[17] This suggests that in a situation in which the urgency of the present was dominant, both aesthetically and politically, the Greek myth provided a field in which shared cultural encounter with the ancient could lead to cultural inter-action in the present.

15 Selaiha (2002).
16 Mezzabotta (2000); Steinmeyer (forthcoming).
17 Steinmeyer (forthcoming).

This process of *political and cultural development in a new and autonomous space* is the third main characteristic of diaspora situations. Theatrical space becomes both a physical and a metaphorical site for a variety of developments. Fémi Òsòfisan's *Women of Owu* (2004), based on Euripides' *Women of Troy*, was subtitled "A Tale of Women as the Spoils of War," a description that applied equally to the ancient play and its modern adaptation. Òsòfisan's version highlighted the interdependence of art forms, cultural hybridity, and multiple political expressions. At the time when Euripides' play was first performed (415 BCE) the war between the Athenians and the Spartans had led to a series of destructions of smaller poleis, the most recent being Melos (416) in which the male citizens were killed by the Athenians and the women and children sold into slavery (Thucydides 5.116). Òsòfisan gave the play a West African setting and, more importantly, a setting in the past that encouraged reflection on African history. In the early 1820s the city of Owu was sacked after a seven-year siege in which many people were displaced and the city itself reduced to rubble. The male population was massacred by the combined forces of two neighboring Yoruba kingdoms. So one layer of meaning in the play is recognition of the abuse of power in nineteenth-century Yorubaland, in which suffering was imposed by African upon African, just as in the fifth century BCE it was imposed by Greek upon Greek. However, the fact that *Women of Owu* was being written in 2003 and staged in 2004 created resonances with the war in Iraq, to which there were verbal and semiotic allusions (the besieging army was called "the allied forces"; there was parody of the rhetoric of liberation and its relationship with material greed). The Chorus, sang, danced, and spoke mainly as a group, stressing commonalities in suffering and insight. They faced out to include the audience, challenging it to make connections with suffering anywhere. Òsòfisan also exploited and adapted the Greek theatrical conventions of the Messenger Speech so that the Herald (the Talthybius figure) addressed the audience on child-killing and the slaughter of Astyanax stood for the death of children in Iraq as well as Africa.[18]

This multiple layering of text and counter-texts is characteristic of modern West African adaptations of Greek drama.[19] They are not polemical or narrowly partisan. Blame is not unequivocal. The plays not only critique colonial oppression (past and present) but also challenge internal and localized injustices and complicities. They intervene to transform perspectives on West African sociopolitics both historically and after independence. This has exposed dramatists such as Òsòfisan, Rotimi, and Soyinka to charges of political and cultural disloyalty and even complicity with neocolonialism.[20] There are also significant tensions

18 Some audiences found the historical and cultural agility that was required to follow the layering of meaning too challenging; see the review by the theater critic Joyce MacMillan, *The Scotsman* (February 21, 2004), 11.
19 Budelmann (2004 and forthcoming).
20 McDonald (2000); Okpewho (1991); Simpson (forthcoming).

between, on the one hand, claims that adaptations of Greek drama by African writers have revalidated African history and theater traditions and incidentally restored to Greek drama in performance the awareness of song, dance, body and vocal texture, design, and color that European and North American performance traditions may have marginalized; and, on the other hand, that many African adaptations have resulted from commissions from Western Europe and North America, rather than from communities in Africa, and may cater for the perceived tastes of Western audiences.[21] So far as *Women of Owu* is concerned, the Choral songs were in the Yoruba language, with new lyrics set to traditional music and drawing on traditional forms such as the Oriki (praise song) which can be both religious and profane. The role of dance also witnessed to its historical importance in cultural resistance to oppression and slavery and the baring of their breasts by the female Chorus represented the significance of nudity in Yoruba culture as the last resort of resistance. All these factors contributed to a performance style that combined protest, lament, and comedy to ensure the involvement of the audience and exploited the formal elements of both Greek and Yoruba theater.[22] This suggests a recontextualization and reconceptualization of tragedy, initially within the cultural framework of the author, director, and actors but also aiming to transform the experience of audiences (in this case in the West).[23]

The challenging impact on contemporary cultural and political debates that has been created by performances of Greek plays is not, however, confined to the multiple perspectives created by African drama migrations. In Glasgow, Scotland, in 2000 three leading Scottish playwrights were commissioned to adapt Greek tragedies as a mark of the flourishing of theater arts in Scotland in the years before and following devolution. The reconvening of the Scottish Parliament after a gap of almost 300 years was marked by celebrations of Scottish culture and identity and a reexamination of sociopolitical traditions and assumptions. One of the three Greek plays chosen for the occasion was Sophocles' *Oedipus Tyrannos*, adapted by David Greig as *Oedipus*.[24]

21 Òsòfisan's *Women of Owu* had its world premiere commissioned by Chipping Norton theater in Oxfordshire, UK and his *Tegonni: An African Antigone* was commissioned and produced by Emory University, Atlanta, GA, USA in 1994. Soyinka produced major critical and theatrical work while in Cambridge, England in the 1970s, and his *The Bacchae of Euripides* (1973) was commissioned by the National Theatre in London.

22 Source: interview with the director, Chuck Mike, by Felix Budelmann, London, May 13, 2004, documented in entry 2719 in the database of the Open University Reception of Classical Texts Research Project at <http://www2.open.ac.uk/ClassicalStudies/GreekPlays>.

23 For discussion of recontextualization in African theater and techniques for creating audience participation, see Djisenu (forthcoming).

24 The other plays were Sophocles' *Electra*, adapted by Tom McGrath, and Euripides' *Medea*, adapted by Liz Lochhead, which subsequently toured internationally and was published (Lochhead (2000)).

Greig's version explored ambivalences about identity which were mythical, historical, and contemporary. At the time of devolution, there was a sense that Scotland was emerging from domination by the English, that its situation was in some sense postcolonial. However, as part of Great Britain the role of Scots in the growth and administration of the British empire had been extensive and Scottish identity in the eighteenth and nineteenth centuries had been closely interwoven with that of empire – as slave-traffickers, settlers, soldiers in armies of conquest and occupation, and in administration and policy-making. Furthermore, Gaelic speakers were evicted from their crofts in the Highlands of Scotland and forced to emigrate, as were many of the urban poor.[25]

Greig's adaptation resonated with these ambivalent aspects of the identity of Scots as both colonizers and colonized, agents for displacement and themselves displaced, nostalgic for a home society that existed only in the memory and for a past in which that status of victim and oppressor was confused. He drew on the psychology and politics of unwitting incest as a metaphor for colonial relationships and through setting, design, and language the production, directed by Graham McLaren, reworked the Greek dramatic conventions to address current debates through exposure of the complexities of the past.[26] The costume and setting suggested the India of the British Raj and explored the semiotics of class and race in the Indian context. Set design suggested ironically that the sun was setting over a colonized and plague-ridden city. The language and acting styles ensured that there was never an easy definition of what or who was colonized. Creon and Oedipus spoke in Scots accents and idiom and through his use of the *agon* Greig charted how their roles of usurper and liberator fluctuated throughout the play. The Chorus of villagers associated the plague with old wounds – "Its cut open scars? And picked at scabs / Leave it alone' (text 27).[27] The closing Chorus looked at what Oedipus stood for and what also destroyed him – "This is Oedipus. Dam builder / Road maker / Visionary / He has been consumed by the fire of his own life . . ." (text 53–4). Thus at the end, Greig's Oedipus became in retrospect a flawed and yet Promethean figure in the collective memory, just as the action of the play itself revealed the deep fissures and complicities in the exercise of imperial power.

Nostalgia, Cultural Memory, and Identity

This range of diaspora situations problematizes all three aspects of cultural and political engagement. Notions of "home," of nostalgia, and of contested identities and genealogies emerged alongside the ongoing political dynamic as equally

---

25 Devine (1999, 2003).
26 Hardwick (2004c).
27 I am grateful to David Greig for allowing me to study his as yet unpublished play-text.

significant features of diaspora situations. This section of the chapter discusses some examples of how dramatization of Greek material has worked through these dilemmas, in practices that engage in dialogue with both the positive and negative aspects of diaspora theory that might otherwise be polarized. Problematic conceptions and realizations of "home" highlight the ways in which diaspora situations involve not only migration and even scattering of displaced individuals and groups but also desires and aspirations of resettlement, either in a return "home" or in a reconstruction in another place, time, and sometimes language of the "home" that exists in the individual or collective memory. Both "home" and "host" communities may be involved in this process and alignment. Exploration of these dilemmas in the contexts of staging may involve improvisation in response to present pressures as well as mining of the structural and formal aspects of the text, its themes, language, and fields of reference. Improvisation may create startling new connections with the Greek material that illuminate the ancient and modern texts and contexts. Equally it may overburden the ancient and the modern with the weight of the concerns of the moment.

Greek drama has become a significant site for working out these antinomies of nostalgia for a past which is unrecoverable. The continuing vibrancy of the experiences associated with "home" and the desire for a future that can embrace both past and present has become a feature of community drama projects in which both amateur and professional actors can work through their own experiences and then combine to reach out to audiences who then in terms of their theatrical experiences become metaphorical if not actual members of a diasporic community. In 2004 this process was exemplified in the production of Aeschylus' *Agamemnon* staged by Foursight Theatre and directed by Dorinda Hulton at an arts center in a multicultural community in Wolverhampton, England. The production, part-sponsored by the Arts Council, was in a studio theater. At each end of the traverse acting space were altars surrounded by objects. One end represented "war," the other "home," so there was a metatheatrical comment on the construction of both in the cultural frameworks of Aeschylus and of the audience, each context having its attendant myths. The open space between the two "ends" provided a place for encounter, conflict, and, perhaps, resolution. The traverse allowed the moves of the Chorus to take place in the space between the polarized elements. This was especially effective given the diversity in gender, age, ethnicity, and social status represented in the Chorus. They were not the Elders of Argos, as in Aeschylus, but a cross section of those left behind by the war or caught up in its aftermath. This diversity was reflected in the languages used by the Chorus. Sections of the text were sung and/or spoken in Gujerati, Turkish, Spanish, and Jamaican patois, translated by members of the cast themselves from the English version – significantly the company had chosen a close translation by Philip de May.[28] Music for the words sung in languages other than English was

28 De May (2003).

specially composed from the musical traditions associated with those languages. Ritual from Muslim, Hindu, and Christian traditions was integrated into the actions of the Chorus on the basis of the previous knowledge or special research of the cast into their own backgrounds.[29] Thus the Chorus created a new collective voice, one that recognized the value of rituals remembered from the traditions of individuals and used these to invent a new community. The effect of the linguistic and cultural diversity of the responses to the Greek context and to the Trojan war was to put the audience in the place of those caught up in something that was both familiar and strange, a war and its aftermath in which they sometimes directly understood the words and actions and sometimes watched as cultural strangers.

This is one example of the contribution of Greek plays to a wider trend of productions in which as many languages are used as are naturally spoken by the cast.[30] Such multilingualism is also embedded in the production style. The important point is not that it seeks to create cross-cultural performance across national or ethnic borders but that it reflects diversity *within* communities and marks new cultural collaborations. In so far as multilingualism is used within and alongside translations into English, it also makes a significant statement about the ambivalent status of English as a language which is both associated with imperial cultural and political domination (including the dissemination of classical culture as appropriated by the West) and yet is also a lingua franca among nations and communities with disparate traditions, whether in Nigeria, the Caribbean, or Wolverhampton. So far as de-appropriation and reappropriation of Greek plays is concerned it both allows a variety of languages and cultures to "mark" the plays, claiming them as their own, and acts as a reminder that the English language also has a history as an anti-colonial mechanism.[31]

Return to the "home" represented by the past can, however, be devastating for the present and this situation was confronted in Derek Walcott's *The Odyssey: A Stage Version*, first performed in 1992.[32] This play, an example of the trend towards cross-genre explorations of Greek material, took up the Homeric trope of the deferred homecoming. The narrative centered on the figure of the blind singer Billy Blue who sang at the interface between diaspora and aesthetic invention, representing the traveling bard of Homeric Greece and also the blues singer, an expression of twentieth-century black consciousness that shaped cultural responses in Europe and North America. This framing device articulated disparate

29 Sometimes this research crossed generations – help from the actor's grandfather was needed for the translation into Gujerati.

30 There are other recent examples in Glasgow (Scotland), Ife (Nigeria), Minnesota (USA), and South Africa (Òsòfisan (1999); Mezzabotta (2000); Hardwick (2005c)).

31 Brathwaite (1984); Friel (1981); Hardwick (2005c), Kiberd (1998); Ngugi (1986); Soyinka (1999); Talib (2002).

32 Published text Walcott (1993).

cultural horizons that both actualized and subverted the correspondences between the ancient episodes and their modern analogues. The experiences of Odysseus resonated with twentieth-century articulation of the post-traumatic stress disorders of returning soldiers but they also explored ambivalences in conceptions of the "home" Odysseus had come from and that to which he would return.[33] His "past" was revisited in the visit to the underworld, a *katabasis* achieved through the medium of both Shango and Christian rituals drawn from the Caribbean context that had shaped Walcott's awareness.[34] This strand of the play explored variations on Caribbean cultural consciousness that recognized the contribution of but denied the hegemony of either African or colonial antecedents.[35]

These uncertainties about "home" and cultural mediations exploded in Odysseus' confrontation with Penelope over the slaughter of the suitors, the proposed hanging of the serving maid, and the fumigation of the house. Aesthetic and ethical plausibility became criteria for the audience's authentication of the commonalities and differences between Homeric culture and that represented in the play. It was culturally and politically plausible for the Homeric bard to be a blues singer (and for the Cyclops to be a totalitarian tyrant) but Penelope, a woman of intelligence and *kleos* in Homer, could not plausibly be sent back to the upper room as she was in *Odyssey* 21. 350–8. In Walcott's play Penelope did not prevent the slaughter of the suitors who represented the pollution of war – "Troy's mulch. Troy's rain? Wounds. Festering diseases."[36] But she could and did protest at the house becoming an abattoir[37] and she could and did prevent the hanging of the black maid Melantho in a scene that has become a crux of modern classical reception practice, resonating with the unspoken history of the sexual abuse of women in war and slavery.

The ways in which Odysseus' return to Ithaca has been handled in the most recent adaptations of *The Odyssey* for the stage reveal a deep-seated unease in modern Western perceptions of the cultural force of the poem. Peter Oswald's 1999 version concentrated on Odysseus' psychological trauma as a returning warrior and his reestablishment at home was explored in terms of the healing of his mind. Collision between ancient and modern values was denied and the killing of the maids and fumigation of the house were omitted.[38] In 2005, David Farr's version brought together the personal and social trauma of displacement represented by Trojan asylum seekers.[39] Homeric techniques were used to achieve a

33   Hardwick (2004a, 2004b).
34   Hardwick (1995).
35   For Caribbean reaction against the controlling influence of myths of African origins, see Hardwick (2002) and Greenwood (2004).
36   Walcott (1993), II.vi.151.
37   Walcott (1993), II.vi.153.
38   Oswald (1999) discussed in Hardwick (2004b) 349–50.
39   David Farr, *The Odyssey: A New Retelling After Homer*, Bristol Old Vic/West Yorkshire Playhouse, performance documented, Leeds, April 9, 2005.

reordering of chronology in which the killing of the suitors was foreshadowed in Odysseus' visit to the underworld and the play ended with Odysseus landing in Ithaca and being asked by Eumaios, "Who are you?" This ending left his future actions open, but the maids were expunged from the narrative and an element of suppression of ethical collision remained. Walcott's handling was more radical. His rejection of a closure in which the return "home" would legitimize slavery and the treatment of human beings as objects required the renegotiation of the norms that were to be "restored." In this sense the closing scene of Walcott's version of the *Odyssey* became a kind of performative *katabasis*, an exploration of the complicities of a literary tradition of which the writer himself was a part. Transplantation to the stage of the epic motifs of *nostos* and *katabasis* provides a formal as well as psychological framework for denying the absolute recovery of the past. At the same time it becomes a vehicle for developing a double (or even multiple) consciousness that precludes submission to nostalgia.

Walcott associates nostalgia with the psychology of affliction and acceptance of the status of victim and has explored this both in his critical writing and in his poetry, especially in the figure of Philoctete in *Omeros*.[40] This problematic nexus between notions of affliction, identity, ethnicity, historical experience, and their articulation in the cultural memory underlies the conflicts over the status of *négritude* as a source of cultural energy and as a marker for critical debate. Fémi Òsòfisan has used the phrase "the trenches of négritude" to characterize a situation of out-dated but damaging stalemate in cultural conflict.[41] *Négritude* is itself a linguistically ambivalent term associated particularly with the work of Césaire, Damas, and Senghor in the 1950s when it was used to celebrate pride in black identity and in the past origins of present culture.[42] The concept was important for political and cultural liberation but has been criticized on the grounds that it can encourage a backward-looking concern with genealogies and suffering. This militates against active shaping of the future in contexts that require awareness of multiple and overlapping identities and spheres of activity, both within Africa and in African diasporas. The concept of *négritude* has been criticized for running together histories, circumstances, and senses of identity that were historically different and for privileging the imposition of unifying but potentially oppressive political structures and cultural identities.[43] Receptions of Greek drama and epic have developed practices which both engage with these critiques and also move beyond them.

Thus examination of adaptations and stagings of Greek plays in diasporic situations shows that they have provided a field both for revisiting the sites of past conflicts and for recognizing the problematic relationship between constructions

40   Walcott (1990, 1998); Ramazani (1997); Hardwick (1997).
41   Òsòfisan (1999).
42   Greenwood (2004); Davis (1997a).
43   Soyinka (1999).

of the past and aspirations for the future. The themes and the distant cultural provenance and complex migratory patterns of the Greek plays enable recontextualizations that recognize particularity and yet perform this in interaction with commonality. They recognize the force of ethical and political energies without subsuming these in metanarratives of progress and enlightenment. Receptions in performance thus constitute counter-texts that contest the dominance of any one diasporic perspective. This artistic and cultural praxis has been possible because the Greek plays themselves are diasporic; their migrations and receptions in different aesthetic, cultural, and political contexts have created spaces for the remapping and reevaluation of the theory and practice of Greek drama and its associated traditions and also for the invention of new ones.

18

Reception, Performance, and the Sacrifice of Iphigenia

Pantelis Michelakis

The relation between dramatic text and performance has often developed along the lines of an opposition between the authenticity and originality of the text and the derivative and ministerial role of performance. Throughout their history, theater theory and practice, with all their aesthetic, ethical, psychological, and social frames, have repeatedly promoted a hierarchical order which has reduced performance to an illustration, translation, or fulfillment of the text.[1] Similarly, theories of the theater have often privileged a model of analysis of the theatrical performance which has replicated the textual model of authority, favoring the director and the canonical actor or spectator, and operating within a concept of finality of explanation familiar from literary studies. The director, actor, and spectator have often become sources of monologic authority which have driven the author out of the theater only to take his place. This is true not only for the commercial stage but sometimes for the avant-garde theater as well, whose driving force has often been associated with a nostalgia for origins.[2]

Complicity with authority, then, is not to be associated only with textual practices. It has been central to visual and performance practices as well. This is an important reason why in the last couple of decades performance studies has emerged not within but in opposition to theater or drama studies, sidestepping the whole Western theatrical tradition and prompting one of its "founding fathers," Richard Schechner, to declare the demise of theater with the notorious statement that the staging of written dramas "will be the string quartet of the twenty-first century: a beloved but extremely limited genre, a subdivision of performance."[3]

For valuable suggestions and comments I am grateful to audiences in Bristol and Oxford, and particularly to the editors of the present volume, as well as to Duncan Kennedy, Miriam Leonard, and Kostas Valakas.

1 Carlson (1985).
2 See, for instance, Derrida's (1997) critique of Artaud; Fuchs (2003).
3 Schechner (1992) 8.

Performance has become a mode of resistance to textual authority, or, as Reinelt puts it, a means of "breaking down hierarchies of elite art, recovering the history of forms of performance by including rituals, festivals and other civic events, which previously were the provenance of ethnography or anthropology."[4] With its critique of agency, subjectivity, language, and law, performance has come to define itself in direct opposition to a rigid model of textuality, and along the way it has exposed the elusive singularity of theater based on claims of presence, contingency, and the physicality of the actor's body. Performance studies has sought to relocate theater within the context of a much wider range of artistic, social, and behavioral activities, all under the umbrella of the "performative." "[P]lay, reality, and culture," Carlson argues, "are all involved in a continually shifting pattern of concepts and practices that condition each other, and rather than attempt to separate or privilege any of these terms, the critic or theorist of human activity should have as a goal the explanation of 'how this nature-culture manifests itself in different historical and cultural contexts.'"[5]

In its long history, theater may have encountered formidable enemies who fought it from outside and from within. However, it has also won loyal friends and admirers for whom it has served as a paradigm. Theater has pushed onto center stage aspects of the construction of meaning often concealed in other art forms – most notably the roles of space and frame and of the interaction or collaboration between participants in the experience of the artistic event. Some of the best work in this area has been done by theory critics who have drawn on theater to debate the various forms and problems of reading and the limits of textuality. Theater and theatricality have been used as models to explain the activity and to define the object of a number of theories, including narratology, structuralism, psychoanalysis, gender studies, and philosophy. As Mária Brewer argues, each of these theories has drawn on theater for different reasons, and as a result it has constructed a different type of theater.[6] By and large, though, the theater of theory has been cast to play one or the other of two antithetical roles. On the one hand, theatricality has been used as a conservative force, a force of closure thought to pose a threat to the disruptive potential of radical art. To quote from Brewer, "the imaginary theatre that theory sets up to account for . . . mise-en-scène, is a surprisingly conventional and unproblematic one of textual self-presentation that is at odds with the challenge to narrative representation in contemporary writing."[7] On the other hand, theatricality has served as a metaphor for division and difference, for polyvalence, for a "play of limits and borders."[8] Theater has served to emphasize self-reflexivity

4   Reinelt (2003) 160–1.
5   Carlson (1996) 29, quoting Ehrmann (1968) 50.
6   Brewer (1985). On theatricality in French theory see a collection of articles in Murray (1997).
7   Brewer (1985) 15.
8   Brewer (1985) 19.

and polyphony, enabling the shift, and I quote from Brewer again, "from thought as seeing and knowing, originating in the subject alone, to the many decentered processes of framing and staging that representation requires but dissimulates."[9]

Reception studies has not systematically drawn on theater as an art form, nor has it deployed it as a frame of reference for interpretation to the extent that some of the disciplines mentioned above have. Since its emergence in the 1960s, reception theory has been preoccupied with literary texts and with the practice of reading. Its more recent shift towards cultural and media studies has similarly bypassed theater. For instance, in Machor and Goldstein's introduction to the recent collection of articles entitled *Reception Study: From Literary Theory to Cultural Studies* the reception of *Hamlet* is reduced to different strategies of reading a printed text, with the theatrical character of the play going unacknowledged.[10] A genealogically related concept, though, which both Hans Robert Jauss and Wolfgang Iser have derived from anthropology and sociology via Gadamer, is that of the "play."[11] The transformation of the text into a playground takes us back to the two theaters of theory. Jauss has used the notion of the "play" in his *Aesthetic Experience and Literary Hermeneutics* for the insights it provides into ritual acts whose opposition to the constraints of the everyday may be liberating but which also enforce the servitude of new roles and of collective identities.[12] Iser, on the other hand, has drawn on the concept of the "play" both in *Prospecting* and especially in *The Fictive and the Imaginary* as a way out of mimetic notions of representation and as a mode of resistance against the finality of explanation and the certainties it provides.[13]

If theater theory and practice had a limited impact on reception theory, the opposite holds true for the reception of reception theory in the world of theater studies. Since the late 1970s, European theater scholars such as Patrice Pavis, Anne Ubersfeld, and Erika Fischer-Lichte, have drawn systematically on reception theory to redefine the theatrical event from a semiotic point of view and to reinvent the role of the spectator not as passive and detached but as creative and participatory.[14] Less preoccupied with the performative turn than their American colleagues and more interested in the comeback of theatricality, European scholars have turned to reception theory to recast their subject and to reinstate its paradigmatic force.[15] In the world of classical studies, on the other

---

9   Brewer (1985) 16.

10 Machor and Goldstein (2001) xi–xii.

11 On Gadamer's definition of play in relation to the work of art see Gadamer (1975) esp. 91–119. The single most influential study of the significance of play in culture is Huizinga (1970).

12 Jauss (1982c) 164–7.

13 Iser (1989) 249–61 and esp. (1993b) 247–303.

14 See Calandra (1993) and Pavis (1993).

15 On the American affiliations of performativity and the European ones of theatricality see Reinelt (2003).

hand, performance reception has evolved into a rather different phenomenon, not only because of its thematic focus on Greco-Roman drama and its different geographical spread – it is in Britain that it has been embraced most enthusiastically – but also because of its disciplinary affiliations which are with theater history and historiography, as well as cultural studies, rather than theater theory or reception theory.[16] In contrast with the performance reception theorized about in European theater studies, that practiced by British classicists has oscillated between empiricism and historicism, dramatic analysis and cultural relativism, an openness to interpretative frameworks and cultural practices and a defense of its methodological eclecticism and of the autonomy of its field.

What I would like to do here is to go back to dramatic texts, exploring ways in which they can be subjected to a performance-oriented analysis. Rather than locating "the meanings of the stage in the contours of the dramatic text,"[17] rehearsing the priority of text to performance, I want to try the reverse, to look at how texts and their readings can embody performance theory and practice. Rather than trying to master theatrical performance with textual explanations or reading theories, I want to look at some of the ways in which "the conceptual tools of performance studies and performance theory can be used to expand the ways of talking about" dramatic texts.[18] If performances have often been read as versions of texts, versions which fail to do justice to the multiplicity and ambiguity of an authoritative, original text, this chapter sets out to explore an alternative model in which readings, like performances, substitute and redeem the text even when they seem simply to reproduce it. There are two concepts on which I will draw to define the performative nature of the relation between text and reading: transformation and substitution. I take the terms from Richard Schechner and Joseph Roach respectively. Interpretation, like performance, transforms something into something else; it takes a material object and turns it into a sign of a sign, into something which is both "not itself" and "not not itself," "not familiar" and "not not familiar." It is this transformative process that makes interpretation performative and, like memory or perception at large, potentially creative and pleasurable.[19] Transformation can of course fail. It can also become mechanically repetitive, or standardized within the limits of a certain tradition. However it can also produce something new, something which establishes itself on the grounds not of what it repeats but of the fact that it will be repeated.[20] The process of transformation is not always smooth. Substitutes often meet with distrust and

16 See, most recently, Hall (2004); Hardwick (2003a); Goldhill (1999).
17 Worthen (2003) 86.
18 Worthen (2003) 96.
19 States (2003) 127.
20 This is the taxonomy introduced by the philosopher Robert Crease in his discussion of performance in scientific experimentation: see further Crease (2003) and States (2003) 126–8.

resistance and need to be mobilized by what Joseph Roach calls "narratives of authenticity and priority," narratives which "may congeal into full-blown myths of legitimacy and origin."[21] Such narratives do not relate to the material substituted, but to the often concealed conventions of interpretation or framing devices which make the substitution possible. Acts of substitution neither reproduce the original material, nor do they gain their validity by it. Rather, they produce "the terms of its authorization in performance" embodying its memories or traces.[22]

Like theater itself, the reputation of Euripides' *Iphigenia at Aulis* (hereafter *IA*) has undergone extraordinary changes since it was first performed in, or around, 405 BCE. Today the play is best known for the corruption of its moral universe and the corruption of its text. If the *Bacchae*, together with which it was first performed, is unanimously accepted as Euripides' final masterpiece, an example of how well a "classic" has stood the test of time, *IA* is generally thought of as a counter-example of how badly a play has suffered from the passing of time. That this is a rather narrow perspective of the two plays becomes evident as soon as we look at earlier canons of Greek plays translated and performed, where the *Bacchae* is virtually absent and the now doomed *IA* central.[23] Here I will focus on three moments in the reception history of *IA* in terms more heuristic than historical, looking at the terms of discourse, the systems or conventions of interpretation deployed, and the models of theater summoned in each of them. It is the final scene of the play to which I will confine my attention, the scene of Iphigenia's sacrifice and her miraculous last-minute disappearance and substitution by a deer. If the dismemberment of Pentheus in the *Bacchae* and the fragmentary nature of that play's ending have been seen as metaphors for the fragmentation of the narrative, authority, and meaning,[24] the miracle of Iphigenia's disappearance and substitution puts forward an alternative model of interpretation based on the drama of sacrificial substitution. The stag which replaces Iphigenia restores ritual and social order not only by *becoming* the sacrificial victim it substitutes but also by pointing towards the invisible forces (Artemis, the gods) which make this transformation possible and which invest Iphigenia's disappearance with positive meaning. As a ritual practice, the act of the sacrifice conjures up "ideas of an interminable return, the reproduction and reduplication of patterns of social interaction and of symbolic meaning."[25] Yet as a piece of theater dramatizing the fate of an

21 Roach (1996) 2–3.
22 Worthen (2003) 98.
23 The modern reception history of the *IA* started as early as the beginning of the sixteenth century, with the translation of the play into Latin by Erasmus, whereas the *Bacchae* did not capture the modern imagination until the end of the nineteenth century. On the reception history of the *IA* see Reid (1993) 599–605 and Gliksohn (1985).
24 See, for instance, Segal (1997) index, s.v. *sparagmos*, and Fischer-Lichte (1998) 258–62.
25 Thompson (2003) 148.

extraordinary victim, the scene can also conjure up ideas of an interminable division and difference, becoming a site not for the concealment but for the revelation of patterns of social interaction and symbolic meaning.

My first case study is Jean Racine's *Iphigenia*. "It is to [Pausanias]," Racine writes in the preface to the first edition of his play in 1675,

> that I owe the fortunate discovery of [the character of] Eriphile without which I would never have dared to set my hand to this tragedy . . . I was most happy to find among the ancients this other Iphigenia, whom I was able to represent as I wanted, and who, as she meets the fate which, in her jealousy, she wished to bring upon her rival, in a way deserves to be punished, without being, however, altogether unworthy of compassion . . . And one need only have seen my work on the stage to understand the pleasure I have given the spectator both by saving in the end a virtuous princess in whom he has taken such a lively interest in the course of this tragedy, and by saving her by means other than a miracle, which he would not have tolerated because he would never have believed in it.[26]

Racine replaces the implausible miracle of Euripides' play with a near-tragedy of errors. In order to save Iphigenia and to restore the good name of Euripides' play, he comes up with a new character, the illegitimate child of Helen's affair with Theseus, who first rivals the "virtuous" Iphigenia for the heart of the hero Achilles and for the attention of the spectators and then replaces the deer slaughtered in her place by committing suicide. What legitimizes this double of Euripides' Iphigenia and her substitute? First, Racine points out, it is the textual authority of an ancient source, Pausanias. Second, it is the moral imperative of rewarding virtue and punishing jealousy and rivalry. Third, it is the adherence to verisimilitude, a neoclassical rule for the construction of the tragic plot. Fourth, it is the pleasure derived from seeing the play on stage. Eriphile is not "altogether unworthy of compassion," but her nature (both her illegitimate birth and her unpleasant character) make her self-inflicted punishment look just and desirable. Racine does not claim her as his brainchild but as a fortunate discovery which he felt entitled to develop according to his needs and eventually to dispose of, for everyone's benefit. Eriphile threatens to steal the (theatrical) show, but she eventually becomes the protagonist of a ritual which restores the moral framework of the myth and reaffirms Racine's ties to his primary source and his audiences. She is a character that Racine sacrifices to save Euripides' work from its implausibilities and to offer the spectator pleasure. In this benevolent world where virtue is eventually rewarded with good fortune and vice is punished, the reader of the play's printed text who has missed its performance – and the opportunity to see the spectator deriving pleasure from it – cannot be left empty-handed. Racine may be modest about what exactly the reader has missed – the play in an open

---

26 Quoted from the translation in Cairncross (1963) 50.

air theater set up for the occasion in the gardens of Versailles for the enjoyment of Louis XIV – but he offers a compensation for the loss, his preface.[27] What kind of replacement to such a performance the preface offers – whether it should be likened to the jealous Eriphile who rivals the virtuous Iphigenia or to the sacrificial Eriphile who replaces the original deer to bring a happy ending to the reader's tragedy – is for the reader to decide. Whatever his or her decision might be, Racine set not only the moral but also the theatrical standards for the celebration of the miraculous transformation of Euripides' Iphigenia for more than a century since the play was first performed and published in 1674: playwrights and, with the emergence of opera, librettists and composers, kept the miracle of moral justice and social order alive through lavish displays of Eriphile's death and Iphigenia's escape.

I will now move forward to 1934 to look at another preface, this time by the classical scholar Denys Page, to his classic study, *Actors' Interpolations in Greek Tragedy*:

> [s]ince the middle of the eighteenth century most scholars have agreed that *Iphigeneia in Aulis* is much interpolated. And it has always been the fashion to adduce reasons for calling some verses genuine and others spurious, and to build a text on this distinction.[28]

The first printed editions and translations of Euripides' *IA* date back to the early 1500s. Yet it was not until the second half of the eighteenth century and the emergence of textual criticism that the play gained its reputation as the subject of serious academic study. In the course of the century and a half which separated Page from the earliest textual critics of the age of the Enlightenment, *IA* became one of the most famous examples of the limitations imposed on our knowledge of ancient texts by centuries of copying and interpreting, a paradigm of the need for scientific criteria and methodologies to separate the ancient authors from their imitators. If neoclassical theater subjected Euripides to the moral gaze of the benevolent monarch (playwright, spectator, reader . . .), nineteenth-century philology turned Euripides into the object of the penetrating gaze of the textual critic. The arguments against the authenticity of the scene of the sacrifice, which scholars were going to rehearse enthusiastically (Page speaks of a "fashion") for generations to come, were first outlined as early as 1802 when Richard Porson, Regius Professor of Greek at Cambridge, published his second edition of Euripides' *Hecuba*. The extant ending of *IA*, it was argued, could not have been written by Euripides on linguistic and metrical grounds, as well as on the basis of a small fragment which the third-century author Aelian (*On the Nature of Animals*

---

27   Forestier (1999) 168–72. A detailed account of the event can be found in Félibien (1994) 141–3.

28   Page (1934) ix.

7.39) attributed to the play and which was delivered by the goddess Artemis herself (who is absent from the epilogue as we have it). If Euripides died before the play's first performance, then the task of completing or rewriting the epilogue – and perhaps other passages such as the prologue – could well have fallen to the dramatist who was involved in the play's production. If the text was mutilated in later times, it is Hellenistic or even Byzantine scribes and scholars who might have stepped in to complete it. Textual criticism recast and so recreated the text in a new idiom (Page speaks of building *a* text), which on the one hand opened up new possibilities for interpretation but on the other hand worked as a ritualized practice reiterating a specific vision of hierarchical order to the exclusion of others. The invention of Euripides' incompetent imitators and the projection onto them of all the problems of interpretation legitimized the replacement of the extant scene of the sacrifice by an absent one, authenticated by the textual authority of Aelian and Euripides' poetic genius. The mediocre epilogue of the manuscript tradition became the sacrificial deer whose death was a small price to pay for the revelation of Euripides' missing conclusion in all its transcendental glory.

In a review of Michael Cacoyannis' film *Iphigenia*, released in American art theaters in 1978, the classicist Bernard Knox notes how the director

> works with a succinct modern Greek version of Euripides' play; the speeches are reduced but the essentials are all there. The great scenes lose none of their power and those between father and daughter produce the almost unbearable pathos which explains Aristotle's statement that Euripides, in spite of his faults, is the most tragic of the poets. I heard the same judgement, expressed in different terms, from the Washington cinema owner who organized the premiere of the film at the Kennedy Center prior to its exclusive run at one of his theaters: "It's a four-handkerchief movie."[29]

It would certainly be interesting to reflect on what might constitute the *same*ness of judgments between Knox, Aristotle, and the Washington cinema owner, but here I would like to concentrate on the relation between Euripides' play and Cacoyannis' film. In Cacoyannis' performance of the play's epilogue, Iphigenia does not escape the sacrifice. There is no god from the machine in it to intervene and change the fate of the young virgin, nor any messenger to communicate the event to the spectator. The cloud that conceals the scene of the sacrifice reveals not the mystery of divine benevolence but the horror of human greed. Iphigenia is slaughtered to satisfy the bloodthirsty Greek army and its ambitious leaders. With Cacoyannis, Euripides' play becomes a celebration of female resistance against male oppression and a warning that violence can only generate more violence. The film closes with a long shot of Clytemnestra, who has tried in vain to save her daughter, looking with hatred at the departing Greek army. Her gaze

---

29   Knox (1979) 351.

prepares the audience for the revenge she is going to exact on Agamemnon when the war at Troy is over. From *mater dolorosa*, Clytemnestra is transformed into an avenging spirit, setting a pattern for the spectator's emotional response to the film as a whole. Can we reconcile Clytemnestra's hatred and the promise for revenge, mobilized by the unlawful killing of her innocent daughter, with the pathos of the scenes between father and daughter promised by Knox and authorized by Aristotle and the Washington cinema owner? What does Knox sacrifice to celebrate the preservation of Euripides' "essence" in Cacoyannis' film? And what does Cacoyannis himself sacrifice in the closing shot of his film to celebrate female martyrdom and revenge? If Knox draws unproblematically on the discourses of authentication of ancient dramatic criticism and of cinema as a form of popular entertainment and as an institution, Clytemnestra's gaze draws on a discourse of female oppression which only superficially differs from that of Knox. Taking revenge on Agamemnon will not give new life to Iphigenia, nor will it punish the Greek army which imposed her death. It will however give a strong sense of closure to the film and much needed reassurance to an audience used to problems being addressed on a personal level rather than on a social one. It should come as no surprise that today, some 25 years after Cacoyannis' adaptation of Euripides' play, the film retains its relevance. The generic boundaries of tragedy and the inscription of the female in patriarchal systems of representation are issues that resonate forcefully in contemporary critical responses towards Euripides, both in the classroom and on the professional stage.[30]

What I have done so far is to explore the drastic and far-reaching revaluation of Euripides' *IA* between the Renaissance and the present day by enacting three different moments in its reception history. The differences between the theatrical, academic, and cinematic readings of *IA* we have looked at should not obscure the fact that all of them, rather than reproducing Euripides' text, have sought to replace it, to reduce it to a trace or a memory. This drama of sacrificial substitution informs the creative work of all the various readers or spectators of the play over the centuries but it is not confined to them. The scene of the sacrifice features a number of internal spectators whose views on the sacrifice not only rival one another but also seek to replace the sacrifice itself. I will conclude the chapter by looking at two of these spectators, Agamemnon and Clytemnestra.

"And when King Agamemnon saw the girl coming into the grove to be slain," the messenger reports in his speech, "he groaned loudly, turned his head away from her and burst into tears, pulling his robe in front of his eyes." (1547–50)[31]

Agamemnon's response to the sacrifice is concealed not only under the reported speech of the messenger but also under his veil and inarticulate sounds. What is

30   See, for instance, the contributions in Mitchell-Boyask (2002).
31   Translation by Morwood (1999) 130.

concealed, and how it is revealed in the act of being concealed, has been hotly debated over the centuries. One may want to relate Agamemnon's response to the tears he sheds as a bad father and a good politician earlier in the play; or to the visual articulation of grief in the funerary iconography of the fifth century; or to the veiled characters that Aeschylus first brought onto the tragic stage, whom Aristophanes parodied in his *Frogs* (911–13) the year *IA* was first produced. Similarly, Agamemnon's response can be related – either as an inspiration or as an imitation – to the now famous painting on the subject by the late fifth-century painter Timanthes, a piece of visual art whose loss excited the imagination and sharpened the critical edge of the (textual) reflections of Cicero, Pliny, and Lessing.[32] What interests me here is that the figure of the shrouded Agamemnon, like Racine, Porson, or Cacoyannis, has acquired its own, almost autonomous, reception. Agamemnon may be a spectator of the scene of the sacrifice, but it is in his role as a performer that he has been revisited through the centuries. It is not for what he sees (or rather for what he refuses to see) that he has mattered, nor for what he does, but for the way in which his act gestures towards different genealogies of interpretation. Agamemnon's act makes use of the sacrifice, but it is not authorized by it. Agamemnon does not *look* at the otherness of Iphigenia's pain, death, and absence. He enacts them in a self-centered performance which, whether it shows compassion or rivalry or both, refuses to enter into a dialogue with them. Whether Agamemnon's act is mobilized by Timanthes, early tragedy, funerary iconography, or subjective interiority, it steals the show. It cites the suffering Iphigenia and the innocent deer that replaces her and at the same time it restores faith in the presence of absence: the presence of content behind the emptiness of form, the presence of meaning behind the veil, the narrative of the messenger, and the narrative of Iphigenia's disappearance.

In my analysis, Agamemnon becomes the silent and "blind" spectator of modern realistic theater who, to quote from Worthen, "removed from participation" and immobilized, consumes the spectacle from his individual seat, "disciplined by and into the illusion of community created by the powerful but coercive conventionality of the modern stage."[33] I will now turn to Clytemnestra:

> My child, which of the gods has stolen you? How can I speak to you? How can I not say that this story has not been made up to console me so that I can lay to rest my cruel grief over you? (1615–18)[34]

Clytemnestra distances herself from the reported spectacle and interrogates her relation with it in a post-Brechtian fashion. She both acknowledges the interpretative

32 On Timanthes' painting, its relation to Euripides, and its ancient and modern reception see Montagu (1994).
33 Worthen (2003) 92.
34 Translation by Morwood (1999) 132, adapted.

model of Iphigenia's miraculous disappearance offered by the messenger and re-enacted by Agamemnon, and at the same time she resists it. Clytemnestra does not embody Iphigenia's pain, whether as a rival or as a substitute, but her own pain. She does not perform, verbally or with her body, Iphigenia's transcendental presence-in-absence, but exposes it as fiction. For Clytemnestra, absence is not a role to be reenacted as a key to meaning and authority but a framework to be problematized as devoid of authority. Clytemnestra sacrifices the prospect of consolation and closure offered by Agamemnon and the messenger to the cruelty of an open dialogue with the dead. She has nothing to reveal because her role resides not in the performance of the imaginary but in its unmaking, the undoing of the opposition between form and meaning, illusion and reality.

In its long history in the West, theater has often been perceived as a paradigm of the representational, imitative, and illusionist nature of art, as a shorthand for lies and deceit, as an enemy of truth, authenticity, and morality. The so-called antitheatrical prejudice has made itself manifest across temporal, cultural, and disciplinary boundaries, encompassing philosophy, religion, literary and art criticism.[35] For all their declared hostility, enemies of theater have often betrayed a profound ambivalence towards what they have undoubtedly recognized as a formidable opponent – and this must surely be one of the reasons why theater has survived their criticisms. Theater may not have always managed to defend itself against the prejudices of its foes. However, as a mobile notion, it has also been deployed as a force for change, as the scene of inclusivity, diversity, and crisis.

What I have tried to do in this chapter is to put forward a performance-oriented model of interpretation which foregrounds the concepts of transformation and substitution and collapses the differences between readings and performances of a dramatic text. What I have called "reenactments" of a dramatic text do not empty it of its multiplicity and ambiguity but add to it. Each one of them becomes a site of its production deriving its power from different conventions of interpretation. These conventions can be concealed, as in modern realistic theater, or exposed as in anti-realist theater. My own reenactment of *IA* has sought to expose the framework of performance-oriented criticism on which it draws and to distance itself from the dramatic text as a source of authority. I am aware of the fact that while doing so, my chapter has not only derived from the *IA* some of its conceptual vocabulary, but it has also located the text in different interpretative traditions, cited some of its interpretations, and discussed narratives of its priority and authenticity. However, none of this is incompatible with my attempt to dissociate theater reception from rigid definitions of theater practice or textuality and to model it on theater theory. The answer to the question "what are dramatic performances perfomances *of*?"[36] may not hold the promise of finality but it offers the compensating pleasures of polyphony and self-reflexivity.

35 Barish (1981).
36 Worthen (2003) 96.

19

Reception and Ancient Art

The Case of the Venus de Milo

Elizabeth Prettejohn

We here propose to do just what Copernicus did in attempting to explain the celestial movements. When he found that he could make no progress by assuming that all the heavenly bodies revolved round the spectator, he reversed the process, and tried the experiment of assuming that the spectator revolved, while the stars remained at rest.

Kant, *Critique of Pure Reason*[1]

The modern discipline of art history began, according to the most prevalent genealogy, with Winckelmann's *History of Ancient Art* (1764). Thus, we can add, it began with the frankest possible acknowledgment of the radical unfathomability of the past. Winckelmann's book ends without a conclusion, as he notes the destruction of virtually all the monuments of ancient art:

Still I could not refrain from searching into the fate of works of art as far as my eye could reach; just as a maiden, standing on the shore of the ocean, follows with tearful eyes her departing lover with no hope of ever seeing him again, and fancies that in the distant sail she sees the image of her beloved. Like that loving maiden we too have, as it were, nothing but a shadowy outline left of the object of our wishes, but that very indistinctness awakens only a more earnest longing for what we have lost, and we study the copies of the originals more attentively than we should have done the originals themselves if we had been in full possession of them.[2]

Today's students of ancient art are bound to acknowledge the same difficulties; as much as discoveries since Winckelmann's time have expanded the archive, we still have knowledge only of the most minuscule fraction of the artistic production

I owe thanks to Mary Beard, John Betts, Shelley Hales, Lin Holdridge, John House, Kathy McLaughlan, Pantelis Michelakis, and Jason Rosenfeld.

1 Kant (1993) 15.
2 Winckelmann (1881) 2.364–5.

of the ancient world. Winckelmann's achievement was to transform this fundamental problem into an intellectual adventure – as Hegel put it, to "have opened
up for the spirit a new organ and totally new modes of treatment."[3] Yet today's
students of ancient art are content, for the most part, to tinker with such data as
an avowedly inadequate archive can supply.[4] Can reception theory offer a new
method, one in which the study of ancient art may once again lead the discipline
rather than lagging hopelessly behind other fields in which the archive has more
to offer?

It is strange that reception theory has made so little impact on the historical
study of the visual arts. Perhaps that is because the basic tasks of identifying, attributing, and cataloging the physical objects of the art historian's study are so difficult
that they have dominated what is still a relatively young scholarly discipline; these
tasks concentrate on establishing the origin or genesis of works of art. Yet the
survival of objects from the past into the present, more tangible and concrete than
in the case of literary works, together with the multifarious and intractable physical changes that objects undergo, ought to place reception at the forefront of
the art historian's concerns. In the study of ancient art such issues are particularly urgent given the loss of so much of the physical evidence, the impossibility
of establishing origins or provenances for much of what does survive, and the
exceptionally high status that these objects have nonetheless enjoyed throughout the period since antiquity. Yet there is so far very little in the way of either
theory or art-historical practice to indicate what might constitute a reception study
of ancient art.[5] This essay proposes to make a start by addressing these issues through
a single case study: the Venus de Milo (fig. 19.1). I shall sketch three possible
approaches to the study of this exceptionally famous object in order to begin
exploring the theoretical and practical implications of a reception-based approach to
ancient art in general.

I

First, it is necessary to consider a traditional art-historical approach to the object,
one which might be called "positivist" or "historicist" and which aims to discover

---

3 Hegel (1975) 1.63.
4 Both of the methods described in Smith (2002) for the study of ancient art are
   positivist. Brunilde Sismondo Ridgway's surveys of the field are scrupulous in their
   skepticism about our positive knowledge, but do not contemplate the possibility of
   a different method; see Ridgway (1986, 1994). I am not arguing against positivist
   methods per se, only against the restriction of the discipline to such methods; there is,
   of course, great value in continuing to collect and publish such data as become available. Cf. Elsner (2004) 807.
5 See however Barkan (1999), Brilliant (2000), Gazda (2002). The only general history
   that takes reception fully into account is Beard and Henderson (2001).

Figure 19.1 *Venus de Milo* (*c*.100 BCE). Parian marble, 211 × 44 cm. Musée du Louvre, Paris. © Photo RMN – Daniel Arnaudet/Jean Schormans.

as much as possible about the object's making, the social and historical contexts in which it was made, and its meanings within those contexts. In the case of the Venus de Milo there is very little to be done along these lines. In common with the overwhelming majority of objects that survive from the ancient past, there is no documentary or textual evidence that can securely be associated with this work; it is not mentioned in any of the ancient writings on art and was wholly undocumented until its discovery on Melos in 1820. Thus the positive data about the work's origin fine down almost to a single fact: it can be assumed to be Greek. Moreover the examination of its physical characteristics has failed to produce any kind of scholarly consensus about the artistic school or milieu in which it was created, or its basic subject matter (and thus any meanings it may have had at the time of its origin). A fragmentary inscription on a block found with the statue might identify part of the sculptor's name ("... andros of Antioch on the Maeander"), but the interpretation of the inscription has always been disputed and in any case the block was misplaced (intentionally?) at some point in the nineteenth century. Some have seen the deep undercutting of the drapery folds as similar to the Parthenon marbles; the facial type has often been called Praxitelean, and the fine working of the marble is a documented aspect of Praxitelean style; yet the specificity of rendering, of both flesh and drapery, appears Hellenistic to many eyes. Scholarly consensus now tends to identify it as dating from around 100 BCE, but reflecting some kind of revival of an earlier style or styles; since there is no concrete evidence for this interpretation, a strict historicist might be tempted to regard it as a compromise. A fragment of a hand bearing an apple, also found near the statue, has suggested to some that the subject might be Venus with the apple of Paris, to others that it is a deity of the island of Melos, but again it is disputed whether the apple belongs to the statue. (A peculiarity of the Venus's discovery is that the two main blocks of which it is composed and the fragments found nearby all differ in grain of marble and quality of workmanship, so it is difficult either to prove or to disprove their relationships to one another.) The statue has also been seen as a Muse, a Nemesis, a Sappho, an Amphitrite, a toilette of Venus, or a bather surprised; as Salomon Reinach observed in 1890, in the face of such diverse possibilities it may be preferable simply to call it, with Heinrich Heine, "Notre-Dame de Beauté."[6] Thus there is too little positive data about the work to write more than an impoverished history of the traditional art-historical kind. Moreover, a similar conclusion, *mutatis mutandis*, is inevitable for virtually all other extant works of ancient art. There is, then, a serious argument to be made that it is not possible to write a history of ancient art at all, along the positivist lines of traditional art-historical inquiry.

Most of those who have studied the statue since 1820 have acknowledged it to be exceptionally fine in workmanship and aesthetic impact; but that judgment

---

6 Reinach (1890) 388. For interpretations of the subject see also Pasquier (1985) 35.

has no bearing on the work's original status. We simply do not have enough surviving ancient statues to decide whether it is better or worse than average (even if we did, we know too little about ancient methods of estimating sculptural quality to be sure that our judgment would correspond to those of its original viewers). Recent scholarship has been increasingly honest about such limitations to our knowledge, but with a result that can only be called bizarre. The Venus has fallen out of favour, in relation to works universally acknowledged to be of lower technical quality, so long as those can be linked in some way to documentary evidence. Thus most textbooks and general histories give considerable space to statues presumed to be later copies of Praxiteles' Aphrodite of Cnidus (a work mentioned prominently in ancient sources), but mention the Venus de Milo only briefly, if at all.[7] Yet the Melian is a fine example of ancient sculptural technique and of the articulation of the female body, while everyone admits that the putative copies of the Cnidian are comparatively feeble.[8] Surely this is evidence of a persistent prejudice against the visual; the merest fragment of text is permitted to override the kinds of knowledge that the eye can provide. That raises a different kind of problem: how can we account for the statue's undeniable, and undiminished, capacity to fascinate its audiences? If we find we can make no progress in establishing data about the statue itself, then perhaps we should reorient the inquiry, to explore instead the responses of the statue's viewers.

7   Compare the discussions, respectively, of the Cnidian and Melian sculptures in Robertson (1975) 1.390–4, 553–4; Stewart (1990) 1.177–8 (plus 16 further references), 1.224 (plus 3 further references); Spivey (1996) 178–83, 185. Among those who discuss the Cnidian, but not the Melian, are Spivey (1997) 306–12; Stewart (1997) 97–107. An exception is the fine study by Christine Mitchell Havelock, which treats the Venus de Milo in relation to other female nudes; see Havelock (1995). See also Hales (2002).

8   It is remarkable that the identification of the copies with the Cnidian is invariably presented as fact (a rare exception is Beard and Henderson (2001) 125), since the numismatic evidence is far from conclusive (as a careful reading of Havelock (1995) 11 will show). Anyway the copies contradict aspects of the ancient evidence, which should at least induce greater caution; they are clearly designed for two principal views, front and back, whereas Pliny states that the statue was famous for being equally admirable from all sides (*Natural History*, XXXVI.iv.21). Moreover the conspicuous vase and drapery impede the view, and are not mentioned in any ancient source – nor is the bathing subject apparently implied by the accessories (Havelock skillfully demonstrates the ideological entailments of modern scholars' enthusiasm for the bathing subject; see Havelock (1995) 19–37). A feature of scholarship on ancient art is the occlusion of the historical contingency of identification and dating (in this case, by Visconti in the 1780s; see Haskell and Penny (1982) 331); thus a previous identification is repeated tralatitiously as if it were a fact, rather than a historically specific judgment. A recent text even takes the copies of the Cnidia as the principal evidence for Praxiteles' "personal style"; see Ajootian (1996) 99.

II

A second approach might then be to explore the history of the work's reception since its discovery. It is immediately obvious that this can provide a much richer narrative, not only because of the sheer abundance of scholarly, literary, and artistic interpretation of the statue since 1820, but also because we know a great deal about the social and cultural contexts for these modern interpretations. Thus the reception history of the Venus de Milo has just the qualifications that the history of its origins lacks, for treatment according to the dominant art-historical method of the late twentieth century: the social history of art.[9] The statue's acquisition by the French state just a few years after the defeat of Napoleon placed it at the center of the nationalist cultural politics of the period. The Venus instantly took pride of place in the Louvre, struggling to maintain its status after the forced restitution of the ancient works Napoleon had plundered from Italy, and after the British Museum's acquisition of the Parthenon marbles. Thus the question of just how good the statue was had implications far beyond classical scholarship. A related issue, whether the statue was an original or a copy, had ramifications no less far-reaching in an art world where questions of artistic originality were assuming central importance; indeed, we shall see that the Venus has remained a focus for such questions up to the present day. Writers of the 1820s were right, then, to compare the discovery to those of the ancient statues unearthed in the Renaissance.[10] Like the Laocoon and the Apollo Belvedere, the Venus de Milo has played a crucial role in the cultural and artistic debates of the modern world ever since the time of its discovery.

   Within months of the statue's arrival in the Louvre, three distinguished French scholars produced detailed interpretations: Antoine-Chrysostome Quatremère de Quincy, Permanent Secretary of the Institut des Beaux-Arts; the Comte de Clarac, the Louvre's curator of antiquities; and Toussaint-Bernard Éméric-David, an eminent art historian who had collaborated on the catalogue of the antiquities of the Musée Napoléon. Understandably, all three were concerned to establish the status of the new French acquisition; it is telling that they all referred to the Parthenon marbles early in their papers.[11] But recent scholars are mistaken to discount these interpretations as mere propaganda. The three agreed on nothing else,

---

9   R. R. R. Smith calls for a social history approach to ancient art (belatedly, given the predominance of such approaches in art history since the 1970s); see Smith (2002) 72–102. There is a serious problem with his contention (p. 73) that a history based on consumption and context is more appropriate to classical antiquity than one based on artists and artistic development, since the main ancient source (Pliny) is (as he acknowledges) the paradigmatic example of a history of the latter kind.

10   Clarac (1821) 28. On the Renaissance discoveries see Barkan (1999).

11   Quatremère (1821) 5; Clarac (1821) 2; Éméric-David (1853) 189.

and for reasons that remain valid: then (as now) procedures for identification and attribution depended heavily on comparison with other extant examples, but the Venus has no precise parallels (we do not, of course, know whether this is due to the statue's uniqueness, or to the non-survival of comparable examples). Moreover, the absence of the arms, which creates the distinctive silhouette so important to the statue's modern celebrity, also permits the most extravagant range of conjecture about the figure's action, and thus its subject matter and meaning. Quatremère reasoned from the figure's gaze to her left, and the less finished drapery on that side, that she must originally have appeared in a group with Mars; this conveniently explained the loss of the arms, which Quatremère argued must have been broken when the two figures were separated, for unknown reasons, some time in antiquity. Quatremère drew on extant sculptural groups and Roman coins to describe this subject as *Venus Victrix*, or *Vénus victorieuse*: Venus victorious over Mars. Thus he could allegorize the subject in a way that had clear contemporary relevance, as "peace succeeding war." Ingeniously, too, he supplied the textual authority that the undocumented statue signally lacked: it may have been just such a group, he declared, that inspired Lucretius to write his invocation to Venus.[12] (Interestingly, a relationship to Lucretius, ignored during the intervening period, has recently reappeared in a study of 1995 by Christine Mitchell Havelock; in her account, the generative power of Aphrodite is a crucial religious idea of the Hellenistic period to which the Venus de Milo, and many other representations of the nude Aphrodite, are now generally dated.[13] Havelock's emphasis on sexuality is perhaps as characteristic of the date of her book as Quatremère's allegory of peace is of early nineteenth-century France.)

Éméric-David easily picked out the flaw in Quatremère's argument: if the statue is to be prized as a Greek original, then how could Quatremère justify his identification through the use of Roman evidence? He counters with a moral argument: the Greeks, he claimed, would not sanction the adulterous relationship between Venus and Mars in an important sculptural monument. Moreover, the assertive movement of the figure and the firm contours of her body, which for Éméric-David suggested "quelque chose de mâle," did not answer to the Greek character of Venus, always youthful, smiling and passive, awaiting her lover in repose. Instead, he proposed that the statue represented the tutelary deity of the island of Melos.[14] Then as now, each interpreter was able to emphasize the aspects of the archeological evidence that suited his case; thus Éméric-David accepted the authenticity of the hand holding an apple, dismissed by Quatremère because of its inferior workmanship, since the fruit could refer to the name of the island. Clarac, by contrast, was the only one to dwell on the inscription.[15] But if this

12   Quatremère (1821) 15–25; quotation from p. 24.
13   Havelock (1995) 118.
14   Éméric-David (1853) 195–226; quotation from p. 190.
15   Clarac (1821) 48–55.

names the artist, there are implications for the date; although the name is half
missing, the inscription clearly indicates that he came from Antioch, not founded
until the third century BCE. In keeping with the romantic subject he proposed, as
well as the fine working of the marble (a point much emphasized in his account),
Quatremère had attributed the sculpture to the circle of Praxiteles, in the mid
fourth century;[16] for Éméric-David the "masculine" character of the figure, as well
as the resemblance of the drapery to that of the Parthenon sculptures, suggested
an even earlier date, midway between Phidias and Praxiteles.[17]

Thus these three preliminary estimates of the statue differed in date, in attribution, and in the identification of the subject (Clarac implausibly but engagingly
suggested that the statue might be a later repetition of Praxiteles' Aphrodite of
Cos, the draped counterpart to the nude Cnidian[18]). It should be emphasized that
each of these three experienced scholars made a thorough study of the archeological evidence and of available comparisons; their observations, although not
their conclusions, are very similar to those of today's scholars (indeed they are
more detailed and precise than most). No doubt there was considerable pressure
to demonstrate an early date, which would give the Venus a status comparable
to the Parthenon marbles. But a larger issue was also involved: that of the statue's
originality, and by extension of the importance of originality in the evaluation of
a work of art. Since he accepted the inscription, Clarac disputed the importance
of originality; as he observed, even the Parthenon marbles are not from Phidias'
own hand, but productions of his school.[19] Éméric-David, although he could not
name a sculptor, considered his date of *c*.420–380 BCE to add special interest to
the statue, since that was a period from which few original works survived.[20]
Quatremère acknowledged that the evidence was insufficient to resolve the question
of originality, observing that this was the case not only for "the most beautiful
antiques that we admire," but even for much of the art of more modern periods.
But perhaps there is another way to think about originality:

> If, however, we understand this word in a sense relative to the superiority in merit
> among the doubles of the same composition, there will be no reason, I think, to
> doubt that the Venus of Melos . . . was the original of those which we have cited.
> The distance that separates them is without measure.[21]

---

16 Quatremère (1821) 32; he has just (p. 31) quoted Pliny on Praxiteles, "marmore feli-
    cior" (*Natural History*, XXXIV.xix.69). With great rhetorical skill, Quatremère builds
    the suspense until he reveals his attribution in the final sentences.
17 Éméric-David (1853) 191–2.
18 Clarac (1821) 43–6. It is interesting that Clarac is both the strictest archeologist of
    the three and the most extravagant in his interpretation.
19 Clarac (1821) 14.
20 Éméric-David (1853) 192.
21 Quatremère (1821) 26–7.

Thus Quatremère, unlike modern scholars, is prepared to permit a judgment of quality to take the place of positive evidence in confirming his conclusions.

Quatremère was right in one respect: despite the notable absence of consensus on the statue's author, date, or subject matter, its quality quickly established it as one of the most famous antiques in Europe. Whether or not it had been an "original" in antiquity, then, it certainly became one in modernity, as it was constantly reproduced in all of the media available in the nineteenth century. Casts were disseminated in the traditional way (the Berlin Academy had one as early as 1822[22]), but the statue was also taken up in the newest reproductive media such as photography and mechanical reproduction in bronze, in a variety of reduced sizes.[23] Thus its celebrity as an antique was inextricably linked to the reproductive techniques of modernity, and from the start it was addressed not only to scholars and connoisseurs but to audiences of all social levels. In the Greek Court at the Crystal Palace in Sydenham, opened as a popular tourist attraction in 1854, a cast of the Venus was presented as number one in the catalogue: "One of the finest statues that has ever been discovered. It may be regarded as the utmost extent to which grandeur of form can be united with feminine beauty."[24] The Crystal Palace was a commercial venture, but its displays also aimed at public education; accordingly the cast was juxtaposed with others of half-draped ancient statues of the female nude, for comparison.[25]

Quatremère had successfully recommended that the arms should not be restored, on the grounds that without the figure of Mars he believed had originally accompanied the Venus, the action of the arms would appear unmotivated. The consequence, perhaps unintended, was that (like the Parthenon marbles, also unrestored) the Venus helped to initiate a new taste for the fragmentary and time-worn.[26] Its armless silhouette was both immediately recognizable, in whatever form it was reproduced, and specially resonant, perhaps, for the sensibility of the Romantic period; thus its visual appearance was modern, in one way, as well as ancient in another. The writer and art critic Théophile Gautier, a notorious sensualist, noted another advantage of the non-restoration: "it seems that, if one were to

---

22   Haskell and Penny (1982) 329–30.
23   For a selection, with illustrations, see Cuzin et al. (2000) 444–53. See also Bergstein (1992) 486–8.
24   Scharf (1854) 49.
25   For a contemporary illustration see Piggott (2004) 71. The Venus de Milo is given clear priority over the two flanking half-draped casts, of the Townley Venus (British Museum) on the left and the Venus of Capua (see n. 38 below) on the right.
26   See Nochlin (1994), a classic study which concentrates on the modern aesthetic of the fragment; the role of ancient sculpture deserves further attention (see however Prettejohn (2004) 55–9). A depressing consequence of the increasing marginalization of ancient art from the rest of art history is the concomitant loss of conversancy with classical art, formerly a central point of reference, among art historians, who often drastically underplay the role of the classical tradition in later art.

rediscover the arms, they would hamper the pleasure of the eye by preventing the view of this superb chest and this admirable breast." Gautier was also the leading critic of the Romantic generation, and it is telling that in his guidebook to the Louvre he singled out the Venus as the sole ancient sculpture worth discussing; so dazzling was its effect, for Gautier, that it eclipsed all the sculptures traditionally revered as exemplars of classical form. Moreover, Gautier does not assume that its popular appeal requires an attribution to a famous name; instead he marvels that "in the temple of a little island there shone forth this masterpiece of an unknown sculptor."[27] It seems, indeed, that the Venus did not supplant the traditional casts of ancient sculptures, generally male, in French academic art education, although young artists frequently drew more informally from it; in the 1860s Frédéric Bazille drew the Venus with a pipe in her mouth, an early example of the way the statue's celebrity could encourage irreverence or parody.[28]

At the same time, though, the statue could serve as a key point of reference for the new classicizing projects of the middle of the century. A poem of 1852 by Leconte de Lisle turned the statue into an icon for the "Parnassian" reaction against Romantic emotionalism:

> Du bonheur impassible ô symbole adorable,
> Calme comme la mer en sa sérénité,
> Nul sanglot n'a brisé ton sein inalterable,
> Jamais les pleurs humains n'ont terni ta beauté.

(O adorable symbol of impassive blitheness, calm as the sea in its serenity, no sob has riven your unchangeable breast, never have human tears tarnished your beauty.)

In the following decades, the French artist Pierre Puvis de Chavannes developed a novel neoclassicism, pared down to utmost simplicity of figural form and muted colour, in allegorical compositions whose symbolism remained elusive. A recurring element in these scenes is a half-draped figure, sometimes seen from behind, with the left shoulder elevated and the weight on the right leg – these figures can perhaps be understood as multiple repetitions of the Venus de Milo, inexplicit symbols of a majestic ideal of silent grandeur amidst the variously grouped classical figures of Puvis's rarefied Arcadian world.[29] For the English artists who adopted classicism in the 1860s, the Venus was scarcely less important than the Parthenon marbles. Albert Moore restored the statue in painted form, in a work exhibited in 1869 with the title *A Venus* (fig. 19.2); perhaps the indefinite article hints at

---

27 Gautier (1882) 191–2.
28 Illustrated in Cuzin et al. (2000) 434.
29 Jennifer Shaw tentatively identifies one example (Shaw (2002) 131–4) but fails to note the recurrence of the figure (see n. 26 above); see e.g. d'Argencourt et al. (1976) nos. 54, 97, 134, 155, 174.

Figure 19.2 Albert Moore, *A Venus* (1869). Oil on canvas, 160 × 76.2 cm. York Museums Trust (York Art Gallery).

the mysteries surrounding the statue, or the vexed issue of distinguishing an original from a copy (we know that this is "a" Venus, but not which one, precisely). Moore's close associate, the American-born and French-trained James McNeill Whistler, reportedly kept a cast of the Venus de Milo in his studio, so that he could refer to its ideal forms while he was drawing from the living model. His unfinished painting of *Venus* (fig. 19.3), from about the same date as Moore's, presents a different interpretation of the statue, emphasizing the suggestion of movement in the pose and surrounding the figure with wind-blown draperies. Later, in his famous "Ten O'Clock" lecture of 1885, Whistler made the statue into a symbol of Aestheticism, a visible proof of the superiority of art to mere nature: "and the Gods stand by and marvel, and perceive how far away more beautiful is the Venus of Melos than was their own Eve."[30]

Thus the statue had become a cultural icon in the fullest sense by the mid nineteenth century, and its fame had spread far beyond France. But nationalist politics resurfaced in dramatic fashion at the time of the Franco-Prussian war. As the Germans approached Paris, the Louvre's curator of sculpture, Félix Ravaisson, thought it advisable to protect his most famous work from plunder; under cover of night, he removed it to the basement of a police building, where it was hidden behind a wall, distressed to look old.[31] Heaps of official documents were then deposited and a second wall, similarly distressed, was erected, on the theory that the German troops, if they penetrated the outermost wall, would assume that only the documents were being concealed, and would never discover the more precious artistic treasure behind the farther wall. In the event the statue survived intact. Nonetheless, the event had important consequences. When the statue was recovered from its hiding place, Ravaisson discovered that its two blocks had been assembled on a slight slant when they first arrived at the Louvre, so that the upper section leaned forward and to the side.[32] Ravaisson had casts made both of the assemblage of 1821 and of the rebalanced form he thought more authentic. Gautier, who was among the scholars and critics invited to compare the two versions, noted a striking difference of effect: the newly equilibrated version seemed to Gautier younger, more svelte, less voluptuous, more a goddess and less a woman. For the moment, it was decided that the French public needed the reassurance of seeing their icon in its familiar form, and the statue was not restored to equilibrium until 1883, when the slight repairs of 1821 were also removed; once again, the Venus was in the forefront of the latest thinking on restoration, increasingly non-interventionist as the nineteenth century progressed. In a reception history, though, it is important to remember that the statue we see today is not quite the one that viewers experienced between 1821 and 1883. As Gautier put it, the statue

30 Whistler (1967) 146.
31 For a vivid account see Gautier (1871) 348–59.
32 Ravaisson (1871) 3–27.

Figure 19.3 James McNeill Whistler, *Venus* (*c*.1868, reworked 1879–1903). Oil on millboard mounted on wood panel, 61.9 × 45.6 cm. Freer Gallery of Art, Smithsonian Institution, Washington, DC: Gift of Charles Lang Freer, F1903.175.

in its equilibrated state is no longer the Venus, "adorablement épuisée," of which Goethe had spoken.[33]

From this date, too, French and German opinions of the statue began to diverge markedly, and sometimes acrimoniously. The nationalist dimension of this scholarly disagreement is already hinted in a short story of 1873 by the realist novelist Champfleury, "Les Bras de la Vénus de Milo," an attack at once on the classical ideal and on German cultural pretensions, with an unpleasant caricature of a German archeologist named "M. Protococus." Protococus becomes obsessed with the idea of uniting the Venus in a group with the Borghese Mars, also in the Louvre; in fact this was a French idea, derived from Quatremère's original theory and advocated by Ravaisson.[34] But in Champfleury's tale the scholarly exercise leads to disaster, as Protococus is forced ignominiously to retire to Berlin after the utter failure of his experiment.[35]

In 1893 the eminent German scholar Adolf Furtwängler published a detailed account of the Venus de Milo, in his magisterial demonstration of the techniques of *Meisterforschung* (attribution) and *Kopienkritik* (comparison of extant versions of the same sculptural composition), translated into English two years later as *Masterpieces of Greek Sculpture*. Furtwängler was utterly committed to the originality of the Hermes, unearthed in German excavations at Olympia in 1877 and hailed as a work by Praxiteles, documented in Pausanias. But he abruptly demoted the Venus de Milo, which he saw as a late and derivative copy, unsuccessfully attempting to amalgamate two prototypes, neither of them Praxitelean.[36] Many of today's scholars believe that archeological evidence disproves the Praxitelean authorship of the Hermes.[37] This ought to raise doubts about Furtwängler's other conclusions, which depend heavily on his view of the Hermes, yet the authority of his critical methods remains almost unchallenged, and most scholars still accept his dating of the Venus de Milo.[38] For Furtwängler the inferiority of the Venus was inextricably linked to its late date, and although current scholars no longer despise the Hellenistic, it is arguably the case that the Venus's reputation has never quite recovered – at least in classical archeology and

33   "Adorably exhausted" (Gautier (1871) 357).
34   Ravaisson (1871) 27–66.
35   Champfleury (1874) 243–69.
36   Furtwängler (1895) 367–401.
37   See Ridgway (1986) 21 and n. 125.
38   For example, Robertson (1975) 553–4; this account also repeats Furtwängler's (conjectural) reconstruction of the arms and other details, without attributing or dating the scholarly opinion (see n. 8 above). Havelock, by contrast, notes the dependence of later scholars on Furtwängler's account, including his contention that the Venus de Milo derives from an original seen more clearly in a manifestly inferior Roman copy, the Venus of Capua (National Museum, Naples); as she notes, "The logic seems absurd." See Havelock (1995) 96, 139.

scholarship, where the German critical techniques of the later nineteenth century remain authoritative for questions of attribution and dating.[39]

The reverse is true of the Venus's status as cultural icon.[40] The utterly distinctive – original? – silhouette of the armless statue remains "ideal" for use in advertisement and caricature. In the early twentieth century the Surrealists were fascinated both by the statue's mutilation and by its status as a paradigm of the classical ideal, on which artists such as Magritte and Dalí could draw in paradoxical subversion of the modernist mainstream (fig. 19.4).[41] In 1962 Niki de Saint-Phalle shot bullets of paint at a plaster reproduction of the Venus in a performance that manifested, perhaps, both feminist and anti-establishment anger.[42] But at about the same date Yves Klein returned attention to Venus's beauty. He imbued the forms of a headless, armless, and undraped Venus with his signature color, "International Klein Blue" or "I.K.B." (cover image).[43] The luminous ultramarine calls to mind the limitless blues of the sky or sea; colored thus, the Venus seems almost to float, released from the gravity of ancient marble. In recent decades the Venus de Milo has attracted, if anything, a growing variety of rich and subtle responses from contemporary artists in all media. The Irish performance artist Mary Duffy has photographed herself in a haunting series of images that reconfigure perceptions of disability through reference to the beauty of the Venus (fig. 19.5).[44] The French artist Arman cuts through the body of the Venus, in bronze replica, with industrial wheels or film reels, repeating the breakage of the ancient original with modern technology; photographers explore the marble in close-up or distant views, sharply focused or suggestively veiled, sometimes including the mesmerized audiences of tourists.[45] In Bernardo Bertolucci's film of 2004, *The Dreamers*, a character mimics the Venus de Milo.[46] The American artist Jim

39 See however Hales (2002), which persuasively links the Venus de Milo to a positive estimate of Hellenistic art.

40 See e.g. Curtis (2003); Salmon (2000). Other discussions for wider audiences include the classic book on the nude, Clark (1987) 83–4; an interesting psychoanalytical study marred by poor research, Fuller (1980); and Arenas (2002).

41 See Cuzin et al. (2000) 460–7.

42 Wilson (2000) 158.

43 Klein's *Blue Venus* is based on a cast of another Venus in the Louvre (inv. no. Ma 2184), but has often been mistaken for a replica of the more famous Venus de Milo, whose armless silhouette it certainly recalls. Klein also made a blue *Victory of Samothrace* in 1962.

44 See Nead (1992) 77–8, which does not, however, note the relationship to the Venus de Milo (see n. 26 above). The representations of the disabled artist Alison Lapper by Marc Quinn and by Lapper herself also recall the Venus de Milo; Quinn's white marble sculpture, *Alison Lapper Pregnant*, was chosen in 2004 for exhibition on the fourth plinth in Trafalgar Square (*Independent* (March 16, 2004), 13).

45 For a selection, with illustrations, see Cuzin et al. (2000) 477–99.

46 For a still see Thompson (2004) 22.

Figure 19.4 Salvador Dalí, *Venus de Milo with Drawers* (1936/1964). Painted bronze and fur, 98 × 32.5 × 34 cm. Collection Museum Boijmans Van Beuningen, Rotterdam. © Salvador Dali, Gala–Salvador Dali Foundation, DACS, London 2005.

Figure 19.5 Mary Duffy, from *Cutting the Ties that Bind* (1987). Series of
8 photographs, overall dimensions 56 × 80 cm. Courtesy the artist.

Figure 19.6 Jim Dine, *Looking Toward the Avenue* (1989). Patinated bronze in three parts, 14 ft, 18 ft, and 23 ft high. Installation at 1301 Avenue of the Americas, New York. © ARS, NY and DACS, London 2005. Photo © Bill Jacobson, courtesy PaceWildenstein, New York.

Dine has replicated a decapitated Venus de Milo in media ranging from colored woodcuts to monumental public sculpture.[47] Dine's *Looking Toward the Avenue* of 1989 (fig. 19.6), at 1301 Avenue of the Americas in New York, is composed of three magnified Venuses de Milo (14, 18, and 23 feet tall) in rugged, textured bronze; soaring above the street corners, the Venuses recreate their ancient majesty on the scale of the modern city. Examples could be multiplied. The statue has proved supremely adaptable to the concerns of the art we call "postmodern," such as celebrity, replication, normativity and deviance in the representation of the body. Yet these may also be seen as versions of the perennial concerns of the study of ancient art: high cultural status, copying versus originality, the ideal human figure. At the present moment, it seems to be practicing artists, rather than classical scholars, who maintain faith in the intellectual and aesthetic power of classical art.

47 See Cuzin et al. (2000) 468–76.

III

The previous section offered only the barest preliminary sketch of the statue's reception history, but even this is enough to demonstrate its central importance not only to the history of modern scholarship on ancient art, but also to the history of modern art, up to and including the contemporary. Nonetheless, we are entitled to ask whether such an approach tells us more about the statue's interpreters – from Quatremère to Saint-Phalle – than it does about the statue itself, particularly since the various responses seem often to contradict one another. If the statue can be seen either as "the eternal feminine" or as "male";[48] as ideally chaste or sensually enticing; as high culture or kitsch – can we learn anything of value from its reception? It is here that theories of reception may be of use. Each of the receptions of the Venus is "subjective," yet each is also a response *to* the object. Moreover we cannot have the one without the other; since Kant's Critiques we have come to accept that we cannot understand, or even see an object (such as the Venus), except insofar as it is *we* who do so, with our peculiar intellectual and sensory capacities. But we should not forget the other side of Kant's insight: it is the Venus (in our example) that puts our capacities into fruitful play. Thus, at a minimum, we can say that each reception potentially has something to tell us about the Venus, as well as something about the subjective perception of the receiver. It may be impossible to disentangle the two – or to disentangle either from our own reception of the response and of its object. That, I want to argue, is precisely the value of a reception-based method.

Take, for example, Éméric-David's perception that there is "quelque chose de mâle" about the statue. This is clearly to do with the gendered assumptions of Éméric's historical period; for him, the action of the left leg, elevated on some object (now lost), connoted pride of possession or some form of command, which he associated with masculinity. But the perception also relates to the clearly articulated body parts and internal markings of the figure, characteristics more often seen in male than female nudes from antiquity. So far as we know, that is – a high proportion of the surviving female nudes are generally thought to be copies, feebler in detail than their putative originals. Thus a recent scholar remarks, apropos of copies of the Cnidia: "The soft forms of the body have few of the points and internal lines of articulation that helped so much in the replication of male statues, and the effect of the copies is varied, often weak."[49] It is not quite clear whether this refers to the representation of the female body in Greek art, or to the female body in general. Should we, then, attribute the stronger bodily articulation of the Venus de Milo to its superior quality among ancient statues, to its status as an "original," to the rising social prominence of women in the Hellenistic period,

48 Gautier (1871) 349; Éméric-David (1853) 190.
49 Smith (1991) 79.

or even, perhaps, to the unique personal style of the unknown sculptor? Should we relate the perception that this is a "male" characteristic to the patriarchal society of ancient Greece, to that of early nineteenth-century France, to that of our own time, or to the essential characteristics of the gendered human body? Given the limitations of our data, we shall never be able to provide final answers to these questions. The virtue of a reception study is that it encourages us to ask them.

Albert Moore's *A Venus* emphasizes this aspect of the statue (see fig. 19.2); indeed contemporary critics complained that its internal markings were too prominent. But Moore has thought deeply about the articulation of the body in the ancient statue. He represents the torso and the action of the legs quite faithfully, although in reverse (this suggests that he consulted an engraved reproduction). However, he also carefully corrects the "error" in the balance of the statue that Ravaisson would not identify until two years later: a plumb-line from a point midway between the clavicles falls directly to the supporting foot. In this respect Moore's picture is closer to the statue as it has been displayed since 1883 than it is to the one he actually saw, on visits to the Louvre or in contemporary reproductions. He also reorients the head and invents a plausible action for the missing arms, which again helps to balance the pose. This is a sophisticated exploration of a crucial aspect of ancient art and its reception, the ideal or normative presentation of the human body. For Ravaisson, it seemed important to restore the statue to normative equilibrium – to bring it closer to what he understood as the Greek ideal. But Moore's painting still looks more stable than the Venus de Milo itself, even in its "correctly" restored state. This is partly an effect of the unequal severing of the missing arms; again, we shall never be certain about how the statue looked "originally." Salvador Dalí's witty reinterpretation provided the statue with a series of open drawers at the front, intensifying the sense that it might topple forward (see fig. 19.4). The revision makes the statue "modernist." But it is also a salutary reminder that our notions of the ideal classical body may be oversimplified.

Moore's painting decisively rejects theories such as Quatremère's, which would make the statue part of a group and supply a focus for her faraway gaze. Moore's figure is autonomous, self-sufficient, and expressionless. In these respects it accords with Hegel's characterization of the classical art form, succinctly paraphrased by Walter Pater in his essay on Winckelmann, published two years before Moore's painting was exhibited:

> But take a work of Greek art, – the Venus of Melos. That is in no sense a symbol, a suggestion, of anything beyond its own victorious fairness. The mind begins and ends with the finite image, yet loses no part of the spiritual motive. This motive is not lightly and loosely attached to the sensuous form, as its meaning to an allegory, but saturates and is identical with it.[50]

50   Pater (1980) 164; compare e.g. Hegel (1975) 1.77–9.

This is an eloquent description of the Venus as it now appears, stripped of its original coloring and jewelry, and deprived also of specific subject matter. But Pater knew that this was only one aspect of the statue, and five years later he presented a different view:

> What time and accident, its centuries of darkness under the furrows of the "little Melian farm," have done with singular felicity of touch for the Venus of Melos, fraying its surface and softening its lines, so that some spirit in the thing seems always on the point of breaking out, as though in it classical sculpture had advanced already one step into the mystical Christian age, its expression being in the whole range of ancient work most like that of Michelangelo's own: – this effect Michelangelo gains by leaving nearly all his sculpture in a puzzling sort of incompleteness, which suggests rather than realises actual form.[51]

The startling transhistorical comparison, so different from the careful *Kopienkritik* of the German scholars whose work Pater read attentively, nonetheless has a serious point to make about the Venus: the over-lifesize statue has a commanding presence that we may describe, in modern terms, as Michelangelesque. Perhaps Pater hints, too, that the statue might postdate the height of the classical age; at the same time, though, he negates the importance of the date, by identifying the aesthetic of the statue with its time-worn condition. This could be called a "romantic" interpretation – or a "Hellenistic" one, for it responds to qualities of the sculpture that scholars tend to characterize as Hellenistic, such as the surface texture of the marble or the chiaroscuro of the drapery folds. In a painting of the same year as Pater's comment, the Prussian artist Adolph Menzel represented the fragmentary and brilliantly lit cast of a Venus, in startling oblique perspective, hanging on a studio wall with other casts, life and death masks (fig. 19.7). The malleable texture of the plaster and the nuanced shadows give the cast a startling realism that makes it difficult to identify, with certainty, as a representation of the Venus de Milo;[52] nonetheless the painting explores a crucial issue in the Venus's reception, the relationship between real and ideal (as well as that constant theme, the relationship between original and copy).

Menzel's painting might also be called a Hellenistic interpretation of the Venus, while Moore's is a classicizing one – but each responds to something observed in the Venus de Milo itself. Moreover, it is precisely the apparent stylistic discrepancies

---

51 Pater (1980) 52–3.

52 Françoise Forster-Hahn has tried to associate the cast, traditionally identified as the Venus de Milo, with the copies of the Aphrodite of Cnidus. She discredits her own argument by illustrating the Aphrodite of Arles (not a copy of the Cnidia); anyway the resemblance (either to the Cnidia copies or to the Aphrodite of Arles) seems no closer than to the Venus de Milo. See Forster-Hahn (2002) 221–3. As noted above, the Berlin Academy, where Menzel attended the antique class in 1833, included a cast of the Venus de Milo.

Figure 19.7 Adolph Menzel, *Studio Wall* (1872). Oil on canvas, 111 × 79.3 cm ©
Bildarchiv Preussischer Kulturbesitz (bpk) Berlin/Hamburger Kunsthalle/Elke Walford.

that have caused scholarly disagreements about the statue; the Venus is valuable above all for challenging our preconceptions about the orderly progression of styles in ancient art, and the various visual receptions can help to clarify the stylistic points at issue. Thus the receptions are not merely new interpretations (although they are immensely imaginative in that sense); they are also serious explorations of the ancient statue itself, including all of the problems that have troubled the scholars.

What they do not do is solve those problems. But do we want to solve them? To discover the supposed historical "truth" about the statue would be to fore-close further interpretation – our own, as well as that of others. Furtwängler's account of 1893 has threatened to do just that; its debunking tone, its air of demys-tifying or deromanticizing the statue, have perhaps lent it a greater authority than its often debatable arguments should warrant. Furtwängler states forthrightly that we ought to "find out, not what the statue ought to have been or how it would answer best to our preconceived notions, but what it actually was."[53] This is a classic statement of historical positivism, instantly reminiscent of Ranke's famous phrase, "wie es eigentlich gewesen."[54] But why should we limit our interpreta-tions to what we can prove with hard evidence? Since the evidence inexorably diminishes in the passage of time, what we have left is merely a minimum – not the "original" meaning of the statue at all, but something much less, something lamentably impoverished. The receptions of the Venus – scholarly, literary, artistic – constantly range beyond what Furtwängler thought permissible. But the imaginative collaboration of many minds produces a fuller account of the statue than the bare minimum our facts can provide. Such an account may be closer in its richness and complexity to the "original" import of the statue. Reception-based accounts have often been accused of privileging the subjective to the point of sol-ipsism, but we may argue that the reverse is the case: it would be solipsistic indeed to ignore the receptions of others in our exploration of the Venus. What the statue "actually was" may even seem to slip farther into the distance, like the departing lover at the end of Winckelmann's *History*. But Winckelmann may have been right: that should only make us study the Venus more attentively.

---

53 Furtwängler (1895) 384.
54 On the historiographical issues see Bann (1984) 8–31.

20

The Touch of Sappho

Simon Goldhill

This chapter approaches some of the most insistent and difficult questions facing reception theory, via the small scope of a single picture. It is concerned first with a double process integral to classical reception. An artist (or writer) produces a work, which engages with the classical past. Such productions are often the focus of author-centered *Rezeptionsgeschichte*; and how an artist (or writer) recognizes and treats the classical is a traditional topic of scholarly discussion. But viewers (or readers) also respond to such a work as part of their own engagement with the classical past (and with the present). The picture becomes the site of an ongoing and active response to the classical past. This reception is multiform at the time of the work's production, and also changes over time. Our contemporary understanding of a Victorian painting's view of the classical past necessarily passes through the prism of such layered receptions, as viewing in the here and now performs its own gestures of appropriation, (mis)recognition, and revelation. Putting the viewer back into *Rezeptionsgeschichte* reminds us that reception is best seen as a continuing, dynamic process, where our object of study is not the picture as a static and stable receptacle of meaning, but rather the viewer's engagement with the picture as a cultural event.

A viewer is not simply an abstract construct, however, even though art history often makes a generalization out of the multiform subject positions from which art is viewed. To focus on a viewer's reception is to broach not just constructions of class, gender, and education, but also of the relation between the margins and the center of cultural life, and how such mapping affects the comprehension of a cultural work. A picture on display in the Royal Academy is not the same event as a privately circulated image. A picture viewed by 90,000 people in a gallery in Liverpool has a different cultural significance from a picture seen and debated by the London critics. A picture may be viewed differently by a man and by a woman. What's more, as viewers change over time, what can be seen alters over history.

Thanks to the editors and, above all, to Liz Prettejohn for expert help with this piece.

This is nowhere more pertinent than with texts and images that treat the expression, recognition, and regulation of desire. Desire cannot be expressed without its veils, feints, and silences. As Freud teaches us, it *always* cannot speak its name, at least its clear and real name: it cannot *stop* speaking of its aliases and alibis. There are always silences in the exchange that makes up the recognition of desire, and the reception of silence is inevitably a hermeneutic crisis. My interest in this chapter, then, is the shifting recognition of desire in readers' receptions of a Victorian image of the classical past – and the interpretative lures and snags of such an inquiry.

The picture in question is a painting exhibited in the Royal Academy by Lawrence Alma-Tadema in 1881, titled *Sappho*, though now usually called *Sappho and Alcaeus* (fig. 20.1).[1] I want to use this image as a route into the more general questions of the contours of cultural normativity which I have been outlining. It is a most striking canvas, which immediately attracted a good deal of attention in the press. It is one of Alma-Tadema's larger works (it measures 66.1 × 122 cm), and it is now in the Walters Art Gallery, Baltimore. The setting is a marble terrace, an *exedra*, where the Mediterranean glistens in the background, and a bright sky can be glimpsed through a canopy of pines. On the right, a beautiful young man, Alcaeus, the poet, is playing on the cithara (a type of lyre) and his mouth is slightly open, perhaps singing. Across the performance space – the empty center of the painting – sits Sappho, staring intently at him. On her lectern is a laurel wreath, a victor's crown awaiting a head, and under the lectern stands a statue of Winged Victory, holding out a laurel wreath too. Behind Sappho, arranged on the marble benches, are three girls in various states of concentration, rapture, critical observation, and concert-goer's inattention. The middle of these three girls looks out at us the viewers, enforcing a self-conscious sense of looking: it is in part a picture that represents gazing and listening: acts of interpretation, appreciation, and performance. A fourth girl stands behind Sappho. She alone is crowned with brightly colored daisies, which match her decorated dress, and while she looks at Alcaeus, her arm is draped across Sappho's shoulders in an affectionate and protective manner. The stone benches are scratched with graffiti, the clearest of which spell out in Greek the names of the girls named in Sappho's love poetry – Anactoria, Atthis, Gongyla, Gyrinnos, as well as some less clear syllables.[2]

Now, Alma-Tadema painted a series of well-known paintings of *exedrai* which are often peopled by young lovers: in *Pleading* (1876), a young man lies prone on a marble bench looking up at a seated girl, who with her hand to her mouth is poised in a moment of doubtful hesitation. The same pose is adopted by the two figures in *Xanthe and Phaon* (1883). *Ask Me No More* (1906) has a young

1 It is already listed as *Sappho and Alcaeus* in Dircks (1910).
2 The names are taken from Sappho's own poetry: see fragments 16 (where Anactoria is named); 8, 49, 96, 131 (Atthis); 22, 95 (Gongyla); 82a (Gyrinno(s)). For a text and wonderful translation of Sappho (with good notes also), see Carson (2002).

Figure 20.1 Lawrence Alma-Tadema, *Sappho* (1881). Oil on panel, 66.1 × 122 cm. Walters Art Gallery, Baltimore.

man kiss the hand of a woman, who turns her head and body away from his approach. *Amo te, ama me* (painted in 1881, the same year as *Sappho and Alcaeus*) shows another courting couple against a Greek backdrop. In *A Reading from Homer* (1885), a full-scale canvas now in the Philadelphia Museum of Art, four listeners, posed around the *exedra*, are held transfixed by a poet reciting from a scroll: a young man with a lyre and a young woman leaning on a marble bench with a tambourine hold hands; in front of them, a youth dressed incongruously in animal skins, as if in satyr costume, languishes on the floor; a fourth figure, shrouded in a cloak and garlanded, stands in the shadows behind them. In all these pictures of *exedrai*, the sea can be glimpsed, blue against the white marble, and the figures are caught in a moment of longing and looking and listening.[3] In *Sappho and Alcaeus*, then, both poetry and erotics are cued by the scenery of the *exedra* as well as the title of the painting.

There is a long tradition linking Sappho and Alcaeus erotically (as well as a less well-defined tradition that has them share in ill-judged political activity against Pittacus, the tyrant of Lesbos[4]). According to one story, usually taken back to the authority of Aristotle (*Rhet.* 1.9.20), Sappho rejected an indecent proposal from Alcaeus.[5] For Madame de Staël, Alcaeus was a lover of Sappho, who later, as a friend, became the preserver of her literary record.[6] For others, he was the jealous rival of Phaon, the man for whose love Sappho leapt to her death.[7] The discovery of a fifth-century Greek pot in 1822 with paired images of Sappho and Alcaeus gave their relationship the romance of an apparently authentic material embodiment.[8] Alma-Tadema's image looks back through the long history of modern representations of Sappho as poet and lover.

The physical tensions of the painting seem carefully calibrated. Sappho, leaning on her arms, is intent and fully focused in her gaze at Alcaeus – across the central gap of the *exedra* and the painting. Is this poetic appreciation? Or even rivalry? The laurel wreath is set between them, as is the little statue of Victory,

3 These pictures are reproduced and discussed in Barrow (2001).

4 This story was made popular by Jean-Jacques Barthélemy in his *Voyage de jeune Anacharsis en Grèce* (1788), who based his claim on the fragmentary *Marmor Parium* which said that Sappho fled Mytilene and went to Sicily. He states that this must have been because of her political involvement with Alcaeus against the tyrant. This is discussed by DeJean (1989) 158–60.

5 DeJean (1989) 153. Georg Ebers thinks the picture is inspired by a poem of Hermesianax, quoted in Athenaeus, *Deipnosophists* 13.598b, which simply states, "You know how many revels Lesbian Alcaeus enjoyed as he sang and played his yearning love for Sappho."

6 DeJean (1989) 190.

7 DeJean (1989) charts this most fully. See also Williamson (1995) 8–12 and in general the fine collection of essays in Greene (1996).

8 A wine cooler now attributed to the Brygos Painter (Munich 2416). Both figures are named on the pot.

reaching out towards him. The girl with her arm on Sappho's shoulder, and the girl on the seats behind them to the left also stare at the poet, creating a trio of shared attention, and a strong line of sight between them and the man on the other side of the *exedra*: a transfixed audience. And the wood of the lectern set against the marble matches the wood of the chair and of Alcaeus' lyre, visually linking the two poets. A scene, then, of poetic appreciation.

Or is the tension between the protagonists of the painting (also) a sexual tension, as one might expect in such a setting and from the tradition of these two characters? The drinking cup casually discarded underneath the chair of Alcaeus suggests a certain decadence. Alcaeus, depicted as a very beautiful young man, seems to stare past the lyre directly towards Sappho's eyes. Sappho and Alcaeus, who are the only two figures not to have their bodies largely obscured by the seating and the dais, are dramatically foregrounded, both dark-haired and olive-skinned, both intent apparently on each other and the moment of musical performance. Yet Sappho is set amid her girls, and the names of her female lovers are all around her, like plaques on the seats, an erotic history, purloined from her own poetic fragments. And she is being touched by a beautiful young woman garlanded with flowers.

It might well be thought that if there is a sexual tension here it is a tension between the tradition that makes Sappho a lover of women and the tradition that has her dally with men – and indeed kill herself for love of a man. Is Sappho to cross the line between her band of girls and Alcaeus? The empty center of the picture is a question. The picture asks the viewer to read desire in the painting. Who wants whom and in what terms? Reading the mute expression of desire is always fraught with danger, however, and we need a more developed frame for this question. The first element of the frame is made up by the Victorian concern about the expression of sexualized beauty in art, and the feelings aroused in the viewers of such art. The depiction of the nude, of flesh, and of the moral horrors of adultery, lust, and failing self-control, was explicitly debated in contemporary society, and this debate has been very well discussed by recent critics to show how the public performance of prudishness contrasts with a flourishing market for such art.[9]

Alma-Tadema himself became a focus of such worries four years before *Sappho and Alcaeus* with his painting of *A Sculptor's Model* (fig. 20.2). This painting is based primarily on the Venus Esquilina, which was excavated only in 1874 (Alma-Tadema visited Rome in 1875–6). It also recalls the (male) *diadoumenos* of Polycleitus. But his painting of a life-size naked woman has no pretensions to mythic veils. It should be remembered that Lord Haddo had proposed to Parliament in 1860 that all funding should be removed from art schools which used life classes, because of the immorality necessarily involved – and that against

9 Bullen (1998); Nead (1988); Pointon (1990); Pollock (1988); Smith (1999a); Smith (1999b) and esp. Smith (1996).

Figure 20.2 Lawrence Alma-Tadema, *A Sculptor's Model* (1877). Oil on canvas, 195.5 × 86 cm. Private collection.

the background of the Contagious Diseases Act of 1860.[10] Haddo was resoundingly defeated but the concern over the relation between artist and model rumbled on through the last quarter of the century. Interestingly, this painting was produced because Robert Collier, Lord Monkswell, had asked Alma-Tadema to take on his son as a pupil. Alma-Tadema refused, but agreed to let the student attend his studio while he painted the painting, provided that Monkswell bought it afterwards.[11] It is a painting where an artist stares at the nude from behind in his studio, while the viewer stares at her from the front, painted to teach a watching student: Lord Haddo would have had apoplexy.[12]

The Bishop of Carlisle was vexed by the Alma-Tadema picture. He wrote to a friend: "For a living artist to exhibit a life-sized almost photographic representation of a beautiful naked woman strikes my inartistic mind as somewhat if not very mischievous."[13] It would be much easier if the artist were dead, it seems, or the woman less obviously sexy and, well, big. Jenkyns is right that this is a private letter and written in a tone which is sophisticated and self-ironizing.[14] But when the picture was exhibited in Liverpool in 1878, a whole series of outraged letters was published in the press, often signed with such sobriquets as "An Offended Father," expressing strong moral objections to the painting and its display – utilizing a familiar contrast between the Plain Man and the Sophisticated Artist.[15] As usual with such press-fomented scandals, the public responded by going to the gallery in droves: 89,110 people visited the exhibition, 20 percent more than in any previous year. The painting was a *cause célèbre* and a *succès de scandale*.

The degree to which art stimulates or expresses desire between artist and model, or between picture and viewer, is an area where maximum care is needed in Victorian culture, and where particular attention is required concerning what is publicly articulated about such feelings.

The second element of the frame is scholarly. In the academy and beyond, there was, as Jean DeJean and Yopie Prins have outlined, a lengthy and often heated debate, led by German scholarship, on the nature of Sappho's desire – a debate to be set against the background of new homosexual legislation, high profile trials, and the very invention of the words "homosexual," and "lesbian" in the attempt to pathologize the desiring subject.[16] Alma-Tadema was obsessive about his scholarly accuracy (and it was a topic of much press commentary).[17] He was

10 On Haddo's attempted legislation see Smith (1996) 30–2.
11 Swanson (1990) 52.
12 Smith (1999a) 202–7 is particularly good on responses to this painting in context.
13 Stirling (1926) 63–4. He also comments that "*Punch* was evidently a little staggered."
14 Jenkyns (1991) 125–8.
15 See Smith (1999b) on "the British Matron."
16 DeJean (1989); Prins (1999); see also in general (from a huge bibliography) Porter and Hall (1995); Gilman (1985); Bland and Doan (1998).
17 Typical is this comment of Meynell (1887) 15: "His subjects, as a general rule, are in no sense connected to the feelings; they are the learned revivifications of the past, delighting only in their scholarly accuracy."

forced to defend the chair on which Alcaeus sits, and did so stridently, citing archaic pots whose design he was imitating.[18] He wrote the girls' names in Greek letters. He – and a good part of his audience – was likely to know well the potential in the figure of Sappho for highly transgressive sexuality.

What's more, there is a long tradition of paintings of Sappho *as* expressions of female desire. These are usually associated, however, with her love of Phaon, a man, and her suicidal leap from the rocks into the sea. Let me contrast two of these, which will be particularly useful for thinking about the centers and margins of cultural normativity. Figure 20.3 shows Charles-Auguste Mengin's painting of Sappho. Mengin has not been a well-known or celebrated artist, and this painting of 1877 was donated to the Manchester City Art Gallery in 1884, where it has been exhibited without much notice since. I have not been able to trace any contemporary review of the painting, although it was exhibited in the Salon at Paris in 1877, and there has been no study of Mengin the artist. This is a picture that did not enter the mainstream culture.[19] Sappho is dark, as Ovid describes her, though not exactly short and ugly, as Ovid also adds.[20] Rather, she appears as a passionately moody romantic artist – she is carrying her lyre – contemplating death and love. She stares with an inward gaze, her face shadowed by her hair and robe which run into each other, as she melds into the dark rocks. This is not the Greece of light and purity, sunshine and rationality, but the physical embodiment of a dangerous passion, "where burning Sappho loved and sang." But Mengin in an extraordinary gesture has bared Sappho's breasts and shoulders. The light burns as brightly here as the rest of her is shaded. It is not at all easy to see how any light source could produce this effect. It is as if her breasts illumine what we can see of her face. Archaeological accuracy is not what is at stake here. Rather, *this* dream of Greece lets the viewer stare full on at the young girl's exposed and fleshly body (such images still help to sell paintings as well as cars and newspapers). We could intellectualize the image and say the burning love in her breast is a passion which lights her face, the mirror of the soul – a metaphor for the passion of artistic creativity – but, whatever the rationalizations, the viewer is obviously being offered an erotic stare at the girl's body – and invited to take pleasure in looking. This is a very *sexy* painting about a poet of love.

The second Sappho (in fig. 20.4) is also preparing for a suicidal leap. Her hair is in a neat bun – a few strands have escaped in the most refined distress. Her hands are joined not in simple prayer, but probably to indicate her inner turmoil. Her dress is standard Greek issue – uncovered arms and shoulders, with the barest hint of bodily form beneath. The "fallen woman" is one obvious image recalled

---

18 Swanson (1977) still feels the need to regret the shocking anachronism of the furniture. The Victory is based on a table-stand from Pompeii, with a lectern added.

19 It is used on the cover of Prins (1999), and has had a certain brief flurry of notoriety in Sappho studies at least.

20 *Heroides* 15.31–5. The authenticity of this poem does not affect its importance for the tradition of representations of Sappho.

Figure 20.3 Charles-Auguste Mengin, *Sappho* (1877). Oil on canvas, 230.7 × 151.1 cm. Manchester City Art Gallery.

SAPPHO

Figure 20.4   Queen Victoria, *Sappho* (1841). Ink on paper. Reproduced from
The Critic (June 1900).

here.[21] What makes this sketch interesting is not just the telling contrast with
Mengin's image, but that this was drawn by Queen Victoria, as a young woman,
in 1841: it began as a private sketch but was actually published in 1900.[22] Here
is one critical response from the press. "It will be hard to refine upon the poetic
beauty and romantic intensity of Sappho as etched by her Majesty the Queen . . .
It is simple and impassioned."[23] This may be a courtier's flattery, but the reviewer
is insistent on seeing this sketch as an intense and impassioned embodiment of
female desire. If this sketch started as a private and marginal self-expression of
female desire and loss, when published as the work of a now aged Queen, it must

21   See Nead (1988).
22   Brinton (1900). It is discussed well by Prins (1999) 187–8.
23   Brinton (1900) 509–10.

be seen as an image from the very center of British culture, but it also becomes a deeply layered and complex opportunity of recognizing desire. The dignity of the queen, the aged queen's recollection of youth, the queen allowing the publication of a formerly private image after all these years, all provide filters which manipulate the viewer's recognition. The courtier's reaction is only an extreme version of the dynamics of power and publicity which make the valence of this picture so hard to judge.

An image of Sappho, then, invokes a tradition of desire, of female desire. But in that tradition, it is extremely rare indeed to have Sappho *touch* anyone. A touch is always a charged moment in Victorian art, a moment of embodied emotion, a significant gesture. I have found, however, only two paintings where Sappho is touched by a human.[24] The first is David's *Sappho and Phaon* (fig. 20.5). There are two points I need to make about this complex canvas. The first is that this picture barely enters the tradition of Western cultural knowledge. It was painted for Prince Youssoupoff who took it to Russia where it remained in private hands. David himself had to ask Youssoupoff for a sketch of the canvas to remind himself of it.[25] It is not even clear whether the one contemporary critical comment on it that has survived was based on a description of the painting or on seeing the painting itself. This painting, despite being by the celebrated David, is marginal in that almost no one saw it, and hence no one could have been influenced by it.

The second point is that the touch does something extraordinary to the painting. David himself, in a brief description of the work, and says that Phaon has come in to surprise her, and as he touches her cheek from behind she drops her lyre, which Eros picks up to play the Hymn to Aphrodite.[26] The word "Phaon" can be seen written on the scroll on Sappho's lap. But modern viewers have had more trouble with the picture than this narrative gloss may suggest. The strange way in which Sappho and Phaon gaze out of the frame at the viewer (and not at each other), coupled with Sappho's odd look – a "sensuous, self-satisfied and

24   I have excluded from this survey prints of an erotic/pornographic nature where Sappho is in a sexual embrace with another woman, of which the most well known is probably *Songe de Sapho* by Girodet-Trioson, which is conveniently reproduced in Reynolds (2003) 64 fig. 3, who discusses such images on pp. 53–67. I have also not included such images as the frontispiece of Blin de Sainmore's *Lettre de Sappho à Phaon* (1766), where Sappho languishes on a seashore like Ariadne and is supported by a female companion (conveniently reproduced in DeJean (1989) 144 fig. 2); nor a painting such as Angelica Kauffman's *Sappho Inspired by Love*, where Cupid rests a hand on Sappho's shoulder. One could say that both the pornographic images and the images of Sappho as deserted or inspired lover would add to the erotic expectations of the Alma-Tadema picture. In each case, the touch is a significant moment.

25   See Adams (1977–8); Crow (1995) 262–4.

26   See Schnapper (1980) 268–70. The painting is now in the Hermitage.

Figure 20.5 Jacques-Louis David, *Sappho and Phaon* (1809). Oil on canvas, 222 × 260 cm. Hermitage Museum, St. Petersburg.

somewhat fatuous smile," as one critic puts it[27] – is less easy to fit into the apparent allegory of the production of erotic lyric. What's more, this is an erotic narrative that we know will lead to Sappho's death. The picture has consequently provoked some intensely uncomfortable readings.[28] When Sappho is touched and passion erupts, the regulation of the imagery of desire fractures. The story becomes much harder to control.

The second painting of Sappho being touched is a lush Pre-Raphaelite water-color now in the Tate Collection in London (fig. 20.6), painted by Simeon Solomon in 1864, and called *Sappho and Erinna in a Garden at Mytilene*. Two "wasted and weary" Pre-Raphaelite beauties, complete with fawn and flowers, nearly brush lips in what looks like a sexualized clinch. The dark Sappho on the right is

27 Johnson (1993) 245–6.
28 See Johnson (1993) 244–7, "compelling in its strangeness"; Crow (1995); Adams (1977–8).

Figure 20.6   Simeon Solomon, *Sappho and Erinna in a Garden at Mytilene* (1864).
Watercolor on paper, 33 × 38.1 cm. Tate Collection, London.

hugging and leaning over a rather resistant Erinna. Erinna was also a poet, who
was said by a very late Greek encyclopedia, in the usual way of such things, to be
a student of Sappho (though it would have been impossible given their dates).[29]
If there is a hint of an image of poetic inspiration here, it is outweighed by the
less salubrious teacher–pupil relation on display.

Again I have two brief points on an image that could bear more extensive discussion. First, Solomon is as marginalized and self-marginalizing as you can get
in Victorian high culture. He was a Jew. He was flamboyantly open about his
sexuality, was reputed to have cavorted naked with Swinburne, and illustrated
Swinburne's unpublished poem on flogging. He was explicitly shunned by all good
society after he was arrested for soliciting in a public urinal, and died a destitute

29   Sappho does mention an Eirana (fr. 91; 135) who is implausibly linked with Erinna
      the poet, who almost certainly lived at least 200 years after Sappho: see Williamson
      (1995) 18–19.

alcoholic.[30] Because of this, quite a lot of shocking people in the know talked about him quite a lot – for example, Symonds, Wilde, Pater, and Rossetti.[31] As the poet John Gray wrote in 1891, "People no longer speak of him, except in whispers."[32] There was a flurry of retrospective exhibitions of his work between his death and World War I, but many of his pictures circulated not only in private circles but between self-selected aesthetes. That he was both so marginal and so connected shows how intricate and intimate the dynamic of celebrity and influence can be. The second point is that this picture comes out of – or rather stays in – a specifically homosexual environment, which privileged Greekness as a coded expression of desire.

There is a more precise evocation here, however, than the generalities of "Greek love" and "Sapphism." For this painting functions as a visual instantiation – an illustration almost – of Swinburne's notorious poem "Anactoria." Swinburne as a young writer was the great white hope of English poetry, closely linked to the Oxford Aesthetic movement and a man-about-town. After a debilitating episode of alcoholic dysentery, he spent his last years in the suburb of Putney, although his poetry remained popular and in print.[33] The turning point in his career was the publication in 1866 of the volume which included "Anactoria" – published against the advice of his closest friends. The following lines convey the poem's thrill – as it describes Sappho's desperate desire to put her lips to Anactoria's body:

> Ah that my lips were tuneless lips, but pressed
> To the bruised blossom of thy scourged white breast!
> Ah that my mouth for Muses' milk were fed
> On the sweet blood thy sweet small wounds had bled!
> That with my tongue I felt them, and could taste
> The faint flakes from thy bosom to thy waist!

The vividly portrayed longing for flagellation and blood, licked from the "sweet small wounds," "from thy bosom to thy waist," is only part of what makes these verses (still) outrageous. When Sappho touches and is touched – especially by a woman – the eruption of fleshly desire is, within Victorian cultural norms, deeply disturbing. Swinburne is knowingly scandalous because of what he publicly expressed and how he expressed it. Sapphic desire needs careful control.

30 On Solomon's career see Davis (1999); Donoghue (1995) 38–9; Reynolds (1984); Cruise (1995); and the brief but salient comments of Dellamora (1990) 170–1.

31 Pater praised him in print – anonymously but very recognizably: "a young Hebrew painter" – three years after his disgrace (rpr. in Pater (1922) 42). The description of Solomon's painting of Dionysus included this "homosexual code" (Donoghue (1995) 39): "the sea-water of the Lesbian grape become somewhat brackish in the cup."

32 Cited in McCormack (1991) 28.

33 Prins' chapter on Swinburne and Sappho is particularly good (Prins (1999) 112–73). See also Dellamora (1990) 69–85.

Figure 20.7 Frederic Leighton, *The Fisherman and the Syren* (1858). Oil on canvas, 66.3 × 48.7 cm. Bristol Museums and Art Gallery.

Even in the context of classical mythologizing, the touch – like the naked body – is a charged area, where female desire becomes visible and hence frightening. Figure 20.7 is Frederic Leighton's *The Fisherman and the Syren*, where the intensely liquid form of the siren is pressed against a fisherman, looking like a crucified Christ by Michelangelo, a martyr to desire. Her desire kills him, and he appears as a troubling victim, unable to resist her embrace and her feelings. The physical interface – the touch – between man and woman is here a source of fascinated horror.[34] But consider this sequence of pictures of Oedipus and the Sphinx. The famous Ingres painting of Oedipus (fig. 20.8), from the early nineteenth century (1808), shows an Oedipus who is posed in the act of thinking, faced by the protuberant breasts and enigmatic smile of the statuesque Sphinx. She merely reaches out a shadowy paw towards him. Figure 20.9 is the painting that made the name of Gustave Moreau in 1864. The Sphinx has leapt violently on Oedipus. But he resists, like a Desert Father, and dominates with a stern gaze. The Sphinx symbolizes the lascivious and tempting woman, wrote one contemporary critic, a "bestial humanity" which the man conquers. "Faithful and calm in his moral strength he looks at her without trembling," as Moreau himself put it. She is the image of "modern female beauty," wrote another overheated critic (whose experience of modern females must have been very upsetting).[35] Stuck's *The Kiss of the Sphinx* from 1895 (just fourteen years after Alma-Tadema's *Sappho and Alcaeus*) takes the involvement of man and monstrous female a step further (fig. 20.10). The Sphinx and Oedipus are locked in a carnal embrace. The scarlet palette embodies the unclassical and degenerate. The artist's own features make up the face of Oedipus. There is no question of faithful and calm resistance here. The artist portrays himself lost in the swirls of a mythological and rapacious desire.[36] There can be little doubt about which poem was in Stuck's mind, however: Heine's "Sphinx."

> Before the gate there lay a Sphinx –
> Terror and lust cross bred!
> In body and claws a lion's form
> A woman in breast and head.
>
> A lovely woman! Her white eyes
> Spoke of desire grown wild;
> Her lips gave silent promises,
> Her mute lips arched and smiled.

34 See Østermark-Johansen (1999) 119–20.
35 See Mathieu (1994) 72–9: the quotations are my translations, and the critics quoted are Désiré Laverdant, and Maxime du Camp, cited on p. 78. Moreau's own comments are taken from *L'Assembleur de rêves: écrits complets de Gustave Moreau*, ed. P.-L. Mathieu (Fontfroide, 1984) 60.
36 For Stuck's work and references to the contemporary response to it, see Voss (1973).

Figure 20.8   Jean-Auguste-Dominique Ingres, *Oedipus and the Sphinx* (1808).
Oil on canvas, 189 × 144 cm. Musée du Louvre, Paris.
© Photo RMN/© René-Gabriel Ojéda.

Figure 20.9 Gustave Moreau, *Oedipus and the Sphinx* (1864). Oil on canvas, 206.4 × 104.8 cm. Metropolitan Museum of Art, New York, bequest of William H. Herriman, 1920 (21.134.1).

Figure 20.10 Franz von Stuck, *The Kiss of the Sphinx* (1895). Oil on canvas,
160 × 144.8 cm. Szépmüvészeti Museum, Budapest.

The nightingale! she sang so sweet –
I yielded, passion tossed –
and as I kissed that lovely face,
I knew that I was lost.

The marble image came alive,
Began to moan and plead –
She drank my burning kisses up
With ravenous thirst and greed.

She drank the breath from out my breast,
She fed lust without pause;
She pressed me tight, and tore and rent
My body with her claws.

Heine, the sardonic Jewish poet despised by the growing racism of German nationalism, was an icon for the artists of high Expressionism, and typically here the
Oedipus myth becomes a Pygmalion-like tale of artistic self-destruction, in which
female desire, as so often in this period of "decadence," is seen as violent,
destructive, frightening, something to lose yourself in – vampiric and monstrous.[37] The trajectory of Greek mythological imagery of sexual desire is another
frame in which to view the touch of Sappho.

All this should make Alma-Tadema's painting a remarkable image. It seems
to be one of the very few public, privileged works of art to suggest, however
carefully, a tension between a woman's sexual love for a woman and a woman's
sexual love for a man. This should be a very transgressive picture indeed, bringing a dangerous and marginal desire into the very center of the image world of
Victorian high culture. So it is fascinating to see what viewers and critics made
of it. *Punch* imagines an "academic dialogue" which might seem to recognize this
tension.[38] A "Critical Lady" asks a "Wise Young Judge" which figure Sappho is.
He points to one. "Which? The man?" asks the woman. "Oh is that a man? I
didn't see exactly –." "But," asks the Critical Lady, "was Sappho a man or a woman?"
The Wise Young Judge can't answer ("Ah – was Sappho a he or a she?"), but
eventually decides she was one of the Muses. This might seem to play with the
sexual ambivalence of Sappho or the soft beauty of Alcaeus. But it seems to me
that the joke is actually on the pretentious buffoon who doesn't know what
we know – and goes no further than that. It is yet another *Punch* joke about
the insufficiently educated and pretentious. The same week a cartoon in *Punch*,
entitled "Sap-pho-tography", parodied the painting as Alcaeus taking a photo-
graph of Sappho and the other girls on the *exedra*.[39] It is equally unrevealing,
except of the current fame of the picture and artist.

The Times, however, published a review after *Punch* had appeared (it refers explicitly to the *Punch* parodies of the show) and it is the one dissenting voice in the
chorus of lavish praise which greeted Alma-Tadema's picture in reviews of the
exhibition. It too focuses surprisingly on the problem of identity: "we hardly know
which is Sappho, and, what is worse, we do not care . . . (F)or Sappho and what
she is reading or singing we do not care a straw, nor did the artist, if appearances
may be trusted."[40] That the reviewer seems to think that it is Sappho who is singing
or reading in this picture seems uncannily to embody the *Punch* joke! This confusion over the subject of the canvas (which may have motivated its change of
title) can be seen in the range of identifications. Edmund Gosse in the upmarket
Fortnightly Review had no difficulty in identifying Alcaeus, nor did the reviewer
of the *Athenaeum*. Other reviewers offer no name or, in the case of a somewhat

37   See Auerbach (1982).
38   *Punch* (May 14, 1881) 226.
39   *Punch* (May 14, 1881) 217.
40   *The Times* (June 6, 1881) 4.

overheated article in the *Daily Telegraph*, identify him as Phaon.[41] A viewer's response depended on what narrative the picture was taken to capture – and different narratives reveal different interests and silences.

Particularly telling was a lengthy article published in New York five years after the exhibition, which found the painting outrageous and attacked it viciously – for its archaeological inaccuracies.[42] The author was particularly upset that the little statue of Victory could not have been produced until at least 200 years after Sappho, and, worst of all, that the graffiti is not written in the letters of sixth-century Lesbian but fifth-century Attic! It is a long and strident article. Equally odd to my mind is the response recorded in the *American Journal of Philology*.[43] One critic, we are told, says that the object of the poet, Alcaeus, is to "enlist Sappho's support in a political scheme of which he is the leader, if not chief prophet, and he has come to Sappho's school in Lesbos with the hope of securing another voice and other songs to advocate the views of his party."[44] This is a direct though unattributed quotation from the review in the *Athenaeum*.[45] We are meant to see in the painting, in other words, a piece of lobbying for a political campaign – the poets as the spin-doctors of ancient Lesbos. But the editor of the *American Journal of Philology* knows better. What is at stake here is not politics but metrics. Alcaeus is singing "new songs with new rhythms" – as Sappho "hears it, she feels that there is a strain of balanced strength in it that she has not yet reached." The editor does think that the clausula at the end of a Sapphic stanza is "the incomplete echo of the cry of yearning love, a passionate invocation." But the tension in Alma-Tadema's painting stems from the discovery of a new metrical scheme.

In 1885, four years after the painting, Wharton published what was to prove the most influential translation of Sappho for the next 50 years and more.[46] It was the first English translation to be explicit about the female gender of the object of Sappho's desire. And Wharton took the head of Sappho from the Alma-Tadema painting for his frontispiece. But 25 years later, in 1910, Mary Mills Patrick still had no doubts about Sappho: she was a woman with high moral ideals. And her proof was that Sappho was headmistress of a school, and "There never has been an age of the world when society was so corrupt that young women would be sent from a distance to study under a teacher who had a sullied reputation."[47] (It is no surprise that Mary Mills Patrick was herself a headmistress, of the far-off

41   *Fortnightly Review* 29 (1881) 689–703; *Athenaeum* 2782 (April 30, 1881) 597; *Daily Telegraph* (April 30, 1881) 5; see also *Magazine of Art* (1881).
42   *Nation* (September 16, 1886) 237–8. It is an anonymous review of Georg Ebers's biography of Alma-Tadema.
43   *American Journal of Philology* 34 (1913) 106–7.
44   For the story see n. 4 above.
45   *Athenaeum* 2792 (1881) 597.
46   For the importance of Wharton see Prins (1999) 52–73.
47   Patrick (1912) 100.

Constantinople College, the leading American school in Turkey.) Sappho's words "do not describe love at all," she writes, "but the unhappiness occasioned by the loss of the affection of her friend."[48]

Contemporary reviewers were not swift to see desire in Alma-Tadema's painting. The *Athenaeum* might be thought to show us the effort of repression. It noted that the image "depicted a political as well as a poetical flirtation between two of the greatest lyric poets of antiquity," where the word "flirtation" may suggest a *frisson* between the protagonists. Like Gosse, he calls Sappho "a *précieuse*," which at least notes a certain self-consciousness in the image of Sappho (or in the reviewer).[49] But he adds: "He has avoided giving to her physique any impression of that voluptuous temperament which the scandals of a later age attributed to her" – a statement that tellingly reminds us of what not to see in this image. He immediately adds a novel identification: "The figure of Sappho's daughter, who sits at her side, is charming."[50] The juxtaposition of these two sentences (and Freud would note the misrecognition of the girl as sitting when she is standing) may indicate by their emphatic sense of propriety some of the potential anxiety for viewers of this painting.

Only the *Daily Telegraph* saw a "burning Sappho" – "the quick-witted full-blooded, passionate daughter of Scamandronymus."[51] Indeed, for him "Sappho reminds us much more of Sappho the amorous matron . . . than of Sappho, the sentimental and love-lorn maiden." She stares with "the eyes of a love-sick jaguar from Java." Alcaeus is identified as Phaon, and it is suggested that Sappho's companions were rather sniffy about their leader's infatuation. But, he adds, with knowing tone, "Sappho was a very literary lady indeed. A terribly literary lady." And with this hint the review drifts into direct comedy with a fantasy that Phaon was connected to the press and Sappho threw herself over the cliff because of bad reviews. This article has a quite different tone from the other notices of the exhibition, and it alone seems to flirt with recognizing in Sappho a figure of potentially improper desire: a "terribly literary lady" – though even here the joke is primarily on the "modern woman" in publishing, a stereotypical concern of the 1880s. She may appear as infatuated with a man, Phaon, but he turns out to be, like the reviewer himself, "associated with the Press," as the story reverts to a tale of literary ambition.

48   Patrick (1912) 110.
49   Gosse, *Fortnightly Review* 29 (1881) 692: "something of a *précieuse*"; *Athenaeum* 2792 (April 30, 1881) 597: "it may be that the painter intended a little satire in importing to her garments and her air something that is *précieux*, while it is refined and dignified." The tension in the response here is again in evidence.
50   This identification is also made by Helen Zimmern, *Art Journal* special supplement (1886) 22, rpr. in Singleton (1912).
51   This and the remaining quotations in this paragraph come from *Daily Telegraph* (April 30, 1881) 5.

If this painting of Alma-Tadema, like so many of his works, seems to express a sense of sexual desire in classical dress, it is hard to find significant comment on it in contemporary Victorian society. Where *A Sculptor's Model* unleashed a barrage of shocked private and public response, *Sappho and Alcaeus* seems to have evoked no sexualized narrative at all, except for the jokey and knowing *Daily Telegraph*, which emphasizes all too clearly what is missing in the other notices. For almost all the Victorian viewers it seemed to be a picture about politics, meter, education, architectural features, coloring[52] – anything but erotics.

This raises some fascinating questions, not just about the recognition of desire, but also about how we conceive of centrality and how transgression is negotiated. Swinburne and Solomon, when they represented the touch of Sappho, were deeply scandalous, and their scandalous flouting of acceptable social normativity focused attention on the norms against which they were judged. In this way, they became icons of transgression for others, and had an effect on the center, and at the center, by making the transition across boundaries visible. When Queen Victoria, located at the apex if not the center of the social system, represented Sappho, however, she may have opened a narrative of remembrance of things lost, but her very position, and the consequent response to her, also produced its own blindnesses and silences. The very center here is also wholly exceptional. Even marginalized.

Yet when Alma-Tadema, protected by his social position, his artistic reputation, the classical subject, and the restraint of his portrayal, opened a space where desire may be viewed, the response was either silence, or a careful turning of the head, or a retreat into humor. It could not be seen, or rather, it could not be directly said to have been seen.

The question, therefore, could be asked like this: when it comes to recognizing an eroticized relationship between Sappho and Alcaeus, Sappho and her girl friends, named on the walls of the *exedra*, does the silence of Victorian viewers mean there is nothing there to be seen, because there is no eroticized look except in the eyes of a modern observer? So Reynolds, usually swift to find the *jouissance* in an image of Sappho, wrote dismissively that Alma-Tadema placed Sappho "in her schoolroom . . . surrounded by some of her girls on a marble rank of benches engraved with the names of her pupils and listening to a performance of Alcaeus."[53] Or did the Victorian viewers of this painting maintain silence because silence is the proper reaction – proper because it does not publicly recognize any sexy feelings either in the viewer or between the characters in the painting? An anthropologist aims to reveal the tacit knowledge of a community, to reveal the

---

52 *Magazine of Art* 4 (1881) 309; *Art Journal* (1883) 66; Helen Zimmern, *Art Journal* special supplement (1886) 22; *Schreiber's Magazine* 18 (1895) 670; all comment on the coloring of the sky and sea, but make no comment on the dynamic of the central figures.

53 Reynolds (2003) 81.

structures of belief that a society cannot say of itself. Since Thucydides, historians have been committed to the polarity *logo men, ergo de*: "what was said . . . but what really was the case." The threat of any historical or anthropological analysis, however, is the imposition of modern assumptions where different assumptions exist in the people or culture being studied. When you have a hammer, everything looks like a nail . . . Nowhere is this tension more insistent than in recognizing desire. Being too quick to see the signs of desire is the sneer at the psychoanalyst and the fool in love. Being unable to see how desire is not expressed directly but always veiled is the sneer at the naive literalist – and the fool in love.

At the time of its first exhibition, this picture was viewed by many different people. It was exhibited in a central gallery in London, and entered the public domain more broadly through reviews, commentary, reproductions, and satirical magazines.[54] It was viewed through a set of overlapping frames – philhellenism, the expectations of the genre and iconography of Alma-Tadema's classicizing art, the changing sense of how sexuality and desire were part of the artistic world, the history of images of Sappho, the knowledge of Sappho and Alcaeus as ancient figures and as redrawn by subsequent generations, the protocols of touch and the representation of the fleshly body, the recognized use of Greekness to talk about same-sex desire. It was also viewed by different individuals and groups of individuals: the characters imagined by *Punch* are at one end of a spectrum; the circle of Wilde, Swinburne, and Solomon at the other. The event of this painting's reception takes place within these different and overlapping variables with their different patterns of marginality and centrality, of being in the know and out of the picture.

Yet what the central empty space of the picture, the silence or veils of its language of desire, provokes is a heightened sense of the grounding problem of all such historical analysis. Not only must a modern viewer explore the complex dynamics of the historical moment of the picture's reception, but we must also negotiate our own processes of appropriation – the (inevit)ability of seeing ourselves in the mirror of painting. How much does *our* desire to construct a particular image of the Victorians affect the narrative we tell of the Victorian reception of classical antiquity as a scene of desire?

Reception is a process of more complex dynamics and more intricate and constant negotiation than the standard model of influence and impact allows – or the static image of a map would suggest. I am drawn back again and again to the space between Sappho and Alcaeus, and to the viewer faced by that space. What does this picture know? What does it expect the viewer(s) to know? How *knowing* is this learned painter's image of classical antiquity? It is here that the social expression of this picture becomes evident, and where the reception of the classical takes place.

---

54   The reproductions are conveniently listed by Swanson (1990) 213–14.

21

(At) the Visual Point of Reception

Anselm Feuerbach's Das Gastmahl des Platon; or, Philosophy in Paint

John Henderson

This essay first explores the history of a magniloquent painting which visualizes in epic dimensions the denouement of Plato's *Symposium*.[1] After investigating operative factors in its rise to celebrity, I point to the opportunity it provides for contributing to interpretation of the classic text, sowing the suspicion that this has been missed because mainstream philosophy disregards ekphrastic art as partner for theoretical dialogue. This particular representation even parades its role as wordless twin for Platonic textuality in figuring its status as fictional vector of the truth of the Socratic myth's dependence on fictional representation. Philosophy is risked to the reception given to the reimagining of wisdom in Plato, as in every successive reimaging of that *reception* held at the house of Agathon in the wake of Plato's. Literary-focused rereading of Plato has in recent times revalued the purchase of his graphic writing on the arguments presented:[2] visual artists, too, have plenty to show philosophers about the art *in* philosophy. Mine host, be my guest.

The painter Anselm Feuerbach (1829–80) has been a national treasure throughout the history of modern Germany from its inception.[3] Born into a genealogy of established intellectuals, he grew knowing he would live up to criminologist grandfather, his uncle the political philosopher, and father, professor of philology specializing in archeology (art history) at Freiburg (publishing on the Vatican's

---

1 For Feuerbach's *Gastmahl* and Plato's *Symposium* through iconography and framing see Henderson (2006); for Plato's knotted narration see Henderson (2000) esp. 290–7; and for portraiture of Socrates see Henderson (1996).

2 Esp. Nightingale (1995) on genre; Blondell (2002) on character; and Charalabopoulos (2002) on metatheatricality.

3 See esp. Malyon (1999–2004) for full guide to distribution of the oeuvre; cf. <http://wwar.com/masters/f/feuerbach_anselm.html>. *The* art book (from Hirmer) is Ecker (1991).

idealizing beauty, the classical sculpture *Apollo Belvedere*, in 1833). Hard not to see in those culture heroes entertained in Feuerbach junior's megalographic masterpiece his own ancestors – the destiny they promise and premise (see figs. 21.0–21.2).[4]

Anselm trained in the university studios of Düsseldorf, and Munich, where he fell for Rubens in the Alte Pinakothek, finding undeniable flair for central European landscape under Karl Rahl. Success arrived in Paris, with *Hafiz at the Well* (1852), now in the Munich Schackgalerie (named for his principal patron in the 1860s, the collector Baron A. F. von Schack). From Thomas Couture's studio, he turned out technically skilled, easily liked, pictures – the 1853 *Mädchenkopf*, for example, donated in 2004 to the Leo Baeck Institute (New York) on its return after Nazi seizure. Picking up the "Colorism" idiom on a first trip to Venice, he settled to work in Rome (1856–73), supplying the full range of commissioned portraits and genre pictures which ensured a working artist's living. Back in Baden, his stepmother Henriette fostered his career all through his life and then hers, managing his business and massaging his considerable ego, gusto, and aggro. Married in 1834, widowed in 1851, Henriette plotted Anselm's fame until her death in 1892, eliciting, gathering, and promoting their correspondence into a legacy of writing which has cemented his position as a key witness, theorist, and polemicist in the art world of mid-nineteenth-century Europe.[5]

Today, Feuerbach is an agreeably cosmopolitan chunk of classic *German* culture, a versatile painter who fetches appreciative pleasure to a wide constituency of art lovers; a principal figure in the ex-patriate fraternity of daubers dubbed in their day, arsy-versy, "Deutschrömer." The house in Speyer where he was born has been a tourist attraction since 1971, and the local Historische Museum in Pfalz boasts the attractive *Portrait of Giacinta Neri*.[6] A 50-pfennig stamp with an *Iphigenie* from the ever popular series of post-Goethean gals gazing nostalgically seawards commemorated the centenary of his obit (1980).[7] Outside Germany, the painter is little known despite millennium events such as the exhibition *Anselm Feuerbach e l'Italia*,[8] and in particular the exhibition (and book) curated

4 Agathon combines the type of Winckelmann's idolized-idealized beauty, the Villa Albani *Antinous Relief*, with individualizing traits of *self*-portraiture: Keisch (1992) 27; Muthmann (1951).

5 For "their" biography see Kupper (1993), with *Zeittafel* (136–8) and full *Bibliographie* (143–52). Massively continuous and unguarded, the letters have made Feuerbach as much of a force in print as on canvas. See oft-reprinted Uhde-Bernays (1911; 1912); Kern (1977 [1882]); Kupper (1992). Text twinned with graphics: Fischer (1922).

6 See the regional Art Society's 1976 Heidelberg exhibition: Küffner-Arndt (1976).

7 Product that sells, from 1862, 1871, 1875, *Iphigenie* sits, half-sits, then stands in ever popular *Weltschmerz*; her putative ancestress, by his putative ancestor the classical pot-painter, butts into the vase foregrounding the final *Gastmahl* (Kupper (1993) 72–9).

8 Museo Civico Giovanni Fattori Livorno: <http://www:encanta.it/Anselm_Feuerbach.html>

by Direktor Claude Keisch, *Spirit of an Age: Nineteenth Century Paintings from the Nationalgalerie, Berlin*, which took advantage of the thorough overhaul of the Alte Nationalgalerie within the stupendous facelift given the restored capital of unified Germany – and took in the National Galleries of both London and Washington, DC. The nineteenth-century collection of pictures was reintegrated for the reopening (minus the original sculpture installation), and Feuerbach's monumental *chef d'œuvre* required spectacular crating, hoisting and lowering by crane through a window back to its original position of honor on the staircase, second-floor.[9] The gigantic canvas, *Das Gastmahl des Platon*, had always been glory-bound – purchased *for* the grand opening of the newly imperial capital's mecca for Art in the late 1870s.

Feuerbach the practicing art theorist became victim of his own spin. Strong but unremarkable idealist-humanist sloganizing on Art as the realization of perceptible concepts, a creative poetry rather than any reprise of actuality, rapidly yielded to that perilous persona of the Renaissance genius *drei Jahrhunderte zu spät auf die Welt gekommen*;[10] he just *knew* a great talent is fated to deliver great – enormous, impossible – works. The idea for a *Gastmahl* in oils dated from 1854, first sketches were made in 1857;[11] a color sketch fixing the schema evolved through 1860–6 (fig. 21.0). As the decade wore on, Feuerbach negotiated with an increasingly exasperated, eventually despairing, von Schack to swing serious financial support for a titanic canvas on which the party-goers could appear at full life-size. For all the patron's protestations (who would have a wall to hang a whopper on that scale?), the painter persisted, bargaining (so he gambled, and lost) with pledges of a stream of saleable, admirable, stand-bys. *Folie de grandeur* went still deeper, or higher, for his sketchbook and easel were occupied with a companion project – a vast *Amazonenschlacht* (1857–74) designed and, he willed, destined to face *Gastmahl* in a cosmic showdown between mutually corrosive polarities founded in the conquest of the wild and its incorporation within the civilized: *Chaos* to *Kultur*. Stepmother tried her best to prevent the rift to ruin (1865), but her increasingly obsessive *raison d'être* and meal-ticket went for broke, finishing the *blue* version's dawn mist in 1869, a spread of 295 × 598 cm (fig. 21.1). This he hustled into that year's Munich International Exhibition, whereupon reviews panned it (mucky hue, mediocre talent, frigidity – sick aesthetic aberration . . .). Henriette might wow at the presencing of the figures, proclaim Truth and Discretion, sighing "Only a Colorist . . . ," but the technorama flopped, though an elderly painteress up in Hanover did pay a moderate price – for a reminder of

9   For hauliers' photos of the move see <http://www.hasenkamp.com/en/news/main_archiv.html>

10 Frau Henriette Feuerbach, fighting for all Anselm was worth, to Baron von Schack, Heidelberg (April 21, 1866): Ahlers-Hestermann (1946) 31; see p. 17 on fig. 21.2, "denkt Man im ersten Augenblick mehr an die Hochrenaissance als an die Antike."

11 For the narrative ahead: Ahlers-Hestermann (1946), Keisch (1992), Kupper (1993).

Figure 21.0   A. Feuerbach, Color sketch for *Das Gastmahl*, (first version, 1860–6). 100 × 550 cm. Privately owned, reproduced with permission from Prof. Keisch (1992) 79, Katalog no. 82. My thanks to Prof. Keisch and Martin Dinter.

Figure 21.1   A. Feuerbach, *Das Gastmahl* (first version, 1869). 295 × 598 cm. Staatliche Kunsthalle, Karlsruhe, with permission. My thanks to Karin Merkel.

Rome.[12] Our hero redoubled efforts, pressing on with a portentous version which no world could conceivably resist (1870–3): "it will make me rich and revolutionize the German art world," he wrote mama. Elevation to a chair in Vienna in 1872 coincided with approaching completion of the monsterpiece second

12   See esp. Bringmann (1976).

Figure 21.2 A. Feuerbach, *Das Gastmahl* (second version, 1871–4). 414 × 764 cm. Nationalgalerie, Berlin A I 279, with permission. My thanks to Norbert Ludwig.

Gastmahl, stretching to 414 × 764 × 15 cm (fig. 21.2), along with its counter-weight *Embattled Amazons* (now in Nuremberg). At this crest of his wave, an "up" Anselm packed for the Austrian capital, then at the pitch of its own overhaul into modernity. Refused space in Vienna's World Exposition of 1873, the achieved *Gastmahl* would get a fortnight's showing in its Arthouse the following February, when Feuerbach sanctified Agathon's white "toga" with its gold filigree, but the painting then went on tour in search of cheque and home, reaching Berlin in May (and its final touches). Four years of messy bidding and fuming beat the price down to a flattening mediocrity before the new (now Alte) Nationalgalerie finally stumped up in 1878.

By then, Prof. Feuerbach had launched onslaught in Vienna (where his *entrée* coincided with a massive financial crash) against the – inevitably "pathological" – "New-Baroque" fad that fêted the painter-cum-prater Maqart, in a war of pamphleteering that Anselm could only win in hagiography.[13] He resigned and quit for Venice in 1876–7, to die in 1880 still fizzing indignation and with four years' work wasted on a heroic ceiling for the Vienna Academy which would have apotheosed the Professors in a colossal *Titanensturz* (1875–8). Far from pioneering and/or fitting into, any artistic Zeitgeist, he'd wound up as the final dodo of a historical-monumental paintdom.

Back in 1870, when the Berlin Royal Academy of Arts exhibited the pick of living artists, including Feuerbach's *Judgment of Paris* and his best *Medea*, the "Gründerjahre" of his fame were permanently stitched onto those of his nation and its shrine to Painting. In Feuerbach's decade, Frederick William III succeeded as king of Prussia (1861), appointed Bismarck his chancellor the following year, annexed half of Denmark (1864), smashed Franz Joseph's Habsburg Austria (1866), blitzed through France (1868–71). Empire was acclaimed at Versailles, *Kaiserreich* inaugurated (1871). A long-decreed National Gallery for Prussia was bump-started by a serious donor, recognized in the title *Wagenersche und Nationalgalerie* (1859–61). Relocation (1865–73) to the newly triumphant Museuminsel complex secured expanded and upgraded housing for the king's, then the emperor's, collection of paintings to suit pan-German horizons, and successive directors (with "our Fritz," culture-vulture Crown Prince Frederick III, pitching in) set about augmenting the standard mix of mid-European genres by backing lines likely to suit future taste and ideology. Nascent impressionism among them; Maqart, too. And, of course, a vein of vague-through-crass nationalist heroics, long before Kaiser Bill exerted pressure for more militarism on parade in his capital (from 1888).

In 1890 the "blue" *Gastmahl* (fig. 21.1) was bought for the Kunsthalle by the Rhine-side city of Karlsruhe (where his 1860s output had almost landed

---

13   Feuerbach's "manifesto" on Art derives from this 1873–8 feud: *Über den Makartismus, pathologische Erscheinung der Neuzeit* and *Aus meinem Leben*, consecrated by Henriette in the engrossed collection *Vermächtnis* (Kupper (1992) 96).

Feuerbach a chair). One day it would attract the Führer, but in the nick of time Hitler (devoted to a Feuerbach *Parklandschaft*) would be eased from the idea of displaying Platonic pederasty in his office. Quality plus sibling tie to the Berlin icon have swelled its reception history: both as treasured gem of its collection (for example, Zimmermann (1961)) and as hook-up with the NG, linking the north–south historic art capitals of Germany, and in their time the countries Germany, East and West, through press and curatorial cooperation between Munich and Berlin (whence Vey (1976)). The Kunsthalle staged the closest moment Feuerbach's *Gastmahl* has yet come to figuring in exegesis of Plato, when the legendary NYU guru Seth Benardete expounded *Symposium* with fig. 21.1 for backdrop: to introduce the publication, H. Meier scrutinizes the painting – strictly in terms of (in)fidelity to Plato's text (1994).[14]

By 1906, fig. 21.2 was Hauptwerk of 76 Feuerbachs amassed by the NG. He retained the high profile acquired by being in there at the start, in every revision of "German" art through the twentieth century. No Berliner or Prussophile, mostly working from Italy or Austria, this artist's oeuvre fits no nationalist blueprint, however assertively he was coopted by the Third Reich for some approvable "Munich school" in those greatesque 1930s exhibitions of Germanness. No, Anselm Feuerbach's was and remains "a German's art": soon after Ahlers-Hestermann wrote his account of fig. 21.2 from a black and white print supplemented by keen memories in Berlin 1941, the NG was badly hit, and by the time the monograph was cleared for publication by American Sector control (1946), the massive national heirloom had been removed intact from blitz-time storage – and removed to Russia by the Red Army as prize loot, actual and symbolic. The Alte Nationalgalerie reopened in part by 1949, fully in 1955. Comradely negotiations regained the Berlin *Gastmahl* its berth in 1958 within the DDR. Once "BERLIN WIRD MAUERFREI,"[15] the end to partition could be celebrated not least on the walls of the Galerie. A spectacular occasion in the nation's history and the most spectacular in the painting's came with Keisch's exhibition dedicated to the gestation of *Gastmahl* (1992). As Berlin quit the twentieth century for a lovingly reunified and lavishly revamped future, the NG shut down (1998–2000). Since the reopening, the *Gastmahl* hangs in its traditional place within the original configuration.

In the same years that Strack, "Architekt des Kaisers," built the Nationalgalerie, he also masterminded the 69-meter tall *Siegessäule* that would dominate Berlin's Königsplatz, topped with bronze giantess Victory, tailed with trappings of ongoing military success (1865–73). In those heady years of emergence into *Kaiserreichtum*, images of Victory mushroomed everywhere in public space. The

---

14 Strenuous efforts to name that cast: Ahlers-Hestermann (1946) 8; Keisch (1992) 8; Benardete (2002) on Socratic-Platonic erotics.

15 "– Die Mauer ist in euern Köpfen": 1988 graffito plus scholion on the remaindered Berlin Wall ("Berlin's now wall free – The wall's in our heads"; Waldenburg (1990) 67).

type of a bronze statuette from the second-century CE, in the Antikenmuseum, found particular favor, and became *the* Victory, of Berlin.[16] The most striking alteration to *Gastmahl* from fig. 21.1 → 21.2 replaces a Silenus and Bacchante wall-painting with a gleaming golden Victory niche, *à la* Graeco-Roman "house-hold shrine" – in *the* tradition of Art culture, the spirit that the final *Gastmahl* breathes.[17] Even given the variation in meaning that the painting has borne through its history, surely this mimetic analogue of the advent of supremacy must iden-tify Feuerbach as "Artist of Empire, 1870–4"? As Prussia gasped for acclamation, this Victoria has *forced* her way into the scene (while *Amazonomachy* should sprawl mythological spoils of naked Schadenfreude opposite). Certainly the ponderously multiplied symbols and fetishes of classical cult strewn all round the heavyweight new frame and infiltrating a stack of details across the picture-space endow the picture with sacral power, at once offering and shrine, both decoration and rep-resentation of *ex voto* and altar, and no less apotheosis of Art than beatification of the *work* of Art.[18] But this power need not convert effortlessly and without remainder into *Weltpolitik*, let alone *Weltmacht*, and should not pass itself off uninterrogated.

Reflection back from the production and ultimate destination of the Berlin *Gastmahl* to its genesis in student-days' idolization of Rubens, plus a stimulating Düsseldorf tutor's investment in another *Symposium* sketch (copied by Carstens in 1795),[19] will deliver us to the painting on a very different trajectory. One where *Plato* can matter, and the picture bear on *his Symposium*. Let's *see*.

Feuerbach makes his playwright artiste and dummy-self Agathon host wisdom. The schema acclaims the artist-figure who fetches us to Socratic education through mimesis, through montage, through the triumph of art. For access to vision of whatever kind lies in the pointing of those painted hands, all the way through figs. 21.0 → 21.1 → 21.2. One outstretched arm gestures a welcome that stretches back deep into its intensifier, a square glare of interior light (fig. 21.2). Where thinking should go, behind the appearances, where the mind's eye can be trained to look. Through the appearances, into the light. In the other fist, for those with eyes to see, Socrates' final victory is securely grasped, up-front and at centerfold.

No doubt about it. The one who awards victory *is* Victory. But – look – Victory's crown is targeted on the ugly old Sage and the ugly old crown of his ugly old skull. There will be no party and no picture without reception and orchestration

16   Arenhövel (1979) 2.49–50, Katalog no. 47: height 13 cm.
17   Coers (1999).
18   See Keisch (1992) 33, on bukrania, garlands, etc.
19   Rubens: McGrath (1983); the teacher – W. von Schadow – and the sketch: Keisch (1992) 9, Katalog no. 54. No *tradition* existed for representing the scene, though *Last Supper* traits and allusions recurred.

of reception by victorious Feuerbach–Agathon, but *Socrates* is lit up with his beati-
fying inner victory, of the mind. For underpinning the dramatist's dramatics there
has lurked from figs. 21.1 → 21.2 a hulking background figure of authority that
delivers us through painterly intertextuality to the Passion scene of Platonism. And
his tale centers on the jaundiced old boy sat jawing, off to right, by candlelight.

At the point of visual reception, the design delivers symbolic teaching from
resources of its own kind. There, sat between the columns to back up the producer-
director, the greybeard attests and assures *lovers of art* that Plato is right behind
this artist. As the (hostile) critic F. Pecht saw at once in 1869, the side-lined
Philosopher producer-director-writer has come straight round to join the party
from his appearance in David's classic version of the *Death of Socrates* (1787).
There, the brooding writer faces left, sat at the foot of Socrates' death-bed, away
from the ring of apostles, pondering the eucharistic scene he will recreate in writing the *Phaedo* as it plays out behind his back. And *there*, sat up straight as the
lamp-stand by his bed, Socrates bosses the scene, scourging human imbecility
with up-thrust forefinger while *his* right hand reaches to take his goblet, ready to
down mere death.[20] *You see*, next time, that goblet will be – will have been on
its way to becoming – the poisoned chalice of hemlock, Socrates' martyrdom to
the incivility of society. Art is using the mimetic power of depiction to pierce through
to myth, and retell the story of Philosophy cornered within the confines of agreeable exchange as prefiguration of its ultimate consecration.[21]

And Plato's *Symposium?* Now Plato the sage is recognizable through the ven-
erable age David awarded him as incarnation of classical antiquity. Yet, as is widely
recognized,

> Jacques Louis David's *Death of Socrates* shows Plato seated at the scene in despair.
> In the *Phaedo*, Plato says he was sick and not there. (Markson (1996) 35)

Once we retroject this ancient of days back from his master's death row (399 BCE)
to the occasion of the follow-up party for Agathon's first victory (416), we'll be
obliged to think through the mytho-logic of idealizing representation where it
concerns visual valorization of authority. For if Plato visibly ages not a whit between
the writing of *Phaedo* and of *Symposium* (say, pre-385 and post-385!), nor

---

20   Feuerbach's figure recognized as David's "Plato": Keisch (1992) 9, Katalog no. 50.
     No traditional iconography for Plato existed, but Raphael's figure of the Old
     Testament prophet cum venerable sage claims that role in postclassical art: in *The School
     of Athens* (*c*.1510), Plato's up-thrust forefinger points our souls to the otherwheres
     of Immutable Being, inspiring David to father the gesture on his expiring Socrates
     (Hall (1997) 96, fig. 24). Raphael's Socrates faces away from Plato, holding forth to
     his group that stars the hip Alcibiades at its far left, right elbow jutting out our way
     from the hip, as in his *Gastmahl* group (Hall (1997) 26, fig. 18).
21   Gotshalk (2001).

between those and his *non*-appearances in the scenarios he portrays for 416 and 399, this must serve to promote above verisimilitude the age-old wisdom of the words that authorize the worlds he imagines for Socratic praxis.[22] As personification of nous, Socrates too must *look*, not his age, but his totemic status: the arch-patriarch in the genealogy of western philosophy cannot lose seniority along the way back in time from 399 to 416, between the legendary occasions handed down by Plato's graphic texts. But Plato – the artist Plato is eternal scourge of representation, artistic bane of Art. To "rewrite" the *Symposium* into visual terms is necessarily to resist and recast its dynamic, to press its (Socratic) teaching of "the symposium" and teaching with the sympotic – whether Plato's, Feuerbach's, ours, or anyone else's – from antiquity to the present.

A visual *Symposium* is bound to address structure, repress narrative. *Gastmahl* follows Plato in triangulating the space between the coordinates "Agathon + Socrates + Alcibiades, *their* co-presence/getting it together" (*Symposium* 172a7). Feuerbach's supporting cast loses touch with the text in no time, not troubling to secure the pairing of lovers recounted through the mind-watering course of the dialogue, before Alcibiades arrives with the induction story of his bungled attempt to couple bodily with Socrates. One uncanny case concerns the snake-entwined candlestick that moves along the table as Victory intrudes between figs. 21.1 and 21.2, thereby disestablishing this apparently Asclepian identifier of the recumbent as Dr. Eryximachus, and implying that he and comic poet Aristophanes, and Aristophanes and he, can swap iconographies as easily as they swap positions in the round of Plato's speeches. Most glaringly of all, Feuerbach has made it impossible to *see* how Agathon can be answering the door without tearing up our Plato text, which precludes his getting up and going anywhere of the sort (*Symposium* 213a). How on earth even a dead drunk Alcibiades could land in a vacancy plumb next to Socrates[23] will get no answer from figs. 21.0, 21.1, or 21.2. For sure, *some* brands of loyalty to the Platonic moment are no priority of the composition. Yet Plato's *Gastmahl* itself insists on the *composite* hybridity of its relay of narration, the *combined* narration of narration. Its voices belong to apostles, disciples, fans, as well as celebs, legends, and Sage, conjoined in group adulation. They talk sex-talk in awe of sex-talk, featuring sexy talk about sex-play, weaving in and out of sublimation and seduction, the loves that lurk in *philo-sophia*. So *Symposium* is *in some sense* about the dethroning, as well as the enthroning, of Socrates and crew – about terms and conditions of Socratic philosophy.

The writing pressurizes and polices tension between the monological exegesis of the framing narration (set as Apollodorus') and the sociality of the narrated *symposium*. Here the structure parades: standard *eranos* protocols, of resources pooled

22 Nightingale (2002).
23 *Symposium* 212d–213b: Usher (2002) 224.

between guests and host; plus ad hoc rules for "tonight's" sober party drawn up by Eryximachus in consideration for the gang's hung-over condition after "last night's" victory banquet for Agathon's success with his play; and their *disruption* – by Aristophanes, then by Socrates, and "now," thirdly, by Alcibiades (and, "soon," again, by the arrival of a second komos of anonymous revellers: 223b); not to mention, *passim*, by Eros. Sure, Plato recounts his polished repeat narration of the story as a script, and a theatrically presented script, at that. *His* art soups up all the twists and scrapes of improvised spontaneity for his mimetic narrative: chancy foregathering of the cast; surprise allocation of roles; epiphanic peripeteia to bring the house down . . . ; and takes us "backstage," where we can watch philosophy trying to operate, away from the city's hubbub, in a particularly intimate privacy. Here, if anywhere, dialectic through dialogue should find congenial conditions, as talented "high-culture" friends bring along their varieties of Attic pzazz, back at the acme of rampant democracy? Make no mistake, the rules of sympotic conviviality direct proceedings at Agathon's.[24] For those communal laws of politesse elaborately frame every vocal drop of sagacity: interrogation is off limits, together with every other form of face-threatening, divisive, insistence. Here is a communal clearing for pooling and sharing solidarity, not jousting and criticism. The guests agree to their round of contributions, they distribute the airwaves and the attention in a clockwise ring. Searchers for truth may chafe at the game of charades, but each party-goer takes their turn, adding one more link to the love-chain of uninterrupted praise. Matey variation on what has preceded takes priority; this privacy turns out to host more showbiz, after hours. So Plato's *Symposium* is not about storying the symposium of Agathon–Alcibiades–Socrates. No, it is about (dramatizing) what that tale is *about* – what (any) "symposium" is about, in internally differentiating competition with what (any) Platonic script is about. Namely, what purchase (if any) can Socratic philosophy get on society, when embedded in sociality? Agreeable enough for philosophy to dine out, play civil for a change, stop picking on public figures for their unexamined pretensions. Necessary, too, for the gadfly to fall into the sticky jar of bonhomie, if Plato is to sting erotics, and get real close to the topic(ality) of "Love." The trappings of loving interpersonal relations trap the agent of the intellect, as Socrates is denied free range of tongue and cannot flex his mind. We came to hear the legend of one of Socrates' finest hours, specially prized (loved) by devotees past and future. Instead he must for once join the queue, and *listen*. When his turn comes, he must praise love, too, among lovers, loving and loved, not least himself. He will resort to narration (what else?) solo, unchecked, unexamined. The more blatantly so, *because* of his ruse of recounting a dialogue, his tête-à-tête, on and of desire, with Diotima. Out of reach. Even when Alcibiades disrupts the party, philosophy is still put in its place. Unruly vinous tale-telling brings in his train regression to the temporarily repressed carnival of the traditionally carnal Greek symposium; but all the sex

24   Lissarrague (1990) *passim*, esp. 116.

dripping from the sex-bomb's body and mouth cannot put Socrates together again. Instead, soporiferous fade-out will mumble disremembered, losable afterthoughts, and the sternest of tasks awaits acolytes who would wrest that crown from Agathon and plant it on Socrates.

On this account, the synectic dynamics of Plato's *Symposium* turn on the temporal plot of the sympotic round of speaking in line. *That* is what stymies Socrates; *that* is what Alcibiades disrupts. Hard indeed to see how a pictured *Gastmahl* can put *that* where we can see it? Where the text worked through its line-up of stars at its leisure, dramatizing the views, values, designs for life, "philosophies," personated by the participants, the picture must iron these ingredients out, and present configuration: interactive group bonding. And yet there *is* empathetic power in selecting this moment for the painting to "take place."

The emphatic spatiality of visual design *does* capture in its one sweep of metonymy what should be seriously entertained as one likely candidate for cardinal principle of Plato's text. As sympotic protocol strings the individual guests into the pecking-order according to seating 'plan', all these virtuosoandsos are put in their places. As we noticed, the differences between them are flattened out by intricate manoeuvres of displacement which sees neighbours and partners (ex)change places. Phaedrus and Eryximachus, to inaugurate the entertainment: take eros partners for the dance. Before that, Aristodemus is shunted up-front to arrive before Socrates. Afterwards, Plato's Eryximachus and Aristophanes swap science and farce, as scientifically/comically interchangeable, as they are artistically, in Feuerbach's iconographic replacement of fig. 21.1 by fig. 21.2. On the grand scale, the whole vista of Plato's and Feuerbach's *Symposium* is strung between "Enter Socrates" and "Enter Alcibiades." Agathon must welcome both these uninvited guests, and good hospitability even persuades him to change places himself, rather than setting places for one-and-all. Alcibiades' supervenience drastically changes the place, and changes everyone's places. Literally, by shifting Socrates and coming between Agathon and the Sage; discursively, by changing the rules of exchange, the rules for discourse. The shuffle of placement situates the party around cooperation. A garland, a crown. And this *can* be shown, and paraded.

In his own company, before he arrived at Agathon's, the philosopher's meditation was anti-sociable trance: however magnetic, the guru withdrew, a presence brandishing the absenting of self. So who needs friends, lovers, love – to *think* love? Socrates does. But the party is the best *and* worst place to think anything of the kind. For interrogation is blocked, dialectic outplayed. The primacy of *access* to (the logic of) camaraderie, devotion, fame, myth, desire is on display: the philosopher is caught within the group dynamics of the group dynamics he would analyse. So it is the orchestration of the *Gastmahl* which dominates the spectacle.

The iconography of Plato's *Symposium* has no settled schema, and the underwhelming figure of the lurking Sage is not in itself heavily marked *as* Socrates, whether by posture or by physiognomy, for all that a host of visual and written cues point to his perverse focality. Tradition has pinned no face to Alcibiades, let

alone to Agathon, so insurgent drunken reveler and welcoming crowned host
are only indirectly identifiable. The Alcibiades troupe patently articulates as a
Dionysus tableau,[25] and the *sight* of Alcibiades' Dionysiac *komos* must steal the
scene against all comers, irrupt into eye-catching psychedelic saturation. Just watch.
Ekphrasis can try, then try some more, but no paraded Alcibiades *could* show us
how excited *he* is by the thought, presence, sight, of . . . Socrates. So when painting articulates the asymptotic topic of superior insight, philosophy's inner eye of
meditation, cerebration, and reason must yield in charisma to the phanopoeic melo-
drama of mystic revelation. Socrates' tale of Diotima and the epiphanic "vision
beyond" gets painted into its becoming lamplit corner; and yet the awkward truth
is that *Symposium* is the founding text of Socratic desire, and *philosophical* desire
radiates and orbits around Socrates, as discussant, participant, guru, advocate, focus,
obsession, fetish, and text-case, while the tale advocates, holds a beauty contest
between, theories of desire, pure and applied. Painting can but intercede, since
making desire visible visibly intervenes. Art may pay tribute to the difficulty of
philosophy, but itself constitutes a difficulty for philosophy. A t(h)reat, of metaphysics impigmented, in your face epistemology.

But *Symposium* is more intimately tied to visual take and retake of Socrates than
this. For this central work of Hellenism is, not least, urtext for the iconography
of Socrates, boasting the words that generate and sponsor his imagery. And
yet, as *Gastmahl* underscores, this same piece of writing is busy teaching Plato's
lesson in dethroning imagery. The impossibility of ever "seeing" Socrates is the
doctrinal pay-off for venturing to imagine Socrates, who can only be misrecog-
nized by mere eyes. Withdrawal of valorization from visual cognition models the
denial of sensory knowledge which will characterize mainstream philosophy after
Plato. Its utility is to dramatize the impossibility of representing reality. And the
attendant paradox that *only* images can be seen, since all that can be seen is image,
not thing, depends on deprecation of visual mimesis: since illusion is delusion,
sensed beauty can but denote snare, whereas the ugly exterior functions as a dis-
rupted sign, gesturing beneath and beyond superficiality.

Finally, let Feuerbach's art engage with the dialogue's narrativity. Text-into-art
latches onto the visual theory scripted in the mimetic energy of rhetoric; but
picturing *also* restructures and reconstitutes philosophical propositions and their
argumentation, testing their generalizability – their applicability beyond the
limits of writing codes and book culture. Now this painterly version, like *all*
takes on *Symposium*, enjoys the status of a retake (hence, all are tied to mis-takes,
to mistakenness, as are we). Because the elaborate, abyssal, montage of this
classic text insists at length on its difference within both Platonic corpus and

25 Keisch (1992) 30–1, "Der Hauptzweck aller Veränderungen, die die zweite
    Bildfassung bringt, liegt darin, diese Affinität in eine Identität zu verwandeln"; see
    61–2, Katalog no. 46.

itself: at Agathon's, we read no "witnessed" or "overheard" conversation or group discussion starring Socrates, but rather the iterated, multi-take, narration of a narrative already relayed and replayed at one or more or many removes from its events. None of those layered pages are Plato's own, he is cast as but one (more) reimaginer in the chain: Socrates–Aristodemus–Phoenix–Apollodorus–Glaucon–Plato . . . Yet no other hosts his party of narrators and narration, every word in the script is down to Plato. Now scrutinize Feuerbach for montage. In fig. 21.2, both elephantine frame and crush of inset imagery insist that this art work hosts *art work*: the legend ÆFEUERBACH.R.73 painted onto the gold frieze at bottom left claims the whole production number for the artist; and the titular dedication SUMPO-SION sits atop the paint that colors the central bucranium which stands proud of both the outer and the inner frames, as well as poking into the painted room to cover both the floor covering and the gold-hemmed skirt that covers the body of the host with newly embroidered floral opulence. So the image pictures outside and inside as one, in this complementary engine of self-acclaiming artifice. Similarly, blue sheeting tumbles forward in a cascade of folds that billow over into the picture frame. To left, too, rose chaplets edge down and out into the frame, while grapes dangle and greenery straggles down the sill into the room to waft over and pick out both Bacchic rout and our host. To obtrude on viewers still further that this frame is the same painted expanse of flatness as all the rest of the splash of pigment hung on the gallery wall, watch fruit, vegetable, and flower garlands both lodge within and overspill onto the grey frame, while at once tucking under and encroaching upon the inner frame of repeating "egg-and-dart" rows. Further "inside" yet, those 2-D cupids bestrew and enchain with their garlands the latecomers' route from the door, down those steps, and onto the stage. Bind together all the floral crowns of the revelers with the host's gilded crown and the wreath held out by Victory to crown her chosen winner (gold outside, gold inside, gold, more gold). And bind together all the be-garlanded binding that runs rings of roses and the rest of the floral tribute flat-out all around the frame. Here high culture reflects (on) high culture, matching Plato with oil painting as tickets to the elect. This palette's vision of Socrates is good for imagining Plato, witnessing philosophy, attending (to) *Symposium*; for seeing *through* the ekphrasis, to (do) the work of philosophical response, engagement, reasoning . . . Anselm Feuerbach saw himself as titanic poet, and delivered. He *knew* how to hide where we (philosophers) cannot miss it – to *show* – that it takes art to host undying love. *Das platonische Gastmahl des Feuerbach.*

22

Afterword

The Uses of "Reception"

Duncan F. Kennedy

The chapters in this volume demonstrate the range of work that is currently being carried out in the discipline of classics under the sign of "reception." They embrace histories of reading and of the reception traditions of individual authors or works, interventions which seek to reconfigure traditions and cultural genealogies, reception as theory and as an arena for the contestation of ideologies, and these concerns severally intersect these chapters in varying degrees. Not only are they themselves receptions, but they are also reception *studies*, and thus enact a distinctively scholarly desire for knowledge, (self-)understanding, and authority, and I in turn will use this as a way of organizing my response, and in particular to probe how this desire may find that term "reception" a congenial but in some respects problematical one under which to operate. A recurrent feature of what I have to say is the way in which time, particularly the distinctions between past, present, and future, is differently configured and deployed within reception studies.

The central dictum of reception theory invoked, and put under various sorts of pressure, by a number of contributors to this volume is that "meaning is realized at the point of reception." A constitutive move of reception theory is that there is always a gap between a text (or utterance) and its reception. This gap may be perceived as minuscule, but is theoretically crucial. Batstone puts it thus:

> Words always mean differently: if I want you to understand my words, I want you to understand them from your position. I want you to understand differently . . . what I say here and now, in this place and time, can never be said again, not by me or by you, not even if we repeat these words. The event will always be different. (p. 16)

For all that the impression of similarity may be overwhelming, this gap introduces difference, and it is in this gap that history operates. Crucially, the act of "reception" opens out a distinction between "present" and "past," and confines what it receives to the "past." Suppose that this gap (which, of course, may not simply be a *temporal* one) is opened out to the extent that the sense of difference is sufficiently great that understanding presents explicit challenges. Writing of Lucian's *True Stories*, Tim Whitmarsh says that "[t]he reception of this text shows a marked desire to refashion it so that it *refers*, becomes *about something*" (p. 114; emphasis in original). The text is "refashioned" in the act of reception, which is therefore an act of re-presentation: the text, now from the "past," is made "present." It is but a short step from here to allegorical interpretation (allegoresis). Allegory ("speaking otherwise") explicitly acknowledges the distance between writer's text and reader's text: the enduring value or interest of the writer's text is endorsed, but not its comprehensibility, and it is reconfigured to speak in the reader's terms. Many texts – including scholarly studies – rewrite earlier texts without calling themselves "allegories"; but are the processes we associate with allegoresis no less operative, even if occluded? Viewed thus, Hegel's treatment of Sophocles may not seem very far removed from Neoplatonist readings of Homer. The writer's text is refashioned in its reception in the name of understanding: what are construed *retrospectively* as the "obscurities," the "omissions," or the "suppressions" of the writer's text are "illuminated," "made good," or "revealed" in the reader's interpretation.

Issues of knowledge, and the will to knowledge, are at work here. It is in the apprehension of such gaps that we construct the temporal distinction between past and present crucial to interpretation, a distinction that is thus at one level an epistemological one. In this regard, some philosophers of knowledge invoke what they call the "principle of charity," though that loaded term "charity" is often applied with a greater or lesser degree of condescension. If the writers of the past were more like us (the fortunate inhabitants of a more enlightened age), so the argument goes, *this* is what they would have written – and "would" often shades into "should"; did they but know what we know, this is what they *really* wanted to say.[1] The writer's horizon is seen as opaque or limited in contrast with the reader's, but this, as Batstone suggests, is to "place ourselves above rather than in the complexity of reading and writing" (p. 14). One challenge reception theory

---

1   A term often invoked in such discussions is "modernity," and it is worth briefly pausing to consider it. Charles Martindale remarks: "modernity can be modern only insofar as it postdates or supersedes the past" (p. 8). In the distinction between "postdates" and "supersedes" lies an important debate. "Postdates" suggests "later but not necessarily superior" whilst "supersedes" suggests "later and superior," maybe even "later and thereby superior." In the terms in which I'll be developing my response in this piece, the latter outlook is associated with classic realism, the former with anti-realism. In *We Have Never Been Modern*, Bruno Latour throws out the constructivist, anti-realist challenge to see "modernity" not as a metaphysical reality but as a modality of thought. See Latour (1993).

can pose, as he emphasizes, is to see the reader's horizon as no less partial; to see
ourselves, we might say, "within" history rather than "outside" it, as subjects not
wholly present to ourselves, awaiting our reception in turn. This take on the point
of reception sees it as not simply linking past and present but operating under
the shadow of the future as well. It also carries with it some very specific epistemological assumptions, as we shall see in a moment.

The so-called "principle of charity" would have it that *this* is what the writers
we are rewriting were *really* saying, did they but know it. Our horizon is represented as capable of supplying the plenitude that is – now – so obviously lacking
in theirs (what Batstone calls "the imperfect of our past" (p. 18)). The effect of
this is to grant an epistemological confidence to the here and now in relation to
the past; the present is endowed with a sense of closure or finality, the triumph
of "modern" thinking. If meaning is realized in this way at the point of reception, it comes to the reading subject in a flash of *realization*, of making real, in
which he or she *knows*. Texts are thought to have a "real" meaning, existing
in concealment, but "discovered" in the act of reception to have been there all
along. In this way meaning is *realized*, made *real*, at the point of reception.
Epistemologically, this is classic realism, and its rhetoric, particularly the trope of
"discovery," of uncovering what has "been there all along," can be detected in
many reception studies. Realism reifies, variously making "things" of texts and
subjects, and, thus construed as "things," they are made to stand outside rather
than within history. But reception theory, at least insofar as it emphasizes the
constructedness of meaning and the "*active* role" of readers (Martindale, p. 11),
also has strongly anti-realistic tendencies. So for Batstone, "[t]he point of reception . . . is not some thing-like point 'within' the consciousness of the objective
Thing-like reader" (p. 17), and for Martindale, "[t]here is no Archimedean point
from which we can arrive at a final, correct meaning for any text" (pp. 3–4). Such
anti-realism resists reifications, but does not necessarily escape them, as we shall
see, and it copes with the gestures and tropes of realism by disrupting them or
displacing them rather than by simply abolishing them.

I have suggested that allegoresis can be a useful way of conceptualizing what
is involved in the tenet of reception theory that "meaning is realized at the point
of reception." But what, or when, is the point of reception? This is an issue that
arises in relation to virtually all work done in reception studies. Is "the point of
reception" Derrida reading Hegel or Miriam Leonard reading Derrida? Or me
reading her paper? Derrida can be figured as a "reader" of Hegel, but when he
becomes part of Leonard's text, he is also, though less obviously, configured as
a writer whom she in turn reads. Explicitly the point of reception is Derrida reading Hegel (reading Sophocles), but implicitly it is also Leonard reading Derrida
(reading Hegel . . .). And if Derrida allegorizes Hegel's discussion of Antigone in
such a way as to "reveal" a hitherto "concealed" telos of anti-Semitism that was
there "in" Hegel all along, then Leonard configures Derrida's reading of Hegel
as an allegory of, amongst other things, the implications of reception theory. She

gives a very deft account of the way in which reception treats the text it rewrites as "exemplary" in some respect or other, but as Antigone is an example for Hegel, so Derrida is an example for Leonard.

Often in reception studies (and I'm conscious of doing it myself here), the point of reception is shunted one place back in this way, on to Derrida from Leonard, and on to her from me, and I wonder to what extent that is an inescapable part of a discourse that operates under the sign of "reception," and to what extent it is the pull of a received realist rhetoric from which some practitioners of reception studies strive to escape, but have not yet succeeded? Leonard remarks that "[Derrida's] version is no more committed to predicating an 'original text' than even the most revisionist of literary histories; it rather reveals the *necessity of coming clean* about the ideological drive of the moment of reception" (p. 123; emphasis mine). But can one, as she puts it, "come clean" *only* about the moment *before*? This is where the challenge posed by William Batstone to the self-understanding of the reading subject becomes acutely relevant: we do not yet understand ourselves. If this is valid, it does not, of course, erase the importance of our attempts to understand the process of our self-realization, but these attempts will be historically contingent and open to revision. We can *try* to come clean, *desire* to come clean, but arguably, to come clean we must await the moment of our reception, when we are shunted one place back, possibly by ourselves, as we read our (now past) selves and reflect upon them. If we are not wholly "present" to ourselves, our orientation must be to the future as much as to the past, a future that will retrospectively supply the plenitude that we presently feel to be lacking. And in this way of thinking about reception, the revelatory moment of self-*reali*zation, the reificatory moment when we "discover" rather than "construct" ourselves, is infinitely deferred.

A contest is thus taking place within reception studies between the epistemological claims of realism and anti-realism. Reification is part of the process of reception (the rhetoric of exemplification, as we have seen, effects this, but more broadly any citation of a text, any characterization of a subject works to fence their open-endedness with a determinate meaning), but its temporality can be differently configured. Here the constraints of the inherited terminology of reception can chafe those whose impulse is towards anti-realism. Words beginning with *re-* enact the reifying displacement backwards we have noted: re-use, re-vision, re-construction, re-search, re-velation, and, of course, re-*cep*tion – an act that retrospectively *captures* elusive meaning. Perhaps the key term is "representation" (re-*present*-ation), a term which signals presence in the object of representation, as in the text we are "receiving." As the object of representation, it is endowed with a sense of plenitude, and the process of representation, the act of reading, is endowed with a sense of epistemological confidence. The "present" is a very slippery term. Within the argument I have been developing, the present is less a point in time (though any particular "present" can be assigned a date), than a point of epistemological privilege, in which the reader has that flash of realization in which she *knows*.

And if her impulses are anti-realist, that "knowledge" may very well be that her horizon is partial, or that as a subject she is incomplete.

Tim Whitmarsh is particularly conscious of the constraints of the term "reception," and at the end of his paper proposes the alternative "recipience" in an attempt to emphasize the open-endedness of the project. He writes:

> In short, I propose a "pragmatics" of reception, whereby the Platonist language of knowledge and truth is replaced by an emphasis upon the *provisional* status of historical knowledge. This "provisionality," indeed, is a complex phenomenon: for not only do we not "know" the past, we also do not "know" what we are doing with it in the present. (pp. 106–7; emphasis in original)

A position of epistemological certainty is a comfortable one to inhabit, particularly if you are a scholar, but reception theory has the capacity to challenge that confidence if the predisposition to a retrospective view that the term "reception" encourages is set against the possibility that knowledge is *provisional*, in the strong sense: looking towards the future, toward a desired plenitude that is not yet there (and indeed may never be) – what William Batstone describes as "the future perfect of our present (our desire)" (p. 18).[2] Viewed thus, if meaning is realized at the point of reception, the real is not characterized by plenitude, as in classic realism, but is felt most vividly by us in relation to what we do not *yet* know;[3] plenitude is a prospect. "Discovery" and "revelation" of the truth are not abolished as we move from realism to anti-realism, but displaced temporally. Realism seeks revelation in the present in respect of the past; anti-realism anticipates revelation in the future in respect of the present.[4] Those with anti-realist sympathies, with their orientation towards the future, sometimes use the language of "redemption," even "apocalypse." Timothy Saunders gives a nice characterization of this rhetoric:

> At the same time, one of the futures looked towards by reception theorists extends far beyond anything achieved in practice to date. Instead of remaining content with replacing the question "What did the text say?" with the further question "What does the text say to me, and what do I say to it?" reception theory, in common with several other instances of hermeneutic inquiry, occasionally dreams of a moment of redemption, or even apocalypse. When that future comes, all previous techniques and methodologies will finally fall back into their long awaited obsolescence and interpretation will take place under a new heaven and over a new earth. (p. 42)

2   From this perspective, the meaning of a text *is* what it *will have been*.
3   Compare Saunders: "it is precisely our ignorance of the future which seriously constrains and contextualizes our knowledge of the past" (p. 42), and also Batstone: "the past is always imperfect, always awaiting tomorrow to become what it will have been" (p. 20).
4   We may note in passing how a sense of plenitude is temporally located in this sentence by another *re-* word: "in respect of."

Theoretically, however, that moment is infinitely deferred. "Horizon" is a favored trope in reception studies; from this point of the view, the horizon ever recedes as one moves towards it. This orientation towards the future is also invoked in a number of the papers here as offering the possibility, indeed the infinite possibility, of as yet unthought-of interpretations of valued texts. For some, this can be harnessed for a rhetoric of "liberation" from past attitudes and procedures, whilst in Martindale's peroration we are offered a new imperialist vision of the discipline of classics, a distinctively Virgilian *imperium sine fine*, destined ever to advance without boundaries of time and space:

> Two things above all I would have classics embrace: a relaxed, not to say imperialist, attitude towards what we may study as part of the subject, and a subtle and supple conception of the relationship between past and present, modern and ancient. Then classics could again have a leading role among the humanities, a classics neither merely antiquarian nor crudely presentist, a classics of the present certainly, but also, truly, of the future. (p. 13)

We shall see.

Bibliography

Compiled by Katherine Harloe

The following list contains details of all the works referred to in the text and notes, as well as certain other items (mostly in English) likely to be of interest to readers of this book and recommended for further reading. It is not, however, a complete bibliography to the subject.

Abish, W. (1977), *In the Future Perfect*, New York.

Adam, P. (1992), *The Arts of the Third Reich*, London.

Adams, B. (1977–8), "Painter to Patron: David's Letters to Yousoupoff about the *Sappho, Phaon and Cupid*," *Marsyas* 19, 29–36.

Adams, J. N. (1981), "A Type of Sexual Euphemism in Latin," *Phoenix* 35, 120–8.

Adams, J. R. R. (1987), *The Printed Word and the Common Man: Popular Culture in Ulster 1700–1900*, Belfast.

—— (1989), "The Determination of Historical Popular Reading Habits: A Case Study," *Journal of Documentation* 45, 318–26.

—— (1998), "Swine-Tax-him and Eat-him-all-Magee," in Donnelly and Miller, eds., 99–117.

Addison, J. (1720), *Notes upon the Twelve Books of Paradise Lost*, London.

Adorno, T., and Horkheimer, M. (1947), *Dialektik der Aufklärung: Philosophische Fragmente*.

Affron, M., and Antliff, M., eds. (1997), *Fascist Visions: Art and Ideology in France and Italy*, Princeton.

Aglen, A. S. (1896), *The Odes and Carmen Saeculare of Horace translated into English Verse*, Glasgow.

Ahlers-Hestermann, F. (1946 [1941]), *Anselm Feuerbach, Das Gastmahl des Platon*, Der Kunstbrief nr. 16, Berlin.

Aicher, P. (2000), "Mussolini's Forum and the Myth of Augustan Rome," *Classical Bulletin* 76, 117–39.

Ajootian, A. (1996), "Praxiteles," in Palagia and Pollitt, eds., 91–129.

Albistur, M., and Armogathe, D., eds. (1977), *Histoire du Féminisme Français*, Paris.

Alcorn, M. (1994), *Narcissism and the Literary Libido*, New York and London.

Allen, G. (2000), *Intertextuality*, New York and London.

Alpers, P. (1997), *What is Pastoral?* Chicago and London.

Altick, R. D. (1998), *The English Common Reader: A Social History of the Mass Reading Public 1800–1900*, 2nd edn., Columbus, OH.

Anonymous (1799), *Essay on the Present State of Manners and Education among the Lower Class of the People of Ireland*, Dublin.

Arenas, A. (2002), "Broken: The Venus de Milo," *Arion* (3rd series) 9, 35–45.

Arenhövel, W. (1979), *Berlin und die Antike: Architektur, Kunstgewerbe, Malerei, Skulptur, Theater, und Wissenschaft vom 16. Jahrhundert bis heute*, 1–2, Berlin.

Armstrong, Isobel (2003), "A Fine-Knit Tribute," review of *Literature, Science, Psychoanalysis, 1830–1970: Essays in Honour of Gillian Beer*, ed. H. Small and T. Tate, *Times Literary Supplement* (November 21), 29.

Armstrong, Richard H. (2005), *A Compulsion for Antiquity: Freud and the Ancient World*, Ithaca and London.

Arscott, C., and Scott, K., eds. (2000), *Manifestations of Venus: Art and Sexuality*, Manchester and New York.

Arteaga, A., ed. (1994), *An Other Voice: Nation and Ethnicity in the Linguistic Borderlands*, Durham, NC.

Attridge, D., Bennington, G., and Young, R. (1987), *Post-structuralism and the Question of History*, Cambridge.

Auerbach, N. (1982), *Woman and the Demon*, Cambridge, MA.

Auslander, P., ed. (2003), *Performance: Critical Concepts in Literary and Cultural Studies*, vols. 1–4, London.

Azim, F. (2001), "Post-colonial Theory," in Knellwolf and Norris, eds., 237–47.

Baer, W., ed. (1996), *Conversations with Derek Walcott*, Jackson, MS.

Bakhtin, M. M. (1981), "Discourse in the Novel," in *The Dialogic Imagination*, trans. C. Emerson and M. Holquist, ed. M. Holquist, Austin, TX, 259–422.

—— (1986a), "The Problem of the Text in Linguistics, Philology, and the Human Sciences: An Experiment in Philosophical Analysis," in *Speech Genres and Other Late Essays*, trans. V. W. McGee, ed. C. Emerson and M. Holquist, Austin, TX, 103–31.

—— (1986b), "The Problem of Speech Genres," in *Speech Genres and Other Late Essays*, trans. V. W. McGee, ed. C. Emerson and M. Holquist, Austin, TX, 60–102.

—— (1986c), "From Notes Made in 1970–71," in *Speech Genres and Other Late Essays*, trans. V. W. McGee, ed. C. Emerson and M. Holquist, Austin, TX, 132–58.

—— (1993), *Toward a Philosophy of the Act*, trans. V. Liapunov, Austin.

Bakker, E., and Kahane, A., eds. (1997), *Written Voices, Spoken Signs: Tradition, Performance and the Epic Text*, Cambridge, MA and London.

Baldick, C. (1983), *The Social Mission of English Criticism, 1848–1932*, Oxford.

Bann, S. (1984), *The Clothing of Clio: A Study of the Representation of History in Nineteenth-Century Britain and France*, Cambridge.

Barish, J. (1981), *The Antitheatrical Prejudice*, London.

Barkan, E., and Shelton, M.-D. (1998), *Borders, Exiles, Diasporas*, Stanford, CA.

Barkan, Leonard (1986), *The Gods Made Flesh: Metamorphosis and the Pursuit of Paganism*, New Haven and London.

—— (1991), *Transuming Passion: Ganymede and the Erotics of Humanism*, Stanford, CA.

—— (1999), *Unearthing the Past: Archaeology and Aesthetics in the Making of Renaissance Culture*, New Haven and London.

Barringer, T., and Prettejohn, E., eds. (1999), *Frederic Leighton: Antiquity, Renaissance, Modernity*, New Haven.

Barrington, J. (1830), *Personal Sketches of His Own Times*, London.

Barron, S., ed. (1991), *"Degenerate Art": The Fate of the Avant-Garde in Nazi Germany*, Los Angeles.

Barrow, R. J. (2001), *Lawrence Alma-Tadema*, London.

Barthes, R. (1970), *S/Z*, Paris.

—— (1973), *Le Plaisir du texte*, Paris.

—— (1974), *S/Z*, trans. R. Miller, New York.

—— (1975), *The Pleasure of the Text*, trans. R. Miller, New York.

Bartsch, S. (1984), *Decoding the Ancient Novel: The Reader and the Role of Description in Heliodorus and Achilles Tatius*, Princeton.

Barzun, J. (1974), *The Use and Abuse of Art*, Princeton.

Batstone, William W. (2002), "Catullus and Bakhtin: The Problems of a Dialogic Lyric," in Branham, ed., 99–136.

Baudelaire, Charles (1964), *The Painter of Modern Life and Other Essays*, trans. and ed. Jonathan Mayne, New York.

Baumbach, M. (2002), *Lukian in Deutschland: eine Forschungs- und Rezeptionsgeschichtliche Analyse vom Humanismus bis zur Gegenwart*, Munich.

Bayoumi, M., and Rubin, A., eds. (2001), *The Edward Saïd Reader*, London.

Beames, M. (1983), *Peasants and Power: The Whiteboy Movements and Their Control in Prefamine Ireland*, New York.

Beard, Mary (2000), *The Invention of Jane Harrison*, Cambridge, MA and London.

Beard, M., and Henderson, J. (1995), *Classics: A Very Short Introduction*, Oxford and New York.

—— and —— (2001), *Classical Art: From Greece to Rome*, Oxford.

Beck, U. (1998), *Was ist Globalisierung? Irrtümer des Globalismus – Antworten auf Globalisierung*, Frankfurt am Main.

Beissinger, M., Tylus, J., and Wofford, S., eds. (1999), *Epic Traditions in the Contemporary World. The Poetics of Community*, The Joan Pavlesky Imprint in Classical Literature, Berkeley, Los Angeles, and London.

Benardete, S. (1994), *On Plato's* Symposium, ed. and intro. H. Meier, Munich.

—— (2002), *Socrates and Plato. The Dialectics of Eros*, Munich.

Ben-Ghiat, R. (2001), *Fascist Modernities: Italy, 1922–1945*, Berkeley.

Benjamin, Walter (1983), *Charles Baudelaire: A Lyric Poet in the Era of High Capitalism*, trans. Harry Zohn, London and New York.

—— (1992), *Illuminations*, ed. H. Arendt, trans. H. Zohn, London.

Bentley, R., ed. (1732), *Milton's* Paradise Lost, London.

Bergstein, M. (1992), "Lonely Aphrodites: On the Documentary Photography of Sculpture," *Art Bulletin* 74, 475–98.

Berve, H. (1993 [1934]), "Antike und nationalsozialistischer Staat," in W. Nippel, ed., *Über das Studium der Alten Geschichte*, Munich, 283–99.

Bery, A., and Murray, P. (2000), *Comparing Postcolonial Literatures: Dislocations*, London and New York.

Bhabha, H. (1993), *The Location of Culture*, London.

Bion, W. (1959), *Second Thoughts*, London.

—— (1962), *Learning from Experience*, London.

Blanchard, A. (1969), *Trésor de la poésie baroque et précieuse (1550–1650)*, Paris.

Bland, L., and Doan, L., eds. (1998), *Sexology in Culture: Labelling Bodies and Desires*, Cambridge.

Bleicher, J., ed. (1980), *Contemporary Hermeneutics*, London.

Blessington, F. (1979), Paradise Lost *and the Classical Epic*, Boston, London, and Henley.

Block, E. (1984), *The Effects of Divine Manifestation on the Reader's Perspective in Vergil's* Aeneid, Salem, NH.

Blondell, R. (2002), *The Play of Character in Plato's Dialogues*, Cambridge.

Bondanella, P. (1987), *The Eternal City*, Chapel Hill, NC.

Borges, J. L. (1992 [1932]), "Some Versions of Homer," trans. S. J. Levine, *PMLA* 107, 1134–8.

—— (1998 [1939]), "Pierre Menard, Author of the *Quixote*," in *Collected Fictions*, trans. Andrew Hurley, London.

Botley, P. (2004), *Latin Translation in the Renaissance: The Theory and Practice of Leonardo Bruni, Giannozzo Manetti and Desiderius Erasmus*, Cambridge.

Boudhors, C.-H. (1939), *Nicolas Boileau-Despreaux, Épîtres, Art Poétique, Lutrin*, Paris.

Bourdieu, P. (1990), *The Logic of Practice*, trans. R. Nice, Stanford.

Bowra, C. M. (1948), *From Virgil to Milton*, London.

Boyd, B. W., ed. (2002), *Brill's Companion to Ovid*, Leiden.

Bradshaw, Graham (1987), *Shakespeare's Scepticism*, Brighton.

Brah, A. (1996), *Cartographies of Diaspora: Contesting Identities*, London.

Branham, R. B. (1985), "Introducing the Sophist: Lucian's Prologues," *TAPA* 115, 237–43.

—— (1989), *Unruly Eloquence: Lucian and the Comedy of Traditions*, Cambridge, MA.

—— (2002a), "A Truer Story of the Novel?" in Branham, ed., 161–86.

—— ed. (2002b), *Bakhtin and the Classics*, Evanston, IL.

—— ed. (2004), *The Bakhtin Circle and Ancient Narrative*, *Ancient Narrative* supplementum 3, Groningen.

Brathwaite, E. K. (1984), *History of the Voice*, London.

Braund, S. M., and Gill, C., eds. (1997), *The Passions in Roman Thought and Literature*, Oxford.

Brenan, M. (1935), *Schools of Kildare and Leighlin*, Dublin.

Brenner, H. (1963), *Die Kunstpolitik des Nationalsozialismus*, Hamburg.

Breslin, P. (2001), *Nobody's Nation: Reading Derek Walcott*, Chicago and London.

Brewer, M. M. (1985), "Performing Theory," *Theatre Journal* 37 (1), 13–30.

Brilliant, R. (2000), *My Laocoön: Alternative Claims in the Interpretation of Artworks*, Berkeley, Los Angeles, and London.

Bringmann, M. (1976), "Ein erträumter Lorbeerkranz und die Flohsticke der Realität. Feuerbachs Selbstgefühl und die zeitgenössische Pressekritik," in Vey, ed., 124–46.

Brinton, C. (1900), "Queen Victoria as an Etcher," *The Critic* (June), 501–10.

Brodsky, Joseph (1986), *Less than One: Selected Essays*, New York.

Brooks, P. (1994), *Psychoanalysis and Storytelling*, Oxford and Cambridge, MA.

Brooks, R. A. (1966), "*Discolor Aura*: Reflections on the Golden Bough," in Commager, ed., 143–63.

Brown, Sarah Annes (1999), *The Metamorphosis of Ovid: From Chaucer to Ted Hughes*, London.

Buck, A. (1964), "Einleitung," *Julius Caesar Scaliger: Poetices libri septem*, Stuttgart, pp. iv–xx.

Budelmann, F. (2004), "Greek Tragedies in West African Adaptations," *Proceedings of the Cambridge Philological Society* 50, 1–28 (in Goff (2005), 118–46).

—— (forthcoming), "*Trojan Women* in Yorubaland: Femi Osofisan's *Women of Owu*" in Hardwick and Gillespie, eds.

Bullen, J. B. (1998), *The Pre-Raphaelite Body*, Oxford.

Burke, P. (1998), *The European Renaissance: Centres and Peripheries*, Cambridge.

Burke, S. (1992), *The Death and Return of the Author: Criticism and Subjectivity in Barthes, Foucault and Derrida*, Edinburgh.

Burrow, C. (1993), *Epic Romance: Homer to Milton*, Oxford.

Butler, E. M. (1935), *The Tyranny of Greece over Germany: A Study of the Influence Exercised by Greek Art and Poetry over the Great German Writers of the Eighteenth, Nineteenth and Twentieth Centuries*, Cambridge.

Butler, G. F. (1997), "The Wrath of Aeneas and the Triumph of the Son: Virgil's Aegaeon and *Paradise Lost*," *Comparative Literature Studies* 34, 103–8.

Butler, J. (1993), *Bodies that Matter: On the Discursive Limits of "Sex"*, New York.

—— (2000), *Antigone's Claim: Kinship between Life and Death*, New York.

Cairncross, J., trans. (1963), *Jean Racine: Iphigenia, Phaedra, Athaliah*, London.

Calandra, D. (1993), "The Aesthetic of Reception and Theatre," in Hilton, ed., 13–24.

Cambiano, G. (1988), *Il ritorno degli antichi*, Rome.

Camerotto, A. (1998), *Le metamorfosi della parola: studi sulla parodia in Luciano di Samosata*, Pisa and Rome.

Campiglio, P., et al. (2003), *Scultura Lingua Morta. Sculpture from Fascist Italy*, Leeds.

Canfora, L. (1980), *Ideologie del classicismo*, Turin.

—— (1989), *Le vie del classicismo*, Rome and Bari.

Cannistraro, P. V. (1975), *La fabbrica del consenso: fascismo e mass media*, Rome and Bari.

Carleton, W. (1896), *The Autobiography*, Belfast.

Carlson, M. (1985), "Theatrical Performance: Illustration, Translation, Fulfilment, or Supplement?" *Theatre Journal* 37 (1), 13–30.

—— (1996), *Performance: A Critical Introduction*, London.

Carne-Ross, D. S., and Haynes, K., eds. (1996), *Horace in English*, London.

Carrington, C., ed. (1978), *Kipling's Horace*, London.

Carroll, D. (1995), *French Literary Fascism: Nationalism, Anti-Semitism, and the Ideology of Culture*, Princeton.

Carson, A. (2002), *If Not, Winter: Fragments of Sappho*, New York.

Casey, D. J., and Rhodes, R. E., eds. (1977), *Views of the Irish Peasantry 1800–1916*, Hamden, CT.

Cave, T. (1988), *Recognitions: A Study in Poetics*, Oxford.

Champfleury [J. Fleury-Husson] (1874), "Les Bras de la Vénus de Milo," in Champfleury, *Madame Eugenio*, 243–69, Paris.

Charalabopoulos, N. (2002), *The Stagecraft of Plato: The Platonic Dialogue as Metatheatrical Prose Drama*, PhD, University of Cambridge.

Christ, K. (1986), "Spartaforschung und Spartabild: Eine Einleitung," in K. Christ, ed., *Sparta*, Darmstadt, 1–72.

Cioran, E. (1987 [1960]), *History and Utopia*, trans. Richard Howard, Chicago.

Cixous, H. (1974), "The Character of Character," *New Literary History* 5, 383–402.

Clarac, Comte de (1821), *Sur la statue antique de Vénus Victrix découverte dans l'île de Milo en 1820*, Paris.

Clark, K. (1987 [1956]), *The Nude: A Study of Ideal Art*, London and Harmondsworth.

Clarke, M. L. (1945), *Greek Studies in England, 1700–1830*, Cambridge.

—— (1959), *Classical Education in Britain 1500–1900*, Cambridge.

Clausen, W. (1994), *A Commentary on Virgil* Eclogues, Oxford.

Coers, B. (1999), "Zitat, Paraphrase und Locution: zur Funktion der pompejanischer Wandmalerei im Historienbild am Beispiel von J. A. D. Ingres' 'Antiochus und Stratonice' und Anselm Feuerbach's 'Gastmahl des Plato'," in *Tradita et Inuenta. Beiträge zur Rezeption der Antike*, ed. M. Baumbach, Heidelberg.

Cohen, R., ed. (1974), *New Directions in Literary History*, Baltimore.

Collobert, C., ed. (2002), *L'avenir de la philosophie est-il grec?* Ottawa.

Commager, S., ed. (1966), *Virgil: A Collection of Critical Essays*, Englewood Cliffs, NJ.

[Commissioners of Education Inquiry], *First Report of Commissioners of Education Inquiry. Appendix 221: List of Books used in Various Schools*, 1825, London.

Comparetti, D., ed. (1896), *Vergilio nel medio evo*, 2 vols., Florence.

—— ed. (1908), *Vergil in the Middle Ages*, trans. E. F. M. Benecke, London, rpr. Hamden, CT (1966) and (with a new intro. by J. M. Ziolkowski), Princeton (1997).

Conington, J. (1863), *The Odes and Carmen saeculare of Horace, Translated into English Verse*, London.

Connell, P. (1995), *Parson, Priest and Master: National Education in Co. Meath, 1824–41*, Dublin.

Conradie, P. J. (1996), "Debates surrounding an Approach to African Tragedy," *South African Theatre Journal* 10 (1), 25–34.

Conte, G. B. (1994), "Genre between Empiricism and Theory," in *Genres and Readers*, trans. C. Segal, Baltimore and London, 105–28.

Cooper, H. (1977), *Pastoral: Mediaeval into Renaissance*, Ipswich.

Coppock, V., Haydon, D., and Richter, I., eds. (1995), *The Illusions of "Post-feminism"*, London.

Corcoran, T. (1916), *State Policy in Irish Education AD 1536 to 1816*, Dublin.

—— (1932), *Some Lists of Catholic Lay Teachers and their Illegal Schools in Later Penal Times*, Dublin.

Crease, R. P. (2003), "Performance and Production: The Relation between Science as Inquiry and Science as Cultural Practice," in Auslander, ed., vol. 3, 11–31.

Crofton Croker, T. (1824), *Researches in the South of Ireland*, London.

Crow, B., with Banfield, C. (1996), *An Introduction to Post-Colonial Theatre*, Cambridge.

Crow, T. (1995), *Emulation: Making Artists for Revolutionary France*, New Haven.

Cruise, C. (1995), " 'Lovely Devils': Simeon Solomon and Pre-Raphaelite Masculinity," in E. Harding, ed., *Reframing the Pre-Raphaelites: Historical and Theoretical Essays*, Aldershot, Hants., 195–210.

Culham, P. (1990), "Decentering the Text: The Case of Ovid," *Helios* 17 (2), 161–70.

Cullen, L. M. (1990), "Patrons, Teachers and Literacy in Ireland," in Daly and Dickson, eds., 15–44.

Culler, J. (1975), *Structuralist Poetics: Structuralism, Linguistics and the Study of Literature*, London.

Cunningham, B., and Kennedy, M., eds. (1999), *The Experience of Reading: Irish Historical Perspectives*, Dublin.

Curtis, G. (2003), *Disarmed: The Story of the Venus de Milo*, New York.

Cuzin, J.-P., Gaborit, J.-R., Pasquier, A., et al. (2000), *D'après l'antique*, exhibition catalog, Musée du Louvre, Paris.

Dacier, M. (A.) (1724 [1719]), *Madame Dacier's Remarks upon Mr Pope's Account of Homer*, trans. Mr. Parnell, London.

Dallmayr, F. R., and McCarthy, T. A., eds. (1977), *Understanding and Social Inquiry*, Notre Dame, IN.

Daly, M., and Dickson, D., eds. (1990), *The Origins of Popular Literacy in Ireland: Language Change and Educational Development*, Dublin.

d'Argencourt, L., Foucart, J., et al. (1976), *Puvis de Chavannes 1824–1898*, exhibition catalog, Grand Palais, Paris.

Darnton, R. (1990), *The Kiss of Lamourette: Reflections in Cultural History*, New York.

Davidson, A., ed. (1997), *Foucault and His Interlocutors*, Chicago.

Davies, J. K. (2002), "Greek History: A Discipline in Transformation," in Wiseman, ed., 225–46.

Davis, G. (1991), *Polyhymnia: The Rhetoric of Horatian Lyric Discourse*, Berkeley and Los Angeles.

—— (1997a), *Aimé Césaire*, Cambridge.

—— (1997b), " 'With No Homeric Shadow': The Disavowal of Epic in Derek Walcott's *Omeros*," in Davis, ed., 321–33.

—— ed. (1997c), *The Poetics of Derek Walcott: Intertextual Perspectives, The South Atlantic Quarterly* 96 (2) (Spring 1997), Durham, NC.

Davis, W. (1999), "The Image in the Middle: John Addington Symonds and Homoerotic Art Criticism," in Prettejohn, ed., 188–216.

De Boer, C., ed. (1921), *Piramus et Tisbe: Poème du XIIe siècle*, Paris.

—— ed. (1966 [1915–18]), *Ovide moralisé: Poème du commencement du 14ième siècle. Publié d'apres tous les manuscrits connus*, Wiesbaden.

de Certeau, Michel (1999), "Writings and Histories," in *De Certeau Reader*, ed. G. Ward, London, 23–36.

Decreus, F. (forthcoming), "The Same Kind of Smile? About the Use and Abuse of Theory in Defining the Relations between Classics and Post-Colonialism," in Hardwick and Gillespie, eds.

—— and Kolk, M., eds. (2004), *Rereading Classics in East and West: Post-colonial Perspectives on the Tragic*, Documenta 22.4, Gent.

DeJean, J. (1989), *Fictions of Sappho: 1546–1937*, Chicago.

Delaporte, P. V. (1970 [1888]), *L'Art Poétique de Boileau commenté par Boileau et ses contemporains*, Geneva [1st edn. Lille].

Dellamora, R., *Masculine Desire: The Sexual Politics of Victorian Aestheticism*, Chapel Hill and London, 1990.

de May, P., trans. (2003), *Aeschylus: Agamemnon*, Cambridge.

Dennis, J. (1943 [1717]), *Some Remarks upon Mr. Pope's Translation of Homer*, in *The Critical Works of John Dennis*, ed. E. N. Hooker, vol. 2, Baltimore, 115–58.

Derrida, J. (1973), *Speech and Phenomena and Other Essays on Husserl's Theory of Signs*, trans. N. Garver, Evanston, Ill.

—— (1986), *Glas*, trans. J. P. Leavey, Jr. and R. Rand, Lincoln, NE and London.

—— (1997), "The Theatre of Cruelty and the Closure of Interpretation," in Murray, ed., 40–62.

De Vere, S. E., Sir (1888), *Translations from Horace, with Notes*, London and New York.

Devine, T. (1999), *The Scottish Nation*, London.

—— (2003), *Scotland's Empire 1600–1815*, London.

Dimmick, J. (2002), "Ovid in the Middle Ages: Authority and Poetry," in Hardie, ed., 267–87.

Dinshaw, C. (1989), *Chaucer's Sexual Poetics*, Madison, WI.

Dircks, R. (1910), "The Later Work of Sir Lawrence Alma-Tadema O.M. R.A. R.W.S.," *The Art Journal*, Christmas Special edition.

Djisenu, J. (forthcoming), "Cross-Cultural Bonds between Ancient Greece and Africa: Implications for Contemporary Staging Practices," in Hardwick and Gillespie, eds.

Dollimore, Jonathan (1991), *Sexual Dissidence: Augustine to Wilde, Freud to Foucault*, Oxford.

Donaldson, Ian (1982), *The Rapes of Lucretia: A Myth and Its Transformation*, Oxford.

Donnelly, J. S., Jr. and Miller, K. A., eds. (1998), *Irish Popular Culture, 1650–1850*, Dublin.

Donoghue, D. (1995), *Walter Pater: Lover of Strange Souls*, New York.

Doody, M. A. (1997), *The True Story of the Novel*, London.

Dörrie, H. (1968), *Der heroische Brief. Bestandsaufnahme, Geschichte, Kritik einer humanistisch-barocken Literaturgattung*, Berlin.

Dougherty, C. (1997), "Homer after *Omeros*: Reading a H/Omeric Text," in Davis, ed., 335–57.

Dowling, P. J. (1968), *The Hedge Schools of Ireland*, Cork.

—— (1971), *A History of Irish Education: A Study in Conflicting Loyalties*, Cork.

Dubois, Page (1995), *Sappho is Burning*, Chicago and London.

Du Faur, E. (1906), *Horace: The Odes, Epodes (selected) and Carmen saeculare*, Sydney.

Dunsany, Lord (1947), *The Odes of Horace*, London and Toronto.

DuPlessis, R. B. (1985), "For the Etruscans Sexual Difference and Artistic Production: The Debate over a Female Aesthetic," in Showalter, ed., 271–91. Rev. version rpr. in Rick Rylance, ed., *Debating Texts: A Reader in Twentieth-Century Literary Theory and Method* (1988), Milton Keynes, 259–74.

Dutton, H. (1808), *Statistical Survey of the County of Clare*, Dublin.

Easterling, P. E. (1984), "The Tragic Homer," *Bulletin of the Institute of Classical Studies* 31, 1–8.

—— ed. (1997), *The Cambridge Companion to Greek Tragedy*, Cambridge.

Ecker, J. (1991), *Anselm Feuerbach, Leben und Werk: kritische Katalog der Gemälde, Ölskizzen und Ölstudien*, Munich.

Eco, U. (1979), *The Role of the Reader: Explorations in the Semiotics of Texts*, Bloomington, IN.

Edgeworth, R., and Edgeworth, M. (1820), *Memoirs of Richard Lovell Edgeworth*, vol. 2, London.

Edmonds, L. (2001), *Intertextuality and the Meaning of Roman Poetry*, Baltimore and London.

Edwards, C., ed. (1999), *Roman Presences: Receptions of Rome in European Culture: 1789–1945*, Cambridge.

Ehrmann, J. (1968), "Homo Ludens Revisited," in J. Ehrmann, ed., *Game, Play, Literature*, Boston, 31–57.

Eilon, D. (1991), *Fiction's Factions: Ideological Closure in Swift's Satire*, London and Toronto.

Elam, K. (2002), *The Semiotics of Theatre and Drama*, 2nd edn., London and New York.

Elias, N. (1969 [1939]), *Über den Prozess der Zivilisation. Soziogenetische und Psychogenetische Untersuchungen*, 2nd edn., 2 vols., Bern and Munich [1st edn. Basel].

Eliot, T. S. (1951), "Tradition and the Individual Talent," in *Selected Essays*, London, 13–22.

Elkins, C. (1980), "The Voice of the Poor: The Broadside as a Medium of Popular Culture and Dissent in Victorian England," *Journal of Popular Culture*, 262–75.

Ellmann, R. (1983), *James Joyce*, Oxford.

Elsner, J. (2004), "Some Recent Publications in Roman Art," *Art History* 27, 806–14.

Éméric-David, T.-B. (1853), "Observations sur la statue antique de femme, découverte dans l'île de Milo, en 1820," rpr. in T. B. Éméric-David, *Histoire de la Sculpture Antique*, Paris, 189–234.

Escarpit, R. (1964), *Sociologie de la littérature*, Paris.

Evans-Pritchard, E. E. (1937), *Witchcraft, Oracles, and Magic among the Azande*, Oxford.

Falasca-Zamponi, S. (1997), *Fascist Spectacle: The Aesthetics of Power in Mussolini's Italy*, Berkeley.

Fallon, S. M. (1984), "Satan's Return to Hell: Milton's Concealed Dialogue with Homer and Virgil," *Milton Quarterly* 18, 78–81.

Fantham, E. (1997), "'Envy and Fear the Begetter of Hate': Statius' *Thebaid* and the Genesis of Hatred," in Braund and Gill, eds., 185–212.

Farrell, J. (1997), "Walcott's *Omeros*: The Classical Epic in a Postmodern World," in Davis, ed., 246–73, rpr. in Beissinger, Tylus, and Wofford, eds. (1999), 270–96.

Feldherr, Andrew, and James, Paula (2004), "Making the Most of Marsyas," *Arethusa* 37, 75–103.

Félibien, A. (1994), *Les fêtes de Versailles*, Maisonneuve and Larose.

Felice, R. de (1996), *Le interpretazioni del fascismo*, Roma-Bari.

Felson, N., and Slatkin, L. (2004), "Gender and Homeric Epic," in Fowler, ed., 91–114.

Ferguson, M. W. (2003), *Dido's Daughters: Literacy, Gender, and Empire in Early Modern England and France*, Chicago and London.

Fetterley, J. (1978), *The Resisting Reader: A Feminist Approach to American Fiction*, Bloomington, IN.

Finley, M. (1975), *The Use and Abuse of History*, London.

Fischer, O., ed. (1922), *Anselm Feuerbach, Briefe und Bilder*, Stuttgart.

Fischer-Lichte, E. (1997), *The Show and the Gaze of Theatre: A European Perspective*, Iowa City.

—— (1998), "Invocation of the Dead: Festival of People's Theatre or Sacrificial Ritual? Some Remarks on Staging Greek Classics," in S. Patsalidis and E. Sakellaridou, eds., *(Dis)Placing Classical Greek Theatre*, Thessaloniki, 252–63.

Fish, S. (1967), *Surprised by Sin: The Reader in* Paradise Lost, London.

—— (1971), *Surprised by Sin: The Reader in* Paradise Lost, Berkeley.

—— (1972), *Self-consuming Artifacts: The Experience of Seventeenth-Century Literature*, Berkeley.

—— (1980), *Is There a Text in This Class? The Authority of Interpretive Communities*, Cambridge, MA.

—— (2001), "Yet Once More," in Machor and Goldstein, eds., 29–38.

Fitzgibbon, G. (1868), *Ireland in 1868, the Battlefield for English Party Strife, etc.* London.

Flashar, H. (1991), *Inszenierung der Antike: Das Griechische Drama auf der Buhne der Neuzeit, 1585–1990*, Munich.

Fleishman, M. (1990), "Workshop Theatre as Oppositional Form," *South African Theatre Journal* 4 (1), 88–118.

Foley, H. (2001), "Tantalus," *American Journal of Philology* 122, 415–28.

Foley, T., and Ryder, S., eds. (1998), *Ideology and Art in the Nineteenth Century*, Dublin.

Forestier, G., ed. (1999), *Jean Racine: Iphigénie*, Paris.

Forster-Hahn, F. (2002), "Public Concerns – Private Longings: Adolph Menzel's *Studio Wall* (1872)," *Art History* 25, 206–39.

Foucault, M. (1966), *Les mots et les choses: une archéologie des sciences humaines*, Paris.

—— (1969), "Qu'est-ce qu'un auteur?" *Bulletin de la Société Française de Philosophie* 63, 73–104.

—— (1977), "What is an Author?," in *Language, Counter-Memory, Practice*, trans. D. Bouchard and S. Simon, ed. D. Bouchard, Ithaca, NY, 124–7.

—— (1980), *The History of Sexuality*, vol. 1: *An Introduction*, trans. R. Hurley, New York.

—— (1983), "On the Genealogy of Ethics: An Overview of Work in Progress," in H. L. Dreyfus and P. Rabinow, eds., *Michel Foucault: Beyond Structuralism and Hermeneutics*, Chicago, 229–52.

—— (1984), "What is Enlightenment?" in *The Foucault Reader*, ed. P. Rabinow, New York, 2–50.

—— (1985), *The History of Sexuality*, vol. 2: *The Use of Pleasure*, trans. R. Hurley, New York.

—— (1986), *The History of Sexuality*, vol. 3: *The Care of the Self*, trans. R. Hurley, New York.

—— (1988a), *Politics, Philosophy, Culture: Interviews and Other Writings, 1977–1984*, ed. L. D. Kritzman, New York and London.

—— (1988b), *Technologies of the Self: A Seminar with Michel Foucault*, ed. L. H. Martin, H. Gutman, and P. H. Hutton, Amherst, MA.

—— (1989), "The Birth of a World." Interview with Jean-Michel Palmier. In *Foucault Live: Interviews, 1966–84*, ed. Sylvère Lotringer, New York.

—— (2001), *L'Herméneutique du sujet: Cours au Collège de France, 1981–1982*, Paris.

Fowler, D. (2000), "On the Shoulders of Giants: Intertextuality and Classical Studies," in *Roman Constructions: Readings in Postmodern Latin*, Oxford, 115–37.

Fowler, R., ed. (2004), *The Cambridge Companion to Homer*, Cambridge.

Frankland, G. (2000), *Freud's Literary Culture*, Cambridge.

Freud, S. (1905–6), "Psychopathic Characters on the Stage," in *Penguin Freud Library*, vol. 14: *Art and Literature*, Harmondsworth, 119–27.

—— (1907–8), "Creative Writers and Day-Dreaming," in *Penguin Freud Library*, vol. 14: *Art and Literature*, Harmondsworth, 131–41.

—— (1914), "On Narcissism," in *Penguin Freud Library, On Metapsychology*, Harmondsworth, 59–97.

—— (1921), "Group Psychology and Analysis of the Ego," in *Penguin Freud Library*, vol. 12: *Civilization, Society and Religion*, Harmondsworth, 91–178.

—— (1953–74), "The Uncanny," in *The Standard Edition of the Complete Psychological Works of Sigmund Freud*, ed. J. Strachey with A. Freud, assisted by A. Strachey, A. Tyson, and An. Richards, 24 vols., London, vol. 17, 219–56.

Freudenburg, Kirk, ed. (2005), *The Cambridge Companion to Roman Satire*, Cambridge.

Friedman, S. S. (1991), "Post/Poststructuralist Feminist Criticism: The Politics of Recuperation and Negotiation," *New Literary History* 22, 465–90.

Friel, B. (1981), *Translations*, in *Selected Plays*, London.

Fuchs, E. (2003), "Presence and the Revenge of Writing: Re-thinking Theatre after Derrida," in Auslander, ed., vol. 2, 109–18.

Fuller, P. (1980), "The Venus and 'Internal Objects'," in *Art and Psychoanalysis*, London, 71–129.

Fumagalli, M. (2001), *The Flight of the Vernacular: Seamus Heaney, Derek Walcott and the Impress of Dante*, Cross/Cultures: Readings in the Post/Colonial Literatures in English 49, Amsterdam and New York.

Furtwängler, A. (1895), *Masterpieces of Greek Sculpture: A Series of Essays on the History of Art*, trans. and ed. E. Sellers, London.

Fusillo, M. (1988), "Le miroir de la lune: l'*Histoire vraie* de Lucien, de la satire à l'utopie," *Poétique* 19/73: 109–35, trans. in S. Swain, ed., *Oxford Readings in the Greek Novel*, Oxford, 351–81.

Gadamer, H. G. (1975), *Truth and Method*, trans. G. Barden and J. Cumming, London.

—— (1976), *Philosophical Hermeneutics*, Berkeley, and Los Angeles.

—— (1993), *Truth and Method*, New York.

—— (1998), *Truth and Method*, New York.

Gaisser, J. H. (1993), *Catullus and His Renaissance Readers*, Oxford.

—— ed. (2001), *Catullus in English*, London.

—— (2002), "The Reception of Classical Texts in the Renaissance," in A. J. Grieco, M. Rocke, and F. Gioffredi Superbi, eds., *The Italian Renaissance in the Twentieth Century*, Florence, 387–400.

Galinsky, K. (1993–4), "Reading Roman Poetry in the 1990s," *Classical Journal* 89, 297–309.

Gamble, S. (2001a), "Postfeminism," in Gamble, ed., 43–54.

—— ed. (2001b), *The Routledge Companion to Feminism and Postfeminism*, London and New York.

Gamel, M.-K. (1990), "Reading Reality," *Helios* 17 (2), 171–4.

Garnsey, E. R. (1907), *The Odes of Horace: A Translation and an Exposition*, London.

Gautier, T. (1871), *Tableaux de siège: Paris, 1870–1871*, Paris.

—— (1882), *Guide de l'amateur au Musée du Louvre*, Paris.

Gazda, E. K., ed. (2002), *The Ancient Art of Emulation: Studies in Artistic Originality and Tradition from the Present to Classical Antiquity*, Ann Arbor.

Gentile, E. (1993), *Il culto del littorio. La sacralizzazione della politica nell'Italia fascista*, Rome.

Georgiadou, A., and Larmour, D. H. J. (1998), *Lucian's Science Fiction Novel* True Histories: *Interpretation and Commentary*, Leiden.

Gibbons, L. (1998), "Between Captain Rock and a Hard Place: Art and Agrarian Insurgency in Ireland," in Foley and Ryder, eds., 23–44.

Gibbons, S. R., ed. (2004), *Captain Rock, Night Errant: The Threatening Letters of Pre-Famine Ireland 1801–1845*, Dublin.

Gidel, A. Ch. (1872), *Œuvres complètes de Boileau accompagnées de notes historiques et litteraires*, Paris.

Gilbert, H., and Tompkins, J. (1996), *Post-colonial Drama: Theory, Practice, Politics*, London and New York.

Gildenhard, I., and Ruehl, M., eds. (2003), *Out of Arcadia: Classics and Politics in Germany in the Age of Burckhardt, Nietzsche, and Wilamowitz*, London.

Gilman, S. (1985), *Difference and Pathology: Stereotypes of Sexuality, Race and Madness*, Ithaca, NY.

Gilroy, P. (1993), *The Black Atlantic*, London and New York.

Glaser, H. (1978), *The Cultural Roots of National Socialism*, trans. E. A. Menze, London.

Gleason, M. W. (1995), *Making Men: Sophists and Self-presentation in Ancient Rome*, Princeton.

Glendinning, R. (1986), "Pyramus and Thisbe in the Medieval Classroom," *Speculum* 61, 51–78.

Gliksohn, J.-M. (1985), *Iphigénie: de la grèce antique à l'europe des lumières*, Paris.

Goff, B., ed. (2005), *Classics and Colonialism*, London.

Goldhill, S. (1999), "Programme Notes," in S. Goldhill and R. Osborne, eds., *Performance Culture and Athenian Democracy*, Cambridge, 1–29.

—— (2002), *Who Needs Greek? Contests in the Cultural History of Hellenism*, Cambridge.

—— (forthcoming), "The Genre of the Ancient Novel," in T. Whitmarsh, ed., *The Cambridge Companion to the Greek and Roman Novel*, Cambridge.

Golsan, R. (1992), *Fascism, Aesthetics, Culture*, Hanover.

Gotshalk, R. (2001), *Loving and Dying: A Reading of Plato's* Phaedo, Symposium, *and* Phaedrus, Lanham, MD.

Gow, A. S. F., ed. (1950), *Theocritus*, ed. with a translation and commentary, 2 vols., Cambridge.

Grafton, A. (2005), *What was History? The Art of History in Early Modern Europe*, The George Macaulay Trevelyan Lectures, delivered at the Cambridge History Faculty, 20 Jan.–1 Feb.

Graziosi, Barbara (2002), *Inventing Homer: The Early Reception of Epic*, Cambridge.

Greenblatt, S. J. (1980), *Renaissance Self-fashioning: From More to Shakespeare*, Chicago.

Greene, E., ed. (1996), *Re-reading Sappho: Reception and Transmission*, Berkeley and Los Angeles.

Greenwood, E. (2004), "Classics and the Atlantic Triangle: Caribbean Readings of Greece and Rome via Africa," *Forum of Modern Language Studies*, 40 (4), 365–76.

Greig, D. (2000), *Oedipus* (unpublished, archive of Reception of Classical Texts Research Project at the Open University).

Griffin, J. (1995), *Iliad: Book Nine*, Oxford.

Griffin, R. (1991), *The Nature of Fascism*, London.

—— (1996), "Staging the Nation's Rebirth: The Politics and Aesthetics of Performance in the Context of Fascist Studies," in G. Berghaus, ed., *Fascism and Theatre: Comparative Studies on the Aesthetics and Politics of Performance in Europe*, Providence, RI, 11–29.

—— (2001), "Notes towards the Definition of Fascist Culture: The Prospects for Synergy between Marxist and Liberal Heuristics," *Renaissance and Modern Studies*, 42, 95–115.

—— (2003), "The Palingenetic Core of Generic Fascist Ideology," in A. Campi, ed., *Che cos'é il fascismo? Interpretazioni e prospettive di ricerche*, Rome, 97–122.

Grimm, G. (1977), *Rezeptionsgeschichte, Grundlegung einer Theorie mit Analysen und Bibliographie*, Munich.

Gugelberger, G. M. (1991), "Decolonizing the Canon: Considerations of Third World Literature," *New Literary History* 22, 505–24.

Günther, H. F. K. (1929), *Rassenkunde Europas: Mit besonderer Berücksichtigung der Rassengeschichte der Hauptvölker indogermanischer Sprache*, Munich.

Habermas, J. (1977), "A Review of Gadamer's *Truth and Method*," in Dallmayr and McCarthy, eds., 335–63.

—— (1980), "The Hermeneutic Claim to Universality," in Bleicher, ed., 181–211.

—— (1984), *The Theory of Communicative Action*, vol. 1: *Reason and the Rationalization of Society*, Boston.

Hahn, Stephen (2002), *On Derrida*, Belmont, CA.

Hainsworth, Bryan (1993), *The Iliad: A Commentary*, vol. 3: *Books 9–12*, Cambridge.

Hales, S. (2002), "How the *Venus de Milo* Lost Her Arms," in Ogden, ed., 253–73.

Hall, E., (2004), "Towards a Theory of Performance Reception," *Arion* 12 (1) (Spring/Summer), 51–89.

—— and Macintosh, F. (2005), *Greek Tragedy and the British Theatre 1660–1914*, Oxford.

——, ——, and Taplin, O., eds. (2000), *Medea in Performance 1500–2000*, Oxford.

——, ——, and Wrigley, A., eds. (2004), *Dionysus since 69: Greek Tragedy at the Dawn of the Third Millennium*, Oxford.

Hall, M., ed. (1997), *Raphael's* School of Athens, Cambridge.

Hall, S. (1990), "Cultural Identity and Diaspora," in J. Rutherford, ed., *Identity, Community, Culture, Difference*, London, 222–37.

Hall, S. C. (1841), *Ireland, Its Scenery, Character, etc.*, London.

Halliwell, S. (1998), *Aristotle's Poetics*, 2nd edn., London.

Halperin, D. M. (1983), *Before Pastoral: Theocritus and the Ancient Tradition of Bucolic Poetry*, New Haven and London.

—— (1990), *One Hundred Years of Homosexuality: And Other Essays on Greek Love*, New York.

—— (1995), *Saint Foucault: Towards a Gay Hagiography*, New York.

——, Winkler, J. J., and Zeitlin, F. I., eds. (1990), *Before Sexuality: The Construction of Erotic Experience in the Ancient Greek World*, Princeton.

Hamilton, Paul (2003), *Historicism*, 2nd edn., London.

Hamner, R. (1997), *Epic of the Dispossessed: Derek Walcott's* Omeros, Columbia, MO and London.

Haraway, D. J. (1991), *Simians, Cyborgs, and Women: The Reinvention of Nature*, London.

Hardie, P. R., ed. (2002), *The Cambridge Companion to Ovid*, Cambridge.

Harding, D. (1962), *The Club of Hercules: Studies in the Classical Background of* Paradise Lost, Urbana, IL.

Hardwick, L. (1992), "Convergence and Divergence in Reading Homer," in C. Emlyn-Jones, L. Hardwick, and J. Purkis, eds., *Homer: Readings and Images*, London, 227–48.

—— (1995), "Classical Distances," in D. Sewart, ed., *One World Many Voices*, Birmingham, vol. 1, 283–6.

—— (1997), "Reception as Simile: The Poetics of Reversal in Homer and Derek Walcott," *International Journal of the Classical Tradition* 3 (Winter), 326–38.

—— (2000a), *Translating Words, Translating Cultures*, London.

—— (2000b), "Theatres of the Mind: Greek Tragedy in Women's Writings in English in the Nineteenth Century," in L. Hardwick et al., eds., *Theatre Ancient and Modern*, Milton Keynes, 68–81.

—— (2000c), "Walcott's Philoctete: Imaging the Post-colonial Condition," in Hardwick (2000a), 97–111.

—— (2001), "Who Owns the Plays? Issues in the Translation and Performance of Greek Drama on the Modern Stage," *Eirene* 37 (Theatralia special edition), 23–39.

—— (2002), "Classical Texts in Post-colonial Literatures: Consolation, Redress and New Beginnings in the Work of Derek Walcott and Seamus Heaney," *International Journal of the Classical Tradition* 9 (2) (Fall), 236–56.

—— (2003a), *Reception Studies*, Greece and Rome New Surveys in the Classics 33, Oxford.

—— (2003b), "Classical Drama in Modern Scotland: The Democratic Stage," in Hardwick and Gillespie, eds.

—— (2004a), "Greek Drama and Anti-colonialism: Decolonizing Classics," in Hall, Macintosh, and Wrigley, eds., 219–42.

—— (2004b), "'Shards and Suckers': Contemporary Receptions of Homer," in Fowler, ed., 344–62.

—— (2004c), "Sophocles' *Oedipus* and Conflicts of Identity in Post-colonial Contexts," in Decreus and Kolk, eds., 376–86.

—— (2005a), "Refiguring Classical Texts: Aspects of the Post-colonial Condition," in Goff, ed., 107–17.

—— (2005b), "Staging *Agamemnon*: The Languages of Translation," in Macintosh et al., eds., 207–22.

—— (2005c), "The Praxis of What is 'European' in Modern Performances of Greek Drama," *Parodos*.

—— and Gillespie, C., eds. (2003), *The Role of Greek Drama and Poetry in Crossing and Redefining Cultural Boundaries*, Milton Keynes.

—— and —— eds. (forthcoming), *Classics in Post-colonial Worlds*, Oxford.

Harpham, G. G. (1987), *The Ascetic Imperative in Culture and Criticism*, Chicago.

Harrison, S. J., ed. (2001), *Texts, Ideas, and the Classics*, Oxford.

Hart-Davies, R., ed. (1962), *The Letters of Oscar Wilde*, London.

Haskell, F., and Penny, N. (1982), *Taste and the Antique: The Lure of Classical Sculpture 1500–1900*, New Haven and London.

Havelock, C. M. (1995), *The Aphrodite of Knidos and Her Successors: A Historical Review of the Female Nude in Greek Art*, Ann Arbor.

Haynes, K. (2001), "John Dryden: Classical or Neoclassical?" *Translation and Literature* 10, 67–77.

—— (2003), *English Literature and Ancient Languages*, Oxford.

Hebel, U. J. (1991), "Towards a Descriptive Poetics of Allusion," in Plett, ed., 135–46.

Hegel, G. W. F. (1948), *Early Theological Writings*, trans. T. M. Knox, Chicago.

—— (1975), *Aesthetics: Lectures on Fine Art*, trans. T. M. Knox, 2 vols., Oxford.

—— (1977), *Phenomenology of Spirit*, trans. A. V. Miller, New York.

—— (1986), *Werke*, vols. 13–15: *Vorlesungen über die Ästhetik I–III*, Frankfurt.

Heidegger, M. (1967), *What is a Thing?* trans. W. B. Barton, Jr. and Vera Deutsch, London.

—— (2000), *An Introduction to Metaphysics*, trans. G. Fried and R. Polt, New Haven and London.

Held, G. (1951), *De Papoea: Cultuurimprovisator*, The Hague.

Henderson, J. (1996), "Seeing through Socrates: Portrait of the Philosopher in Sculpture Culture," *Art History* 19, 327–52.

—— (2000), "The Life and Soul of the Party: Plato, *Symposium*," in A. Sharrock and H. Morales, eds., *Intratextuality: Greek and Roman Textual Relations*, Oxford, 287–324.

—— (forthcoming 2006), "Umm, Anselm Feuerbach's 'Gastmahl des Platon'," in M. Trapp, ed., *Socrates in the 19th and 20th Centuries*, London.

Henigan, J. (1994), "For Want of Education: The Origins of the Hedge Schoolmaster Songs," *Ulster Folk-Life* 40, 27–38.

Hesk, J. (2003), *Sophocles: Ajax*, London.

Hexter, R. (1986), *Ovid and Medieval Schooling: Studies in Medieval School Commentaries on Ovid's* Ars Amatoria, Epistulae ex Ponto *and* Epistulae Heroidum, Münchener Beiträge zur Mediävistik und Renaissance-Forschung 38, Munich.

—— (1988), "The Metamorphosis of Sodom: The Ps-Cyprian *De Sodoma* as an Ovidian Episode," *Traditio* 44, 1–35.

—— (1989), "The *Allegari* of Pierre Bersuire: Interpretation and *the Reductorium morale*," *Allegorica* 10, 49–82.

—— (1990), "What was the Trojan Horse Made Of?," *Yale Journal of Criticism* 3, 109–31.

—— (1992), "Sidonian Dido," in Hexter and Selden, eds., 332–84.

—— (1999), "Ovid's Body," in Porter, ed., 327–54.

—— (2002), "Ovid in the Middle Ages: Exile, Mythographer, Lover," in Weiden Boyd, ed., 413–42.

—— and Selden, D., eds. (1992), *Innovations of Antiquity*, New York.

Heywood, L., and Drake, J., eds. (1997), *Third Wave Agenda: Being Feminist, Doing Feminism*, Minneapolis and London.

Hickey, W. (1833), *Hints to Small Holders and Peasantry of Ireland*, Dublin.

Hilton J., ed. (1993), *New Directions in Theatre*, London.

Hinds, S. (1998), *Allusion and Intertext: Dynamics of Appropriation in Roman Poetry*, Cambridge.

Hoberman, Ruth (1997), *Gendering Classicism: The Ancient World in Twentieth-Century Women's Historical Fiction*, Albany, NY.

Hodgson-Wright, S. (2001), "Early Feminism," in Gamble, ed., 3–15.

Holland, N. (1975), *Five Readers Reading*, New Haven.

Hollis, M., and Lukes, S., eds. (1982), *Rationality and Relativism*, Cambridge, MA.

Holmes, G. (1801), *Sketches of Some Southern Counties of Ireland*, London.

Holquist, M. (1990), *Dialogism: Bakhtin and His World*, London.

Holub, R. C. (1984), *Reception Theory: A Critical Introduction*, London.

Holzberg, N. (1988), "Lucian and the Germans," in A. C. Dionisotti, A. Grafton, and J. Kraye, eds., *The Uses of Greek and Latin: Historical Essays*, London, 199–209.

Hopkins, David (2004), "The English Homer: Shakespeare, Longinus and English Neoclassicism," in C. Martindale and A. B. Taylor, eds., *Shakespeare and the Classics*, Cambridge, 261–76.

Horton, R. (1993), *Patterns of Thought in Africa and the West*, Cambridge.

Hubbard, T. K. (1998), *The Pipes of Pan*, Ann Arbor.

Huizinga, J. (1970), *Homo Ludens: A Study of the Play Element in Culture*, London.

Hulubei, A. (1938), *L'Églogue en France au XVIe siècle*, Paris.

Humboldt, W. v. (1903), *Wilhelm von Humboldts gesammelte Schriften*, ed. A. Leitzmann, B. Gebhardt, et al., 17 vols., Berlin.

—— (1960–81), *Werke in fünf Bänden*, ed. A. Flitner and K. Giel, 5 vols., Stuttgart.

Hume, P., ed. (1695), *The Poetical Works of John Milton . . .* , London.

Hunter, R. (1999), *Theocritus: A Selection*, Cambridge.

Iser, W. (1971), *Die Apellstruktur der Texte: Unbestimmtheit als Wirkungsbedingung literarischer Prosa*, Konstanz.

—— (1978a), *The Implied Reader: Patterns of Communication in Prose Fiction from Bunyan to Beckett*, Baltimore.

—— (1978b), *The Act of Reading: A Theory of Aesthetic Response*, Baltimore.

—— (1989), *Prospecting: From Reader Response to Literary Anthropology*, Baltimore.

—— (1993a), "Renaissance Pastoralism as a Paradigm of Literary Fictionality," in Iser (1993b).

—— (1993b), *The Fictive and the Imaginary: Charting Literary Anthropology*, Baltimore.

Jameson, F. (1981), *The Political Unconscious: Narrative as a Socially Symbolic Act*, London.

Jardine, A. A. (1985), *Gynesis: Configurations of Woman and Modernity*, Ithaca, NY and London.

Jauss, H. R., ed. (1968), *Die nicht mehr schönen Künste: Grenzphänomene des Ästhetischen*, Poetik und Hermeneutik 3, Munich.

—— (1970), "Literary History as a Challenge to Literary Theory," *NLH* 2 (1), 7–37.

—— (1982a), *Toward an Aesthetic of Reception*, trans. T. Bahti, Minneapolis.

—— (1982b), *Ästhetische Erfahrung und literarische Hermeneutik*, enlarged edn., Frankfurt am Main.

—— (1982c), *Aesthetic Experience and Literary Hermeneutics*, Minneapolis.

—— (1994), "Rezeptionsgeschichte als Provokation der Literaturgeschichte," in Warning, ed., 126–62.

—— (1999), "Theory of Genres and Medieval Literature," in *Toward an Aesthetics of Reception*, trans. T. Bahti, Minneapolis, 76–109.

Jenkyns, R. (1980), *The Victorians and Ancient Greece*, Oxford.

—— (1991), *Dignity and Decadence: Victorian Art and the Classical Inheritance*, London.

Jeyifo, B., ed. (2001), *Conversations with Wole Soyinka*, Jackson, MS.

—— ed. (2002), *Modern African Drama*, New York and London.

J. J. M. (1910), "Irish Chap Books," *The Irish Book Lover* 1 (12), 157–9.

Johnson, D. (1993), *Jacques-Louis David: Art in Metamorphosis*, Princeton.

Jowett, B. (1994), *Plato: Symposium and Phaedrus*, New York.

Jung, M. R. (1994), "Aspects de l'*Ovide moralisé*," in Picone and Zimmerman, eds., 149–72.

Kallendorf, C. (1994), "Philology, the Reader, and the *Nachleben* of Classical Texts," *Modern Philology* 92, 137–56.

—— (1999a), "Historicizing the 'Harvard School': Pessimistic Readings of the *Aeneid* in Italian Renaissance Scholarship," *Harvard Studies in Classical Philology* 99, 391–403.

—— (1999b), *Virgil and the Myth of Venice: Books and Readers in the Italian Renaissance*, Oxford.

—— (2003), "Representing the Other: Ercilla's *La Araucana*, Virgil's *Aeneid*, and the New World Encounter," *Comparative Literature Studies* 40, 394–414.

Kallendorf, H., and Kallendorf, C. (2000), "Conversations with the Dead: Quevedo and Statius, Annotation and Imitation," *Journal of the Warburg and Courtauld Institutes* 63, 131–68.

Kant, I. (1987), *Critique of Judgment*, trans. Werner S. Pluhar, Indianapolis, IN.

—— (1993), *Critique of Pure Reason*, trans. J. M. D. Meiklejohn, rev. and ed. V. Politis, London and Vermont.

Kaufmann, W. (1950), *Nietzsche: Philosopher, Psychologist, Antichrist*, Princeton.

Keisch, C. (1992), *Um Anselm Feuerbachs "Gastmahl": Katalog, Ausstellung in der Alten Nationalgalerie auf der Museuminsel vom 15. Juli bis zum 13. September 1992*, Berlin.

—— ed. (2000), *Spirit of an Age: Nineteenth Century Paintings from the Nationalgalerie, Berlin*, Berlin.

Kelly, J. (1982), "Early Feminist Theory and the *Querelle des femmes*, 1400–1789," *Signs* 8 (1).

Kennedy, D. F. (2001), Review of *Literature in the Greek and Roman Worlds: A New Perspective*, ed. Oliver Taplin (Oxford, 2000), *Greece and Rome* 48, 87–8.

Kermode, F. (1983), *The Classic: Literary Images of Permanence and Change*. Cambridge, MA and London.

Kern, G. J., ed. (1977 [1882]), *Anselm Feuerbach: Ein Vermächtnis. Hg. von Henriette Feuerbach. Wien 1882*, Hildesheim.

Kerrigan, J. (1996), *Revenge Tragedy: Aeschylus to Armageddon*, Oxford.

Kershaw, I. (2000), *The Nazi Dictatorship: Problems and Perspectives of Interpretation*, London.

Keuls, E. (1990), "The Feminist View of the Past: A Comment on the 'Decentering' of the Poems of Ovid," *Helios* 17 (2), 221–4.

Kiberd, D. (1998), "Romantic Ireland's Dead and Gone," *The Times Literary Supplement*, 12 June, 12–14.

Kinsley, J., ed. (1958), *The Poems of John Dryden*, Oxford.

Kirk, G. (1990), *The Iliad: A Commentary*, Cambridge.

Klancher, J. P. (1987), *The Making of English Reading Audiences 1790–1832*, Madison, WI.

Klein, M. (1977 [1946]), "Notes on Some Schizoid Mechanisms," in *Envy and Gratitude and Other Works 1946–1963*, London.

Knellwolf, C., and Norris, C. (2001), *The Cambridge History of Literary Criticism*, vol. 9: *Twentieth-Century Historical, Philosophical and Psychological Perspectives*, Cambridge.

Knox, B. (1979), *Word and Action: Essays on the Ancient Theater*, Baltimore.

Kopff, E. C. (2000), "Italian Fascism and the Roman Empire," *Classical Bulletin* 76, 109–15.

Kostof, S. (1978), "The Emperor and the Duce: The Planning of the Piazzale Augusto Imperatore in Rome," in H. A. Millon and L. Nochlin, eds., *Art and Architecture in the Service of Politics*, Cambridge, MA and London, 270–325.

Kristeva, J. (1984), *Revolution in Poetic Language*, trans. M. Waller, New York.

—— (1991), *Strangers to Ourselves*, New York.

—— (1995), *New Maladies of the Soul*, New York.

—— (1996), *Interviews*, ed. R. M. Guberman, New York.

—— (2002), *The Portable Kristeva*, New York.

Küffner-Arndt, M. (1976), *Ausstellungskatalog Anselm Feuerbach als Zeichner: Kunstverein Heidelberg, historiches Museum der Pfalz*, Heidelberg.

Kühnl, R. (1996), "The Cultural Politics of Fascist Governments," in G. Berghaus, ed., *Fascism and Theatre: Comparative Studies on the Aesthetics and Politics of Performance in Europe*, Providence, RI, 30–8.

Kupper, D., ed. and comm. (1992), *Feuerbach, Anselm: "Vermächtnis". Die originalen Aufzeichnungen. Herausgegeben und kommentiert*, Berlin.

—— (1993), *Anselm Feuerbach*, Hamburg.

Lacoue-Labarthe, P. (1987), *La fiction du politique*, Mesnil-sur-l'Estrée.

Laird, A. (2003), "Roman Epic Theatre? Reception, Performance, and the Poet in Virgil's *Aeneid*," *PCPS* 49, 19–39.

Landry, D. (1990), *The Muses of Resistance: Labouring-Class Women's Poetry in Britain, 1739–1796*, Cambridge.

Laplanche, J., and Pontalis, J.-B. (1973), *The Language of Psychoanalysis*, London.

Larmour, D. H. J., Miller, P. A., and Platter, C., eds. (1998), *Rethinking Sexuality: Foucault and Classical Antiquity*, Princeton.

Latacz, J. (1987), "Frauengestalten Homers," *Humanistische Bildung* 11, 43–71.

Latour, B. (1993), *We Have Never Been Modern*, Cambridge, MA and London.

Lattimore, R. (1951), *The Iliad of Homer*, Chicago and London.

—— (1962), *The Iliad of Homer*, Chicago and London.

—— (1965), *The Odyssey of Homer*. New York.

Lazarus, N. (1999), *Nationalism and Cultural Practice in the Postcolonial World*, Cambridge.

Leonard, M. (2005), *Athens in Paris: Ancient Greece and the Political in Post-War French Thought*, Oxford.

Leoussi, A. S. (1998), *Nationalism and Classicism*, London.

Levene, D. S., and Nelis, D. P., eds. (2002), *Clio and the Poets: Augustan Poetry and the Traditions of Ancient Historiography*, Leiden, Boston, and Köln.

Levine, J. M. (1991), *The Battle of the Books: History and Literature in the Augustan Age*, Ithaca, NY and London.

Levine, S. J. (1992), "Translator's Introduction. J. L. Borges, Some Versions of Homer," *PMLA* 107, 1134–5.

Lipstadt, D. (1994), *Denying the Holocaust: The Growing Assault on Truth and Memory*, New York.

Lisle, Leconte de (1852), *Poèmes antiques*, Paris.

Lissarrague, F. (1990), *The Aesthetics of the Greek Banquet: Images of Wine and Ritual*, Princeton.

Liversidge, M., and Edwards, C., eds. (1996), *Imagining Rome: British Artists in Rome in the Nineteenth Century*, London.

Lloyd, D. (1994), "Adulteration and the Nation: Monologic Nationalism and the Colonial Hybrid," in Arteaga, ed., 53–92.

Lobel, E., and Page, D. (1955), *Poetarum Lesbiorum Fragmenta*, Oxford.

Lochhead, L. (2000), *Theatre Babel's Medea; After Euripides*, London.

Loeber, R., and Stouthamer-Loeber, M. (1999), "Fiction Available to and Written for Cottagers and their Children," in Cunningham and Kennedy, eds., 124–72.

Long, G., ed., (1996), *Books beyond the Pale*, Dublin.

Longinus (1907), *On the Sublime*, trans. W. Rhys Roberts, Cambridge.

Loraux, N. (1993), "Éloge de l'anachronisme en histoire," *Le Genre Humain* 27, 23–40.

—— (1996), "Back to the Greeks? Chronique d'une expédition lointaine en terre commune," in Revel and Wachtel, eds., 275–94.

Losemann, V. (1977), *Nationalsozialismus und Antike: Studien zur Entwicklung des Faches Alte Geschichte 1933–1945*, Hamburg.

—— (1999), "The Nazi Concept of Rome," in Edwards, ed., 221–35.

Loughrey, B., ed. (1984), *The Pastoral Mode: A Casebook*, London and Basingstoke.

Lytton, The Right Hon. Lord (1869), *The Odes and Epodes of Horace*, Edinburgh and London.

Macé, S., (2002), *L'Éden perdu: La pastoral dans la poésie française de l'âge baroque*, Paris.

Machor, J. L., and Goldstein, P., eds. (2001), *Reception Study: From Literary Theory to Cultural Studies*, New York and London.

Macintosh, F. (1994), *Dying Acts: Death in Ancient Greek and Modern Irish Tragic Drama*, Cork.

—— (1997), "Tragedy in Performance: Nineteenth and Twentieth-century Productions," in Easterling, ed., 284–323.

—— (2000), "Introduction: The Performer in Performance," in Hall, Macintosh, and Taplin, eds., 1–31.

——, Michelakis, P., Hall, E., and Taplin, O. (2005), *Agamemnon in Performance, 458 BC–AD 2002*, Oxford.

MacIntyre, A. (1970), "The Idea of a Social Science," in Wilson, ed., 112–30.

Mailloux, Steven (1998), *Reception Histories: Rhetoric, Pragmatism, and American Cultural Politics*, Ithaca, NY and London.

Malvano, L. (1988), *Fascismo e politica dell'immagine*, Turin.

Malyon, J. (1999–2004), <http://www.artcyclopedia.com/artists/feuerbach_anselm.html> (accessed May 9/10, 2005).

Mandela, N. (1994), *Long Walk to Freedom*, London.

Mandelbaum, Allen, trans. (1971), *The Aeneid of Virgil*, New York.

Marchand, S. (1996), *Down from Olympus: Archaeology and Philhellenism in Germany, 1750–1970*, Princeton.

Markson, D. (1996), *Reader's Block*, Chicago.

Marshall J. (1907), *The Odes and Epodes of Horace translated into English Verse corresponding with the Original Metres*, New York and London.

Martin, T. (1860), *The Odes of Horace translated into English Verse*, London [2nd edn 1861].

Martindale, C. (1984a), "Unlocking the Word-Hoard: In Praise of Metaphrase," in Shaffer, ed., 47–72.

—— ed. (1984b), *Virgil and His Influence: Bimillennial Studies*, Bristol.

—— (1986), *John Milton and the Transformation of Ancient Epic*, London and Sydney [2nd edn Bristol 2002].

—— ed. (1988), *Ovid Renewed: Ovidian Influences on Literature and Art from the Middle Ages to the Twentieth Century*, Cambridge.

—— (1993), *Redeeming the Text: Latin Poetry and the Hermeneutics of Reception*, Cambridge.

—— (1996), "Troping the Colours, or How (Not) to Write Literary History: The Case of Rome" (review essay of G. B. Conte, *Latin Literature: A History* (1994)), *History of the Human Sciences* 9, 93–106.

—— ed. (1997a), *The Cambridge Companion to Virgil*, Cambridge.

—— (1997b), "Introduction: 'The Classic of All Europe'," in Martindale, ed., 1–18.

—— (1997c), "Green Politics: The *Eclogues*," in Martindale, ed., 107–24.

—— (2002), "Virgil," in *John Milton and the Transformation of Ancient Epic*, 2nd edn., London, 107–52.

—— (2004), *Latin Poetry and the Judgement of Taste: An Essay in Aesthetics*, Oxford.

—— and Hopkins, D., eds. (1993), *Horace Made New: Horatian Influences on British Writing from the Renaissance to the Twentieth Century*, Cambridge.

—— and Martindale, M. (1990), *Shakespeare and the Uses of Antiquity: An Introductory Essay*, London and New York.

—— and Taylor, A. B., eds. (2004), *Shakespeare and the Classics*, Cambridge.

Mathieu, P.-L. (1994), *Gustave Moreau*, Paris.

McClure, Ch. (1993), "Helen of the 'West Indies': History or Poetry of a Caribbean Realm," *Studies in the Literary Imagination* 26 (2), 7–20.

McCormack, J. (1991), *John Gray: Poet, Dandy and Priest*, Hanover.

McDonald, M. (1992), *Ancient Sun, Modern Light: Greek Drama on the Modern Stage*, New York.

—— (2000), "Black Dionysus: Greek Tragedy from Africa" in Hardwick et al., eds., 95–108.

—— (2003), *The Living Art of Greek Tragedy*, Bloomington, IN.

—— and Walton, J. M., eds. (2002), *Amid Our Troubles: Irish Versions of Greek Tragedy*, London.

McGann, J. J. (1985), *The Beauty of Inflections: Literary Investigations in Historical Method and Theory*, Oxford.

McGrath, E. (1983), " 'The Drunken Alcibiades': Rubens' Picture of Plato's *Symposium*," *Journal of the Warburg and Courtauld Institutes* 46, 228–35.

McManus, A. (2002), *The Irish Hedge School and Its Books*, Dublin.

McManus, B. (1990), "Multicentering: The Case of the Athenian Bride," *Helios* 17, 225–35.

McNamara, D. (1853), *Eachtra Ghiolla an Amaráin*, ed. S. H. Hayes, Dublin.

Medvedev, P. (1985), *The Formal Method in Literary Scholarship: A Critical Introduction to Sociological Poetics*, trans. A. Wehrle, Cambridge, MA.

Meier, H. (1994), [introduction], in Benardete, 6–27.

Merten, K. (2004), *Antike Mythen–Mythos Antike: Posthumanistische Antikerezeption in der englischsprachigen Lyrik der Gegenwart*, Münchner Studien zur neueren englischen Literatur 14, Munich.

Meynell, W. (1887), *The Modern School of Art*, 4 vols., London.

Mezzabotta, M. (2000), "Ancient Greek Drama in the New South Africa," in Hardwick et al., eds., 246–68.

Milton, J. (1957), *The Complete Poems and Major Prose*, ed. M. Y. Hughes, Indianapolis.

Mishra, V. (1996), "The Diasporic Imaginary: Theorizing the Indian Diaspora," *Textual Practice* 10 (3), 421–47.

Mitchell-Boyask, R., ed. (2002), *Approaches to Teaching the Dramas of Euripides*, New York.

Modleski, T. (1991), *Feminism without Women: Culture and Criticism in a "Postfeminist" Age*, New York and London.

Möllendorff, P. v. (2000), *Auf der Suche nach der verlogenen Wahrheit: Lukians Wahre Geschichten*, Tübingen.

Momigliano, A. (1969), "Prospettiva 1967 della storia greca," in *Quarto Contributo alla storia degli studi classici e del mondo antico*, Rome, 43–58.

Monk, S. H. (1935), *The Sublime: A Study of Critical Theories in XVIII-Century England*, New York.

Montagu, J. (1994), "Interpretations of Timanthes's Sacrifice of Iphigenia," in J. Onians, ed., *Sight and Insight*, London, 305–25.

Morales, H. (2004), *Vision and Narrative in Achilles Tatius' Leucippe and Clitophon*, Cambridge.

Morson, G. S., and Emerson, C. (1990), *Mikhail Bakhtin: Creation of a Prosaics*, Stanford.

Morwood, J. (1999), *Euripides' Bacchae and Other Plays*, Oxford.

Moss, A. (2003), *Renaissance Truth and the Latin Language Turn*, Oxford.

Mosse, G. (1964), *The Crisis of German Ideology: Intellectual Origins of the Third Reich*, London.

—— (1966), *Nazi Culture: Intellectual, Cultural, and Social Life in the Third Reich*, London.

—— (1980), *Masses and Man: Nationalist and Fascist Perspectives of Reality*, New York.

—— (1999), *The Fascist Revolution*, New York.

Munari, F. (1960), *Ovid im Mittelalter*, Zürich and Stuttgart.

Murray, O. (1985), "Symposium and Genre in the Poetry of Horace," *JRS* 75, 39–50.

Murray, T., ed. (1997), *Mimesis, Masochism and Mime: The Politics of Theatricality in Contemporary French Thought*, Ann Arbor.

Muthmann, F. (1951), "Alkibiades und Agathon: Über die antiken Grundlagen von Anselm Feuerbachs *Gastmahl des Platon*," *Zeitschrift für Kunstgeschichte* 14, 97–112.

Näf, B. (1986), *Von Perikles zu Hitler: Die athenische Demokratie und die deutsche Althistorie bis 1945*, Bern.

—— ed. (2001), *Antike und Altertumswissenschaft in der Zeit von Faschismus und Nationalsozialismus. Kolloquium Universität Zürich 14–17. Oktober 1998*, Mandelbachtel and Cambridge.

Nauta, Ruurd R. (1994), "Historicizing Reading: The Aesthetics of Reception and Horace's 'Soracte Ode'," in Irene J. F. de Jong and J. P. Sullivan, eds., *Modern Critical Theory and Classical Literature* (*Mnemosyne*, Supplementum 130), Leiden, 207–30.

Nead, L. (1988), *Myths of Sexuality*, Oxford.

—— (1992), *The Female Nude: Art, Obscenity and Sexuality*, London and New York.

Nehamas, A. (1985), *Nietzsche, Life as Literature*. Cambridge, MA.

—— (1998), *The Art of Living: Socratic Reflections from Plato to Foucault*, Berkeley.

Nesselrath, H.-G. (1990), "Lucian's Introductions," in D. A. Russell, ed., *Antonine Literature*, Oxford, 111–40.

Neuberg, V. E. (1968), *The Penny Histories: A Study of Chapbooks for Young Readers over Two Centuries*, London.

Newman, F. W. (1853), *The Odes of Horace translated into Unrhymed Metres*, London.

Newton, T., ed. (1750), *Paradise Lost. A Poem in Twelve Books. The Author John Milton. . . .* London.

Ngugi wa Thiong'o (1986), *Decolonising the Mind*, Oxford, Nairobi, and Portsmouth, NH.

Nicholas, L. H. (1994), *The Rape of Europa: The Fate of Europe's Treasures in the Third Reich and the Second World War*, London.

Niderst, A. (1991), "La querelle de la pastorale," *La Pastorale Française. De Rémi Bellau à Victor Hugo*, Biblio 17, Papers on French Seventeenth Century Literature, Paris, Seattle, and Tübingen.

Nietzsche, F. (1967), *On the Genealogy of Morals*, trans. W. Kaufmann, New York.

—— (1967–), *Friedrich Nietzsche: Kritische Gesamtausgabe, Werke*, ed. G. Colli and M. Montinari, Berlin.

—— (1980), *Aus dem Nachlass der Achtzigerjahre*, Munich.

—— (1988), *Friedrich Nietzsche: Sämtliche Werke. Kritische Studienausgabe in 15 Einzelbänden*, ed. G. Colli and M. Montinari, 2nd edn., 15 vols., Berlin.

—— (1990), *Twilight of the Idols, and The Anti-Christ*, trans. R. J. Hollingdale, London and New York.

—— (1997), *Untimely Meditations*, ed. D. Breazeale, trans. R. J. Hollingdale, Cambridge.

Nightingale, A. W. (1995), *Genres in Dialogue: Plato and the Construct of Philosophy*, Cambridge.

—— (2002), "Distant Views: 'Realistic' and 'Fantastic' Mimesis in Plato," in J. Annas and C. Rowe, eds., *New Perspectives on Plato, Modern and Ancient*, Cambridge, MA and London, 227–47.

Nochlin, L. (1994), *The Body in Pieces: The Fragment as a Metaphor of Modernity*, London.

O Canainn, S. (1983), "The Education Inquiry 1824–1826 in Its Social and Political Context," *Irish Educational Studies* 3 (3), 52–83.

O Casaide, S. (1916), "Latin in County Kerry," *Kerry Archaeological Magazine* 3 (16), 301–2.

Ó Ciosáin, N. (1998), "The Irish Rogues," in Donnelly and Miller, eds., 78–96.

Ogden, D., ed. (2002), *The Hellenistic World: New Perspectives*, London.

Ogden, T. (1982), *Projective Identification and Psychotherapeutic Technique*, London.

O'Gorman, E. (2002), "Archaism and Historicism in Horace's *Odes*," in D. S. Levene and D. P. Nelis, eds., 81–101.

Okpewho, I. (1991), "Soyinka, Euripides and the Anxiety of Empire," *Research in African Literatures* 30 (4), 32–55.

Oras, A. (1967), *Milton's Editors and Commentators from Patrick Hume to Henry John Todd (1695–1801): A Study in Critical Views and Methods*, 3rd edn., New York.

Òsòfisan, F. (1998), " 'The Revolution as Muse': Drama as Surreptitious Insurrection in a Post-colonial, Military State," in R. Boon and J. Plastow, eds., *Theatre Matters: Performance and Culture on the World Stage*, Cambridge, 11–35.

—— (1999), "Theater and the Rites of 'Post-Negritude' Remembering," *Research in African Literatures*, 30 (1) (Spring), 1–11.

Østermark-Johansen, L. (1999), "The Apotheosis of the Male Nude: Leighton and Michelangelo," in Barringer and Prettejohn, eds., 111–34.

Oswald, P. (1999), *Odysseus*, London.

O'Tuama, S., ed. (1981), *An Duanaire: An Irish Anthology 1600–1900: Poems of the Dispossessed*, trans. T. Kinsella, Philadelphia.

Owenson, S. (1807), *Patriotic Sketches of the South of Ireland*, London.

Page, D. L. (1934), *Actors' Interpolations in Greek Tragedy: Studied with Special Reference to Euripides'* Iphigeneia in Aulis, Oxford.

Palagia, O., and Pollitt, J. J., eds. (1996), *Personal Styles in Greek Sculpture*, Cambridge.

Parliamentary Debates Series 2, vol. 10: *February 3–March 29, 1824*, London, 1824.

Parliamentary Debates Series 2, vol. 15: *March 20–May 3, 1826*, London, 1826.

Pasquier, A. (1985), *La Vénus de Milo et les Aphrodites du Louvre*, Paris.

Pater, W. (1868), "Poems by William Morris," *Westminster Review* NS 34 (October), 300–12.

—— (1913 [1889]), *Appreciations: With an Essay on Style*, London.

—— (1914 [1894]), *Greek Studies: A Series of Lectures*, London.

—— (1922), *Greek Studies*, London.

—— (1980), *The Renaissance: Studies in Art and Poetry: The 1893 Text*, ed. D. L. Hill. Berkeley, Los Angeles, and London.

Patočka, J. (1996), *Heretical Essays in the Philosophy of History*, trans. E. Kohák, ed. J. Dodd, Chicago and La Salle, IL.

Patrick, M. M. (1912), *Sappho and the Island of Lesbos*, London.

Patsalidis, S., and Sakellaridou, E., eds. (1999), *(Dis)Placing Classical Greek Theatre*, Thessaloniki.

Patterson, A. (1987), *Pastoral and Ideology: Virgil to Valéry*, Berkeley.

Patterson, F., gen. ed. (1931–40), *The Works of John Milton*, 18 vols. in 21. New York.

Pavis, P. (1993), "Production and Reception in the Theatre," in Hilton, ed., 25–71.

Pedrick, V., and Rabinowitz, N., eds. (1982), *Audience-Oriented Criticism and the Classics* (*Arethusa* 19 (2)).

Perkins, D. (1992), *Is Literary History Possible?* Baltimore and London.

Petropoulos, J. (1996), *Art as Politics in the Third Reich*, Chapel Hill, NC.

Picone, M., and Zimmerman, B., eds. (1994), *Ovidius Redivivus: Von Ovid zu Dante*. Stuttgart.

Picot, G. (1963), *Boileau, L'Art Poétique*, Paris.

Piggott, J. R. (2004), *Palace of the People: The Crystal Palace at Sydenham 1854–1936*, London.

Plett, H., ed. (1991), *Intertextuality*, Berlin and New York.

Pocock, G. (1980), *Boileau and the Nature of Neo-classicism*, Cambridge.

Poggioli, R. (1968), *The Theory of the Avant-Garde*, Cambridge, MA.

Pointon, M. (1990), *Naked Authority*, Cambridge.

Pollard, M. (1989), *Dublin's Trade in Books 1550–1800*, Oxford.

Pollock, G. (1988), *Vision and Difference*, London.

Pope, A. (1961), *The Poems of Alexander Pope*, vol. 1: *Pastoral Poetry and An Essay on Criticism*, ed. E. Audra and A. Williams, London and New Haven.

—— (1967), *The Poems of Alexander Pope*, vols. 7–10: *Translations of Homer*, ed. M. Mack, London and New Haven.

—— (1996), *The Iliad of Homer*, ed. Steven Shankman, London.

Porson, R. (1802), *Euripidis Hecuba ad fidem manuscriptorum emendata et brevibus notis emendationum potissimum rationes reddentibus instructa*, Cambridge.

Porter, James I. (1998). "Unconscious Agency in Nietzsche," *Nietzsche-Studien*, 27, 153–95.

—— (1999a), "Nietzsche et les charmes de la métaphysique: 'La logique du sentiment'," *Revue germanique internationale*, 11 ("Nietzsche moraliste"), 157–72.

—— ed. (1999b), *The Construction of the Classical Body*, Ann Arbor.

—— (2000), *Nietzsche and the Philology of the Future*, Stanford.

—— (2002), "Homer: The Very Idea," *Arion* 10 (2), 57–86.

—— (2003), "The Materiality of Classical Studies," *Parallax* 9, 64–74.

—— (2005a), "Introduction," in J. I. Porter, ed., *Classical Pasts: The Classical Traditions of Greece and Rome*, Princeton, 1–65.

—— (2005b), "What is Classical about Classical Antiquity?" in J. I. Porter, ed., *Classical Pasts: The Classical Traditions of Greece and Rome*, Princeton, 301–52.

—— (2005c), "Foucault's Ascetic Ancients," *Phoenix*, 21–32.

Porter, R., and Hall, L. (1995), *The Facts of Life: The Creation of Sexual Knowledge in Britain 1650–1950*, New Haven.

Porter, W. (1993), *Reading the Classics and Paradise Lost*, Lincoln, NB and London.

Potts, A. (1994), *Flesh and the Ideal: Winckelmann and the Origins of Art History*, New Haven.

Preston, C. Lynn (1995), "Introduction," in C. Lynn Preston and M. J. Preston, eds., *The Other Print Tradition: Essays on Chapbooks, Broadsides, and Related Ephemera*, New York, pp. ix–xx.

Prettejohn, E., ed. (1999), *After the Pre-Raphaelites: Art and Aestheticism in Victorian Britain*, Manchester.

—— (2002), "Lawrence Alma-Tadema and the Modern City of Ancient Rome," *Art Bulletin* 84, 115–29.

—— (2004), "Between Homer and Ovid: Metamorphoses of the 'Grand Style' in G. F. Watts," in Trodd and Brown, eds., 49–64.

—— (2005), *Beauty and Art: 1750–2000*, Oxford.

Prins, Y. (1999), *Victorian Sappho*, Princeton.

Pucci, J. (1998), *The Full-Knowing Reader: Allusion and the Power of the Reader in the Western Literary Tradition*, New Haven and London.

Quane, M. (1954), "Banna School, Adfert," *Journal of the Royal Society of Antiquaries of Ireland* 84, 156–72.

Quatremère de Quincy, A.-C. (1821), *Sur la statue antique de Vénus, découverte dans l'île de Milo en 1820*, Paris.

Quayson, A. (2002), *Strategic Transformations in Nigerian Writing*, Oxford and Bloomington, IN.

Quiller-Couch, Sir A. (1943), *Cambridge Lectures*, London and New York.

Quint, David (1993), *Epic and Empire: Politics and Generic Form from Virgil to Milton*, Princeton.

Rabinowitz, N. S., and Richlin, A., eds. (1993), *Feminist Theory and the Classics*, London and New York.

Ramazani, J. (1997), "The Wound of History: Walcott's *Omeros* and the Post-colonial Poetics of Affliction," *Proceedings of the Modern Literature Association* 112 (3), 405–15.

Rancière, J. (1994), *The Names of History: On the Poetics of Knowledge*, trans. H. Melehey, Minneapolis and London.

Rand, E. K. (1963), *Ovid and His Influence*, New York.

Rapin, R. (1947), *De Carmine Pastorali, prefixed to Thomas Creech's translation of the Idylliums of Theocritus (1684)*, Augustan Reprint Society, Ann Arbor.

Ravaisson, F. (1871), *La Vénus de Milo*, Paris.

Rawson, E. (1969), *The Spartan Tradition in European Thought*, Oxford.

Reeve, M. D. (2001), "Reception/History of Scholarship: Introduction," in Harrison, ed., 245–51.

Rehm, R. (2002), *The Play of Space: Spatial Transformation in Greek Tragedy*, Princeton and Oxford.

—— (2003), *Radical Greek Theatre: Greek Tragedy and the Modern World*, London.

Reid, J. D. (1993), *Classical Mythology in the Arts, 1300–1990s*, vol. 1, New York.

Reinach, S. (1890), "La Vénus de Milo," *Gazette des Beaux-Arts* 32, 376–94.

Reinelt, J. (2003), "The Politics of Discourse: Performativity Meets Theatricality," in Auslander, ed., vol. 1, 153–67.

Revel, J., and Wachtel, N., eds. (1996), *Une école pour les sciences sociales: de la VI ième section à l'École des Hautes Études en Sciences Sociales*, Paris.

Reynolds, M., ed. (2001), *The Sappho Companion*, London.

—— (2003), *The Sappho History*, Basingstoke.

Reynolds, S. (1984), *The Vision of Simeon Solomon*, Stroud, Glos.

Richards, I. A. (1929), *Practical Criticism*, New York.

Richardson, J., father and son (1734), *Explanatory Notes and Remarks on Milton's Paradise Lost*, London.

Richlin, A. (1993), "The Ethnographer's Dilemma and the Dream of a Lost Golden Age," in Rabinowitz and Richlin, eds., 272–303.

Ricoeur, P. (1981), *Hermeneutics and the Human Sciences*, ed. and trans. J. B. Thompson, Cambridge and Paris.

—— (1986), *Lectures on Ideology and Utopia*, New York.

Ridgway, B. S. (1986), "The State of Research on Ancient Art," *Art Bulletin* 68, 7–23.

—— (1994), "The Study of Classical Sculpture at the End of the Twentieth Century," *American Journal of Archaeology* 98, 759–72.

Riley, E. H. (1929), "Milton's Tribute to Virgil," *Studies in Philology* 26, 155–65.

Roach, J. (1996), *Cities of the Dead: Circum-Atlantic Performance*, New York.

Robertson, M. (1975), *A History of Greek Art*, 2 vols., Cambridge.

Robinson, C. (1979), *Lucian*, London.

Robinson, D. (1997), *What is Translation? Centrifugal Theories, Critical Interventions*, Kent, OH and London.

Rocco, C. (1997), *Tragedy and Enlightenment: Athenian Political Thought and the Dilemmas of Modernity*, Berkeley, Los Angeles, and London.

Rorty, R. (1989), *Contingency, Irony, and Solidarity*, Cambridge and New York.

Rose, J. (1992), "Rereading the English Common Reader: A Preface to a History of Audiences," *Journal of the History of Ideas* 53, 47–70.

—— (2001), *The Intellectual Life of the British Working Classes*, New Haven.

Rosenmeyer, T. G. (1969), *The Green Cabinet: Theocritus and the European Pastoral Lyric*, Berkeley.

Rosslyn, F. (2000), *Tragic Plots*, Studies in European Cultural Transition 9, Aldershot, Burlington, Singapore, and Sydney.

Rowe, C., et al. (2003), Application to AHRB under Subject Areas for Ring-Fenced Doctoral Awards scheme.

Rudat, W. E. H. (1981), "Milton's Dido and Aeneas: The Fall in *Paradise Lost* and the Vergilian Tradition," *Classical and Modern Literature* 2, 33–46.

Rütten, U. (1997), *Phantasie und Lachkultur: Lukians* Wahre Geschichten, Tübingen.

Safran, W. (1991), "Diasporas in Modern Societies: Myths of Homeland and Return," *Diaspora* 1 (1), 83–99.

Saïd, E. (1993), *Culture and Imperialism*, London.

—— (2001), "Intellectual Exile: Expatriates and Marginals (1993)," in Bayoumi and Rubin, eds., 368–81.

Salmon, D. (2000), *La Vénus de Milo: un mythe*, Paris.

Sanders, V. (2001), "First Wave Feminism," in Gamble, ed., 16–28.

Sandler, J., ed. (1989), *Projection, Identification, Projective Identification*, London.

Sartre, J.-P. (1976), *Situations III*, Paris.

Scharf, G. (1854), *The Greek Court Erected in the Crystal Palace, by Owen Jones*, London.

Schechner, R. (1992), "A New Paradigm for Theatre in the Academy," *The Drama Review* 36 (4), 7–10.

—— (2003), "Performers and Spectators Transported and Transformed," in Auslander, ed., vol. 1, 263–90.

Schmidt, P. L. (1985), "Reception Theory and Classical Scholarship: A Plea for Convergence," in W. M. Calder III, U. K. Goldsmith, and P. B. Kenevan, eds., *Hypatia: Essays in Classics, Comparative Literature, and Philosophy Presented to Hazel E. Barnes on Her Seventieth Birthday*, Boulder, CO, 67–77.

Schmitz, T. (1997), *Bildung und Macht: zur sozialen und politischen Funktion der zweiten Sophistik in der griechischen Welt der Kaiserzeit*, Munich.

Schnapper, A. (1980), *David: Témoin de son temps*, Friburg.

Schnur, H. C. (1970), "Dubious *Dicta?*" *Classical Journal* 66, 70–1.

Schulte, R., and Biguenet, J. (1992), *Theories of Translation: An Anthology of Essays from Dryden to Derrida*, Chicago.

Schweickart, E. A., and Patrocinio, P., eds. (1986), *Gender and Reading: Essays on Readers, Texts and Contexts*, Baltimore.

Scobie, A. (1990), *Hitler's State Architecture: The Impact of Classical Antiquity*, London.

Segal, C. (1997), *Dionysiac Poetics and Euripides' Bacchae*, Princeton.

Segers, Rien T. (1979–80), "An Interview with Hans Robert Jauss," *New Literary History* 11, 83–95.

Selaiha, N. (2002), "Antigone in Palestine," *Al Ahram Weekly* 585 (May 9–15), 16.

Selden, D. (1992), "*Caveat lector*," in Hexter and Selden, eds., 458–512.

Selden, R. ed. (1995), *The Cambridge History of Literary Criticism*, vol. 8: *From Formalism to Poststructuralism*, Cambridge.

Sewell, W. (1850), *The Odes and Epodes of Horace, Translated Literally and Rhythmically*, London.

Shackleton Bailey, D. R. (1982), *Profile of Horace*, London.

Shaffer, E. S., ed. (1984), *Comparative Criticism*, vol. 6, Cambridge.

Sharrock, Alison (2002), "Gender and Sexuality," in Hardie, ed., 95–107.

Shaw, J. L. (2002), *Dream States: Puvis de Chavannes, Modernism, and the Fantasy of France*, New Haven and London.

Showalter, E., ed. (1985), *The New Feminist Criticism: Essays on Women, Literature, and Theory*, New York.

Siegel, D. L. (1997), "Reading between the Waves: Feminist Historiography in a 'Postfeminist' Moment," in Heywood and Drake, eds., 55–82.

Silk, M. S., ed. (1996), *Tragedy and the Tragic: Greek Theatre and Beyond*, Oxford.

Simpson, M. (forthcoming), "The Curse of the Canon: Ola Rotimi's *The Gods Are Not To Blame*," in Hardwick and Gillespie, eds.

Sims, J. H. (1982), "A Greater than Rome: The Inversion of a Virgilian Symbol from Camões to Milton," in *Rome in the Renaissance: The City and the Myth*, ed. P. A. Ramsey, 333–44, Binghamton, NY.

Singleton, E., ed. (1912), *Modern Paintings as Seen and Described by Great Writers*, New York.

Sitterson, J. C., Jr. (1992), "Allusive and Elusive Meanings: Reading Ariosto's Vergilian Ending," *Renaissance Quarterly* 45, 1–19.

Sjöberg, L. (1983), "An Interview with Derek Walcott," *Artes* 1, 23–7, rpr. in Baer, ed. (1996), 79–85.

Skinner, M. B. (1986), "Rescuing Creusa: New Methodological Approaches to Women in Antiquity," *Helios* 13 (2), 1–8.

Skoie, M. (2002), *Reading Sulpicia: Commentaries 1475–1990*, Oxford.

Slater, N. (1990), *Reading Petronius*, Baltimore.

Slater, N. W. (2002), *Spectator Politics: Metatheatre and Performance in Aristophanes*, Philadelphia.

Smith, A. (1996), *The Victorian Nude*, Manchester.

—— (1999a), "Nature Transformed: Leighton, the Nude and the Model," in Barringer and Prettejohn, eds., 19–48.

—— (1999b), " 'The British Matron' and the Body Beautiful," in Prettejohn, ed., 217–39.

Smith, R. R. R. (1991), *Hellenistic Sculpture: A Handbook*, London.

—— (2002), "The Use of Images: Visual History and Ancient History," in Wiseman, ed., 59–102.

Smyth, J. (1998), *The Men of No Property: Irish Radicals and Popular Politics in the Late Eighteenth Century*, New York.

Sontheimer, K. (1968), *Antidemokratisches Denken in der Weimarer Republik*, Munich.

Soyinka, W. (1973), *The Bacchae of Euripides: A Communion Rite*, London.

—— (1976), *Myth, Literature and the African World*, Cambridge.

—— (1999), *The Burden of Memory: The Muse of Forgiveness*, Oxford.

Spargo, J. W. (1934), *Virgil the Necromancer: Studies in Virgilian Legends*, Harvard Studies in Comparative Literature 10, Cambridge, MA.

Spivey, N. (1996), *Understanding Greek Sculpture: Ancient Meanings, Modern Readings*, London.

—— (1997), *Greek Art*, London.

Spotts, F. (2002), *Hitler and the Power of Aesthetics*, London.

Spufford, M. (1981), *Small Books and Pleasant Histories: Popular Fiction and Its Readership in Seventeenth Century England*, Athens, GA.

Stack, F. (1985), *Pope and Horace: Studies in Imitation*, Cambridge.

Stanford, W. (1976), *Ireland and the Classical Tradition*, Dublin.

States, B. O. (2003), "Performance as Metaphor," in Auslander, ed., vol. 1, 108–37.

Steadman, J. (1967), *Milton and the Renaissance Hero*, Oxford.

Steinmeyer, E. (forthcoming), "Mark Fleishman et al.: In the City of Paradise (1998)," in Hardwick and Gillespie, eds.

Sternhell, Z. (1986), *Neither Right nor Left: Fascist Ideology in France*, trans. D. Maisel, Berkeley.

—— et al. (1994), *The Birth of Fascist Ideology: From Cultural Rebellion to Political Revolution*, trans. D. Maisel, Princeton.

Stevens, W. (1972), *The Palm at the End of the Mind: Selected Poems*, New York.

Stewart, A. (1990), *Greek Sculpture: An Exploration*, 2 vols., New Haven and London.

—— (1997), *Art, Desire, and the Body in Ancient Greece*. Cambridge.

Stewart, S. (1984), *On Longing: Narratives of the Miniature, the Gigantic, the Souvenir, the Collection*, Baltimore.

Stirling, A. (1926), *The Richmond Papers*, London.

Stone, M. (1999), "A Flexible Rome: Fascism and the Cult," in Edwards, ed., 205–20.

Stray, C. (1998), *Classics Transformed: Schools, Universities, and Society in England, 1830–1960*, Oxford.

Suleiman, S., and Crosman, I., eds. (1980), *The Reader in the Text: Essays on Audience and Interpretation*, Princeton.

Suzuki, M. (1989), *Metamorphoses of Helen. Authority, Difference, and the Epic*, Ithaca, NY and London.

Swain, S. (1996), *Hellenism and Empire: Language, Classicism, and Power in the Greek World, AD 50–250*, Oxford.

Swanson, V. (1977), *Sir Lawrence Alma Tadema: The Painter of the Victorian Vision of the Ancient World*, London.

—— (1990), *The Biography and Catalogue Raisonné of the Paintings of Sir Lawrence Alma-Tadema*, London.

Swedenberg, H. T., ed. (1972), *The Works of John Dryden*, Berkeley.

Talib, I. S. (2002), *The Languages of Postcolonial Literatures*, London.

Taplin, O. (1977), *The Stagecraft of Aeschylus*, Oxford.

—— (1978), *Greek Tragedy in Action*, London.

—— (2002), "Contemporary Poetry and Classics," in Wiseman, ed., 1–19.

Terada, R. (1992), *Derek Walcott's Poetry: American Mimicry*, Boston.

Thieme, J. (1999), *Derek Walcott*, Contemporary World Writers, Manchester and New York.

Thomae, O. (1978), *Die Propaganda-Maschinerie. Bildende Kunst und Öffentlichkeitsarbeit im Dritten Reich*, Berlin.

Thomas, R. F. (1986), "Virgil's *Georgics* and the Art of Reference," *Harvard Studies in Classical Philology* 90, 171–98.

—— (2000), "A Trope by Any Other Name: 'Polysemy,' Ambiguity and *significatio* in Virgil," *HSCP* 100, 381–407.

—— (2001), *Virgil and the Augustan Reception*, Cambridge.

Thompson, D. (2004), "Undress Rehearsal," *Sight and Sound* 14 (January), 22–5.

Thompson, G. F. (2003), "Approaches to 'Performance': an Analysis of Terms," in Auslander, ed., vol. 1, 138–52.

Thornham, S. (2001), "Second Wave Feminism," in Gamble, ed., 29–42.

Todd, H. J. (1809), *The Poetical Works of John Milton*, 2nd edn., London.

Tompkins, J. P. (1980), *Reader-Response Criticism: From Formalism to Post-structuralism*, Baltimore.

Trevor-Roper, H. R. (1953), *Hitler's Secret Conversations*, New York.

Trodd, C., and Brown, S., eds. (2004), *Representations of G. F. Watts: Art Making in Victorian Culture*, Aldershot, Hants. and Burlington, VT.

Turner, F. M. (1981), *The Greek Heritage in Victorian Britain*, New Haven.

Ubersfeld, A. (1996), *Lire le théâtre: l'école du spectateur*, Paris.

Uhde-Bernays, H., ed. (1911), *Anselm Feuerbachs Briefe an seine Mutter*, 2 vols., Berlin.

—— (1912), *Henriette Feuerbach: Ihr Leben in ihren Briefen [Auswahl]*, Berlin.

Upton, C.-A., ed. (2000), *Moving Target: Theatre Translation and Cultural Relocation*, Manchester and Northampton, MA.

Usher, M. D. (2002), "Satyr Play in Plato's *Symposium*," *American Journal of Philology* 123, 205–28.

Vance, N. (1997), *The Victorians and Ancient Rome*, Oxford.

Van Elslande, J.-P. (1999), *L'imaginaire pastoral du XVIIe siècle: 1600–1650*, Paris.

Van Steen, G. (2001), "'Playing by the Censor's Rules?' Classical Drama Revived under the Greek Junta (1967–1974)," *Journal of the Hellenic Diaspora*, 27 (1/2), 133–94.

—— (2002a), "'The Word's a Circular Stage': Aeschylean Tragedy through the Eyes of Eva Palmer-Sikelianou," *International Journal of the Classical Tradition* 8 (3) (Winter), 375–93.

—— (2002b), "Rolling Out the Red Carpet: Power 'Play' in Modern Greek Versions of the Myth of Orestes from the 1960s and 1970s (I)," *IJCT* 9 (1) (Summer), 51–95.

—— (2002c), "Rolling Out the Red Carpet: Power 'Play' in Modern Greek Versions of the Myth of Orestes from the 1960s and 1970s (II)," *IJCT* 9 (2) (Fall), 195–235.

van Zyl Smit, B. (2003), "The Reception of Greek Tragedy in South Africa," *Eirene* 39, 234–53.

Venuti, L. (1994), *The Translator's Invisibility: A History of Translation*, London and New York.

—— (1998), *The Scandals of Translation: Towards an Ethics of Difference*, London and New York.

Verbart, A. (1995), *Fellowship in* Paradise Lost*: Vergil, Milton, Wordsworth*, Amsterdam and Atlanta, GA.

Vergilius Maro, P. (1969), *Opera*, ed. R. A. B. Mynors, Oxford.

Vey, H., ed. (1976), *Ausstellungskatalog Anselm Feuerbach 1829 bis 1880, Gemälde und Zeichnungen: Ausstellung in der staatliche Kunsthalle Karlsruhe*, Munich and Berlin.

Veyne, P. (1988a), *Did the Greeks Believe in Their Myths? An Essay on the Constitutive Imagination*, Chicago.

—— (1988b), "La médication interminable," in Seneca, *De la tranquillité de l'âme*, trans. Colette Lazam, Paris.

Virgil (1972), *The Aeneid*, trans. A. Mandelbaum, New York.

Volosinov, V. (1973), *Marxism and the Philosophy of Language*, trans. L. Matejka and I. Titunik, New York.

Voss, H. (1973), *Franz von Stuck: Werkkatalog der Gemälder*, Munich.

Walcott, D. (1990), *Omeros*, Toronto, Boston, and London.

—— (1993), *The Odyssey: A Stage Version*, London.

—— (1997), "Reflections on *Omeros*," in Davis, ed., 229–46.

—— (1998), *What the Twilight Says*, London.

Waldenburg, H. (1990), *The Berlin Wall Book*, London.

Walder, D. (1993), "Introduction," in A. Fugard, *Township Plays*, Oxford, pp. ix–xxxiv.

Walton, J. M. (1987), *Living Greek Theatre: A Handbook of Classical Performance and Modern Production*, New York.

—— (2002), "Hit or Myth: The Greeks and Irish Drama," in McDonald and Walton, eds., 3–36.

Waquet, F. (2001), *Latin, or the Empire of a Sign: From the Sixteenth to the Twentieth Century*, trans. John Howe, London and New York.

Warning, R., ed. (1994), *Rezeptionsästhetik*, Munich.

Weeks, J. (1977), *Coming Out: Homosexual Politics in Britain, from the Nineteenth Century to the Present*, London.

Wellek, R. (1973), "Classicism in Literature," in Ph. P. Wiener, ed., *Dictionary of the History of Ideas: Studies of Selected Pivotal Ideas*, vol. 1, 450–6.

Wender, D. (1980), *Roman Poetry: From the Republic to the Silver Age*, Carbondale, IL.

West, D. (1995), *Cast Out Theory: Classical Association Presidential Address*, Alresford, Hants.

West, M. L. (1997), *The East Face of Helicon: West Asiatic Elements in Greek Poetry and Myth*, Oxford.

Wetmore, K. J., Jr. (2002), *The Athenian Sun in an African Sky*, Jefferson, NC and London.

—— (2003), *Black Dionysus: Greek Tragedy and African American Theatre*, Jefferson, NC and London.

Whelan, K. (1996), "The Republic in the Village: The Dissemination and Reception of Popular Political Literature in the 1790s," in Long, ed., 101–40.

Whelehan, I. (1995), *Feminist Thought: From the Second Wave to "Post-feminism"*, Edinburgh.

Whistler, J. A. M. (1967 [1892]), *The Gentle Art of Making Enemies*, New York.

Whitman, C. (1965), *Homer and the Heroic Tradition*, New York.

Whitmarsh, T. (2001), *Greek Literature and the Roman Empire: The Politics of Imitation*, Oxford.

—— (2004a), "Dialogues in Love: Bakhtin and His Critics on the Greek Novel," in Branham, ed., 107–29.

—— (2004b), "The Cretan Lyre Paradox: Mesomedes, Hadrian and the Poetics of Patronage," in *Paideia: The World of the Second Sophistic*, ed. B. Borg, 377–402, Berlin.

—— (2005), "The Greek Novel: Titles and Genre," *American Journal of Philology* 126, 587–611.

—— ed. (forthcoming), *The Cambridge Companion to the Greek and Roman Novel*, Cambridge.

Wiles, D. (2000), *Greek Theatre Performance: An Introduction*, Cambridge.

—— (2003), *A Short History of Western Performance Space*, Cambridge.

—— (2004), "The Use of Masks in Modern Performances of Greek Drama," in Hall, Macintosh, and Wrigley, eds., 245–64.

Wilgus, D. K. (1977), "Irish Traditional Narrative Songs in English: 1800–1916," in Casey and Rhodes, eds., 107–28.

Willcock, M. M. (1978), *The Iliad of Homer*, London.

Williams, G. (1962), "Poetry in the Moral Climate of Augustan Rome," *Journal of Roman Studies* 28–46.

Williamson, M. (1995), *Sappho's Immortal Daughters*, Cambridge, MA.

Wilson, B., ed. (1970), *Rationality*, Oxford.

Wilson, E. (2004), "Tongue Breaks" (review of three books on Sappho), *London Review of Books* (January 8), 27–8.

Wilson, S. (2000), "Monsieur Venus: Michel Journiac and Love," in Arscott and Scott, eds., 156–72.

Winch, P. (1970), "Understanding a Primitive Society," in Wilson, ed., 78–112.

Winckelmann, J. J. (1881), *The History of Ancient Art*, 2 vols., trans. G. H. Lodge, London.

—— (1985 [1755]), "Thoughts on the Imitation of the Painting and Sculpture of the Greeks," in H. B. Nisbet, ed., *Aesthetic and Literary Criticism: Winckelmann, Lessing, Hamann, Herder, Schiller, Goethe*, Cambridge, 32–54.

Winkler, J. J. (1985), *Auctor and Actor: A Narratological Reading of Apuleius'* The Golden Ass, Berkeley.

Winterer, C. (2002), *The Culture of Classicism: Ancient Greece and Rome in American Intellectual Life, 1780–1910*, Baltimore.

Wiseman, T. P., ed. (2002), *Classics in Progress: Essays on Ancient Greece and Rome*, Oxford.

Wood, S. N. C. (1991), "Creative Indirection in Intertextual Space: Intertextuality in Milton's *Samson Agonistes*," in Plett, ed., 192–206.

Woodman, T., and Powell, J., eds. (1992), *Author and Audience in Latin Literature*, Cambridge.

Worthen, W. B. (2003), "Drama, Performativity, and Performance," in Auslander, ed., vol. 2, 86–108.

Wyke, M. (1997), *Projecting the Past: Ancient Rome, Cinema and History*, New York and London.

—— and Biddiss, M., eds. (1999), *The Uses and Abuses of Antiquity*, Bern.

Zimmermann, G. D. (1967), *Songs of Irish Rebellion: Political Street Ballads and Rebel Songs 1780–1900*, Hatboro, PA.

Zimmermann, W. (1961), *Anselm Feuerbach: Gemälde und Zeichnungen aus der staatlichen Kunsthalle Karlsruhe*, Karlsruhe.

Ziolkowski, T. (1993), *Virgil and the Moderns*, Princeton.

—— (2005), *Ovid and the Moderns*, Ithaca, NY and London.

Index

Note: numbers in *italics* refer to illustrations.